PATERNOSTER BIBLICAL MON(

Joseph, Wise and Otherwise

The Intersection of Wisdom and Covenant in Genesis 37-50

PATERNOSTER BIBLICAL MONOGRAPHS

A full listing of titles in both this series and
Paternoster Theological Monographs
appears at the end of this book

PATERNOSTER BIBLICAL MONOGRAPHS

Joseph, Wise and Otherwise

The Intersection of Wisdom and Covenant in Genesis 37-50

Lindsay Wilson

PATERNOSTER PRESS

First published 2004 by Paternoster Press

Paternoster Press is an imprint of Paternoster Publishing,
P.O. Box 300, Carlisle, Cumbria, CA3 0QS, U.K.
and
P.O. Box 1047, Waynesboro, GA 30830-2047, U.S.A.

10 09 08 07 06 05 04   7 6 5 4 3 2 1

British Library Cataloguing in Publication Data
A catalogue record for this book is available from the British Library

ISBN   1-84227-140-7

Unless otherwise stated, Scripture quotations are taken from the New Revised
Standard Version of the Bible, copyright © 1989 by the Division of
Christian Education of the National Council of the Churches
of Christ in the United States of America.

Typeset by Lindsay Wilson
and printed and bound in Great Britain by
Nottingham Alpha Graphics

Series Preface

One of the major objectives of Paternoster is to serve biblical scholarship by providing a channel for the publication of theses and other monographs of high quality at affordable prices. Paternoster stands within the broad evangelical tradition of Christianity. Our authors would describe themselves as Christians who recognise the authority of the Bible, maintain the centrality of the gospel message and assent to the classical credal statements of Christian belief. There is diversity within this constituency; advances in scholarship are possible only if there is freedom for frank debate on controversial issues and for the publication of new and sometimes provocative proposals. What is offered in this series is the best of writing by committed Christians who are concerned to develop well-founded biblical scholarship in a spirit of loyalty to the historic faith.

In memory of my parents,
Jim and Lola Wilson,
who taught me wisdom.

Abbreviations

ABRL	Anchor Bible Reference Library
ATANT	Abhandlungen zur Theologie des Alten und Neuen Testaments
AUSS	*Andrews University Seminary Studies*
BA	*Biblical Archaeologist*
BETL	Bibliotheca ephemeridum theologicarum lovaniensium
Bib	*Biblica*
BibInt	*Biblical Interpretation*
BK	*Bibel und Kirche*
BN	*Biblische Notizen*
BSac	*Bibliotheca Sacra*
BZ	*Biblische Zeitschrift*
BZAW	Beheifte zur Zeitschrift für die alttestamentliche Wissenschaft
CBOTS	Coniectanea biblica Old Testament Series
CBQ	*Catholic Biblical Quarterly*
CBQMS	Catholic Biblical Quarterly Monograph Series
CTJ	*Calvin Theological Journal*
EvQ	*Evangelical Quarterly*
ExpTim	*Expository Times*
FOTL	The Forms of the Old Testament Literature
HAR	*Hebrew Annual Review*
HDR	Harvard Dissertations in Religion
HeyJ	*Heythrop Journal*
HSM	Harvard Semitic Monographs
HTR	*Harvard Theological Review*
HUCA	*Hebrew Union College Annual*
ICC	International Critical Commentary
Int	*Interpretation*
JAAR	*Journal of the American Academy of Religion*
JBL	*Journal of Biblical Literature*
JEA	*Journal of Egyptian Archaeology*
JETS	*Journal of the Evangelical Theological Society*
JNSL	*Journal of Northwest Semitic Languages*
JSOT	*Journal for the Study of the Old Testament*
JSOTSup	Journal for the Study of the Old Testament Supplement Series
JSP	*Journal for the Study of the Pseudepigrapha*
JSS	*Journal of Semitic Studies*
JTS	*Journal of Theological Studies*
NIBC	New International Biblical Commentary
NICOT	New International Commentary on the Old Testament
OBO	Orbis biblicus et orientalis
OTS	*Oudtestamentische Studiën*

RB	*Revue biblique*
RTP	*Revue de théologie et de philosophie*
RTR	*Reformed Theological Review*
SANT	Studien zum Alten und Neuen Testament
SBLDS	Society of Biblical Literature Dissertation Series
SBLMS	Society of Biblical Literature Monograph Series
SBLSS	Society of Biblical Literature Semeia Studies
SBT	Studies in Biblical Theology
ScEs	*Science et esprit*
SJOT	*Scandinavian Journal of the Old Testament*
SJT	*Scottish Journal of Theology*
SNTSMS	Society for New Testament Studies Monograph Series
SVTP	Studia in Veteris Testamenti pseudepigrapha
TOTC	Tyndale Old Testament Commentaries
TynBul	*Tyndale Bulletin*
VT	*Vetus Testamentum*
VTSup	Vetus Testamentum, Supplements
WBC	Word Biblical Commentary
WMANT	Wissenschaftliche Monographien zum Alten und Neuen Testament
WTJ	*Westminster Theological Journal*
ZAW	*Zeitschrift für die alttestamentliche Wissenschaft*
ZTK	*Zeitschrift für Theologie und Kirche*

PART 1

PRELIMINARY MATTERS

CHAPTER 1

Introduction

The recent resurgence in scholarly and popular interest in Old Testament wisdom literature is in no small part due to the perception that it offers productive resources for contemporary society. Old Testament wisdom is no longer viewed as an unwanted and troublesome stepchild, but is increasingly being regarded as a valuable and contributing member of the family. This study has emerged from an interest in understanding the wisdom corpus as part of the whole biblical canon.

This rise of interest in wisdom has inevitably been accompanied by vigorous debate between its proponents and its detractors. Crenshaw has warned about wisdom being made to reach out its tentacles into all parts of the Old Testament, describing this as a kind of 'wisdom imperialism'.[1] Brueggemann, on the other hand, has described the wisdom theology of humans being God's trusted creatures as 'the neglected side of biblical faith'.[2]

The canonical wisdom literature has raised particular difficulties for those seeking to write Old Testament theologies. The distinctive wisdom emphases have forced scholars to consider how these wisdom ideas relate to apparently different concepts in the rest of the Old Testament.[3] In particular, if much of the Old Testament concerns God's mighty acts on

---

1 See J.L. Crenshaw, 'Method in Determining Wisdom Influence Upon 'Historical' Literature', *JBL* 88 (1969): 129-142.

2 Most prominently in W. Brueggemann, *In Man We Trust: The Neglected Side of Biblical Faith* (Atlanta: John Knox, 1972).

3 Recent surveys of this dilemma include L.G. Perdue, *Wisdom and Creation: The Theology of Wisdom Literature* (Nashville: Abingdon, 1994) 19-48; R.E. Clements, 'Wisdom and Old Testament Theology', in *Wisdom in ancient Israel: Essays in honour of J.A. Emerton*. eds. J. Day, R.P. Gordon and H.G.M. Williamson. (Cambridge: Cambridge University Press, 1995), 269-286; and R.E. Murphy, *The Tree of Life: An Exploration of Biblical Wisdom Literature*. ABRL. 2nd edn. (Grand Rapids: Eerdmans, 1996) 111-131, 223-227. I have discussed this briefly in L. Wilson, 'The Place of Wisdom in Old Testament Theology'. *Reformed Theological Review* 49 (1990): 60-69.

behalf of his covenant people - Abraham and his descendants who
ultimately become the nation of Israel - it is proper to ask why this aspect
is so glaringly absent from the canonical wisdom texts.

A plethora of issues arise from this apparent dissonance between the
wisdom books and the rest of the Old Testament. Some ask historical and
sociological questions about the social setting of wisdom in Israel. Others
explore the social and political forces which aided wisdom's integration
into Old Testament thought at the various stages of Israel's history. These
are legitimate and important background matters, but they are not the
concern of this book. Instead, we will focus on the intersection at the level
of ideas in the final form of the text, asking how the concepts of wisdom
relate to the theological themes that emerge out of the covenant strand so
prevalent in the rest of the Old Testament.

This could be attempted in a number of ways. For example, one could
study the key ideas of a foundational wisdom book like Proverbs and the
main ideas of a covenant book like Exodus. That would be a legitimate
enterprise, but is too large a task for our purposes. It would also not reveal
how the authors or editors of the texts understood the interrelationship of
wisdom and covenant. While showing the distinctives of each, it would fail
to indicate their interconnection.

Two main integrative pathways have been taken in the past. The first has
been to highlight 'covenant elements' in the canonical wisdom literature,
attempting to show that wisdom fits the covenant paradigm despite first
impressions to the contrary. This approach is often used to legitimise
wisdom or incorporate it into a covenant-based model of Old Testament
theology.[4]

The second option has been to argue that wisdom, based on a theology of
creation, has its own legitimacy, and is in fact more prominent in the Old
Testament than is commonly thought.[5] This view has been taken one stage
further by a number of scholars who have discerned a wisdom hand in the
Pentateuch (Genesis 2-3; Exodus 1-2; Deuteronomy), in some psalms, in
the historical books (for example, the Succession Narrative), in the prophets
(for example, Amos, Isaiah, Jonah) and in other writings (for example,

---

4 An early example of this approach is G.L. Goldsworthy, 'Empirical Wisdom in
   Relation to Salvation-History in the Psalms', (Dissertation, ThD, Union Theological
   Seminary, Richmond, Virginia, 1973), which is a study of salvation historical
   elements in wisdom psalms. More recently see I.J.J. Spangenberg, 'Old Testament
   Theology and Wisdom Literature', *Theologica Evangelica* 25 (1992): 2-7; R.L.
   Schultz, 'Unity or Diversity in Wisdom Theology? A Canonical and Covenantal
   Perspective', *TynBul* 48 (1997): 271-306, especially at 292-303.
5 As, for example, in the seminal studies of J.F. Priest, 'Where Is Wisdom to be
   Placed?', *JAAR* 31 (1963): 275-282 and W. Zimmerli, 'The Place and Limit of the
   Wisdom in the Framework of the Old Testament Theology', *SJT* 17 (1964): 146-158.

Esther, Daniel).[6] In these sections of the Old Testament, it has been argued that there are wisdom characters, themes, emphases, and/or language that warrant speaking of 'wisdom influence'.[7]

Most of these studies, however, are simply concerned with establishing or denying 'wisdom influence' in a specific non-wisdom text. While that is an important matter, few scholars then consider how the wisdom elements relate to the non-wisdom elements in the text. This book proposes to progress to this next level and explore the intersection of wisdom and covenant in the Joseph Narrative (Genesis 37-50). Of course, it will need to be argued that both wisdom and covenant ideas are present in these chapters. Yet, if these can properly be established, then the question of their interaction may usefully be explored.

The Joseph narrative is potentially a fruitful place in which to quarry. As part of the Pentateuch, it preserves the people of the Abrahamic promise from famine, and moves them to Egypt, enabling the clan of Jacob to grow into the nation of Israel. It thus can be assumed that the Joseph story includes significant elements of God's dealings with his covenant people, and the reasons for this will be reinforced by the exegesis in Part 2 of this book. The presence of covenant elements in the Joseph narrative is not generally contested by scholars.

More hotly disputed is the issue of wisdom influence in the Joseph narrative. While many think that Joseph is wise, some will argue strongly that he, and the concerns of his narrative, are otherwise. A major goal of this book will be to explore the question of whether wisdom ideas and emphases can legitimately be found in Genesis 37-50. With this in mind, the book will commence with a survey of studies considering the question of wisdom and the Joseph narrative. Issues of terminology will then be explored, since this is the source of much confusion. Prior to a more detailed exegetical study of the text, the methodology of discerning wisdom influence in non-wisdom narrative texts will also be discussed.

Once these preliminary matters are concluded, a literary reading of Genesis 37-50 will be undertaken, with a particular brief to discern elements that suggest or negate a wisdom 'family resemblance'. A summary of the nature and location of the Abrahamic covenant emphases will be provided in chapter 9, followed by a drawing together of wisdom

---

6 This is well surveyed in D.F. Morgan, *Wisdom in the Old Testament Traditions* (Oxford: Basil Blackwell, 1981), and briefly but more recently by Murphy, *The Tree of Life*, 97-110, 221-223.

7 For a useful chart outlining the wisdom vocabulary, forms, themes, characters and functions that can lead to the conclusion of wisdom influence, see C.R. Fontaine, 'A Response to 'The Bearing of Wisdom'', in *A Feminist Companion to Samuel and Kings*. Feminist Companion to the Bible, 5, ed. A. Brenner. (Sheffield: Sheffield Academic Press, 1994), 166.

ideas and themes in chapter 10.

Finally, the other major goal of this book is to explore in a preliminary way the intersection of the wisdom and covenant ideas that may emerge from the Joseph story. Can we hold together a Joseph narrative that is both wise and otherwise? An attempt will be made at proposing patterns or models of this interrelationship. Such a study may not exhaust the interconnection of wisdom and covenant ideas, for other parts of the Old Testament (perhaps Daniel, Isaiah) may suggest some different or additional links. However, the consideration of an individual text such as the Joseph story may be suggestive for a more general consideration of the interaction between the wisdom and covenant strands in the Old Testament as a whole.

CHAPTER 2

Wisdom and the Joseph Narrative

A Survey

The idea of Joseph being 'a wisdom figure' is quite recent, but the notion that Joseph's character is portrayed as one for us to emulate is, of course, much older. It is, for example, prominent in early texts such as *Joseph and Asenath* and *The Testament of Joseph*.[1] Indeed, the view that Joseph was a teacher of wisdom is reflected in Ps 105:22, and thus is quite respectably ancient.[2]

G. von Rad

However, the modern debate about wisdom influence in Genesis 37-50 was provoked by an article by von Rad, originally appearing in 1953, in which he claimed that "the Joseph story, with its strong didactic motive, belongs to the category of early wisdom writing."[3] He is here not simply claiming

---

1   See, for example, H.W. Hollander, *Joseph as an Ethical Model in the Testaments of the Twelve Patriarchs*. SVTP, 6. (Leiden: E.J. Brill, 1981); H.W. Hollander, 'The Ethical Character of the Patriarch Joseph', in *Studies on the Testament of Joseph*. ed. G.W.E. Nickelsburg. (Missoula: Scholars, 1975), 47-104; A.W. Argyle, 'Joseph the Patriarch in Patristic Teaching', *ExpTim* 67 (1955/56): 199-201. In more recent times (late 19th century-early 20th century) a number of works sought to explore the model character of Joseph, such as J. Monroe, 'Joseph as a Statesman', *BSac* 54 (1897): 484-500, and A. Black, 'Joseph: an Ethical and Biblical Study', *The Expositor* 6th Series 1 (1900): 63-78, 111-121, 217-230, 289-308, 444-459.

2   J.S. Kselman, 'Genesis', in *Harper's Bible Commentary*. ed. J.L. Mays. (San Francisco: Harper & Row, 1988), 120 comments that "[a]pparently even in antiquity the wisdom character of the Joseph novella was recognized by the authors of Daniel; modern scholarship has only rediscovered it."

3   G. von Rad, 'The Joseph Narrative and Ancient Wisdom', in *The Problem of the Hexateuch and other essays*. trans. E.W.T. Dicken. (London: SCM, 1984), 292-300. The quote comes from 299. The article originally appeared in German in 1953. C. Westermann, *Genesis 37-50*. trans. J.J. Scullion. (Minneapolis: Augsburg, 1986) 26 does not know of any express reference to a connection between the Joseph story

that the narrative showed wisdom influence, but rather that it was a piece of wisdom literature itself.[4]

Von Rad's argument is essentially that the wisdom nature of the Joseph story is reflected both in its portrayal of an educational ideal in the character of Joseph, and in the fundamental theological ideas underlying the text. He posits a literary and theological setting in the early monarchic period, more specifically, a time of 'Solomonic enlightenment'.[5] He sees Joseph as an ideal for an administrator in his outspokenness and good counsel (Genesis 41; Prov 22:29); his avoiding the 'strange woman' (Gen 39:7-12; Prov 22:14; 23:27-28); his patience and self-control (Gen 42:24; 43:30-31; 45:1; Prov 14:29-30; 12:23; 10:19); and his forbearance of revenge (Gen 45:4-8; 50:14-21; Prov 24:29; 10:12).[6]

Von Rad also points to the common theological presuppositions underlying both the Joseph narrative and the wisdom writings. An example of this can be seen in how God's purposes are worked out. Neither the wisdom writings nor the Joseph story contain many statements about God's direct activity, focusing instead on human accomplishment. God's work is hidden rather than explicit, yet God's purposes prevail.[7] In addition, the absence of historico-political interests, the lack of emphasis on cult or aetiology, no theological interest in redemptive history, and the suggestions of Egyptian wisdom influence all point in the same direction.[8]

Thus von Rad concludes that "[t]he Joseph story is a didactic wisdom-story which leans heavily upon influences emanating from Egypt, not only with regard to its conception of an educational ideal, but also in its fundamental theological ideas."[9]

The Critics of von Rad

Von Rad's connection of Joseph and wisdom then prevailed for the next decade and a half, until Crenshaw (1969) and Redford (1970) independently raised objections.[10]

---

and wisdom prior to von Rad's 1953 article.

4   As S.D.E. Weeks, *Early Israelite Wisdom*. Oxford Theological Monographs. (Oxford: Clarendon, 1994) 92 points out.
5   von Rad, 'Ancient Wisdom', 292-293.
6   von Rad, 'Ancient Wisdom', 293-296. He buttresses many of his observations by references in the book of Proverbs as well as parallels in Egyptian wisdom literature.
7   von Rad, 'Ancient Wisdom', 296. He refers in particular to Gen 45:5-8 and 50:20.
8   von Rad, 'Ancient Wisdom', 299.
9   von Rad, 'Ancient Wisdom', 300.
10   D.B. Redford, *A Study of the Biblical Story of Joseph (Genesis 37-50)*. VTSup, 20. (Leiden: E.J. Brill, 1970) 101, footnote 1, cites the following writers who largely followed von Rad: P.A.H. de Boer, 'The Counsellor', in *Wisdom in Israel and in*

J.L. CRENSHAW

Crenshaw primarily raised some methodological objections.[11] Firstly, Crenshaw argues that von Rad's definition of wisdom ('practical knowledge of the laws of life and of the world, based on experience') is too broad, covering all of life. Crenshaw helpfully insists that a distinction must be maintained between wisdom literature, wisdom tradition, and wisdom thinking.[12] Secondly, one needs to identify stylistic or ideological characteristics found primarily in wisdom literature, and not simply those that are part of the common cultural stock. Even the presence of vocabulary used in wisdom texts (for example, 'hear', 'know') is not enough to conclude that there is wisdom influence. Indeed, even when something which seems to be a wisdom word, phrase or motif is found outside of the wisdom literature, it is worth asking whether the accepted sapiential meaning has been retained or modified. In addition, the negative attitude to wisdom in so much of the historical and prophetic literature of the Old Testament should lead us to be cautious about finding wisdom being pictured as a desirable trait in narrative texts.[13] Finally, wisdom thinking underwent changes, so there is a need to be careful in tracing lines of influence. In particular, the incorporation of priestly and salvation historical concern needs to be accounted for, and the co-existence of wisdom and strong nationalism needs to be explained.

When Crenshaw turns to the Joseph narrative, he concludes that there are no stylistic or ideological peculiarities. The anthropological interest, and the rejection of the temptress, arose out of a common cultural stock, and were not due to wisdom influence. Furthermore, the theme of providence is common to both wisdom and the Joseph narrative, but is not restricted to wisdom. Crenshaw suggested that Joseph is given a privileged insight into God's providence through his dreams, while he claims that wisdom elsewhere denies such an insight to anyone. Thus, a common wisdom

---

the Ancient Near East. VTSup, 3, eds. M. Noth and D.W. Thomas. (Leiden: E.J. Brill, 1955), 42-71 at 57-58; C.T. Fritsch, '"God Was With Him": A Theological Study of the Joseph Narrative', *Int* 9 (1955): 21-34 at 33; J.C.H. Lebram, 'Nachbiblische Weisheitstraditionen', *VT* 15 (1965): 167-237 at 170ff.; S.B. Frost, *Patriarchs and Prophets* (London: John Murray, 1963) at 41ff.; J. Hempel, *Geschichten und Geschichte im Alten Testament bis zur persischen Zeit* (Gütersloh: Gerd Mohn, 1964) 194. One might also include O. Wintermute, 'Joseph Son of Jacob', in *Interpreter's Dictionary of the Bible*. 4 vols., ed. G.A. Buttrick. (Nashville: Abingdon, 1962), 2:983-985.

11 Crenshaw, 'Method', 129-142.
12 Crenshaw, 'Method', 130. He sees wisdom literature as the literary deposit; wisdom tradition as the specifically defined movement itself; and wisdom thinking as a particular stance or approach to reality.
13 This point is hardly very strong, for there is a negative attitude to particular kings and prophets in most of the narrative texts as well.

theme is dealt with in an unwisdomlike way. Finally, he points out the presence of a number of what he regards as non-wisdom themes in the narrative.[14]

Crenshaw makes no positive suggestions about genre, setting or provenance, but that is not his intention. He merely seeks to point out some methodological deficiencies in von Rad's work, and thus rightly puts the methodological questions on the agenda.

It is worth observing that Crenshaw was seeking to refute von Rad's specific thesis that the Joseph narrative is wisdom literature *per se*.[15] However, this does not necessarily preclude the possibility of wisdom elements just being one thread of the narrative. Does, for example, Joseph's initial lack of discretion, or the fact that he weeps before his brothers, or that God's hidden action is emphasised, preclude Joseph being pictured as having become a model wise man? If so, then how would one account for Job being among the wise?

It is further noteworthy that Crenshaw has not offered a detailed rebuttal, as his critique of von Rad's work on the Joseph narrative is only two pages long - a fact ignored by many subsequent scholars who quote Crenshaw's seminal argument as if it has settled the issue decisively.[16]

D.B. REDFORD

Redford, an Egyptologist, calls von Rad's view "a misinterpretation of the evidence", largely on the basis that chapters 37 and 42-45 do not portray Joseph as an ideal wise man.[17] He thinks it likely that those who have been influenced by wisdom teaching have left their mark on the story, but argues that the story *per se* cannot be placed in wisdom. In particular, the narrative

---

14 Crenshaw, 'Method', 136-137 cites the following: 1. Joseph's frustration in relationships with his brothers (and father); 2. the ideal administrator was not trained in a school; 3. he was chosen as the counsellor because of his 'spiritual' characteristics; 4. he failed to control his emotions at crucial points; 5. he showed a lack of tact by telling his dreams to his brothers, and later treating them harshly; 6. the story appeals to special revelation and visions, dreams and a divining cup, sacrifice, genealogy and kosher food. It includes an aetiology for taxes and contact with redemptive history in the use of the names of places, patriarchs and God.

15 Crenshaw, 'Method', 142 notes that he has been assessing "the arguments for wisdom influence as the *exclusive background* for the Joseph narrative" (emphasis mine).

16 Indeed, Crenshaw himself does this: J.L. Crenshaw, 'Prolegomenon', in *Studies in Ancient Israelite Wisdom*. Library of Biblical Studies, ed. J.L. Crenshaw. (New York: KTAV, 1976), 11, 18; J.L. Crenshaw, 'Wisdom Literature: Retrospect and Prospect', in *Of Prophets' Visions and the Wisdom of Sages*. JSOTSup, 162, eds. H.A. McKay and D.J.A. Clines. (Sheffield: Sheffield Academic Press, 1993), 161-178.

17 Redford, *Biblical Story of Joseph*, 100-105.

does not have a strong didactic thrust.[18] Furthermore, Redford also argues
that Potiphar's wife is not the 'loose woman' of Proverbs but the scorned
woman or 'spurned wife', a well-known motif in Egyptian literature.[19]

He seeks neither to date the story in Solomonic times, nor attribute it to
the Yahwist. Instead, his distinctive proposal is that it was brought together
between the 7th and 5th centuries BCE. He says we know little about the
court in Solomonic times, and that wisdom probably had a family not court
setting. He observes that when the story deals with family matters, Joseph is
furthest from displaying wisdom. In his dating and in asserting an exclusive
family setting for wisdom, he has not convinced many. Even if the family is
one possible setting for wisdom, surely the royal court is another likely,
indeed crucial, setting.[20]

CONCLUSIONS

What Crenshaw and Redford are both able to establish is that the Joseph
story is not simply a self-contained wisdom tale, for clearly there are wider
concerns. As will be shown in the body of this study, chapters 37-50 play a
crucial role in the book of Genesis as a whole, not least in rounding off the
story of the patriarchs, and in accounting for their descent to Egypt.
Furthermore, it functions as a bridge to link the book of Genesis with the
rest of the Pentateuch, thus playing a vital role in the story of God's
covenant people.

What is important for our purposes, however, is to realise that neither the
critique of Crenshaw, nor that of Redford, has established that there are *no*
'wisdom elements' in the Joseph narrative. They merely seek to establish
that Genesis 37-50 is not *solely* a piece of wisdom literature.

A Mediating Position - G.W. Coats

Coats' first contribution to this debate came in an article published in 1973,
in which he suggests that, from a methodological view, genre, setting and
intention are the best criteria to establish any connection between the
Joseph story and wisdom.[21] His argument was that the 'wisdom elements'

---

18   Redford, *Biblical Story of Joseph*, 105.

19   Redford, *Biblical Story of Joseph*, 91-93.

20   G. von Rad, *Wisdom in Israel.* trans. J.D. Martin. (London: SCM, 1972) 13-38
      shows that it is not so easy to dismiss the royal court setting of wisdom. See also W.
      Brueggemann, 'The Social Significance of Solomon as a Patron of Wisdom', and
      R.N. Whybray, 'The Sage in the Israelite Royal Court', both in *The Sage in Israel
      and the Ancient Near East.* eds. J.G. Gammie and L.G. Perdue. (Winona Lake:
      Eisenbrauns, 1990), 117-132, 133-139.

21   G.W. Coats, 'The Joseph Story and Wisdom: a Reappraisal', *CBQ* 35 (1973), 287-
      288. He has subsequently written an important monograph on the Joseph story:
      G.W. Coats, *From Canaan to Egypt: Structural and Theological Context for the*

form the kernel of the story (chapters 39-41), but are incorporated into wider concerns that are in tension with these wisdom features.[22] Coats views chapters 39-41 as a political legend, which has a setting in the royal court, intending to paint a picture of an ideal administrator for future generations.[23] He makes a useful distinction that the focus here is not on the proper way for a young man to rise to power (as in some other wisdom texts), but rather the proper use of power by an administrator already in office.[24]

Coats examines arguments against wisdom influence in the kernel, arguing that both his reason for rejecting the advances of Potiphar's wife, and his role as interpreter of dreams, are consistent with Joseph being a wisdom figure.[25] Coats finally argues that most of the 'unwisdomlike' aspects suggested by Crenshaw happen outside chapters 39-41.[26] Coats also turns Crenshaw's argument on its head, claiming that the absence of these elements here, and presence in the rest of the story, is explained by a wisdom kernel in a non-wisdom story. He posits a setting for the kernel in the royal court.[27]

Coats then turns to examine the genre, setting and intention of the Joseph story as a whole. In relation to genre, he notes it is intricate and complex, qualifying it as a novella.[28] He observes that the genre 'novella' is not inherently a wisdom genre, the only question being whether the artist(s) were influenced by wisdom tradition. In the light of the non-wisdom concerns and characteristics in the wider narrative, and the function of the story as a whole, he rejects the genre classification of entire narrative as a wisdom novella and also a royal wisdom provenance for the whole story. Coats argues that this can clearly be seen in the characterization of Joseph as a non-wisdom figure in chapters 37 and 42-45.[29] When Coats looks at the question of intention of the Joseph story as a whole, he sees at least three strands - to describe life in a family; to explore the actions of a political

---

Joseph Story. CBQMS, 4. (Washington: Catholic Biblical Association, 1976).

22   Coats, 'The Joseph Story and Wisdom' 288. He argues that the final form of the Joseph narrative has preserved intact an earlier block of text, "a story within a story".

23   Coats, 'The Joseph Story and Wisdom', 288-289.

24   Coats, 'The Joseph Story and Wisdom', 292.

25   *Contra* Crenshaw, 'Method', 136-137; L. Ruppert, *Die Josephserzählung der Genesis: Ein Beitrag zur Theologie der Pentateuchquellen.* SANT, 11. (Munich: Kösel, 1965) 57-59; Redford, *Biblical Story of Joseph*, 103.

26   Coats, 'The Joseph Story and Wisdom', 293.

27   Coats, 'The Joseph Story and Wisdom', 287-288; G.W. Coats, 'Joseph, Son of Jacob', in *The Anchor Bible Dictionary.* 6 vols., ed. D.N. Freedman. (New York: Doubleday, 1992), 3:980.

28   Coats, 'The Joseph Story and Wisdom', 294.

29   Coats, 'The Joseph Story and Wisdom', 295-296.

<u>Unplugged</u>

Awesome

...on the inside

7.30pm Thursday 16th . 23rd, 30th September

@ **Parish Hall**

More info..Dan: 0208 542 2966

Ignition

"Jesus: Meek and mild??"

Sunday 19th September 2010
6pm-8pm
St George's Church
Central Road

leader; and to continue the story of the patriarchal promises.[30]

The article by Coats is thorough and stimulating. It at least demonstrates that chapters 39-41 cannot be excised, but are presupposed in the rest. Furthermore, it establishes that there are wisdom elements, more dominant in some parts of the narrative than in others, although the Joseph story as a whole is not just a wisdom tale. Such a view at least accounts for the presence of, and tension between, wisdom and salvation history, although his explanation of the unevenness of the distribution of wisdom elements - the hypothetical kernel - will need further evaluation after a more detailed study of the text.

The Supporters of von Rad

Two South African writers have sought to defend, nuance and elaborate the views of von Rad. Like von Rad, their approach is largely to find parallel incidents and verses between the Joseph story and the book of Proverbs.[31]

J.A. LOADER

Loader seeks to defend and amplify von Rad's basic position, at times refining it by adding additional references in Proverbs and pointing out some further connections with Proverbs 25-27, and between Joseph and Solomon. He also draws attention to common thematic ideas such as the optimism about human success, humility as the way to honour, and the balancing of God's providence and human action.[32]

His thirteen theses may be set out as follows

i. the practical action and rational dealing with reality is reminiscent of the early wisdom of Proverbs 25-27.
ii. there were contacts between the wise in Egypt and in Israel (such as the Teachings of Amenemope).
iii. The optimism about the success that humans can achieve with wisdom is characteristic of wisdom.
iv. The Joseph story had its *Sitz im Leben* in the royal court, and Joseph's administrative wisdom is seen in Gen 41:38, 39; 47:13-26.
v. The wise person should speak well, correctly and at the right time (Prov 10:20, 31; 12:13; 15:2, 4, 7, 23; 16:13; 17:7 etc), and it is this

---

30   Coats, 'The Joseph Story and Wisdom', 296-297.
31   This is pointed out by J.H. le Roux, 'The study of wisdom literature in South Africa', *Old Testament Essays* 4 (1991): 342-361, especially at 347, 351.
32   J.A. Loader, 'Chokma - Joseph - Hybris', in *Studies in the Pentateuch*. Ou Testamentiese Werkgemeenskap in Suid-Afrika, 17 & 18: Old Testament Essays, ed. W.C. van Wyk. (Pretoria: Ou Testamentiese Werkgemeenskap in Suid-Afrika, 1974/75), 21-31.

which impresses Pharaoh (Gen 41:25ff).

vi. A wise man has nothing to do with immoral women (Prov 23:27; 29:3; 31:3), and here Joseph shows a wisdom greater than Solomon.

vii. The wise were interested in reflecting on psychological processes such as the origin, nature and consequences of emotions like hatred, anger, sorrow, impatience etc. (Prov 10:12, 12:16; 14:10, 13, 29; 15:1, 18), and we see this concern in Gen 37:1-8, 10-11; 42:16 and 44:3-17.

viii. The ability to control himself, holding back tears, is characteristic of the wise (Prov 16:32; 17:27 cf. 15:18).

ix. Joseph does not use an opportunity to take revenge (Gen 45:5; 50:19), a feature reflected in the wise (Prov 17:13; 20:22).

x. A wise man makes timely provision of a stock of necessities when he has opportunity to do so (Prov 20:4; cf. 6:6-8).

xi. To acquire wisdom, it is necessary to accept authority - for a young man, the authority of his parents and others (Prov 10:1; 15:5; 19:20; 1:6, 7). The way to honour is humility (Prov 18:12; 15:33; 14:3; 16:5, 18; 21:4; 22:4; 29:23; 8:13).

xii. In wisdom, all is dependent on the guidance and providence of God, since he establishes order in all realms. God acts in response to the maintenance and disruption of his order (Prov 10:3; 14:27; 15:8; 16:3), and there is a contrast between the action and guidance of God, on the one hand, and practical human action on the other (Prov 16:9; 19:21; 20:24). This same contrast constitutes the backbone of the Joseph novel - Joseph's 'secular' wisdom as well as God directing events according to his will (Gen 45:5-8; 50:20).

xiii. There are a number of similarities between Joseph and Solomon, the wise man par excellence.

Loader's more original contribution is in two other areas. Firstly, in relation to the classical source theory, he notes that wisdom is not confined to any one source, since the putative sources J and E seem to have the same wisdom character.[33] It cannot be that both J and E rely on common groundwork predating both, for he suggests that wisdom in Israel is not older than the monarchy. Since the story is a necessary background for the exodus traditions, some form of 'Joseph tradition' must have been circulating well prior to Solomon. Thus, we have a wisdom novel in which the story is built on "age-old tribal traditions that were useful for his purpose".[34] Thus, the wisdom influence is later than J and E, and the story as we have it is a sapientialising of these older traditions.

Secondly, he argues that identifying the story as a wisdom narrative is a wider issue than whether Joseph is a model wise man, which was the

33   Loader, 'Chokma - Joseph - Hybris', 24-26.
34   Loader, 'Chokma - Joseph - Hybris', 26.

dominant focus in von Rad. In Loader's view, the Joseph story "expounds the most fundamental *theological* structure of the old Israelite wisdom".[35] In other words, the Joseph story is more than a wisdom story in which Joseph is portrayed as a model wisdom figure. Rather, the Joseph story illustrates the wisdom *theme* (seen in Prov 18:12; 15:33) that when Joseph acts wisely, God's guidance of events leads to Joseph enjoying honour and success; but that not acting wisely will lead to humiliation or disaster.[36]

This has some merit in that Loader sees the issue of wisdom elements is wider than simply whether Joseph is a model wise character. His approach allows for a negative view of Joseph in chapter 37.[37]

J.P.H. WESSELS[38]

Wessels' initial concern was the classification of the genre of the Joseph story and he argued that the appropriate genre classification was the novelette.[39] In trying to identify what kind of novelette it was, Wessels noted that the Joseph narrative displayed what Gunkel called '*eine Freude am Fremdartigen*' (a delight in what was foreign), and that this was evident in the many Egyptian aspects of the story.[40] He sees the influence from the Egyptian *wisdom* literature, noting the connection between the wisdom of Amenemope and Proverbs 22-23.[41] With this in mind he explores the elements of wisdom in the narrative based on parallels with Proverbs such as those pointed out by von Rad and Loader. Ultimately he classified the Joseph story as a 'wisdom novelette' because of the following wisdom features[42]

> 1. the purely human and 'secular' level of the story - Joseph does not fast or pray before interpreting Pharaoh's dreams; he uses common sense to solve the future grain crisis. This is reflected in Proverbs 25-27 (for

---

35 Loader, 'Chokma - Joseph - Hybris', 29.

36 Loader, 'Chokma - Joseph - Hybris', 30.

37 Loader, 'Chokma - Joseph - Hybris', 28 suggests, for example, that Joseph's behaviour is marked by hybris in Genesis 37.

38 J.P.H. Wessels, 'The Joseph story as a wisdom novelette', *Old Testament Essays* 2 (1984): 39-60. For an analysis of both Loader and Wessels in a wider context, see le Roux, 'The study of wisdom literature', 342-361.

39 The links with the book of Esther were first pointed out by L.A. Rosenthal, 'Die Josephsgeschichte mit den Büchern Ester und Daniel verglichen', *ZAW* 15 (1895): 278-284.

40 H. Gunkel, *Genesis* (Göttingen: Vandenhoeck, 1910) 397 = H. Gunkel, *Genesis*. Mercer Library of Biblical Studies, trans. M.E. Biddle. (Macon: Mercer University Press, 1997) 383. Wessels, 'The Joseph story', 49-51 outlines many Egyptian elements.

41 Wessels, 'The Joseph story', 51.

42 Wessels, 'The Joseph story', 52-54.

example, 27:19).

2. the educational ideal of developing man according to his potential (Proverbs 10ff). Joseph as a vizier of the king's court (like Ptahhotep and Kagemni in Egypt), a wise administrator, puts high value on righteous speech (Proverbs 16).

3. Joseph's conduct towards Potiphar's wife is the application of Proverbs 23, 29, and 31 (for example, 23:27) and similar sayings in Egyptian wisdom.[43]

4. the ability to speak the right word at the right time, the quality which impressed Pharaoh about Joseph (Prov 15:7, 23).

5. Joseph's self-control (see Prov 16:32; also Ptahhotep, Amenemope). Crenshaw's counter-argument of his tears (Gen 43:30; 50:1) is unsound, since the expression of strong attachment between family members has never been alien to wisdom.[44]

6. the way to treat enemies (Prov 25:21 - Joseph giving a banquet for his brothers). This, however, is hardly strong since the banquet is part of his testing of their hearts.

7. he does not seek revenge (Prov 20:22).

8. he provides for the years of famine while there is plenty (Prov 20:4).

9. the parallels between Joseph and Solomon.[45]

He then addresses what we make of chapter 37, and concedes that Crenshaw is right in asserting that Joseph does not act initially like a wise man. His gossiping, for example, is a breach of Prov 27:2. Joseph, however, learned wisdom, including the precept that a haughty spirit goes before a fall (Prov 16:18). Furthermore, he picks up Loader's point that the basic pattern of the story is that presumption and self-aggrandizement, which is a transgression of wisdom, results in humiliation, while obedience to wisdom precepts leads to order in life, honour and success. The emphasis on God's guidance, characteristic of wisdom (Prov 19:21), is seen clearly in Gen 45:5 and 50:20.

Wessels concludes that the story can thus be read at two levels. Firstly, it

---

43   See H. Schmid, *Wesen und Geschichte der Weisheit*. BZAW, 101. (Berlin: Töpelmann, 1966) 204.

44   He relies here on H.-C. Schmitt, *Die Nichtpriesterliche Josephsgeschichte: Ein Beitrag zur neusten Pentateuchkritik*. BZAW, 154. (Berlin: Walter de Gruyter, 1980) 159.

45   He notes the following: a. both were children of the best loved wife, who was not the first. b. both were considerably younger than most of the other brothers. c. both had fathers who were invalids and no longer able to exercise full authority. d. both had an elder half-brother who demonstrated his claim to the inheritance by entering into his father's harem. e. dreams played an important part in the lives of both. f. both were men of insight and wisdom. g. both married Egyptian wives given them by Pharaoh. h. both stored food in store-cities.

a wisdom novelette since we can "still read and understand it as a story without having to know what precedes it or what follows in Exodus."[46] Like Loader, he understands that the wisdom teacher drew on ancient traditions (sources) as he wrote this story. Secondly, "the story also fits well into its present context, for the very reason that it draws on material from this context … At this level it is seen as part of the 'salvation history' line that explains Israel's entrance into Egypt and provides the substructure for the exodus."[47]

He argues for the need to read the story at both levels, to integrate the wisdom and salvation-historical elements.[48] Unfortunately, he does not explore in any detail how this can be done in such a way as to do justice to both.

Methodological Studies

The following writers were not concerned not so much with the Joseph narrative as such, but with methodological issues that impinge on our discussion.

H.-P. MÜLLER

Müller tries to define a genre of didactic narrative (*Lehrerzählung*) which includes the frame of Job, the Joseph story, the narrative frame of the Aramaic book of Ahiqar, Daniel 1-6, Esther and Tobit.[49] He does not focus on the court as the setting for these narratives, but notes a common morphological-synchronic analysis of the stories. He sees the function of this sapiential narrative as presenting 'a paradigmatic portrayal of a virtue or group of virtues. '[50]

He sets out the common form of these narratives as follows (illustrated by Job and Joseph)[51]

Introduction:
  1a Protagonist is described in respect to his or her virtue (description of Job; Joseph's dream).
  1b Symbolic deed which arises from the virtue, and confirmation of its

46 Wessels, 'The Joseph story', 56-57.
47 Wessels, 'The Joseph story', 57.
48 Wessels, 'The Joseph story', 58.
49 H.-P. Müller, 'Die weisheitliche Lehrerzählung im Alten Testament und seiner Umwelt', *Die Welt des Orients* 9 (1977): 77-98.
50 Müller, 'Die weisheitliche Lehrerzählung', 94.
51 Müller, 'Die weisheitliche Lehrerzählung', 79-94. This analysis is based on the summary of L.M. Wills, *The Jew in the Court of the Foreign King: Ancient Jewish Court Legends.* HDR, 26. (Minneapolis: Fortress, 1990) 10-11.

worth (Job's offering; Joseph loved by father, resented by brothers).

1c Antagonists introduced, with their intermediaries (Job's wife, interlocutors; Joseph's brothers as antagonists; king in court legends as intermediary).

Body

2a Conflict arises, instigated by virtue (Job's arguments, Joseph's brothers' conspiracy, Joseph's restraint with Potiphar's wife).

2b Testing and proving of the virtue (Job's despair, Joseph's sojourn in Egypt).

Conclusion

3a Confirmation of virtue of protagonist through punishment of antagonists (God's answers in Job, Joseph's superior position over his brothers).

3b Confirmation of virtue through rewarding of protagonist (Job upheld; Joseph benefactor of family).

3c Confirmation of virtue sometimes through miraculous demonstrations (Job summons God, Joseph interprets dreams).

Müller concludes that the two-fold purpose of a didactic narrative is firstly to make the virtue(s) of the hero paradigmatic, and secondly, to highlight the order that exists, even if temporarily interrupted.[52] Since this common form can be discerned in Genesis 37-50, then it can be classified as a sapiential didactic narrative.

S. NIDITCH AND R. DORAN

However, Niditch and Doran argue that it is not enough to find common motifs, since a form can only be established by a common ordering of elements.[53] They note that Gen 41:1-45, as well as Dan 2:1-49 and the Syriac version of Ahiqar 5-7:23 fit a common pattern of the following four elements

1. A person of lower status *is called before* a person of higher status *to answer* difficult questions or solve a problem requiring insight.
2. The person of high status *poses* the problem which no one seems capable of solving.
3. The person of lower status *does solve* the problem.
4. The person of lower status *is rewarded* for answering.[54]

---

52 Müller, 'Die weisheitliche Lehrerzählung', 94.

53 S. Niditch and R. Doran, 'The Success Story of the Wise Courtier: A Formal Approach', *JBL* 96 (1977): 179-193.

54 Niditch and Doran, 'The Success Story', 180. They describe it in terms of Aarne and Thompson's folklore type 922 (Clever Acts and Words). At 186-187 they apply the 922 pattern to Gen 41:1-45, and conclude that Genesis 41 is a standard 922

This common pattern, and a number of specific parallels, causes them to speak of these texts belonging to "the folktale genre of wisdom literature."[55] On their view, chapter 41 is a miniature of the rise of Joseph in the story as a whole.[56]

L.M. WILLS

Wills' work deals with the broader methodological question of how to determine whether or not a story like that of Joseph is a 'wisdom narrative'.[57] Since his work moves in some new areas, it is worth analysing carefully.

Wills is critical of what he calls the 'proverbial correlative' view of von Rad, which establishes that a theme in the narrative can be linked to a verse or verses in Proverbs.[58] He makes the important methodological point that "[w]e must think of wisdom narratives as narratives and not as proverbial correlatives. ... it is the narrative structure, and not the proverbial correlative, to which we should pay careful attention."[59] Such an observation rightly implies that the work of von Rad, Loader and Wessels must be pushed much further if they were to establish the wisdom nature of the Joseph narrative.

Furthermore, he is not persuaded that the wisdom orientation of 'Jewish court conflicts' has been established simply by observing the providential working of God in the narrative. In fact, Wills argues, the main theme of the Joseph story is not providence but justice - that the wise and righteous

---

type, "with a marked theological slant" (193).

55 Niditch and Doran, 'The Success Story', 181-182. Sometimes there are quite specific parallels such as being clothed in a certain way (Gen 41:42 and Arabic Ahiqar 7:21). The expressions in common include 'called to' (קרא + ל) + members of court (see Gen 41:8; Dan 2:2; Ahiqar 5:4), and a nuanced reward motif ('set him over', Gen 41:33, 40, 41; Dan 2:48; Ahiqar 7:23).

56 Niditch and Doran, 'The Success Story', 185.

57 Wills, *The Jew in the Court*, especially 1-38, 52-55; L.M. Wills, 'Observations on "Wisdom Narratives" in Early Biblical Literature', in *Of Scribes and Scrolls: Studies on the Hebrew Bible, Intertestamental Judaism, and Christian Origins. Presented to John Strugnell on the Occasion of His Sixtieth Birthday.* eds. H.W. Attridge, J.J. Collins and T.H. Tobin. (Lanham: University Press of America, 1990), 57-66. His article treats the same material as his book but pushes the methodological issues further.

58 Wills, 'Observations', 58. Von Rad, he suggests, was not really interested in formal parallels, merely in observing that wisdom ideals and values were embodied in the protagonist, and that the Joseph story dramatized how to live in the world. Wills, *The Jew in the Court*, 29-30 concludes that "[t]he search for a 'proverbial correlative' as a prime consideration in wisdom narratives, while pointing us in a fruitful direction, was ultimately unsuccessful."

59 Wills, *The Jew in the Court*, 32-33.

hero will succeed and that his wisdom is only a means to this just end.[60] Even so, he regards as too narrow the line championed by Crenshaw that wisdom influence cannot be established unless a clear *Sitz im Leben* can be demonstrated. Wills asks the very important question, "Is it necessary to locate a wisdom text in a definite *Sitz-im-Leben*, or at least in a certain social milieu?"[61] Wills concludes that it is the institution of transmission (be that clan, court or school) which is crucial for identifying wisdom materials.[62] Most contentiously, Wills suggests that, instead of comparing a tale like Joseph to the book of Proverbs, we should compare the figure and story of Joseph to the vast range of legends in the narrative wisdom literature of Asia Minor, Greece and Persia.[63] In the end, Wills concludes that in the court conflict legends (such as Joseph), what is true across the literature from a range of cultures is that the wise, righteous hero or heroine, always succeeds.[64] They can be called wisdom narratives in that the wisdom figure ultimately prospers. The extent to which comparative literature is useful depends, however, on the extent to which Israel's wisdom thought had no theological distinctives. However, Wills' work is still invaluable in showing the clear existence of an ancient literary genre - the didactic narrative, and that this is tied up with wisdom figures. His thesis suggests that didactic narrative is a more legitimate genre description of the Joseph story than a term borrowed from modern literary criticism, such as 'novella'.[65]

Subsequent Studies of the Joseph Narrative

C. WESTERMANN

Westermann's commentary on Genesis 37-50 was published in 1982

---

60 Wills, *The Jew in the Court*, 30-31. He accepts the distinction made by W.L. Humphreys in 'A Life-Style for Diaspora: A Study in the Tales of Esther and Daniel', *JBL* 92 (1973): 211-223. Humphreys distinguished between 'court contests' (those court legends in which a wise person of undistinguished status, but from within the court, against all expectations makes wise judgments, solves a problem, or interprets a dream or omen that no-one else in the court can, and is elevated to a high position in the court) and 'court conflicts' (here the wise courtier begins in a respected position, but is persecuted or conspired against, usually by other courtiers, suffers a fall, and is finally vindicated before the king). The Joseph story is clearly a contest.

61 Wills, *The Jew in the Court*, 27-28; Wills, 'Observations', 58.

62 Wills, 'Observations', 59; Wills, *The Jew in the Court*, 32.

63 Wills, *The Jew in the Court*, 35-37.

64 Wills, *The Jew in the Court*, 37-38, 49.

65 For a critique of 'novella' as a useful category, see D. Garrett, *Rethinking Genesis* (Grand Rapids: Baker, 1991) 48-49.

(English translation 1986). Despite the significance of this commentary, he does not make a major contribution to the debate about wisdom in the Joseph narrative, agreeing in general terms with Crenshaw and Redford - "it is neither a didactic narrative nor a wisdom narrative; the exegesis has shown this and the structure has now demonstrated it."[66]. Although he notes that Coats restricts wisdom to chapters 39-41, he agrees with Redford that chapter 39 must be excluded since it centres on the scorned woman, not the 'loose woman' of Proverbs.[67] Westermann says there is general agreement that sapiential motifs are present in 40-41, but even there he suggests that they are determined by the setting of the narrative - the king's counsellor is in the royal court.[68]

Westermann appears to hold that the narrative form is inconsistent with wisdom literature, for he asks "how can the Joseph story be a short story and at the same time belong to the wisdom teaching?"[69] While Westermann's analysis of the Joseph narrative will be crucial to this study, he does not appear to make a significant or original contribution to the debate about wisdom in the story.

W.L. HUMPHREYS

Humphreys' initial foray into the Joseph narrative was in his doctoral dissertation on the motif of the wise courtier.[70] More recently, he has given a very detailed treatment of Joseph in a careful literary study that raises the issue of wisdom elements as well as how the Joseph story secured its place within the Torah.[71]

Humphreys notes that the Joseph story is set, like Esther and Daniel, in a foreign court, and tells of success despite the odds. He regards chapters 40-41 as pivotal to the story as a whole, detailing the rise of the hero in a court contest.[72] While there is a clear element of the fortuitous in the story, Joseph

---

66 Westermann, *Genesis 37-50*, 247.
67 Westermann, *Genesis 37-50*, 27. At 248, he adds that in a wisdom narrative good would have to be rewarded and wickedness punished in accordance with the act-consequence sequence.
68 Westermann, *Genesis 37-50*, 247-248.
69 Westermann, *Genesis 37-50*, 19.
70 W.L. Humphreys, 'The Motif of the Wise Courtier in the Old Testament' (Dissertation, PhD, Union Theological Seminary, New York, 1970). He also contributed the article, 'Joseph Story, The', in *Interpreter's Dictionary of the Bible, Supplementary Volume* (Nashville: Abingdon, 1976), 491-493.
71 W.L. Humphreys, *Joseph and His Family: A Literary Study*. Studies on Personalities of the Old Testament. (Columbia: University of South Carolina Press, 1988).
72 Humphreys, *Joseph and His Family*, 11. At 176, after identifying the wisdom elements in this kernel, Humphreys suggests that a re-reading of the rest of the Joseph novella shows that this kernel is presupposed. Joseph's own words in Gen

is the model wise courtier who makes the most of whatever opportunities are set before him. He concludes that

> the background traditions against which this story is to be understood are those generally treasured in wisdom circles. Certain admonitions and ideals of the wise find illustration here in a distilled narrative. ... The wisdom themes seem so to permeate the material that some close influence from these circles seems probable.[73]

Humphreys then considers the etiological thrust of Gen 47:13-26, the question of the dreams, and polemic against foreign wisdom. He argues that Crenshaw and others have overemphasised these, but that, while these may not be found in biblical wisdom literature, they are not antithetical to it.[74] Thus, despite the criticisms raised above, "the tale was composed and treasured by those steeped in court wisdom traditions."[75]

He adopts a mediating position about the depiction of Joseph in relation to the story as a whole: "He [Joseph] is in the full novella neither a straightforward illustration of wisdom tenets - a 'type' of the ideal wise courtier - nor the crass antithesis of this ideal that Redford's counter to von Rad would make of him."[76] The change in Joseph between chapters 40-41 and 42-45 is only one of degree, and can be accounted for by his concern being drawn away from national concerns to more personal ones.[77] He concedes that "the theme of the hidden providence of God is too common to be designated as a sure sign of wisdom material", though it is a prominent wisdom theme.[78] He also finds it useful to make a distinction between wisdom literature written by the sages, and others within the 'effective reach' of the wise.[79]

One pregnant aspect of the story is that the climax of Joseph as courtier is not his rise to power in the royal court, but rather the reuniting and

---

    45:8, 9, 12 assume the events of chapter 41; the material in chapters 42-50 - the famine, Joseph's position and authority - require the material given in the story of Joseph's rise to power.

73 Humphreys, *Joseph and His Family*, 147-148. Similarly, in 'Joseph Story, The', 492.

74 Humphreys, *Joseph and His Family*, 148-150.

75 Humphreys, *Joseph and His Family*, 150.

76 Humphreys, *Joseph and His Family*, 181; Humphreys, 'Joseph Story, The', 492 concedes that "he is hardly such a model [of a wise courtier] in much of Gen. 37, 42-48, 50".

77 Humphreys, *Joseph and His Family*, 181.

78 Humphreys, *Joseph and His Family*, 188.

79 Humphreys, *Joseph and His Family*, 189. By this latter category he means those who "write about and possibly under the influence of themes and ideals treated by the wise."

deliverance of his family, who are also the chosen covenant line. In the last chapter of Humphreys' book, he asks the crucial question about how the novella fits within the broader context of the rest of the *Torah*. While he is partially preoccupied here with detailed questions of harmonising tensions within the text, he rightly notes that this broader context reorients the motif of the wise courtier. The focus is no longer on serving Pharaoh, nor even reuniting his family; it is now on Yahweh and Joseph's function in preserving the heirs of the promise on their way to nationhood.[80]

OTHER RECENT STUDIES

A number of other studies have been undertaken of either the Joseph narrative or the book of Genesis more broadly. The recent commentaries by Wenham and Hamilton make important observations on the characterisation of Joseph and the key ideas of Genesis 37-50, but they do not specifically address the issue of whether or not the Joseph story is a wisdom or wisdom-influenced text.[81] Recent German-language commentaries have also not largely focused on this aspect of Genesis 37-50.[82] Green's literary reading of these chapters does not largely consider the question of wisdom elements and themes, although it does explore the literary aspects of characterisation. Wildavsky's monograph focuses quite strongly on the issue of characterisation, arguing that Joseph is a negative model of assimilation. His work has important ramifications for the question of wisdom in the Joseph story, but that is not his primary concern. Issues of characterisation, at least in parts of Genesis 37-50, are also explored in recent monographs by Fung and Pirson, but the focus in each case is not on Joseph and

---

80 Humphreys, *Joseph and His Family*, 200-201. However, it still does not seem to have grappled sufficiently with the interrelationship between the wisdom and covenant strands present within the Joseph narrative.

81 G.J. Wenham, *Genesis 16-50*. WBC. (Dallas: Word, 1994); V.P. Hamilton, *The Book of Genesis Chapters 18-50*. NICOT. (Grand Rapids: Eerdmans, 1995). Similar comments could also be made about the recent commentaries of Brueggemann, Fretheim, Janzen, Ross, Hartley, Sailhamer, Adar, Alter, Sarna, and Scullion.

82 Schmitt, *Die Nichtpriesterliche Josephsgeschichte*; J. Scharbert, *Genesis 12-50*. Die Neue Echter Bibel. (Würzburg: Echter, 1986); L. Schmidt, *Literarische Studien zur Josephsgeschichte*. BZAW, 167. (Berlin: Walter de Gruyter 1986); W. Dietrich, *Die Josephserzählung als Novelle und Geschichtsschreibung: Zugleich ein Beitrag zur Pentateuchfrage*. Biblisch-Theologische Studien, 14. (Neukirchen-Vluyn: Neukirchener Verlag, 1989); N. Kebekus, *Die Joseferzählung: Literarkritische und redaktionsgeschichtliche Untersuchungen zu Genesis 37-50* (Münster: Waxmann, 1990); H. Schweizer, *Die Josefsgeschichte: Konstituierung des Textes*. 2 vols. (Tübingen: Francke, 1991). Generally these have been more concerned with source critical matters and redactional history, rather than how the different elements relate together in the final form.

wisdom. Da Silva's study of dreams and clothing in Genesis 37-50 is also very stimulating, and is especially valuable for a better understanding of chapter 37.[83]

However, since these recent works do not explicitly address the issue of wisdom and the Joseph narrative, it is proposed to interact with them in the exegetical chapters of this study.

Recent Revisionism

S.D.E. WEEKS

A major contribution has been made by Weeks, who questions many 'consensus views' in wisdom scholarship.[84] Three aspects of his arguments are of especial interest to this study - his analysis of the Joseph story itself; his assessment of Solomonic times; and his evaluation of the evidence for schools in Israel. The first deals with the text of Genesis; the latter two with the question of *Sitz im Leben*.

Firstly, he discusses the characterisation of Joseph and argues that, if the text were a didactic one, Joseph's character would be more clearly drawn, and more consistently the ideal.[85] Joseph's rise to power is not a pattern for

---

83 B. Green, *"What Profit for Us?" Remembering the Story of Joseph* (Lanham: University Press of America, 1996); A. Wildavsky, *Assimilation versus Separation: Joseph the Administrator and the Politics of Religion in Biblical Israel* (New Brunswick: Transaction, 1993). The studies by Y.-W. Fung, *Victim and Victimizer. Joseph's Interpretation of his Destiny*. JSOTSup, 308. (Sheffield: Sheffield Academic Press, 2000) and R. Pirson, *The Lord of the Dreams. A Semantic and Literary Analysis of Genesis 37-50*. JSOTSup, 355. (Sheffield: Sheffield Academic Press, 2002) were both published after this study was substantially written, and are thus not dealt with at length. A. da Silva, *La symbolique des rêves et des vêtements dans l'histoire de Joseph et de ses frères*. Héritage et projet, 52. (Québec: Fides, 1994). Other recent literary studies of themes in and sometimes beyond the Joseph story include L.A. Turner, *Announcements of Plot in Genesis*. JSOTSup, 96. (Sheffield: JSOT Press, 1990) and R. Syrén, *The Forsaken First-Born: A Study of a Recurrent Motif in the Patriarchal Narratives*. JSOTSup, 133. (Sheffield: Sheffield Academic Press, 1993). R.E. Longacre, *Joseph: A Story of Divine Providence: A Text Theoretical and Textlinguistic Analysis of Genesis 37 and 39-48* (Winona Lake: Eisenbrauns, 1989) has also studied the textlinguistic aspects of the Joseph story.

84 Weeks, *Early Israelite Wisdom*. This is a revised form of the author's Oxford DPhil dissertation. His material on Joseph is set out in more detail - especially in relation to dreams and the question of mantic wisdom - in S.D.E. Weeks, 'Joseph, Dreams and Wisdom', (Dissertation, MPhil, Oxford University, 1989).

85 Weeks, *Early Israelite Wisdom*, 93-94. He notes that Joseph did not have a fine education nor any experience in the ways of the world; he cannot rightly be seen as a person of self-control; and in chapters 42-44 he was punishing not testing his

aspiring courtiers, for it is not a story of an able counsellor rising through the ranks of bureaucracy.[86] In fact, Weeks suggests that the correspondences between Joseph's behaviour or character and wisdom literature, are more apparent than real. He considers Coats' view that Joseph is characterised in chapters 39-41 as wise, and regards Joseph in these chapters as a pale figure; his conduct described only in general terms; his administrative success due to divine intervention, not his own ability; and Joseph's dream interpretations rather than his administrative activities being the focus.[87] The incident with Potiphar's wife is viewed as having so many parallels in the ancient literary world, that it is improbable that Genesis 39 was composed to illustrate wisdom teachings about adultery.[88] Finally, he finds that the phrase 'fear God' is not used in a distinctively wisdom sense. Thus, Joseph's character and behaviour is unable to be emulated, and the particular concerns of wisdom literature are rather absent.[89]

The second major part of his discussion of Joseph concerns the narrative's portrayal of God and its religious ideas. Since it is the dreams, he argues, that dominate the narrative, he notes that Joseph's ability to interpret is clearly God-given, rather than Joseph's achievement.[90] He seeks to distinguish passages like Gen 45:5-8 and 50:19-20 from the 'parallel' wisdom texts cited by von Rad, suggesting that "the Joseph Narrative integrates human and divine efforts, while the wisdom sayings contrast them."[91] While he concedes that God's action is pictured as somewhat enigmatic, the religious ideas and portrayal of God in the narrative are not consonant with those of the wisdom tradition, and often bear closer parallels with Old Testament texts that have no wisdom provenance.[92] Thus, he has sought to dismantle all of the supposed links between the Joseph

---

brothers. Weeks also comments on Joseph's tale-bearing, his indiscreet revelation of his dreams, his false accusations of his brothers, noting that these are not in accord with the ethical ideals of wisdom.

86   Weeks, *Early Israelite Wisdom*, 94-95.

87   Weeks, *Early Israelite Wisdom*, 96.

88   Weeks, *Early Israelite Wisdom*, 97-99. At 98 he comments "that it is a strange didacticism indeed which promises a prison sentence as the reward for virtue!"

89   Weeks, *Early Israelite Wisdom*, 100-102.

90   Weeks, *Early Israelite Wisdom*, 102-104. This may not be a useful division, for the two are not incompatible.

91   Weeks, *Early Israelite Wisdom*, 107. As shall be shown later, Weeks' argument is quite weak at this point.

92   Weeks, *Early Israelite Wisdom*, 105-109. He argues that there are many places in the Old Testament where unconscious submission to the divine intention is apparent. He cites Assyria and Cyrus (Isa 10:5ff; 45:1ff); the nations in Amos 9:7; Sihon in Deut 2:30ff; Abigail in 1 Sam 25:32ff; various actions in 1 and 2 Kings (for example, 1 Kgs 15:4, 29-30; 16:1-2, 18); and God hardening Pharaoh's heart in Exod 7:3-4.

story and wisdom.

The two other areas can be dealt with more briefly. In relation to the existence of an extensive Solomonic bureaucracy (modelled on Egypt), or early evidence for scribal schools, Weeks' questioning analysis is quite penetrating. He finds little hard evidence for either hypothesis, though it is fair to comment that he cannot, of course, disprove either.[93] Yet he rightly cautions us not to build elaborate theories on the assumption that these hypotheses are true. However, even if his cautions are right, they do not in themselves preclude wisdom literary influence in Joseph; they merely eliminate one or more possible candidates for the setting of the wisdom movement in Israel. Even if Weeks is right, his line of argument does not preclude a dating in the early monarchy, nor the discovery of wisdom elements in the text. This will be explored below.

M.V. Fox

Most recently, Fox has argued against any the Joseph story sharing significant elements with biblical wisdom.[94] After a useful survey of previous studies, Fox proposes that Genesis 37, 39-45 and 50 reveal values and assumptions that do not reflect the didactic wisdom of the proverbial literature. If anything, the wise behaviour of Joseph in these chapters is closer to the mantic wisdom and the tenacity of faith in times of danger that marks the book of Daniel.[95] His article proposes no new methodology, but largely outlines the view that Joseph's actions are best correlated with Daniel not Proverbs. In particular, he argues that Joseph could not be a useful model for an aspiring courtier since his resistance of temptation does not lead to success, and his rise to power is substantially due to God's disclosure to him of the interpretation of dreams, a revelation rather than a skill that can be learned.[96] The wisdom Joseph displays is through God's gift rather than being shaped or trained by the sages. These suggestions can best be dealt in the exegesis of the text of Genesis 37-50.

Some Preliminary Observations

Our survey of these studies of wisdom and the Joseph narrative has only been cursory, and no attempt has been made to fully evaluate them at this stage. What has emerged is that there are still many unanswered questions, and in some ways a serious *impasse* has been reached. However, the

93   He is strongly influenced by the socio-archaeological approach of D.W. Jamieson-Drake, *Scribes and Schools in Monarchic Judah*. Journal for the Study of the Old Testament Supplement Series, 109. (Sheffield: Almond Press, 1991).
94   M.V. Fox, 'Wisdom in the Joseph Story', *VT* 51 (2001), 26-41.
95   Fox, 'Wisdom' 38-40.
96   Fox, 'Wisdom' 30-34.

following observations can already be made:

1. It seems clear that the Joseph narrative as a whole (Genesis 37-50) is not a pure example of wisdom literature, for it has other crucial elements contained in it. There are powerful arguments both for and against some wisdom 'elements' and 'influence' in the narrative.

2. Yet, the studies explored above often do not discuss how any wisdom features - if they can be established - relate to the other aspects of the story. This is especially vital in relation to the covenant or salvation historical elements which are prominent in parts of Genesis 37-50. Previous studies have tended to focus on the presence or absence of these elements, not on their interaction with wisdom features. The interaction of any wisdom aspects of the narrative with the other traditions is largely unexplored. Are they just side by side with no interaction? Does one lead into the other? Does one override the other? Are they in tension with each other, or contradiction, leading to a deconstruction of the text? Has one been supplemented, edited, qualified by the other? A closer study of the text is needed, with these kind of questions being asked.

3. A number of interpretive issues have been raised in the various studies, and loom as crucial. How is Joseph portrayed, especially in chapter 37? What is the role of chapters like 38 and 39, and 46-49, in the story as a whole? How do chapters 39-41 relate to the rest of the story? What is the theme of the story as a whole? Does chapter 50 or chapter 45 mark the end of the Joseph narrative? These issues require a more detailed study of the text, which will constitute a reasonable portion of this study.

4. There is a pressing need for both terminological and methodological clarity. Our survey has revealed widespread differences in methodology, but there is rarely any articulation of the methodology used. The studies above, with a few notable exceptions, do not generally ask the critical methodological question of how to assess whether there is wisdom 'influence', or whether the alleged wisdom elements are simply part of Israel's common cultural stock. An agreed set of criteria has not yet been forthcoming. It is necessary to explore whether matters of vocabulary, genre, setting, characterisation or theme, or perhaps even a cluster of these, can determine the presence or absence of 'wisdom'. Furthermore, little attention has been given to how the narrative form might affect wisdom ideas. For these reasons it is proposed to turn to terminological and methodological questions for the rest of this chapter.

Terminology and Methodology

The Need for Terminological Clarity

A variety of different terms have been used in the debate over wisdom
influence in other traditions, and often the lack of precision has served to
cloud the debate. While some have been advocating the minimal position of
'wisdom echoes' in a text, others have mounted arguments against the
maximal position of a narrative as a whole being viewed as wisdom
literature. Some have pointed to ideas and motifs found in wisdom books;
still others deny that the word 'wisdom' should be used unless a probable
social setting for the text can be reconstructed.[97] A lack of terminological
clarity has resulted in scholars talking past each other, rather than to one
another. There are, of course, no right and wrong terms, but it is vital that
these terms are not regarded as interchangeable, and that writers articulate
the nuances of the terms that they choose to use.

At one end of the continuum are terms like 'wisdom books' which refer
clearly to the mainstream books in the wisdom tradition or movement -
Proverbs, Job, Ecclesiastes, perhaps Song of Songs. In a derived sense,
'wisdom literature' or 'wisdom text' generally implies that a text not only
reflects ideas found in the wisdom books, but that the corpus of literature
thought to come from a wisdom setting should be expanded to include this
text as well - that this text is the product of wisdom writers just as much as
the book of Proverbs. The 'wisdom setting' is often understood to be a
royal court setting, commonly a wisdom school for training courtiers, but
others would argue for the setting of wisdom literature to be in the clan or
family, either in addition to, or instead of a royal court.[98]

Further along the continuum is the category of 'wisdom influence',
which is often a claim that wisdom forms or ideas (or a redactor who
belongs to a 'wisdom setting') are one part of a given text, and that these
wisdom aspects have mingled with, and influenced, the other traditions and
material in the text. Of course, this 'wisdom influence' might vary from a

---

97   The plethora of terms includes: wisdom text, wisdom literature, wisdom influence,
     wisdom echoes, wisdom allusions, wisdom elements, 'wisdom-like' elements,
     wisdom narrative, wisdom tale, wisdom vocabulary, wisdom figures or characters,
     wisdom tradition, wisdom settings, the intellectual tradition, wisdom contact,
     wisdom parallels, wisdom affinities, wisdom distinctives, wisdom themes or
     theology, wisdom ideals, wisdom flavour, trajectories, patterns, motifs, genres, and
     forms. There are also some conceptually broader terms such as inner-biblical
     allusions, inner-biblical exegesis or intertextual links.

98   See, for example, C. Westermann, *Roots of Wisdom: The Oldest Proverbs of Israel
     and Other Peoples.* trans. J.D. Charles. (Louisville: Westminster John Knox, 1995).

minor wisdom influence through to a dominant wisdom influence. Wisdom influence, however, is distinct from a claim that a text is a wisdom text, though there are likely to be some blurred edges between a wisdom text and a text with a dominant wisdom influence. A term like 'wisdom narrative' or 'wisdom tale' is often not clear. Sometimes what is meant is that the whole story is the product of a wisdom writer or setting; at other times it may mean only that there is significant wisdom influence, or a kind of shorthand for 'a tale showing evidence of wisdom ideas'. Such terms are not very satisfactory.

Further along again is the term 'wisdom element', 'wisdom echo', 'wisdom parallel' or clearer still 'wisdom-like element'. This is more a minimal claim that aspects of a text (ideas, motifs, forms, vocabulary etc.) appear to mirror or remind the reader of similar aspects found in wisdom books. There is not necessarily any assertion that they have come from a wisdom setting, or have been added by wisdom writers, though this may have been the case. All that is being claimed is that the particular aspects are prominent in (that is, typical of), and distinctive (not necessarily exclusive) to, other texts that are clearly wisdom literature.[99] Such terms leave open the question of the setting of the text, and the way in which these 'wisdom elements' relate to other parts of the text. Terms like 'wisdom themes', 'wisdom motifs', 'wisdom ideas', or 'wisdom thinking' appear to be a particularisation of a wisdom element - simply specifying the aspect that is alleged to be found in wisdom books.

How does this category relate to the question of 'wisdom influence'? Firstly, identifying a 'wisdom element' logically precedes deciding whether or not there is wisdom influence. It is indicating the data (the 'elements') that are the subject of a theory (for example, that there is 'wisdom influence'). Secondly, identifying 'wisdom elements' neither demands nor precludes that there is wisdom influence in a text. Indeed, the influence could work in either direction, or there could be no identifiable influence at all.[100] Thirdly, the identification of 'wisdom elements' may be for other reasons than determining 'wisdom influence'. This study proposes to use the term 'wisdom literary influence'. By this is meant how the 'wisdom-like elements' in the text relate to the other elements in the text's final form. It

---

99 There are, for example, elements that may be 'wisdom distinctives' but not 'wisdom exclusives' such as 'the fear of God motif'. Of course, debate is inevitable over how distinctive an aspect must be in order to be viewed as a wisdom element. This does not invalidate the approach, but it does suggest that it is a difficult and sometimes disputed process.

100 Thus, S.L. Harris, *Proverbs 1-9: A Study of Inner-Biblical Interpretation*. SBLDS, 150. (Atlanta: Scholars, 1995) argues that certain portions of Proverbs 1-9 (1:8-19; 1:20-33 and 6:1-19) reflect a revitalising of, and borrowing from, earlier biblical traditions (portions of the Joseph story and the book of Jeremiah).

is, in other words, theorising about how the data relates together in the text as we have it, without prejudging the issue of setting or redaction. The goal of this process is to discern the interrelationship of 'wisdom-like elements' with aspects from other traditions. This will be amplified below.

In Search of a Methodology

There has been no agreement in the broader debate on what is and is not a legitimate methodology for assessing wisdom influence in non-wisdom literature. There has been debate - reflected in the Joseph narrative as clearly as anywhere else - between those who find 'wisdom-like elements' everywhere and those who question them anywhere, but little common ground on how to approach the task. Proponents of different views seem to be talking on different planes, and the issue appears no closer to resolution. This study will identify the main approaches, evaluate them, and propose a way forward in relation to the Joseph narrative.

Current Methodologies

Scholars have tended to argue for the presence (or absence) of 'wisdom-like elements' in non-wisdom texts along several lines.[101] These may be classified as formal, linguistic, social setting and content approaches.

THE FORMAL APPROACH

Firstly, there are the formal arguments from literary form, genre or even style. Nel, for example, notes that a number of literary forms are characteristic of wisdom,[102] but there are two possible drawbacks. Firstly, many of the wisdom forms were used by non-wisdom figures (for example, the parable by the prophet Nathan in 2 Samuel 12). This, however, does not negate the identification of wisdom-like elements, but may hamper the process of discerning wisdom influence. Secondly, such approaches have tended to be more effective in discerning wisdom influence on poetic texts, like the Psalms and some prophets, but less effective in narrative, where a

---

101 In relation to the prophets, D.F. Morgan, 'Wisdom and the Prophets', in *Studia Biblica 1978: I*. JSOTSup, 11. (Sheffield: JSOT Press, 1979), 214 observes "[t]he wisdom influence found in the prophets can be separated into three basic categories: form and style; theme and motif; and vocabulary."

102 P.J. Nel, 'The Genres of Biblical Wisdom Literature', *JNSL* 9 (1981): 129-142. For an exploration of the distinctive rhetoric of the sages see J.L. Crenshaw, 'Wisdom and Authority: Sapiential Rhetoric and Its Warrants', in *Congress Volume, Vienna 1980*. VTSup, 32, ed. J.A. Emerton. (Leiden: E.J. Brill, 1981), 10-29. This comes very close to a content approach, but insofar as he explores rhetorical techniques, and the way authority is appealed to, it is still a formal approach.

change in form or genre would quite naturally be expected.[103] It is possible, however, that some wisdom features (such as the tendency to make observations, rather than issue commands) might still be preserved despite the change from poetry to prose, but these are more likely to be material rather than formal aspects.

Another area where formal matters have been used to identify wisdom material is in the study of the pattern of the whole text. Thus Niditch and Doran use formal criteria to establish that a number of tales (Daniel 2, Ahiqar 5-7, Genesis 37-50) have the same inner structure.[104] The work of Müller and Wills in this regard has been discussed already.

Along a similar vein, but keeping to canonical texts in the Hebrew Bible, some have pointed out formal and content parallels between the Joseph story, Esther and Daniel. The conclusion reached by some is that these three are all 'wisdom narratives'.[105] This is, of course, open to the charge of being circular, but may be useful if parallels can be found with 'wisdom narratives' from other Ancient Near Eastern or classical literature, or other Old Testament narratives that can be classified on other grounds as being wisdom tales. It is, at best, a supporting argument only.

THE LINGUISTIC APPROACH

Secondly, there are linguistic arguments, based on a shared vocabulary between wisdom books and a text under consideration. In this vein, Scott has proposed 77 words that are characteristic of wisdom texts or appear in a

---

103 In narrative text, many of the genres are unlikely to be prominent such as the beatitude, the sentence saying, the popular proverb, the riddle, the numerical saying, onomastica. An example of where the formal parallels are explored in relation to poetic/prophetic literature is J.W. Whedbee, *Isaiah & Wisdom* (Nashville: Abingdon, 1971) 23-110. R.N. Whybray, *The Intellectual Tradition in the Old Testament*. BZAW, 135. (Berlin: Walter de Gruyter, 1974) reflects on the distinctives of narrative when it discusses the usefulness of form-criticism. At 72, Whybray writes that "[g]enerally speaking, form-criticism is inappropriate as a method for the detection of the presence of the intellectual tradition [his term for 'wisdom'] because the enterprise is by definition a search for a particular tradition in books or passages whose form *differs* from that of the books in which it is most clearly at home. The form of a narrative, for example, is necessarily different from that of a proverbial saying." Whybray thus acknowledges that the absence of wisdom forms does not disqualify a narrative text from having significant wisdom elements; indeed you would not expect to find them.

104 Niditch and Doran, 'The Success Story', 179-193 insist that the mere accumulation of parallel motifs is not sufficient to establish relatedness between narratives.

105 In relation to the book of Esther, see M. Gan, 'The Book of Esther in the Light of the Story of Joseph in Egypt', *Tarbiz* 31 (1961): 144-149, I-II; J. R. Kriel, 'Esther: The story of a girl or the story of her God?', *Theologia Evangelica* 19 (1986): 2-14.

concentrated fashion in wisdom books.[106] Whybray lists 9 words that are
'apparently' exclusive to the wisdom tradition.[107] When he looks at the
distribution of the root חכם in the the Joseph story, he discerns strong
evidence of wisdom influence.[108]

This line of argument is very promising, but may give a false sense of
objectivity in that the data is fairly limited due to the small size of the text.
Indeed, Whybray may be claiming too much for the linguistic argument. A
text can, for example, have 'wisdom-like elements' in it, even in the
absence of distinctively wisdom words, in the same way that many suggest
that the New Testament has some trinitarian features despite the absence of
words like 'trinity', 'triune', or 'three-in-one'. Similarly, Genesis 3 is
rightly regarded as a foundational passage on the subject of sin, despite the
remarkable absence of the terminology of sin.

Along these lines Thomas has argued that in discerning the influence of
Romanticism in literature, the test is not just whether words like 'feel' or
'romantic' occur regularly, for on this basis both Keats and Rousseau would
be excluded.[109] In considering the 'metaphysical' school of English poetry,
he adopts a Wittgensteinian category in concluding that "it is the 'family
resemblance' that matters and not the presence or absence of any particular
term."[110] Applying this to the question of wisdom influence, Thomas
suggests that the presence or absence of 'wisdom terminology' is not
crucial, but rather whether the tone of the work has the 'family
resemblance' of wisdom. While this necessarily makes the criteria harder to
discern, his point is cogent.

The linguistic approach also seems to make no allowance for the shift
from poetic sayings to prose narrative. In narrative, a mood can be created
by dialogue, narrative interplay (as in Genesis 3), irony, what is not said,
since there is not the tightness of word limits or poetic structure. A narrative
could, for example, teach or illustrate the lesson 'be shrewd with your
money', without using the word 'shrewd' at all. Thus, the presence of
vocabulary typical of, or prominent in, mainstream wisdom texts may be

106 R.B.Y. Scott, *The Way of Wisdom in the Old Testament* (New York: Macmillan,
     1971) 121-122. Whybray, *Intellectual Tradition*, 121 criticises Scott's list, and
     notes that it includes many common words. Interestingly, Scott does not outline
     how he arrives at his list.
107 Whybray, *Intellectual Tradition*, 142-149.
108 Whybray, *Intellectual Tradition*, 85-87. Of course, Whybray's conclusions here
     would be equally consistent with Coats' view that there is a wisdom kernel in a
     non-wisdom tale. See also T. Frymer-Kensky, 'The Sage in the Pentateuch:
     Soundings', in *The Sage in Israel and the Ancient Near East*. eds. J.G. Gammie and
     L.G. Perdue. (Winona Lake: Eisenbrauns, 1990), 280.
109 J.H. Thomas, 'Philosophy and the Critical Study of Wisdom Literature', *HeyJl* 20
     (1979): 292.
110 Thomas, 'Philosophy', 293.

important evidence but the absence of distinctive terminology does not preclude wisdom literary influence.

THE SOCIAL SETTING APPROACH

Thirdly, there are those proposals which attempt to explore a proposed wisdom setting in which the text could have been composed or used. If the author was known it would be possible to study their upbringing or education; if the period of writing was identifiable, one could look at the cultural movements and reactions of the time. This may be useful, but it is rarely attainable with any degree of precision. Since most narratives are quite old, and their authors commonly not known, the value of such an approach will often be quite limited.

This, of course, was one of the pillars of von Rad's contribution, which argued for a dating of the Joseph narrative in the 'Solomonic enlightenment'.[111] The very existence of this *'Aufklärung'* (Enlightenment) has been roundly criticised and remains only a theory.[112] Related to this debate is whether a system of schools was established in 10th century BCE Israel to train officials for service in the royal court. This notion has been argued for by Lemaire, but strongly disputed by Golka, Jamieson-Drake and Weeks.[113] The arguments of Jamieson-Drake are crucial (and largely relied upon by Weeks), suggesting that there is no archaeological evidence

---

111 This was picked up in W. Brueggemann, 'David and his Theologian', *CBQ* 30 (1968): 175-176, then in more detail in Brueggemann, *In Man We Trust*, and, most recently, W. Brueggemann, 'The Social Significance of Solomon', 117-132. See also W. Brueggemann, *Genesis*. Interpretation. (Atlanta: John Knox, 1982); E.W. Heaton, *Solomon's New Men* (London: Thames and Hudson, 1974); T.N.D. Mettinger, *Solomonic State Officials*. CBOTS, 5. (Lund: CWK Gleerups, 1971).

112 See, for example, Crenshaw, 'Prolegomenon', 16-20; R.B.Y. Scott, 'Solomon and the Beginnings of Wisdom in Israel', in *Wisdom in Israel and in the Ancient Near East*. VTSup, 3, eds. M. Noth and D.W. Thomas. (Leiden: E.J. Brill, 1955), 262-279 Weeks, *Early Israelite Wisdom*, 110-131; R.N. Whybray, 'Wisdom Literature in the Reigns of David and Solomon', in *Studies in the Period of David and Solomon and Other Essays*. ed. T. Ishida. (Winona Lake: Eisenbrauns, 1982), 13-26 and R.N. Whybray, 'The Social World of the Wisdom Writers', in *The World of Ancient Israel*. ed. R.E. Clements. (Cambridge: Cambridge University Press, 1989), 227-250.

113 A. Lemaire, *Les Écoles et la formation de la Bible dans l'ancien Israël*. OBO, 39. (Fribourg: Éditions Universitaires, 1981); A. Lemaire, 'Sagesse et écoles', *VT* 34 (1984): 270-281; A. Lemaire, 'The Sage in School and Temple', in *The Sage in Israel and the Ancient Near East*. eds. J.G. Gammie and L.G. Perdue. (Winona Lake: Eisenbrauns, 1990), 165-181. Against Lemaire, see Weeks, *Early Israelite Wisdom*, 132-156, D.W. Jamieson-Drake, *Scribes and Schools in Monarchic Judah*. JSOTSup, 109. (Sheffield: Almond Press, 1991), especially 147-157, and, more moderately, J.L. Crenshaw, 'Education in Ancient Israel', *JBL* 104 (1985): 601-615.

of scribal schools until the 8th century BCE, and one should have expected this from the 10th century BCE if these schools were set up to meet the needs of a growing state bureaucracy in Solomonic times.[114] However, it needs to be said that there is a paucity of data here, which makes any conclusion very tentative, and based largely on an argument from silence. The existence of scribal schools can be neither proved nor disproved on the basis of the available evidence.

Indeed, several other qualifications deserve consideration. Firstly, the value of trying to establish influence on the basis of social setting depends on identifying the right setting for wisdom. The argument of Crenshaw, Jamieson-Drake and Weeks that there is no Solomonic enlightenment, nor widespread bureaucracy, nor early scribal schools, even if this can be established, only precludes wisdom influence from this source, in this period. It does not preclude wisdom influence from 'clan wisdom', nor a family setting (most recently Westermann),[115] wisdom from other Ancient Near Eastern courts, other schools, later royal settings, or a combination of the above. If their argument is accepted, it still only rules out some social settings that may be connected with wisdom. A social setting argument is, at best, only a supporting one.

Secondly, Crenshaw seems to reject wisdom influence on narrative texts if they cannot pass his key requirement - an adequate description of *Sitz im Leben*. Jamieson-Drake and perhaps especially Weeks are taking that as a given, and Weeks thus concludes that Joseph has no wisdom influence because we cannot establish either a Solomonic enlightenment, nor scribal schools at that time. However, it is unlikely that either Job or Ecclesiastes could be established as wisdom literature on the basis of this criterion of *Sitz im Leben*. Any test which would preclude these two wisdom books surely needs to be rethought.

Finally, a social setting argument can easily overlook that a text is in narrative form. Of course, it can be combined with other arguments, as Weeks does. A strength of Weeks' approach is that he deals with the Joseph narrative itself, before thoroughly canvassing the material on Solomon and the scribal schools.[116] Yet, Weeks is consciously reading the narrative against von Rad's interpretation, for von Rad read it in the light of an assumption of Solomonic wisdom and schools for courtiers. What such views fail to deal with is how the distinctive aspects of prose narrative should affect the finding of 'wisdom-like elements' and 'wisdom literary influence'. The social setting approach is also comparatively sterile on its

---

114 Jamieson-Drake, *Scribes and Schools*, 139.
115 Westermann, *Roots of Wisdom*; also Crenshaw in 'Retrospect and Prospect', 161-178.
116 Weeks, *Early Israelite Wisdom*, deals with the Joseph story in chapter 6 before proceeding to the time of Solomon in chapter 7.

own, since it is more concerned to account for the origin of the text than to explain the interrelationship of the ideas in the final form of the text.

THE CONTENT APPROACH

The fourth methodological avenue involves the more broad-ranging proposals of 'wisdom-like elements' based on similarity of theme, content, character or motif. Murphy rightly cautions that this is "a rather slippery criterion".[117] However, its attraction is obvious, in that we would expect that similarity in content or theme would survive the transition from poetic saying to prose narrative. While the language or form may not survive, and the social setting is behind the text, any wisdom-like elements in narrative should be expected to relate to ideas or views prominent in the wisdom books.

The substance of such appeals has been outlined in the survey in the first part of this chapter, and it is already evident that there are three areas of difficulty. Firstly, what ideas, themes, characters and motifs are typical of the wisdom books? The doctrine of retribution, for example, is prominent in Proverbs, but also in Deuteronomy.

Secondly, how can it be determined whether these themes are important to the narrative text, or merely peripheral, or used in a non-wisdom way in the text?[118] Thirdly, given that a wisdom theme could be identified, and given its presence in a narrative, how can it be shown that they are connected or parallel?

What complicates this approach is that scholars are generally seeking to establish 'wisdom influence', or that these are 'wisdom texts' not merely showing the presence of 'wisdom-like elements'. This is an important distinction. The second and third questions above are no obstacle to establishing the presence of wisdom-like elements. Once the general nature of wisdom can be agreed upon, it is then a matter of interpreting the text to discover the presence or absence of such elements. While the conclusions will vary, the process itself can be agreed upon.

A Proposed Methodology for Narrative

All of these are potentially helpful arguments for our purposes, but it is probably a combination of these that will be of most use. Yet none of them take seriously the change from poetic, proverbial text to prose narrative.

---

117 Murphy, *The Tree of Life*, 101. There is often a thin line between the concerns of wisdom and the law (such as the value of landmarks in both Prov 22:28 and Deut 19:14).

118 J. Blenkinsopp, *Wisdom and Law in the Old Testament: The ordering of life in Israel and early Judaism*. Oxford Bible Series. Rev. edn. (Oxford: Oxford University Press, 1995) 42 proposes the test that "the *primary* intent in composing a narrative was to make a point or teach a lesson".

The following principles are therefore proposed as the basis for this study of the Joseph narrative:

1. A vital reason for deciding if there are wisdom aspects in non-wisdom texts is to discover the relationship between wisdom and the other strands or streams of Old Testament thought. The concern of this study is not primarily to look behind the text to discover the nature of Israelite society, the place of schools, nor the nature of court bureaucracy in the early monarchy. All these are legitimate pursuits, but they ought to follow on rather than precede the study of the text itself. For the purpose of determining the interface between wisdom ideas and non-wisdom texts, all that needs to be established are the minimal criteria of 'wisdom-like elements'. The identification of 'wisdom-like elements' is sufficient for determining 'wisdom literary influence' - the influence on the final form of the text by ideas from a particular tradition - even if it does not necessarily establish or clarify any process of influence. Thus, the first task is the need to identify 'wisdom-like elements'.[119]

2. The way to discern how significant the wisdom-like ideas and elements are in a text, and how they are woven into other streams of the text, is by literary analysis of the text in its final form. Just as in the push for final form, synchronic approaches in Old Testament studies generally, so the question of wisdom influence can profitably be studied at the level of the final form. Given the text as a literary entity, how do the 'wisdom-like elements' relate to the other parts of the text, and what can be learnt about the relationship between wisdom and non-wisdom ideas?

3. Any method for detecting wisdom-like elements in a narrative text must take seriously the fact that the text is narrative, and not poetry, hymnic, a prophetic oracle or some other kind of literature. One's methodology for discerning wisdom elements in narrative may coincide with one's methodology for detecting it in other literature, but this ought not to be assumed. Rather, it should be dictated by the kind of text that is studied. There is a need to take seriously that one is dealing with wisdom aspects in a *narrative* text.[120] At its most fundamental level, this asks how the text is to

---

119 This is different from von Rad's 'parallelism' approach in several ways, which simply tries to find parallels or linkages. Firstly, it is asking how central or significant these 'wisdom-like elements' are in a narrative text. Secondly, it will ask whether the ideas are central or peripheral in the wisdom tradition. Twenty parallels from wisdom books - but none of them being central wisdom ideas - do not show a strong interface between the two. Thirdly, it is not just looking for common words or phrases. A narrative might reflect a proverb, not by using its words, but by telling a story in which its truth is illustrated.

120 It is likely that, in a poetic text where there is much greater reflection on and precision in the choice of words, arguments from vocabulary might have greater weight. Perhaps, too, those aspects where narrative is different to a psalm or oracle (such as plot, characterization, narrative theme, narrative pace etc.), are fruitful

be read. Are the implied readers being invited to imitate the character(s) of the story, or are they meant to apply the principles of the narrative theme(s)? Is the purpose of the text more than simply to entertain? Only in the light of the narrative whole - the entire text read as narrative literature, in its broader narrative context - can these questions be suitably answered. Further implications of this will be filled out as the text is studied.

4. A narrative text must be treated as a whole if the interrelationship of wisdom elements and other aspects is to be discerned. An analysis should be undertaken of the whole, and not just those parts of the text that are believed to contain 'wisdom-like elements'.[121] Gispen suggests that the test of 'wisdom influence' is whether the wisdom elements determine the whole of a piece of literature[122] However, it is better to distinguish between the presence of 'wisdom-like elements' in the narrative as a whole, and their presence in every part of a narrative, which would preclude, for example, the absence of wisdom elements in one chapter to highlight a narrative contrast.[123] It is important to allow for narrative artistry in the way that a story is told. A study of the text as a whole may reveal how the wisdom elements of the text are woven into the fabric of the whole.

---

areas to discern wisdom influence in *narrative*. It is worth observing that those who are most interested in the literary aspects of the story (Humphreys, Wills, to some extent Coats) also seem keener to identify wisdom.

121 This is sometimes done out of considerations of space, but it is a criticism that could be levelled at Weeks' study of the Joseph narrative. He studies chapters 37 and 39-41 in some detail, ignores chapter 38, skims quickly through 42-44, focuses of 45:5-8 and 50:19-20, but ignores the rest of chapters 46-50. If chapters 37-50 are the literary unit, then the thrust of the whole narrative, or the narrative as a whole, has not been discerned. A similar criticism could be made of von Rad's initial article, although he has also written a commentary on Genesis.

122 W.H. Gispen, 'What is Wisdom in the Old Testament?', in *Travels in the World of the Old Testament*. eds. M.S.H.G.H. van Vos, P.H.J.H. ten Gate and N.A. van Vehelen. (Assen: van Gorcum, 1974), 79. He warns of the danger of panhokmatism.

123 The insertion of the Judah-Tamar story is chapter 38 may, for example, serve to highlight a contrast between Judah's lack of righteousness in chapter 38 and Joseph's righteousness in chapter 39. See the discussion of these texts below.

CHAPTER 3

The Integrity of Genesis 37-50 as a Literary Unit

This chapter seeks to address the foundational question, 'what are the limits and extent of the Joseph story?'. The following chapters will undertake a literary reading of the Joseph narrative, but this cannot be done until the *prima facie* literary unit is established. Thus there is a need to delimit the text, discerning its boundaries, and to ask whether the whole can be regarded as 'a text'.

Source Analysis and the Joseph Story

Traditional source analysis finds the Joseph story to be an artificial creation caused by the combination of continuous strands, each with its own separate emphasis and theology. Does such an approach prevent identifying Genesis 37-50 as a coherent literary unit?

Traditional Source Criticism

The question of source analysis and the Joseph story has been helpfully explored by a number of scholars.[1] Initially, it seemed to be a fruitful quarry for the source analysts. There is, for example, the doubling of names (Jacob/Israel in 37: 3, 13 and 1, 2, 34), terms (שׂק and אמתחת for sack in 42:27-35), and plot episodes (two sets of dreams; two trips by the brothers; two attempted seductions of Joseph). There are recapitulations (39:10-12, 14-15, 17-18), some apparent discrepancies (37:28 and 36 compared to 37:25; 39:1) and alternatives (Reuben and Judah both trying to prevent Joseph's death in Gen 37: 21-22, 26, 29).[2] Major studies on the Joseph story

---

1 See the survey by Schmidt, *Literarische Studien*, 127-141. Other studies include Coats, *From Canaan to Egypt*, 55-79; Humphreys, *Joseph and His Family*, 3-8; R.N. Whybray, 'The Joseph Story and Pentateuchal Criticism', *VT* 18 (1968): 522-528; R. Rendtorff, 'The Future of Pentateuchal Criticism', *Henoch* 6 (1984): 1-14; Redford, *Biblical Story of Joseph*, 106-186.

2 H.C. White, *Narration and Discourse in the Book of Genesis* (Cambridge: Cambridge University Press, 1991), 232; Coats, *From Canaan to Egypt*, 60-74. D.B. Redford, *Egypt, Canaan, and Israel in Ancient Times* (Princeton: Princeton

that have relied on the source analytical approach include the commentaries by Gunkel and von Rad, and the monograph by Ruppert.[3]

Much of the source analytical interest has been in chapter 37, which Jenks describes as "a parade example of the combination of two originally contradictory strands."[4] Yet even Jenks concedes that the Documentary Hypothesis finds difficulty in the Joseph narrative

> Among the patriarchal narratives the Joseph stories are remarkable both for their length and for their literary unity. This unity makes them resistant to the customary applications of source criticism.[5]

Furthermore, the chapter cannot be unscrambled to provided two complete, continuous sources.[6]

One curious feature is that both Gunkel and von Rad understand the final product to be a work of literary unity, though they do not explore how that can be on the assumption that it is a synthesis of sources.[7] Gunkel concedes that the legends out of which the Joseph story are composed are "very cunningly blended into a whole".[8] Speiser simply argues that the sources are blended so well that they give the (erroneous) appearance of single authorship.[9] This requires a good deal of trust in the theory.

University Press, 1992) 423 makes the interesting comment that "[d]oublets and recapitulation can be deadly; yet in the Joseph story they provide emphasis."

3 Gunkel, *Genesis*; G. von Rad, *Genesis*. OTL, Revised edn., trans. J.H. Marks and J. Bowden. (London: SCM, 1972); Ruppert, *Die Josephserzählung*, seeks to bring out the theology of the J, E and P strands, but not the theology of the final redactor (especially at 205-237). For other studies which focus on the putative underlying sources, see Schmitt, *Die Nichtpriesterliche Josephsgeschichte*; H. Seebass, *Geschlichtliche Zeit und theonome Tradition in der Joseph-Erzählung* (Gütersloh: Gerd Mohn, 1978); Schmidt, *Literarische Studien*; and K.R. Melchin, 'Literary Sources in the Joseph Story', *ScEs* 31 (1979): 93-101.

4 A.W. Jenks, *The Elohist and North Israelite Traditions*. SBLMS, 22. (Missoula: Scholars, 1977) 28. So, too, A. Berlin, *Poetics and Interpretation of Biblical Narrative*. Bible and Literature Series, 9. (Sheffield: Almond Press, 1983) 113. On chapter 37, see also the work of A.F. Campbell and M.A. O'Brien, *Sources of the Pentateuch* (Minneapolis: Fortress, 1993) 223-237.

5 Jenks, *The Elohist*, 27.

6 J.C. Nohrnberg, 'Princely Characters', in *"Not in Heaven": Coherence and Complexity in Biblical Narrative*. eds. J.S. Rosenblatt and J.C. Sitterson. (Bloomington: Indiana University Press, 1991), 70. The image of source analysis being likened to 'unscrambling an omelette' is borrowed from E.R. Leach.

7 See, for example, a good historical analysis in Westermann, *Genesis 37-50*, 19-20.

8 H. Gunkel, *The Legends of Genesis: The Biblical Saga and History*. trans. W.H. Carruth. (New York: Schocken, 1964) 81.

9 E.A. Speiser, *Genesis*. AB (New York: Doubleday, 1964) 292.

A Variation on the Traditional Source View (D.B. Redford)

Redford's significant monograph argues for a different kind of source theory from the traditional Documentary Hypothesis. He claims that the Joseph story is not made up of J, E and P, but rather of one version (the Reuben version), which was supplemented by a secondary Judah version; followed by later, smaller additions (mainly glosses, but also the whole of chapter 39), and finally the rearrangements and additions of the editor of the Book of Genesis.[10] Others have found his theory unsatisfactory in that it is inconsistent and selective. Thus, for example, Redford suggests that the conflicting details of chapter 37, and between 42:11, 13 and 43:7 are due to different sources, but the supposed contradiction of 42:15-16 and 19-20 is explained by the psychology of the hero.[11]

Dissatisfaction with Source Criticism

Roland de Vaux writes of the Joseph story as "one of the most striking instances in the whole of the Pentateuch of a purely 'documentary' form of literary criticism ending in failure."[12] While not all scholars would put it as strongly as de Vaux, several leading mainstream scholars have recently doubted the usefulness of source critical analysis of the Joseph story. Three will be considered briefly in turn.

C. WESTERMANN

Westermann is no opponent of sources, and finds evidence of the P strand in 37:1-2 and chapters 46-50. Yet he argues that Genesis 37, 39-45 is an artistic unity that cannot be broken down into sources, having a unifying tension which reaches from the rupture of family unity in chapter 37 to the family reconciliation of chapter 45. Westermann concludes that the story of Joseph (chapters 37, 39-45) was composed as an expansion of the broader Jacob story to be inserted into the conclusion of that narrative. The wider text of Genesis 37-50 thus has only a redactional unity. Undoubtedly there are sources, but parts of the text resist division according to the classical source theory.[13]

---

10 Redford, *Biblical Story of Joseph*, 182-186.
11 S. Niditch, *Underdogs and Tricksters* (San Francisco: Harper & Row, 1987) 81-82. See also R. Martin-Achard, 'Problèmes soulevés par l'étude de l'histoire biblique de Joseph', *RTP* 21 (1972): 97.
12 R. de Vaux, *The Early History of Israel*. trans. D. Smith. (London: Darton, Longman & Todd, 1978) 294.
13 Westermann, *Genesis 37-50*, 22-25. Similarly, H. Donner, *Die literarische Gestalt der alttestamentlichen Josephsgeschichte* (Heidelberg: Carl Winter, 1976) 24.

R. RENDTORFF

Rendtorff starts with the observation that "it is a strong methodological mistake to identify literary critique with one of its possible results, that means with the documentary hypothesis."[14] When he looks at the book of Genesis, he notes that each of the accounts of Abraham, Isaac, Jacob and Joseph has a distinctive character. The differences in style, literary technique, interests and aims between these four sections leads Rendtorff to conclude that all four cannot be composed of the same interwoven sources.[15] Thus, it is more useful to focus on each of these distinct sections in their own right, and he therefore calls for a fundamentally new method of analysing pentateuchal narratives. Primary to any such approach is that priority should first be given to the studying of the text as a unity, analysing its structure and intention *prior to* identifying any different sources.[16]

R.N. WHYBRAY

Whybray seeks to critique the view that "the Pentateuch is a kind of many-layered *tell* whose strata can be uncovered to reveal the history of Israel's religious beliefs".[17] He claims to demonstrate the deficiencies of both the Documentary Hypothesis and the traditio-historical approach. Von Rad insists that the Joseph story (defined as Genesis 37, 39-47, 50) is both composed of sources, yet has literary uniformity and a wisdom provenance. Whybray suggests that von Rad's view that two stories (J and E) were combined into an even richer, almost seamless narrative is far-fetched.[18] He concludes that "it would seem that we are forced to make a choice in our interpretation of the Joseph story between the documentary hypothesis on the one hand and the view that it is a "novel" of genius belonging to the category of wisdom literature on the other."[19]

From Literary Strata to Literary Strategy

As early in the modern period as 1933, Rudolph was presenting solid

---

14 Rendtorff, 'The Future', 3. He also has some reservations about the criteria used in source analysis, such as the divine names used.
15 Rendtorff, 'The Future', 5-7.
16 Rendtorff, 'The Future', 10-11.
17 R.N. Whybray, *The Making of the Pentateuch: A Methodological Study.* JSOTSup, 53. (Sheffield: JSOT Press, 1987) 9.
18 Whybray, 'Pentateuchal Criticism', 525 comments that "[c]omposite authorship of a novel is not entirely unknown; but it is, to say the least, very difficult to believe that a novel or superlative merit could be the result of a *conflation* of two other novels".
19 Whybray, 'Pentateuchal Criticism', 528. White, *Narration and Discourse*, 233 notes that Whybray's point about the inconsistency of a sophisticated literary text and the documentary hypothesis is compelling.

arguments for the literary unity of the Joseph narrative.[20] His approach was sidelined because of the predominance of the Documentary Hypothesis in Old Testament scholarship. Recently, however, there has been an increasing shift from a focus on the *literary strata* of source analysis, to a concern with the *literary strategy* of the final form.[21] The rationale for this will be explored below. Humphreys' assessment, for example, is that "the analysis of the novella on a synchronic plane ... suggests that, with the exception of Genesis 48, 49, 46:1-4, and 38, the novella is in so many ways an artfully constructed fabric that to pull at bits of thread here and there is to unravel its balanced texture."[22] Indeed, the Joseph story seems to have been incorporated into the Pentateuch as a whole unit.[23]

One observation that is frequently made in relation to the Joseph story is that the final form reveals great literary artistry and skill.[24] Kselman suggests that the difference between the other patriarchal texts, so clearly interwoven from sources, and Joseph, an artistic whole, means that

> the method best suited to the Joseph narrative would seem to be the exercise of 'close reading' in which particular attention is paid to the subtleties and and delicacies of the text under examination and to the recurrent themes and motifs as they are played out in different circumstances and contexts.[25]

With such a polished narrative, Longacre suggests that source analysis "muffles the voice which we want to hear."[26] Once a text is divided into sources, re-arranged and supplemented, it is no longer possible to analyse the whole of the artistic work. This leads Coats into arguing that, from a methodological point of view, the point of departure in exegesis should be the Masoretic Text (hereafter MT) in its final form - "a unified and consistent text open for exegesis as it stands *unless* firm evidence proves to the contrary that it comprises two or more sources or requires reconstruction."[27] Similarly, Humphreys, who recognises the legitimacy of

20 W. Rudolph, 'Die Josephsgeschichte', in *Der Elohist als Erzähler.* BZAW, 63, eds. P. Volz and W. Rudolph. (Giessen: Töpelmann, 1933), 145-184.
21 The contrast is borrowed from J.H. Sailhamer, *The Pentateuch as Narrative: A Biblical-Theological Commentary.* Library of Biblical Interpretation. (Grand Rapids: Zondervan, 1992) xxi. He was talking about the Pentateuch as a whole, rather than simply the Joseph narrative.
22 Humphreys, *Joseph and His Family,* 198.
23 See, for example, M. Noth, *A History of Pentateuchal Traditions.* trans. B.W. Anderson. (Englewood Cliffs: Prentice-Hall, 1972) 208-209.
24 Kselman, 'Genesis', 110. G.A. Rendsburg, *The Redaction of Genesis* (Winona Lake: Eisenbrauns, 1986) 79.
25 Kselman, 'Genesis', 111.
26 Longacre, *Joseph: A Story of Divine Providence,* 12.
27 Coats, *From Canaan to Egypt,* 58.

both the synchronic and the diachronic approaches, argues that priority belongs to the synchronic, at least in order of procedure.[28] He suggests colourfully that

> Certainly for the Joseph narrative, and perhaps for all other material as well, it seems best to begin not with the parts or pieces, the episodes as separate blocks, but with the whole, with the cake as baked and decorated and ready to eat and not the distinct ingredients.[29]

In the end, one must assume either the coherence of a text or its incoherence. While the coherence of a story can only finally be established by a detailed study of its component parts it seems better, in the absence of any contrary external evidence, to work initially on the basis that a given narrative is a literary whole.[30] Northrop Frye has argued for the validity of such an approach

> The primary understanding of any work of literature has to be based on an assumption of its unity. However mistaken such an assumption may eventually prove to be, nothing can be done unless we start with it as a heuristic principle.[31]

Of course, to start with the assumption of coherence has certain dangers, including the possibility of forced and artificial meanings. Yet, to assume incoherence can easily lead a reader to overlook that certain themes or sections need to be held in tension, or to justify the excision of 'inconvenient' aspects of the text.[32] This is not to deny that the text may have had a long pre-history. It is, however, extremely difficult to determine the circumstances of writing, redaction, or the process of compilation of an ancient text like the Joseph narrative.[33] Moreover, to delve into the pre-history of the text *as the first step*, is likely to obscure the literary and

---

28 Humphreys, *Joseph and His Family*, 6. See also R. Polzin, *Moses and the Deuteronomist* (New York: Seabury, 1980) 1-24. At 16 he speaks of the "operational priority of literary over historical criticism".

29 Humphreys, *Joseph and His Family*, 7.

30 So, R.C. Culley, 'Stories of the Conquest: Joshua 2, 6, 7 and 8', *HAR* 8 (1984): 28.

31 N. Frye, cited in R.W.L. Moberly, *At the Mountain of God*. Journal for the Study of the Old Testament Supplement Series, 22. (Sheffield: JSOT Press, 1983) 19.

32 Culley, 'Stories of the Conquest', 42. D. Robertson, *The Old Testament and the Literary Critic*. Guides to Biblical Scholarship, Old Testament Series. (Philadelphia: Fortress, 1977) 6-7.

33 Longacre, *Joseph: A Story of Divine Providence*, 14-15. J.J. Scullion, '"Die Genesis ist eine Sammlung von Sagen" (Hermann Gunkel) Independent Stories and Redactional Unity in Genesis 12-36', in *»Wünschet Jerusalem Frieden« IOSOT Congress Jerusalem 1986*. eds. M. Augustin and K.-D. Schunck. (Frankfurt am Main: Peter Lang, 1988), 243-247.

thematic aspects of the text. Since these are the very aspects that will be vital for this study, it seems best to proceed initially with an assumption that the Joseph story is a coherent literary unit.

This leads quite naturally to the question of whether there are any reasons, other than these methodological ones, for regarding the Joseph narrative as a unit with literary integrity. To answer this, it is necessary to explore the extent and content of the literary unit.

The Text and its Boundaries

Defining the Boundaries of the Text

If it is possible to talk meaningfully about the Joseph story as a literary entity, the first task is to determine where the story begins and ends.[34]

When scholars write about the Joseph narrative as a distinct entity, the narrative is not always delimited in the same way. This is evident from the following table outlining what chapters of Genesis are included:

Brueggemann	37; 39-45; 46:28-47:27 as 'the main narrative'
Coats	37; 39-47:27
Garrett	37:1-46:7, with a wider chiastic unity in 37:3-50:26
Gunkel	37-50, omitting chapters 38 and 49:1-27
Hamilton	37-50
Humphreys	37-50
Kselman	37, 39-45
Longacre	37 and 39-48
Lowenthal	37-50, omitting chapters 38 and 49:1-27
von Rad	37; 39-47, 50
Redford	37:3-36; 39-45; 46:28-47:31; 50:1-21
Wenham	37-50, but as the second part of the Jacob story
Westermann	37:3-36; 39-45 and the non-P passages of 46-50
White	37, 39-45, 50

It appears, therefore, that the minimal position is that the Joseph narrative comprises Genesis 37 and 39-45. In the remainder of this chapter, it will be argued that Genesis 37 is the starting point of a new narrative unit, and that no satisfactory closure comes to this unit until the end of chapter 50. The inclusion of Genesis 38 in the story as a whole will be justified at length in chapter 5.

---

34 J. Muilenburg, 'Form Criticism and Beyond', *JBL* 88 (1969): 8-9.

The Beginning of the Literary Unit

The occurrence in Gen 37:2 of the *toledot* formula ('these are the generations of') is important for understanding where the literary unit starts. This is a formula that occurs eleven times in the book of Genesis, including at the beginning of the narrative cycles of Abraham (11:27 - the *toledot* of Terah) and Jacob (25:19 - the *toledot* of Isaac). This pattern of beginning the other narrative cycles of Genesis with the *toledot* formula of the main character's father, is precisely what is found in Gen 37:2.[35] It is thus quite clearly a structural guide to mark the beginning of a narrative, and it appears to have that function in the Joseph story.

It might be objected that the Joseph story has already started since his birth is described in 30:22-23. However, at the time of Joseph's birth, the implied reader's focus is put on Jacob. There are no predictions about Joseph's character or future prominence. Joseph's birth has a role in the Jacob cycle, as an "event belonging to the tale of rivalry between Rachel and Leah."[36] The Joseph story has not yet started, and there is no further hint of it starting until 37:2.

The second indication that a new literary unit begins in Genesis 37 is that the story about Joseph is significantly different from what precedes. Humphreys expresses this well

> As an artfully designed complex and as extended narrative the last chapters of Genesis do stand apart from what has come before. Its parts are clearly interlocking scenes of a larger whole. ... In this the Joseph narrative has always stood apart from the stories about Abraham and Jacob in Genesis.[37]

There are several distinctive features of the Joseph story. Firstly, the earlier patriarchal accounts are composed of smaller stories, generally no longer than 20 or 30 verses. The Joseph story arguably contains 392 verses.[38] Secondly, it has been claimed that it uses words of Egyptian origin and reflects the customs and institutions of Egypt, in a way not seen in Genesis 12-36.[39] At least, the story appears to reflect a different world, in

---

35 The use of the father of the main character in Gen 11:27 and 25:19 (Terah beginning the Abraham cycle; Isaac beginning the Jacob cycle) also highlights that this is the *Joseph* story, and not the *Jacob* story. Indeed the Joseph story immediately follows the *toledot* formula with a focus on Joseph being seventeen years old and a shepherd. The *toledot* formula does not, then, identify the main character of the story.

36 Niditch, *Underdogs and Tricksters*, 70.

37 Humphreys, *Joseph and His Family*, 8.

38 G. von Rad, 'The Story of Joseph', in *God at Work in Israel*. trans. J.H. Marks. (Nashville: Abingdon, 1980), 20; G.W. Coats, 'Redactional Unity in Genesis 37-50', *JBL* 93 (1974): 21.

39 An early example of such a view is A.H. Sayce, *The Early History of the Hebrews*

which interest and delight in the foreign court of Egypt is evident. Thirdly, it has been commented that the overt intervention of God is absent from the Joseph story, but a strong feature of the previous accounts.[40] The only time that God directly appears in the story is not even to Joseph, but rather to the patriarch Jacob (46:2-4).

Other differences will emerge from a reading of the text, but enough distinctive elements have been raised to indicate that a new narrative starts in chapter 37. This is largely agreed on by scholars, although Westermann regards 'the Joseph story proper' as inserted into the Jacob cycle, which then continues from chapter 46 onwards.[41]

The End of the Literary Unit

The present form of Genesis 50 serves as a most appropriate end to the proposed literary unit. It narrates the death of the main character and resolves the tensions raised in chapter 37. No further resolution needs to take place since Joseph still shows forgiveness to his brothers.

Indeed, chapter 50 presupposes much of the preceding material. The breakdown of family trust (chapter 37), followed by its interim resolution (chapters 42-45), are assumed. Jacob's death is behind the death-bed oracles and blessings of chapters 48-49, and is presupposed in 50:15-21. In fact, his death is the factor that precipitates the brothers' final attempt at deceit (50:15-21).[42] Chapter 50 thus presupposes 47:28-49:33, although there is more detail in these chapters than is necessary. Thus, it seems that the materials about Jacob are either woven into the Joseph story which now encloses it, or that there is a mutual intertwining of these two stories. The argument for 46-50 belonging to the rest - at least redactionally - and drawn in by chapter 50, is, therefore, quite strong.

Secondly, the Joseph story appropriately ends with Joseph's death. As E.M. Forster has commented, "[d]eath ends a book neatly".[43] This is a common method of concluding biblical narratives. However, Joseph is mentioned at the beginning of the book of Exodus, when Moses takes with him the bones of Joseph, and the book of Joshua ends with the burial of his bones in the promised land. Yet, that does not mean that the Joseph story

---

(London: Rivingtons, 1897) 83. More recently, there has been significant debate between those who would support this view (for example, Kitchen, Vergote) and those who oppose it (especially Redford).

40 N.M. Sarna, *The JPS Torah Commentary: Genesis* (Philadelphia: Jewish Publication Society, 1989) 254.

41 Westermann, *Genesis 37-50*, 22-25. See also Wenham, *Genesis 16-50*, 345 who regards these chapters as the second part of the Jacob story.

42 Coats, 'Redactional Unity', 21.

43 E.M. Forster, *Aspects of the Novel* (London: Pelican, 1927) 51 cited in I.B. Gottlieb, '*Sof Davar*: Biblical Endings', *Prooftexts* 11 (1991): 214.

extends beyond Genesis 50, for neither of these narrative incidents adds to our interpretation of the Joseph story. Their role is rather is show a continuity between the patriarchs and the people of Israel. The death of Joseph nicely rounds off his story, and shows that this unit is at an end. 50:22-26 is not an excessively long description and operates as a narrative closure, pushing the implied reader's attention to two Pentateuchal themes - back to the patriarchal promise of land and forward to the exodus.

Interim Conclusions

The above analysis has revealed that there are substantial grounds for regarding Genesis 37-50 as a *prima facie* literary unit. Indeed, chapter 37 sets in train the key issues of the whole unit.[44] The *toledot* formula functions as an initial structural marker, and the contrasts between the Joseph story and the preceding Jacob cycle have been noted. Similarly, chapter 50 has been show to serve as a fitting conclusion, with the death of the main character, and the final resolution of the tensions between the brothers. Chapter 38 is provisionally regarded as part of the Joseph story at this stage.

However, writers such as Coats and Westermann argue that there is not a literary unity in Genesis 37-50, but rather only a redactional unity. It is necessary to be clear on what they are asserting. All that they are pointing out is that the story was not originally one literary whole, that it circulated in earlier forms, and that therefore one cannot do a genre analysis of the text as a whole. In other words, they claim that it never was a genre in its present form, but is rather a composite of other genres.

Yet, even this may be enough for the purposes of this study. The proposed literary unit of Genesis 37-50 is a cohesive whole at the level of the final form of the text. Whether that unit is original or redactional is not crucial, and may in any event emerge from a detailed study of the text. It is possible for redactional *unity* to produce a coherent literary *unit*, since a literary unit is different to literary unity. Establishing that a given text is a literary unit is simply to argue that it is the proper subject of an integrated reading. If Genesis 37-50 is a *prima facie* literary unit, it is proper to study it as a whole in order to discern the presence or absence of any 'wisdom literary influence'.

It is thus not very surprising that quite a number of studies of the Joseph narrative are emerging from the newer literary critics. With their preference for a synchronic over against a diachronic reading of the text, many writers have discovered the literary artistry and aspects of the Joseph story, shedding much new light on the narrative.[45] Insightful, though very diverse

---

44 Humphreys, *Joseph and His Family*, 23.
45 M. Savage, 'Literary Criticism and Biblical Studies: A Rhetorical Analysis of the Joseph Narrative', in *Scripture in Context: Essays on the Comparative Method*.

studies, have been written by White, Alter, Longacre, Ackerman, Coats, Humphreys, King, Culley and Green.[46]

This study proposes to build on such earlier works, and to push them further. This reading of the final form of Genesis 37-50 will therefore proceed with one eye carefully focused on the text, and the other on the issue of whether 'wisdom literary influence' can be discerned in the text as a whole, when it is read as unit with literary integrity.

Pittsburgh Theological Monograph Series, 34, eds. C.D. Evans, W.W. Hallo and J.B. White. (Pittsburgh: Pickwick, 1980), 96-97.

46 See the very useful analysis in R.C. Culley, *Themes and Variations: A Study of Action in Biblical Narrative*. SBLSS. (Atlanta: Scholars, 1992) 156-168. Culley divides the narrative studies of Joseph into two groups - those that focus more on action, and those that focus more on character. Under those who focus on action, he includes White, Alter, Longacre, Ackerman, Coats, Humphreys, and King. Those who focus on character include Alter, Ackerman, Green, Coats and Humphreys.

PART 2

A LITERARY READING

OF THE JOSEPH STORY

CHAPTER 4

Genesis 37

Various aspects of chapter 37 have been viewed as significant in determining the presence or absence of wisdom-like elements in the Joseph narrative. These include the report that Joseph brings of his brothers, Joseph's dreams, the telling of his dreams, and his silence before his brothers. Such elements, however, need to be understood in the light of the text as a whole, and a detailed exegetical analysis of this chapter is therefore required.

Structure

The Joseph story probably begins with the *toledot* formula in verse 2. Verse 1 concludes the previous unit (36:1-37:1) and is therefore outside of the structure in chapter 37.[1]

A number of commentators propose two distinct units in the chapter, with the major structural division of the text coming between verses 2-4 (the exposition) and 5-36 (the complication).[2] However, a more significant

---

1 Wenham, *Genesis 16-50,* 334-335 regards verse 1 as rounding off the discrete unit 36:1-37:1. He argues that 37:1 clearly matches and echoes 36:7-8, and that 36:9-43 is a secondary insertion, so that 37:1 resumes and completes the *toledot* of Edom in 36:1-8. See also Longacre, *Joseph: A Story of Divine Providence,* 21; Sailhamer, *The Pentateuch as Narrative* 20. Green, *What Profit for Us?,* 36 thinks that 37:1 is part of the Joseph narrative, inviting the reader to consider Israel's people in relation to their position in the land. In any event, neither the inclusion or the exclusion of verse 1 will significantly affect the interpretation of the chapter as a whole.

2 Exponents of this view include Brueggemann, *Genesis,* 298; Humphreys, *Joseph and His Family,* 32-37, 57. Coats, *From Canaan to Egypt,* 12-13 regards verses 1-4 as the exposition, with the complication beginning at verse 5, but concedes that verses 5-11 might as easily be considered as part of the exposition, foreshadowing what is to happen in the story as a whole. He includes them in the complication since the dreams (or the telling of them) leads to the brothers' radical action in the verses that follow. Turner, *Announcements of Plot,* 144 prefers, however, to see

divide occurs between verses 11 and 12.

Several aspects of this text support this division into verses 2-11 and verses 12-35/36. Firstly, Joseph's father is found in the narrative at the beginning and end of both sections, but not otherwise. Jacob is present in verses 2-4, seemingly absent in verses 5-9, but reappears in verses 10-11. In the second section, the father is mentioned in verses 12-14, and not again (except incidentally in verse 22) until verses 32-35. In both cases, the material enclosed by the references to Jacob has to do with the relationship between Joseph and his brothers. This similar pattern suggests a two-fold division of the passage, with verse 36 fitting outside this structure.

Secondly, the setting of the events is noteworthy. Verses 2-11 take place in the father's house, while verse 12 begins to move the action into the fields, where it continues until verse 30. The common setting of verses 2-11 argues against the view of those who discern the major break between verses 4 and 5. Verses 31-35 revert again to the father's house, while verse 36 is a hinge verse leading forward into the narrative resumed in chapter 39.[3]

Finally, this chapter will argue that the introduction of the robe and the dream must be kept together in the same literary unit. Both the robe and the dream are connected to, and part of, the motif of the brothers' hatred of Joseph, which is interwoven through verses 2-11. The brothers' hatred is implied in verse 2, and explicit in verses 4, 5, 8, 11. In particular, the motif is present at the 'seam', occurring in both verses 4 and 5 to bind together what might otherwise be a natural division. The omission of this motif in verses 12-17 again shows that the first section ends in verse 11.

Thus, it is proposed to see the text divided into two major sections - verses 2-11 and verses 12-35 - with a hinge or linking verse at the end (verse 36). The whole of verses 2-11 is regarded as the exposition, while verses 12-35 provides the initial complication. In the first section, Joseph is on the ascendancy; in the second, his fortunes steadily worsen. The chapter moves from the dream to the dream apparently frustrated. Verses 2-11 can be subdivided into two subsections: verses 2-4 and 5-11. Verses 12-35 are able to be subdivided into three subsections, on the basis of setting and content: verses 12-17, 18-30 and 31-35.

---

verses 1-4 as a general introduction; verses 5-11 as the exposition and verses 12ff. as the complication. B. Becking, '"They Hated Him Even More": Literary Technique in Genesis 37.1-11', *BN* 60 (1991): 40-47 at 41 examines the internal structure of verses 1-11, which involves verse 1 being regarded as a part of this literary unit.

3   Westermann, *Genesis 37-50*, 35 and A.P. Ross, *Creation and Blessing: A Guide to the Study and Exposition of the Book of Genesis* (Grand Rapids: Baker, 1988), 595 suggest a threefold division in the chapter based on the changes in the setting from the father's house (verses 3-11), to the fields (verses 12-30), and again in the father's house (verses 31-35).

This gives the following structure of the passage

a. Exposition (verses 2-11)
    i. Joseph's report and Jacob's favouritism (verses 2-4)
    ii. Joseph's two dreams (verses 5-11)
b. Complication (verses 12-35)
    i. The father sends Joseph to his brothers (verses 12-17)
    ii. The brothers dispose of Joseph (verses 18-30)
    iii. The brothers return to their father (verses 31-35)
c. Hinge (verse 36) - connecting this passage to chapter 39.

Genesis 37:2-11 - Exposition

37:2-4 - Joseph's Report and Jacob's Favouritism

At the very outset of this story, there are hints of an important question - who is this story about? It does not appear to be about God, who is not explicitly mentioned in chapter 37, and rarely throughout the story as a whole. Verse 2 instead introduces Jacob, Joseph, and some of the brothers, all of whom have been introduced in the earlier chapters of Genesis. Yet, who is at the centre of the story in Genesis 37-50? Jacob and Joseph are named in verse 2, and they appear to be the two most likely possibilities.

THE *TOLEDOT* FORMULA

The opening verse begins with the heading that this is the *toledot* of Jacob. The *toledot* formula occurs ten times in the book of Genesis. On five occasions it introduces genealogies (5:1; 10:1; 11:10; 25:12; 36:1) and in five other instances, including here, it introduces narrative sections (2:4; 6:9; 11:27; 25:19; 37:2).[4]

Goldingay argues that chapters 37-50 are appropriately called the 'story of Jacob'. Jacob is a key player in chapter 37, active behind the scenes in chapters 42-45, and foregrounded in chapters 46-50. Goldingay suggests that "[o]nly in 50:22b-26 is Jacob really left behind and Joseph the focus."[5]

However, the weight of the evidence suggests that chapters 37-50 are really the story of Joseph. They open by considering Joseph's position in Jacob's family (37:2-4) and conclude with a notice about Joseph's death

---

4   J.G. Janzen, *Abraham and All the Families of the Earth: A Commentary on the Book of Genesis 12-50.* International Theological Commentary. (Grand Rapids: Eerdmans, 1993) 143.

5   Goldingay, 'The Patriarchs', 20. See also J. Blenkinsopp, *The Pentateuch.* ABRL. (New York: Doubleday, 1992) 107.

(50:26).[6] Straight after the *toledot* formula, Joseph is introduced (37:2) and there is a description of his dreams. In other words, "[t]he writer immediately begins to tell the story of Joseph."[7] Of all the sons of Jacob, he alone is named in verses 2-11. Thus, although it is headed the *toledot* of Jacob, verse 2 actually begins what is more accurately designated the Joseph cycle.

This view is supported by the way in which the *toledot* formula is used in the book of Genesis. Generally, it focuses on the person's descendants rather than the person named. Some useful parallels can be discerned in its use in 11:27 and 25:19 (the two previous occasions where it has introduced a narrative unit). The *toledot* of Terah (Gen 11:27) is the beginning of the cycle about his son Abraham, but it also includes a member of the wider family - Abraham's nephew, Lot. Yet, the cycle is about Abraham, not about Terah. It is even clearer in the Jacob cycle that precedes, which is called the *toledot* of Isaac in 25:19. In this collection of stories Isaac does not die until the end of chapter 35, and he appears in a few of the episodes. There are even some details about Jacob's brother Esau, yet the real focus of the story is on Jacob. Thus, the use of the *toledot* formula in 37:2 hints that the story is not about Jacob, but about one of his descendants, albeit in the context of the wider family.

Indeed, it may be a helpful way forward to regard Genesis 37-50 as the story of Joseph, but also a story embedded in the larger story of Genesis as a whole. While this duality will be explored in more detail in chapter 9, the wider context must be kept in mind in reading the text.[8] Thus, the reader is being implicitly invited by the text to read it in the light of the earlier patriarchal accounts.

Two particular background issues here are the dissension caused by sibling rivalry, and the question of who will assume the status of the 'first-born' son (Jacob/Esau; Ishmael/Isaac). In the immediately preceding chapters, it appears that Reuben (Gen 35:22), Simeon and Levi (Gen 34:30) may have disqualified themselves from being the 'first-born'. Therefore, the issue of who will Jacob's first-born son is already on the reader's agenda, and verses 2-4 need to be understood in that context.

In its current form, then, Genesis 37-50 appears to be a discrete *toledot*

6   Humphreys, *Joseph and His Family*, 12.
7   J.H. Sailhamer, 'Genesis', in *The Expositor's Bible Commentary*. Vol. 2. (Grand Rapids: Zondervan, 1990), 226.
8   Thus, for example, Coats, *From Canaan to Egypt*, 11; T.E. Fretheim, 'The Book of Genesis', in *The New Interpreter's Bible*. Vol. 1. (Nashville: Abingdon, 1994), 598. Against the need to make these links, see, for example, H.A. Brongers, 'La Crainte du Seigneur (*Jir'at Jhwh, Jir'at 'Elohim*)', *OTS* 5 (1948): 137. P.D. Miscall, 'The Jacob and Joseph Stories as Analogies', *JSOT* 6 (1978): 28 suggests that the Jacob and Joseph stories are to be read as analogous due to the presence of common patterns and elements.

unit, focused on Joseph, but one which is set in a wider literary and canonical context of the patriarchs, and the book of Genesis as a whole.

VERSE 2 - JOSEPH'S REPORT

The fact that Joseph is singled out straightaway may indicate that he will be the favoured son. Certainly he is the son of the favourite wife, Rachel, and fits the 'younger son' motif of Genesis.[9] If so, then the concern of verse 2 is with Joseph's status or role (as it clearly is in verses 3-4), rather than about his character. While many see the content of דבתם רעה (a bad report of them) as an untrue or exaggerated report, with Joseph being portrayed as a 'tattletale', this is based on the assumption that Joseph's character is being assessed here by the narrator.

The phrase דבתם רעה is capable of several different interpretations, and many translate it negatively on the assumption that the text is portraying Joseph in a poor light.[10] The 'report' has been variously understood as true or untrue; malicious, naive or a model of filial piety; a report or an accusation; unfavourable or evil; Joseph's words about the brothers or their words about him.

Wenham is a balanced representative of the view that Joseph is a tattletale.[11] Others discern here a naivety or folly that ignores the admonitions of Proverbs, and would thus be inconsistent with Joseph being pictured here as wise.[12] Some, however, see it referring to the brothers' slanderous words against Joseph.[13] More likely is the view that Joseph's report was true, but unfavourable, revealing the evil deeds of Dan, Naphtali, Gad, and Asher out of Joseph's first loyalty to his father. On this view, Joseph is more one who a purveyor of truth rather than a teller of tales.[14]

The weight of the evidence favours the view that דבתם רעה refers to Joseph's 'report' about his brothers.[15] What is striking, however, is that the

---

9   Redford, *Biblical Story of Joseph*, 88-89 tries to distinguish between younger/elder brother and youngest/older brothers motifs. This is not a very compelling distinction.

10 See the excursus below. The phrase could be understood as any of the following: Joseph's true yet bad report; his untrue bad report; his true or untrue report of their wrongdoing; or their wrong slanders of Joseph (or Jacob).

11 Wenham, *Genesis 16-50*, 350.

12 Weeks, *Early Israelite Wisdom*, 94 sees this as tale-bearing and contrary to Prov 11:13. Also Gibson, *Genesis*, 226.

13 J. Peck, 'Note on Genesis 37,2 and Joseph's Character', *ExpTim* 82 (1970/1971): 343, who argues that the pronominal suffix is subjective not objective. See also Janzen, *Genesis 12-50*, 148; White, *Narration and Discourse*, 295.

14 D. Kidner, *Genesis*. TOTC. (London: Tyndale, 1967) 180; Ross, *Creation and Blessing* 598; and J.G. Baldwin, *The Message of Genesis 12-50: From Abraham to Joseph*. Bible Speaks Today. (Leicester: Inter-Varsity Press, 1986) 158-159.

15 The 'report' may alternatively be understood as an 'accusation', as is argued by

narrator does not make it clear to the readers whether this should be understood as a true or a malicious report, a foolish or a filial action. It is as if that does not matter, as if the reader's attention should be focused elsewhere. Indeed, it has the narrative effect of dividing the brothers into two groups - Joseph and the others. Westermann captures something of this tantalising ambiguity when he writes "it cannot be concluded whether the bad report about the sons of the maidservants was justified or not; nor can Joseph's role be determined with certainty."[16] The reader who is interested in evaluating Joseph's character, will need to read on.

Of course, if verse 2 is read neutrally (for example, that Joseph aligns himself with his father, and perhaps even sees this as a prior obligation), there is no necessary criticism of Joseph's character in verses 2-4. Instead, the focus is on the reality that Joseph is enmeshed in a family characterised by envy, favouritism, and a struggle for pre-eminence. Joseph performs no action at all in verses 3-4, yet is pictured as the favoured son and so perhaps the one who will be the 'first-born'.

On this view, there is no attempt to portray Joseph's character in either a positive or negative light. This is a feature of the narrative which continues right through the chapter. Verse 2 is part of the exposition, which sets out the pattern of relationships (that is, who is aligned with whom) that will be the backdrop to the unfolding of the action. This focus on the pattern of relationships is reflected in the frequent, largely unnecessary and therefore emphatic, use of familial or relational terms in verse 2. In this single verse 'son' is used three times, 'brother' once, 'wife' once and 'father' twice. Of the male members of the family, only Jacob and Joseph are named in the exposition. The brothers are pictured as a group, and none of the Joseph's brothers are named individually until verse 21.[17]

The unusual nature of setting out Jacob's family can be observed by comparing the *toledot* of Esau in chapter 36, which lists his 5 sons, 27 chiefs and 8 kings. There is a clear contrast between the abundance of names in the line of Esau, and the focus here on Jacob, his son Joseph and a group of unnamed brothers.

Indeed, even when Joseph is with his brothers, he is distinguished from them. Thus, he is described separately to his brothers as they shepherd the flock (היה רעה את־אחיו בצאן) and he is called a 'lad', 'helper' or 'assistant' (נער) to the sons of Bilhah and Zilpah.[18]

R.C. van Leeuwen, *Context and Meaning in Proverbs 25-27*. SBLDS, 96. (Atlanta: Scholars, 1988) 58.

16   Westermann, *Genesis 37-50*, 36.
17   Coats, *From Canaan to Egypt*, 11.
18   The word נער is sometimes used to refer to an attendant (1 Sam 9:3, 5, 7) but is also used to describe Joshua's relationship with Moses (Exod 33:11; 1 Sam 20:35-36). Sarna, *JPS Torah Commentary*, 255 citing 2 Sam 5:2; 7:7, suggests that 'he

It is in this context, then, that Joseph brings to his father what is described as דבתם רעה. It is important to note that the phrase occurs in a context where the characters are being introduced rather than evaluated. The focus in verse 2, as in verses 3-4, is on who colludes with whom. The fact that Joseph brings this report to Jacob reveals that he has chosen to align himself with his father instead of with his brothers. Whatever else the bringing of this report may indicate about Joseph's character, its primary function here is to show the nature of the family alliances.

VERSE 3 - JACOB'S FAVOURITISM

Jacob,[19] the patriarch who saw the destructive effects of parental favouritism as he grew up (Gen 25:28), loved Joseph more than his other sons (verse 3). Like the *toledot* formula, and the mention of Jacob's wives and other sons, the motif of parental favouritism is a link with the wider story of the book of Genesis. Just as Jacob had earlier preferred Rachel to Leah, now he prefers Rachel's son to the sons of Leah.[20] As Fretheim notes, "Joseph evidently now has a relationship with his father that the others do not have. It suggests that Joseph becomes the chosen son of the promise; the eleven are 'Esau.' "[21]

The robe (כתנת פסים) is an important part of the detail.[22] Its usage in 2 Sam 13:18-19 suggests it is a royal, perhaps richly-ornamented, robe; others suggest it is a long robe going down to the ankles.[23] On either view, it is

---

shepherded with his brothers' (היה רעה את־אחיו) may carry a subtle suggestion of what follows since it can be translated 'he used to lord it over his brothers'. On both these issues, see Pirson, *Lord of the Dreams* 28-33. R. Pirson, 'What is Joseph Supposed to Be? On the Interpretation of נער in Genesis 37:2'. *Recycling Biblical Figures: Papers Read at a NOSTER Colloquium in Amsterdam, 12-13 May 1997.* (Leiden: Deo, 1999) 81-92 argues for the translation of 'assistant' after a survey of the uses of נער in Genesis.

19   There is a change of name from Jacob (verse 2) to Israel (verses 3, 13), but back to Jacob in verse 34. Perhaps this is due to the redaction of different sources, or it may simply be a literary variation. Wenham, *Genesis 16-50,* 351 notes that unlike Abram/Abraham, both names continue to be used, although some pattern can be discerned.

20   Sailhamer, 'Genesis', 226.

21   Fretheim, 'The Book of Genesis', 598.

22   The clothing motif has been explored by V.H. Matthews, 'The Anthropology of Clothing in the Joseph Narrative', *JSOT* 65 (1995): 25-36. He deals with Joseph's robe on 30-31.

23   It is variously translated in the English versions: 'a coat of many colours' (KJV, based on the LXX and Vulgate); 'a long robe with sleeves' (NRSV); 'a richly ornamented robe' (NIV). The only other use of this expression in the Old Testament is in 2 Sam 13:18-19, where it refers to a robe worn by Tamar, and explained as the clothing worn by the virgin daughters of the king in earlier times). The translation opted for in the NRSV is based on the usual translation of פס to

clearly not 'a set of working clothes', and is thus a sign of parental favour.[24]

The context suggests this even more strongly. Immediately after Joseph is given the robe, Joseph's brothers saw that Jacob loved him more than them. The robe is thus a clear sign of Joseph's pre-eminence in the family. Coats points out that the robe is "a visible sign of his exalted position",[25] and may even signify that Jacob is appointing Joseph as his heir. At the very least, the robe functions as a precursor and then symbol of the dream. In other words, both the robe and the dream proclaim Joseph's pre-eminence, and his future authority over his family.[26]

The gift of the robe thus crystallises the problem for the brothers (that Joseph is preferred to them), and they respond with hatred. Instead of hating their father for his favouritism, they hate the object of Jacob's love - the favoured son Joseph.[27] The extent of this hatred is evident in verse 4, where they could not speak peaceably (לשלם) to him.

A striking aspect of the introduction is the conspicuous absence of Benjamin, who is not mentioned again until Gen 42:4. Benjamin does not seem to be included in the exposition despite the use of the phrases 'all his sons' (verse 3) and 'all his brothers' (verse 4). Calling Joseph 'son of his old age' (verse 3) strikes the reader of the wider story as odd, for Joseph was born in Paddan-Aram (Gen 30:22-24), when Jacob was in his prime, and the real son of his old age was Benjamin (Gen 35:18).[28] A number of plausible explanations could be put forward to account for Benjamin's absence in this chapter.[29] However, it makes sense since there is a focus

---

mean the palm of the hand or sole of the foot. If so, it may be a robe that extends to the palms (wrists?) and soles (ankles?). The significance of this is that most tunics worn by working men were short and sleeveless, for a long, or long-sleeved garment was worn by one who did not have to work. The debate is usefully summarised in Hamilton, *Genesis Chapters 18-50*, 407-409. Speiser, *Genesis*, 289-290 argues for the translation 'ornamented tunic'. Most recently, see Pirson, *Lord of the Dreams*, 33-35.

24   Gunkel, *Genesis*, 390; Z. Adar, *The Book of Genesis: An Introduction to the Biblical World*. trans. P. Cohen. (Jerusalem: Magnes Press, 1990) 139; von Rad, *Genesis*, 351.

25   Coats, *From Canaan to Egypt*, 12.

26   *Contra* Gunkel, *Genesis*, 388 who views the dream and garment as variants belonging to the E and J sources respectively.

27   Westermann, *Genesis 37-50*, 37. Hamilton, *Genesis Chapters 18-50*, however, notes that the phrase 'they hated him' could refer to their hatred of either Jacob or Joseph.

28   However, Rashbam cited in Sarna, *JPS Torah Commentary*, 255, suggests that Joseph was the child of his old age (37:3) in that he was the last of Jacob's sons to be born in Paddan-Aram. This suggestion has not been adopted by many modern commentators.

29   It might be the result of imperfect editing. He may have been omitted to avoid him being implicated in the sale of Joseph, or so that he can become Joseph's

only on the adult sons, and Benjamin is too young to be considered.

Indeed, the narrative reasons for Benjamin's exclusion are even more compelling. Firstly, as part of the exposition, this is a stylised account giving broad brush strokes only. In verses 2-11, the family is being divided into Joseph and rest. Benjamin will enter to nuance the story in chapter 42, but is otiose at the stage of drawing up the boundary lines.

Secondly, the exposition uses the narrative technique of mentioning details that hint at what will happen in the rest of the chapter. The other detail of verse 3 - that he made him a robe, a symbol of Joseph's special position - leads well into the dream, becomes the means by which Joseph is recognised, is taken off him by his brothers, and dipped in blood to deceive Jacob. Thus, it has a significant role in the subsequent narrative.

In the larger narrative that follows, Joseph is distinguished from the brothers as a group. Benjamin will take no significant role in the rest of the chapter, and so is not in view here. The stylised division of the family into Joseph and his brothers is a way of signalling to the reader that this is the crucial line of demarcation in the narratives that follow, and that it will be the source of the tension and conflict that erupts.

Thus, the omission of Benjamin is no more significant than the failure to mention Leah, who is present only incidentally in Gen 46:15, 18, and finally as she is buried in Gen 49:31. Other than these instances, she is not explicitly named in the entire Joseph narrative. She, like Benjamin at this stage, is part of the family, but not significant for the action of the story.

VERSE 4 - THE BROTHERS' REACTION

In verse 4, there are several factors that keep our attention focused on Joseph. Firstly, the object pronoun אֹתוֹ ('him', which refers to Joseph), is used in an emphatic position before אָהַב ('loved'). Secondly, the MT reads אֶחָיו ('his brothers'), which means that the other sons of Jacob are being identified by their relationship with Joseph.[30]

It is significant that in 37:4, the brothers hated Joseph even before the dreams, simply because Jacob favoured him, and not explicitly for his 'bad report' of them. The brothers seem to have taken the initiative in breaking peace with Joseph. While Joseph's previous reporting of the brothers in verse 2 might have triggered off a response from the brothers, that is not mentioned in verse 4.[31] There is irony in the fact that "the love of

---

replacement. See Janzen, *Genesis 12-50*, 149; J.L. Kugel, *In Potiphar's House* (San Francisco: Harper, 1990) 70.

30   The Samaritan Pentateuch opts for what might be expected (בָּנָיו = his sons); the MT records a Joseph-centred text. See Wenham, *Genesis 16-50*, 348.

31   *Contra* Janzen, *Genesis 12-50*, 148-149 who notes that verse 3 is parenthetical so that verse 4 is dependent on verse 2. However, Janzen's conclusion that verse 4 is saying the same thing as verse 2 does not necessarily follow. Verse 4 seems rather

Jacob/Israel is then contrasted with what it subsequently provoked: the hate of the other sons of Jacob."[32] Even at this early stage, the brothers could not speak to Joseph לשׁלם ('peaceably') while later Joseph went on a journey to see about the שׁלום ('well-being') of his brothers (verse 14).

37:5-11 - Joseph's Pair of Dreams

These verses contain Joseph's two dreams, introducing this motif that will be crucial for chapters 37-41. Some suggest that Joseph is being pictured here as wise since he receives dreams, while other writers see him as foolish in telling such dreams to his family. This study proposes that, as in the first part of the exposition (verses 2-4), the text is simply not concerned with evaluating Joseph's character.

The content of the dreams is much more straightforward than their significance. Verse 5 is an anticipatory summary of verses 6-8, and is presumably brought forward for emphasis. Becking argues that this implies that verses 5-11 do not primarily focus on the dreams, but on the growing alienation between Joseph and his brothers. The jealousy aroused then forms the basis of the subsequent actions of the brothers in 37:12-36.[33] Certainly, the mention of the brothers' hatred is foregrounded in verse 5, while the motif of hatred and division in the family is woven through the entire exposition.

However, Becking's proposal appears reductionistic, for there seems to be a twin focus in verses 5-11. On the one hand, there is the recurrent mention of the growing alienation between Joseph and his brothers. Yet, the message of the dreams is also emphasised by virtue of its repetition. Both of these themes are appropriate for the exposition. The second programmatically sets out the story line of Joseph's rise to pre-eminence. The first hints at the source of tension and conflict that will give the text its literary power.

The last four words in verse 5 (ויוספו עוד שׂנא אתו, 'they hated him even more') are not represented in the LXX, and Westermann, among others, regards them as an addition.[34] The difficulty of having these words precede the telling of the dream is removed if their literary function is understood. As suggested above, it draws attention to the theme of alienation within the family, and this is an important emphasis in the exposition. Secondly, it serves to bind together the two parts of the exposition (verses 2-4 and 5-11)

---

to be based on the information given in the parenthetical verse 3 - that Jacob loved Joseph more than his other children.

32   Becking, 'They Hated Him Even More', 42. Similarly, Berlin, *Poetics and Interpretation* 38.
33   Becking, 'They Hated Him Even More', 47.
34   Westermann, *Genesis 37-50*, 34.

by a common motif which is present at the seam (verses 4 and 5). It thus suggests that the dreams and the robe need to be interpreted in the light of the other.

It is important to notice what is omitted in the account of the dreams. In neither dream is there an explicit mention of God as the source of the dream, nor is there any comment on whether it was appropriate or not to pass on the dream. Furthermore, there is no indication of the nature of Joseph's thoughts or motives, either from the dialogue or from the narrator. The reader is not permitted to have these crucial aspects explored, but instead has their attention drawn to the increasing fragmentation of the family, and to the message of the dreams.

VERSES 5-8 - THE FIRST DREAM

Both dreams rely on the transparent use of symbols, and in each case the interpretation is patent. The first dream speaks of Joseph's sheaf rising and standing upright with his brothers' sheaves circling around and bowing down to his sheaf. In itself the dream does not make it clear whether the thrust is on the brothers circling around or bowing down to Joseph, but three factors make it clear that the focus is on their bowing down. Firstly, bowing down appears climactically at the end of the list, so that the ambiguity of their circling or gathering around (to harm him as in verses 23-24, or to acknowledge him) is made clear. Secondly, the response by the brothers show that they interpreted the dream to be about Joseph ruling or reigning over them. Lastly, in the parallel second dream, there is no mention of circling around (though this would have made sense with planetary objects), but only bowing down. Thus, the dream is clearly about Joseph's rise to prominence and the brothers' acknowledgement of this.

The response of the brothers (verse 8) reinforces this theme, and weaves in the hatred motif. The theme of Joseph's pre-eminence is furthered by an emphatic construction (infinitive absolute + imperfect) for both מָשַׁל (rule) and מָלַךְ (reign). Their perception that Joseph wants to rule over them serves both to outline the kind of relationship that the brothers fear, and to heighten their hatred of Joseph. Indeed, the brothers may have hated Joseph not because he had the dreams, nor because he proclaimed their content, but rather because of what the dreams conveyed - Joseph's rise to pre-eminence. Thus, both the robe and the dreams speak of same reality, and both result in the brothers hating Joseph.

It has been suggested above that verse 5 is an anticipatory summary, flagging the key issues to the reader. Verse 8 may be both a closing summary, as well as anticipating the subsequent dream in verse 9. In verse 8 Joseph refers to the plural 'his dreams', although the narrator has so far recorded only one dream. Certainly, this may have been due to imperfect editing, or to the existence of other dreams not mentioned in this partial account. However, it is more likely, following the pattern of verse 5, that this is just an editorial summary anticipating the next dream as well, and its insertion here serves to foreground the hatred motif.[35]

Another puzzling feature in verse 8 is the referent of the phrase 'and for his words'. It could possibly refer to the words of verse 2 (the 'report' brought to Jacob), but Joseph's immediately preceding words are his narration of the dream in verses 6-7. This makes it more probable that 'his words' and 'his dreams' are largely different ways of referring to the same reality - Joseph's rise to pre-eminence set out in the dreams.[36]

VERSES 9-11 - THE SECOND DREAM
This second dream has a similarity with the first, for it too speaks of the rise of Joseph to a pre-eminent position in his family. The main new element is the inclusion of the sun and the moon among those who bow down, which serves a literary function of bringing Jacob into the action. Since Jacob interprets these symbols as referring to him and Joseph's 'mother', much has been made of the discrepancy that arises, for Rachel has died giving birth to Benjamin (one of the eleven stars in 37:9). Some suggest that the second dream is not fulfilled in the narrative, but it is probably best not to press the details and symbols too much.[37] Certainly Rachel's death has preceded the dreams chronologically (Gen 35:19), and her death is assumed right through Genesis 37-50. (for example, 43:27; 48:7). A possible solution, is to see here a stylised picture of Joseph's family, with the whole referred to in order to highlight the extent of his alienation. The emphasis is not on the precise number of sheaves or heavenly bodies, and there is no intention to identify individuals, but simply 'the family as a whole'. In other words, whatever members of the family there are, they will bow down to Joseph.[38] Indeed, it is quite possible - if the details are to be pressed - that the moon is a reference to Leah.[39] As Culley concludes,

> Joseph does achieve a position of authority and his family eventually does come under his direct authority when they arrive in Egypt. Perhaps this is all that is necessary to establish the fulfillment of the dreams.[40]

---

35   Wenham, *Genesis 16-50*, 351 suggests that the narrator uses it to heighten the impact on the brothers.
36   *Contra* Speiser, *Genesis*, 290 who understands 'his dreams and his words' in verse 8 to mean 'his talk about his dreams'.
37   Gibson, *Genesis*, 230-231 argues that the second dream is not fulfilled in the epic and that therefore "Joseph's dream of the sun and moon and stars must have been a false one, suggested by his own arrogance and ambition, and not at all by God's prompting." This is speculative, and based on too little evidence.
38   Along similar lines, see Coats, *From Canaan to Egypt*, 14; Wenham, *Genesis 16-50*, 352.
39   Kidner, *Genesis*, 181; Gibson, *Genesis*, 230.
40   Culley, *Themes and Variations* 157. Sailhamer, *The Pentateuch as Narrative* 207

A further question for some commentators is whether it was wise for Joseph to tell the contents of the second dream, especially in light of his brothers' reaction to the first (37:8). Significantly, the narrator does not focus on this question, but rather on the differing reactions of the father and brothers.[41] The brothers hated Joseph in verse 8, and that presumably was an ongoing state in the light of their animosity in verses 18-28. In verse 11 they are portrayed as being jealous of him. On the other hand, although Jacob 'rebuked' Joseph, he still, kept the matter in mind.[42] Jacob's perception is that Joseph has moved beyond what constitutes proper respect for one's place in the family, yet his knowledge (and perhaps love) of Joseph leave him open to this dream being from God. Thus, the reader is led by the narrator to ponder the possibility that perhaps the dream might come true. Since the matter is kept in Jacob's mind, it is also kept in the reader's, so that the dream lingers, and hovers over the subsequent narrative. The twofold description of Joseph's dreams raises "narrative expectations that the dreams will be fulfilled."[43]

REFLECTIONS ON THE DREAMS IN VERSES 5-11

If, as is claimed in this chapter, the dreams are pivotal for the story as a whole, it is appropriate to pause briefly at this stage of the story and make some observations about the dreams.

It is worth commenting that the fact of Joseph's dream does not make him one of the 'wise'. In the Joseph narrative it is the task of the wise to *interpret* dreams (41:8), not *receive* them. The butler, baker and Pharaoh all receive dreams, but none of them are portrayed as being among the wise.[44] Joseph later *interprets* the dreams of others, but not in chapter 37. At this stage, all that happens is that Joseph receives two dreams that need no interpreter, for his brothers and father can interpret them, and they are not being pictured as wise. It is, however, possible that the dreams are there simply to give the atmosphere, the aroma, the ambience of wisdom. This will depend largely on the meaning and significance of the dream in the

---

also suggests 'bowing down' is a symbol of acknowledging his leadership.
41   This is noted by Berlin, *Poetics and Interpretation*, 48.
42   On the meaning of הדבר (matter) in verse 11, White, *Narration and Discourse*, 246 suggests that "[t]he term הַדָּבָר here includes both the dream report of Joseph, and the brothers' emotional reaction to it." However, this is unlikely since Jacob acts as if he is not aware of the brothers' reaction in verse 13, by sending Joseph out in his coat.
43   Savage, 'Literary Criticism', 91.
44   For example, the chief baker received a dream in 40:16-22, yet this was not to prolong his life, an aspect which Prov 3:1-2 notes is the result of being wise. Of the possible wisdom figures in the Old Testament, Daniel appears to be the only one who receives dreams (Dan 7:1; 8:1 etc.), but this is only after he is a wise interpreter of dreams in chapters 2 and 4.

story as a whole, and whether it is best understood as the expression of a characteristically wisdom theme.

However, the narrative as a whole intimates that these dreams do come from God. Not all are persuaded by this. Westermann, for example, notes that in verses 9-11, "there is not a word about any communication from God to Joseph in the dream."[45] Wenham observes that the latter dreams were interpreted with God's help (40:8; 41:16, 25, 28), yet there is no mention of God in 37:5-11, thus making it uncertain whether the dreams come from God or only from Joseph's ego.[46] However, God is only mentioned in the other dreams at the point of interpretation and this is the one set of dreams that is not interpreted. Thus, many conclude that, despite the lack of explicit mention of God, the dreams are pictured as "God's hidden way in this narrative."[47] It has been further observed that dreams were generally seen in the Ancient Near East as originating from God.[48]

When the dreams of chapter 37 are read as part of the Joseph story as a whole, it is even more evident that the dreams come from God. Later in the story, Joseph shows his own understanding of dreams when he states that dreams come from God (40:8; 41:25, 28).[49] The apparent impossibility of the second dream (since Rachel had died) makes it even more unlikely that it has been fabricated by Joseph.[50]

The very theme of the dream - the rise to pre-eminence of Joseph - is later described in the narrative as God's providential overruling of events being used to bring Joseph to power in Egypt (45:5-7; 50:20). Indeed, when the brothers bow to Joseph, the dream is recalled for the reader (42:6-9). What the dream said would happen, did happen, and this is part of what God intended for good. In other words, the dream announces what God intends for Joseph and the brothers.[51] Turner has argued for the need to discern 'announcements of plot' in Genesis. Joseph's dreams seem to

---

45   Westermann, *Genesis 37-50*, 39.

46   Wenham, *Genesis 16-50*, 351.

47   Von Rad, *Genesis* 351; Brueggemann, *Genesis* 298; Sarna, *JPS Torah Commentary*, 213.

48   Sarna, *JPS Torah Commentary*, 256; N.M. Sarna, *Understanding Genesis*, (New York: McGraw Hill, 1966) 213; Fretheim, 'The Book of Genesis', 601; Ross, *Creation and Blessing*, 600. Green, *What Profit for Us?*, 39-40 sees it as "a biblical truism that dreams are sent by God."

49   Turner, *Announcements of Plot*, 146: comments that "[i]t is surely unlikely that the dreams of one who interprets God's dreams elsewhere with divine aid should himself have dreams which merely reflect his own vaunting ambition. Also, the crucial importance of 37.5-11 for understanding the Joseph story as a whole strongly suggests God as the author of the dreams".

50   Turner, *Announcements of Plot*, 150.

51   Kidner, *Genesis*, 180; Becking, 'They Hated Him Even More', 44.

announce the plot of the rest of the story.[52] At the outset, the dream provides "program notes for the audience" by indicating that Joseph will prosper.[53] Indeed, a crucial literary function of the dreams is that, since the function of the dream is to be fulfilled, the interest of the reader "is shifted from *what* happens to *how* it happens."[54]

However, even if the dreams came from God, not all are convinced that it was appropriate for Joseph to tell them to his brothers, but rather reveals his tactlessness or immaturity.[55] Brisman is representative of this view when he quips "[e]veryone has dreams, but only the fool (perhaps the divinely guided fool) broadcasts unwelcome music."[56]

This suggestion is countered by others, who wonder that, if these dreams have come from God then it might be appropriate for Joseph to pass on the message encoded in the dreams. This may explain why the narrator does not criticise Joseph for telling the dreams. A strong version of this view would be that Joseph was compelled to pass on the message, perhaps even "under divine constraint".[57] A weaker version would be that it was appropriate or permissible - though not obligatory - for Joseph to pass it on.

This study suggests that the text of verses 5-11 focuses not on Joseph's character, but on the meaning of the dreams. The reader is not told Joseph's motives, and the members of his family respond to the *message* of the dreams and not to the fact of him telling them. Thus, one would not expect any implied criticism for Joseph passing on the dreams.

THE TWO DREAMS ARE ONE DREAM

One final issue is whether the focus is on what the two dreams share in common, or rather on the differences between them. In the context of Genesis 37-41, they are clearly a set of dreams, for the six dreams that are found here occur in three pairs of two.[58] However, that does not settle the matter, since the two dreams of chapter 40 have opposite meanings (the cupbearer given life; the baker death).

---

52 Turner, *Announcements of Plot*, 146 notes that it functions like previous announcements of plot in Genesis, which are to do with the inversion of normal expectations. Similarly, S. Zeitlin, 'Dreams and Their Interpretation from the Biblical Period to the Tannaitic Time: An Historical Study', *JQR* 66 (1975) 2-3.

53 Green, *What Profit for Us?*, 44. See also H.C. White, 'The Joseph Story: A Narrative Which "Consumes" its Content', *Semeia* 31 (1985): 60.

54 T.L. Thompson and D. Irvin, 'The Joseph and Moses Narratives', in *Israelite and Judean History*. eds. J.H. Hayes and J.M. Miller. (London: SCM, 1977) 189.

55 White, *Narration and Discourse* 244; Westermann, *Genesis 37-50* 38; Sarna, *JPS Torah Commentary*, 254; Alter, *Genesis*, 209; Coats, *From Canaan to Egypt*, 19.

56 L. Brisman, *The Voice of Jacob* (Bloomington: Indiana University Press, 1990) 102.

57 Peck, 'Note on Genesis 37,2', 343. Similarly, von Rad, *Genesis*, 351-352.

58 Sarna, *Understanding Genesis*, 213; Sarna, *JPS Torah Commentary*, 257.

Yet the parallels seem to be closer between Joseph's dreams in chapter
37 and Pharaoh's in chapter 41. In both pairs of dreams, a similar point is
apparently being made with different imagery. The two dreams of chapter
41 clearly have the same message (41:25, 32). Several factors suggest this
is the case in chapter 37 as well. Both of the dreams of chapter 37 speak
explicitly of bowing down to Joseph (verses 7, 9 and 10), and both are
interpreted as speaking about Joseph's rise to pre-eminence. The concept of
bowing down or submission is not absent in verse 8 either, for this verse
speaks about Joseph reigning or ruling over them. The two dreams have a
single message.

Wenham proposes that the dreams are complementary since once is set
on earth and the other in the heavens.[59] If so, it is again likely that the two
are making one point, rather than saying that his family will bow twice to
him. In 41:32 the doubling of the dream indicates that the matter is firmly
fixed by God, who will shortly bring it about.[60] The force of Joseph's first
dream is also intensified by the second dream.[61] The two dreams appear to
be, in fact, one dream. The focus is on the essential thrust of both dreams,
rather than on their differences.[62]

37:2-11 as a Whole Unit

The structure of chapter 37 is very important, introducing the way that the
dreams of Joseph hang over the whole chapter, and then the entire story.
Verses 2-11 set the scene as the reader is introduced to the family, its
weaknesses and division; and then come these two dreams that will push it
over the brink.[63] Richter observes that dream reports have a standard
structure in the Old Testament, which climaxes in their fulfilment

---

59 Wenham, *Genesis 16-50*, 351.
60 Turner, *Announcements of Plot*, 147 comments that "[w]hen Joseph interprets the
    duplication of Pharaoh's dreams as an indication that their fulfilment is fixed, the
    reader very naturally draws the connection with Joseph's dreams and wonders
    whether their doubling has the same significance." See also T.L. Thompson, *The
    Origin Tradition of Ancient Israel*. JSOTSup, 55. (Sheffield: JSOT Press, 1987)
    117-118.
61 Westermann, *Genesis 37-50*, 38.
62 *Contra* Janzen, *Genesis 12-50*, 149 and most recently Pirson, *Lord of the Dreams*
    47-52, 55-59 and 'The Sun, The Moon and Eleven Stars. An Interpretation of
    Joseph's Second Dream'. *Studies in the Book of Genesis: Literature, Redaction and
    History*. Edited by A. Wénin. BETL 155. (Leuven: Leuven University Press, 2001)
    561-568.
63 D.A. Seybold, 'Paradox and Symmetry in the Joseph Narrative', in *Literary
    Interpretations of Biblical Narratives*. eds. K.R.R. Gros Louis, J.S. Ackerman and
    T.S. Warshaw. (Nashville: Abingdon, 1974) 60.

(*Erfüllung*).[64] He further notes that the dreams in chapter 37 have no immediate notice of fulfilment, and therefore anticipate being fulfilled in the story as a whole. As such, here is a formal argument in favour of that view that the not-yet-fulfilled dream looms over the remaining story. The whole Joseph account, and certainly the rest of this chapter, is founded on these dreams. As Brueggemann comments, "the dream of chapter 37 governs all that follows."[65]

Secondly, in verses 2-11, the focus is on strife between brothers and a dispute over pre-eminence. In this setting, the robe and the dream are merely different aspects of the one reality. They both witness to Joseph's pre-eminence or special position within the family. As far as the brothers are concerned, the robe and the dream are one, for their reaction to *both* is hatred of Joseph. The robe will carry the meaning of, and will symbolise, the dreams for the rest of the chapter.

Genesis 37:12-35 - Complication

37:12-17 - The Father Sends Joseph to his Brothers

This section begins by announcing that the brothers, who so far have been marked by their hatred of Joseph, are grazing the flocks near Shechem. Jacob and Joseph are at the valley of Hebron (verse 14b).[66] There are literally two camps, with the contrast being emphasised by their juxtaposition at the end of verse 14:

וישלחהו מעמק חברון ויבא שכמה
(he sent him from the valley of Hebron and he came to Shechem)

In Shechem, the brothers can no longer be seen or controlled by the patriarch Jacob.[67] This is a situation of potential danger for Joseph, fuelled in verse 13 when Jacob announces that he is going to send Joseph to the brothers. Joseph is to leave the camp of safety (with Jacob), and travel to the camp of risk and uncertainty (with the brothers).[68]

---

64 W. Richter, 'Traum und Traumdeutung im AT: Ihre Form und Verwendung', *BZ* 7 (1963): 204.
65 Brueggemann, *Genesis*, 296.
66 Baldwin, *The Message of Genesis 12-50*, 159 notes that the distance from Hebron to Shechem was 80 kms; it was another 24 kms on to Dothan, through hilly country. The journey from Hebron to Shechem to Dothan was a journey of 4-5 days.
67 Green, *What Profit for Us?*, 44; Kselman, 'Genesis', 112.
68 Humphreys, *Joseph and His Family*, 69; Coats, *From Canaan to Egypt*, 15. In

While this is not made explicit, it appears that the rest of the brothers (though seemingly not Benjamin) are tending the flock, while Joseph is not expected to do that work. He is both away from the work, and near their father. Thus, what was signified by Joseph's robe (in that it was not a functional working garment) is reflected in where he is located.

In verse 14, Joseph is sent to see if all is well with his brothers, and to bring word back to Jacob. For the reader, Jacob's instruction has two parallels to verses 2-4. Firstly, Joseph is to check on the welfare (שָׁלוֹם, verse 14) of his brothers, but the brothers could not speak peacably (לְשָׁלֹם, verse 4) to Joseph. Secondly, in verse 2 Joseph has previously brought back a word (דִּבָּתָם רָעָה, verse 2; דָּבָר, verse 14) about his brothers tending the flock. Their subsequent response (verses 4, 5, 8, 11) was one of hatred and jealousy. If that was their response when Jacob was present, it is unlikely to be favourable when Joseph meets the brothers at a place where Jacob has little control.

While this pericope does not significantly advance the story, it does serve several literary functions. Firstly, it retards the forward movement of the story, since it delays Joseph's arrival.[69] This creates suspense, for the reader knows that Joseph is moving towards a dangerous setting.[70]

Secondly, the episode creates a sense of distance between Jacob and his sons.[71] The intervening verses, which outline events between Joseph's departure and his arrival, draw attention to Joseph moving further away from Jacob's control.

There may well be hints in this pericope of Joseph's character as a dutiful son. His response in verse 13b ('here I am', הִנֵּנִי) to being sent into the 'danger zone' is arguably one of submission.[72] Furthermore, when he arrives in Shechem and cannot find his brothers, he could well have returned home, or when he found out that they were at Dothan, he could have decided not to continue on to there. Had he done either, he could have been fulfilling the letter of his father's command, and returned home safely. His determination to look for his brothers in the fields (verse 15), and to go on to Dothan (verse 17b), shows that Joseph is determined to meet his father's intention, not merely his commands.[73]

---

addition, Shechem could be a dangerous place, even for the brothers, in view of their previous dealings with the Shechemites in Gen 33:18-34:31.

69   Coats, *From Canaan to Egypt*, 16; Ross, *Creation and Blessing*, 607.

70   Berlin, *Poetics and Interpretation*, 49.

71   Westermann, *Genesis 37-50*, 40; N. Leibowitz, *Studies in Bereshit (Genesis)*. trans. A. Newman. (Jerusalem: World Zionist Organization, 1976) 396; White, 'The Joseph Story', 62. Thompson, *The Origin Tradition*, 119 sees a cavalier use of geography here simply to create distance.

72   Leibowitz, *Studies in Bereshit*, 477.

73   So Candlish, *The Book of Genesis*, 122 J. Licht, *Storytelling in the Bible* (Jerusalem: Magnes, 1978) 48.

Yet, there are two balancing factors. Firstly, the words of Joseph are very matter-of-fact, giving little insight into Joseph's motives and thoughts. הנני ('here I am') need not imply submission but perhaps resignation or it may simply be only a conventional or polite response (for example, Exod 3:4). Joseph's words in verse 16 do not enable us to assess Joseph's motivation or character. The incident could have been told in such a way as to give us a window on Joseph's character but, as in the remainder of the chapter, this opportunity seems not to have been taken.

Secondly, if Joseph is wearing his robe as he goes to his brothers (as is likely in the light of verse 23), then the effect of the narrative can hardly be to emphasise his tactfulness. Yet while this is not Joseph's most judicious act in the pericope, the narrator downplays its significance for Joseph's character by not explicitly mentioning the wearing of the robe until verse 23. Therefore it is not arrogance for Joseph to wear the robe, but it is a detail required by the story. Since what the brothers will seek to thwart is Joseph's pre-eminence, this has to be asserted in the narrative by the robe.

On reflection, then, this pericope does not seem to suggest either a positive or negative view of Joseph's character. What is more important is the way the messenger is introduced. In the previous patriarchal accounts, guidance to the leading characters is often given by the appearance of God or angelic messenger.[74] In verse 15, there is no explicit mention of either God or an angel; there is simply a man (איש).[75] If God is active, he is so only behind the scenes and never becomes a character in this part of the story. While Joseph later sees the hand of God in the whole process (45:5-8; 50:20), God is not mentioned here in the foreground.

The Symbolism of the Robe in 37:12-35

In the second section of the chapter, the dreams are referred to explicitly only in verses 19-20. Yet, once it is seen that the robe is a symbol of the dream, it becomes clear that the dream is much more pervasive, and many of the details of this section make better sense.

What is not revealed at first, but seems apparent later in verse 23, is that Joseph was wearing the robe as he travels to his brothers. Prior to verse 23, it is not revealed how the brothers could know from a distance that it was Joseph. It is likely that they recognise him from afar because he was

---

74 See, for example, Gen 12:7; 13:14-17; 15:1-21; 16:7-14; 17:1-22; 18:1-33; 19:1-23; 20:3-7; 21:8-19; 22:1-19; 26:1-5, 23-25; 28:10-17 (though perhaps only a dream); 31:3, 10-13 (a dream context); 32:1-2, 22-32; 35:1, 9-15. The only situation similar to Gen 37:15-17 occurs in Gen 29:1-14, where Jacob meets shepherds in the field who tell him where he can find Laban.

75 *Contra* Leibowitz, *Studies in Bereshit*, 396. Alter, *Genesis*, 211 notes that this incident reinforces the sense of Joseph being 'directed' to an encounter.

wearing the robe. When they see him, they say 'here comes that *dreamer*'. In other words, they see the robe, and recall the dream which it symbolises. The robe and the dream are part of the one reality. As Green remarks, "[t]he coat is a symbol of Joseph's special status in his family, a status which reminds us of his dreams, which were interpreted to make the same point."[76]

This accounts for the logic of verse 23 as well. The first thing the brothers do when 'the dreamer' (בעל החלמות) arrives is that they strip him of his robe, with the parenthetical explanation that this is not just any robe, but the same robe given to him by Jacob.[77] In other words, they are trying firstly to strip his dreams of their power, and only then do they throw him in the cistern. The brothers have apparently disposed of the dream, in stripping Joseph of his robe and spoiling it. They then take the robe back to Jacob not only as evidence of his death, but as the apparent termination of the dream of Joseph's pre-eminence. This, of course, re-opens the issue of pre-eminence in the family, and so it is perhaps natural to focus on Judah in chapter 38. Yet, the story as a whole, and the hint of verse 36, announces that while the robe is a symbol of what the dream reveals, the destruction of the symbol does not finally destroy the dream. The dream is, at least potentially, the larger and more lasting reality.

37:18-30 - The Brothers Dispose of Joseph

This unit begins with the robe-wearing dreamer coming to the brothers on behalf of their father (verse 18). They do not bow down to Joseph, but rather plot to kill him (verse 18). Joseph, by virtue of his symbolic robe, is apparently perceived by the brothers to be asserting his pre-eminence. Hence he is described by them in verse 19 as the dreamer (בעל החלמות).[78]

---

76 Green, *What Profit for Us?*, 51. Similarly, Pirson, *Lord of the Dreams*, 35. For a study of the symbolism of the robe in the Joseph story, see Matthews, 'The Anthropology of Clothing', 25-36, especially 30-31. Matthews notes that the 'garment motif' highlights the theme of Joseph's double rise to a position of power and influence. See also the very useful study by da Silva, *La symbolique des rêves*.

77 *Contra* Redford, *Biblical Story of Joseph*, 29 suggests that the last phrase in verse 23 is an addition.

78 The phrase בעל החלמות is ambiguous on a first reading. It might refer to the one who has the position of lord or master in the dreams (in the dreams he is 'in charge'), or that he is the controller of dreams (he is 'in charge' of the dreams) or that he is one who is obsessed or controlled by the dreams (the dreams are 'in charge' of him). D.J.A. Clines, ed., *The Dictionary of Classical Hebrew Volume II* (Sheffield: Sheffield Academic Press, 1995) 238 notes that בעל החלמות is not used elsewhere, but the combination בעל + construct occasionally occurs. The most significant parallels are as follows: a. In Ecc 10:11 it means 'one characterised or controlled by the tongue', that is a talkative person, not one who controls their tongue; b. In Prov 29:22 בעל המה is in parallel to איש־אף, and means 'one

The label that most characterises Joseph, what the brothers find most odious about him, is that Joseph is the 'dreamer'.[79] Brueggemann suggests that just as verse 5 announced the theme of verses 5-11 ('Joseph had a dream'), verse 19 now states the theme of verses 18-31, ('Here comes the master of the dreams').[80] In the brothers' plot (verses 19, 23) the twin motifs of the robe (verses 3-4) and the dream (verses 5-11) are combined. The movement in the unit involves Joseph being stripped of his robe, sold and sent away to a foreign land (verse 29). Finally the robe is bloodstained (verse 31) so that it can be used as evidence of his apparent death.[81] Thus, there is a movement in this whole unit from the dream being asserted to the dream apparently being frustrated by the 'disposal' of Joseph.[82] In verse 20, it becomes clear that the brothers' ultimate goal is to put an end to Joseph's dreams and make them fail ('we will see what will become of his dreams'). The dreams are thus foreshadowed to be central in the Joseph narrative.

The flip side of this may be seen by focusing on the brothers. The brothers start off as men in the field, without the robe, overwhelmed by the dream. When Joseph, wearing the robe, comes to report on them, they appear to have little power or status. Their initiative in selling Joseph and using the robe for their own deceitful purposes is their attempt to achieve dominance or success by removing the pre-eminent one, and the symbol he wears.

The question of characterisation is an interesting one in verses 18-30. A striking feature is the narrative focus on the brothers and not on Joseph. Joseph is the subject of no main clause, is the subject of, at most, three verbs (verses 18, 23, ?29). He takes no action apart from coming to the brothers (verse 23). Joseph is the one talked about, plotted against and acted upon.[83] There is no indication at all of Joseph's reaction to what was happening, and no mention of his thoughts, feelings or even his words. It is

---

controlled by anger' not one who controls their anger; c. In Prov 22:24, בעל אף is in parallel to איש המות and refers to the inability to control one's anger preventing one making friendships. Thus, it is likely that the expression בעל החלמות in Gen 37:19 means 'one who is characterised or controlled by his dreams' or 'a dreamer', not one who is 'lord in the dreams' or 'lord of dreams'.

79   P.T. Reis, 'Dead Men Tell No Tales: On the Motivation of Joseph's Brothers', *Conservative Judaism* 44 (1992): 57-60, however, suggests that they sought to kill Joseph because he found them where they should not have been (in Dothan, a town on the trade route which would have been frequented by prostitutes).

80   Brueggemann, *Genesis*, 303. Brueggemann sees verses 18-31 as a unit, not 18-30.

81   It might be better to say that this is central in verses 18-35, rather than verses 18-31, for the dipping of the robe in blood in verse 31 is only a preliminary to using the robe to deceive Jacob, which takes place in verses 32-34.

82   Brueggemann, *Genesis*, 304.

83   M. Bal, *Lethal Love: Feminist Literary Readings of Biblical Love Stories*. Indiana Studies in Biblical Literature. (Bloomington: Indiana University Press, 1987) 99.

clear that there is no intention in this passage to give a positive
characterisation of Joseph. Instead, it is curiously avoided.[84] In the chapter
we get the point of view of the narrator, of Jacob, of the brothers, but never
of Joseph, even though he is the object of the chapter's interest. This is
made even more pointed by the later reference (Gen 42:21) to Joseph's
anguish and pleading with his brothers on this occasion.[85] The brothers
remember it thirteen years later, but the narrator has [purposefully] not
recorded it, seemingly to avoid any focus on Joseph's reaction or character.
His strategy works to block us from seeing these events from Joseph's point
of view, and thus using his response as a model. While Joseph may later be
portrayed as a model character, he is in this passage described in neither
positive nor negative terms, and thus is not held up as a person to be
imitated. Joseph is a very flat figure in this opening group of stories, and so
his characterisation must await a later chapter.

By way of contrast, the focus is very much on the brothers. The words
and actions of the brothers as a group are found in verses 18-20, 23-25, and
27b-28; with Judah's words recorded in verses 26-27; and Reuben's in
verses 21, 22 and 30. The narrator provides additional information about
Reuben (for example, verse 29) and tells the reader about his motive, or at
least his intended course of action (verse 22b). In other words, the thoughts,
goals and actions of the brothers as a group and Judah and Reuben as
individuals, dominate this section of the narrative.

There is a consistently negative portrayal of all of the brothers. Verse 18
indicates that they decide to kill when they see him from a distance, and
before he came near to them. This makes it clear that Joseph has done
nothing further to provoke them (except, perhaps, to wear the robe - verse
23). Furthermore, the use of the root הרג ('to kill, slay') in verse 20 has
overtones of ruthless violence (as in Gen 4:8). As a group the brothers
respond to the dream with the 'solution' of fratricide (verse 20), though
they accept the alternative of selling him into slavery (verse 27). In both
scenarios there is an intention to deceive their father (verses 20, 31-32). In
addition, they callously sit and eat their meal while their brother is in the pit
(verses 24-25).[86]

Yet, the chance of success divides the brothers, so that disarray and
confusion dominates them. Once their initial plan is conceived, schism
emerges as Reuben (verses 21-22, 29-30) and then Judah (verses 26-27)
seek to modify it - Reuben to return him to Jacob; Judah to make a profit.[87]

---

84   Savage, 'Literary Criticism', 92.

85   Licht, *Storytelling in the Bible*, 111; Westermann, *Genesis 37-50*, 41.

86   Von Rad, *Genesis*, 354; Kselman, 'Genesis', 113.

87   Judah and Reuben are, of course, two key contenders for the status of first-born in
     the absence of Joseph - Reuben as the actual first-born; Judah as next in line after
     the disgraced three of Reuben, Simeon and Levi (34:30; 35:22).

The brothers' dilemma is an awkward one, since Reuben did not propose his plan until after Joseph was in the pit. If they proceed to kill Joseph after Reuben expresses his disquiet, there is now the danger of discovery, a weak link. But if they let Joseph go, he could take another bad report to their father. Yet, they must act, for Joseph was already in the pit.[88]

Reuben is being pictured, to an extent, as different from the other nine.[89] In verse 21, וַיַּצִּלֵהוּ is probably a conative imperfect, meaning that Reuben tried or attempted to deliver Joseph but was unsuccessful.[90] Yet, Reuben is seen as only partly a responsible son. While he seeks to restore Joseph, his larger goal may have been to ingratiate himself with his father. Thus, Reuben appears to be upset not because of what will happen to Joseph, but rather because it frustrates his plans (verse 30).

In verses 26-28, Judah persuades the brothers to sell rather than kill Joseph and so gain twenty pieces of silver. This may signal that Judah is becoming pre-eminent among the remaining brothers, explaining the focus on him in chapter 38. The narrative in general terms speaks of the apparent dominance or success of the brothers over against Joseph and his dreams, and the possible rise to pre-eminence of Judah among the brothers. Judah may emerge in the chapter as an effective leader, in that his proposal carries the day (verses 26-27), but his plan is motivated more by money (verse 28) than by any brotherly affection.

Thus, while there are differences between the brothers, they are all pictured in a negative light. Despite the fact that they apparently succeed, the continuing rivalries make it unlikely that the removal of Joseph will restore family harmony. In their 'success' there are seeds of future problems, even before Jacob's reaction in verses 32-35.

The other major event in this section is the arrival of a caravan on the way to Egypt, which the brothers 'look up' and see (verse 25).[91] This caravan of Ishmaelites introduces a further complication in that it will thwart Reuben's plan. While some unnecessary information delays the action, the significant detail is that they are going to Egypt. The hidden rule of God is seen in that the caravan that is going past is travelling to the country where Pharaoh and his dreams will be, and where there will be food to preserve the world. Yet, the concerns of this pericope are reflected in the fact that the "journey from the land to Egypt receives less than a line in the Joseph tale".[92] This is in telling contrast to the number of verses devoted to the words of the brothers. The confusion of the brothers acting at cross

---

88   White, 'The Joseph Story', 64.
89   Wenham, *Genesis 16-50*, 360; Brueggemann, *Genesis*, 304.
90   So Westermann, *Genesis 37-50*, 41.
91   Wenham, *Genesis 16-50*, 354 notes that the phrase in verse 25, וַיִּשְׂאוּ עֵינֵיהֶם, always signals that whatever is now seen is to be of great significance, as in Gen 22:4.
92   Niditch, *Underdogs and Tricksters*, 104.

purposes is also reflected in the arrival of Ishmaelites and Midianites, and the uncertainty about who receives the twenty pieces of silver.[93]

The mention of both the Ishmaelites and the Midianites in verses 25-36 has commonly been regarded as strong evidence of the interweaving of underlying sources, although others argue that the verses can be read synchronically.[94] It is not proposed to deal with this complex matter here since, on any unified reading, the brothers *intended* to sell Joseph as a slave into Egypt. If the brothers were the ones who were paid, they are pictured negatively for selling their own flesh and blood into slavery. If the Midianites were the ones who finally received the silver, then this simply makes the brothers look even more inept. On no reading of the passage can the brothers be viewed favourably.

37:31-35 - The Brothers Return to their Father

This section begins ironically in verse 31. The slaughter of a goat would be appropriate if the brothers were planning to make a sacrifice to God, but their intention instead is simply to deceive Jacob. Irony also emerges as the token of the father's love for Joseph (the robe) becomes the means for the brother's deceit and for Jacob's anguish.[95] Indeed, just like Jacob himself had used his brother's clothes to deceive his near-blind father (Gen 27:1-29), now he is deceived by his sons with the use of clothing.[96] The robe of favouritism is ironically used to deceive the deceiver.

The robe is very prominent in this unit. It is mentioned five times in verses 31-33, and it is specifically identified as the robe of verse 3 (verse 32). This is not merely an attack on Joseph, but on the dreams which spoke of his future pre-eminence.[97]

In verses 31-32, the narrator's art is seen in the bare narrative chain that

---

93 Wenham, *Genesis 16-50*, 356 notes that twenty shekels was the typical price of a slave (between 5 and 20 years), in the Old Babylonian period and in Israel (Lev 27:5).

94 For example, E.J. Revell, 'Midian and Ishmael in Genesis 37: Synonyms in the Joseph Story'. *The World of the Arameans I: Biblical Studies in Honour of Paul-Eugène Dion*. Edited by P.M.M. Daviau, J.W. Wevers and M. Weigl. JSOTSup, 324. (Sheffield: Sheffield Academic Press, 2001) 70-91 argues that the Midianites and Ishmaelites are different names for the same group.

95 E.M. Good, *Irony in the Old Testament*. Bible and Literature Series, 3, 2nd edn. (Sheffield: Almond Press, 1981) 107; Brueggemann, *Genesis*, 305.

96 The garment motif is a neglected theme in the Joseph story. Garments will also be used by Tamar to deceive Judah in Genesis 38, and Potiphar's wife uses Joseph's garment to make a deceitful charge against him (Gen 39:12-18). Joseph will also disguise his identity by wearing the garments of an Egyptian official in chapters 42-45.

97 Da Silva, *La symbolique des rêves*, 19; Janzen, *Genesis 12-50*, 151.

appears (they took ... they slaughtered ... they dipped ... they sent ... they brought ... they said). The pace quickens. There is no more discussion, no time for reactions, no conversation. The brothers' tactic of making Jacob identify the robe means that they can avoid telling an explicit lie to their father.[98] Here, then, is the climax of the brothers' plot, but one which will necessarily involve them in an ongoing life of deception.[99]

These verses indicate that the brothers' ambitious plan is at least partially successful. Joseph is certainly disposed of and the brothers' deceitful ploy is not detected by Jacob. His words are exactly what the brothers had themselves planned to say - 'a wild animal has devoured him'

ואמרנו חיה רעה אכלתהו (verse 20)
ויאמר ... חיה רעה אכלתהו (verse 33)

Jacob even adds in verse 33, 'Joseph is surely torn to pieces'. This overstatement ignores the obvious alternative that the breakdown in the family has gone over the edge.

Yet, the removal of Joseph and the destruction of the symbolic robe does not remove Joseph from the centre of Jacob's attention. In verse 34, Jacob tears his garment in mourning, continuing the garment motif. Ironically, the absence of Joseph makes him more present than ever as a result of the excessive grief of Jacob (verses 34-35).[100] Alter notes that the focus on Jacob's mourning is reflected in the half a dozen different activities to do with mourning that are mentioned in verses 34-35.[101]

Jacob mourned for the loss of his son, but the attempted comfort of *all* his other sons and daughters cannot distract from this one son. He speaks not of staying with his other sons, but rather of going down to Joseph ('my son', verse 35). What seems unbalanced here is not Jacob's strong grief, but rather that he appears to value the continued existence of the rest of his children as of little consequence compared to the loss of Joseph. It is as if he has lost the only child, the pre-eminent one, the first-born, the heir. The concluding clause in verse 35 reinforces this impression, for it is *his* father (אביו) not *their* father who bewails the loss of Joseph.[102] The brothers have sought to displace Joseph from their father's affections, but he remains

---

98   White, *Narration and Discourse*, 253; R. Alter, *The Art of Biblical Narrative* (New York: Basic, 1981) 4; White, 'The Joseph Story', 66; Green, *What Profit for Us?*, 52.

99   Brueggemann, *Genesis*, 304; Coats, *From Canaan to Egypt*, 18.

100 Wenham, *Genesis 16-50*, 356-357 points out that normally public grief would last for a week (Gen 50:10), or perhaps even a month for a great public figure (Deut 34:8).

101 Alter, *The Art of Biblical Narrative*, 4-5.

102 In addition, in verse 32 the brothers, in speaking to Jacob, refer to Joseph as 'your son' not 'our brother'.

Joseph's father, and his energy and attention stay fixed on Joseph, despite Joseph's absence.[103] The brothers' goal is thwarted by Jacob's refusal to give Joseph up. Instead of getting rid of Joseph by his apparent death, Jacob focuses on him as much in his 'death' as in his life.

Genesis 37:36 - Hinge

Much attention on verse 36 has been on the relationship of the Midianites to the Ishmaelites in the story, and the possibility of a conflation of sources. Yet, what is often ignored is the literary function of this verse in the narrative as it stands.

At the end of the chapter, the brothers believe that the threat of the dream has been removed (verse 28), and the father believes too that the dreamer is dead (verse 33). Only verse 36 gives a vague hint of another possibility.[104] Joseph had been sold into a position of potential influence. In the light of the whole story he is not only in Egypt, but as a servant to one of Pharaoh's officials. There is the chance, at least, of getting to the heart of the mighty nation of Egypt, though there is also great potential for danger, as will become evident in chapter 40. It is not a position of power, but there is at least the potential of power, in the light of the dream. As long as Joseph is not dead, perhaps the dream is still alive. The symbol is gone, but dream itself might yet prevail.

At the last minute, the narrator changes the focus away from Jacob and turns the reader's attention to Egypt. In the setting of the whole story, it also leads nicely into chapter 38. In emptying Canaan of Joseph, this final verse invites another look at the other brothers, and especially how they will live in the absence of Joseph. Judah and Reuben have been the brothers singled out in chapter 37, so it is perhaps not surprising that there is a focus on Judah in chapter 38 prior to narrowing in on Joseph in Egypt.[105]

Genesis 37 in Retrospect

This chapter is a fitting introduction to the Joseph story as a whole, alerting the reader to some crucial themes, tensions and motifs that extend into the subsequent sections. It is clear that the dream, as well as the robe which

---

103 Campbell and O'Brien, *Sources of the Pentateuch*, 235; Kselman, 'Genesis', 114.

104 Brueggemann, *Genesis*, 301, 307.

105 This, of course, would make chapter 38 something of an interlude which, while purposeful, does not advance fundamental plot of the narrative. The resumptive nature of 39:1, in which the information of 37:36 is virtually repeated, also confirms that chapter 38 is a narrative aside or interlude.

symbolises its basic thrust, reach out over the entire chapter and beyond. The issue of the pre-eminence of Joseph is thus raised for the reader, but it is not yet fulfilled. It arises in the context of, and is complicated by the existence of sibling rivalry, and these two threads will provide much of the dramatic power for the rest of the story. The Joseph narrative, then, starts with this focus, and not a concentration on the character of Joseph. He is, at this stage, passive in his actions, private in his thoughts, and overshadowed by the dream which will determine his destiny.

CHAPTER 5

Genesis 38

Joseph does not appear in Genesis 38, nor is he even mentioned. Yet, a closer reading of this chapter in its context reveals that it is much about wisdom than is commonly imagined. 'Wisdom-like elements' are prominent; it is simply Joseph who is absent.

The story of Judah and Tamar is certainly a perplexing text. Many scholars have regarded the chapter as an originally independent literary unit, and quite out of place in its present context.[1] Even the early retelling of the Joseph story in the pseudepigraphal Book of Jubilees (second century BCE), places the events of this chapter at a different location in the narrative.[2] Other writers have proposed original settings or dates for this chapter which suggest that the Joseph story has not always included the Judah-Tamar story.[3] A more recent trend has been to acknowledge the literary independence of the chapter, but then also to insist on examining its narrative function in its present context.[4] Thus, it is seen as an insertion

---

1 For example, Brueggemann, *Genesis*, 307; von Rad, *Genesis*, 356-357; J.A. Soggin, 'Judah and Tamar (Genesis 38)', in *Of Prophets' Visions and the Wisdom of Sages*. JSOTSup, 162, eds. H.A. McKay and D.J.A. Clines. (Sheffield: JSOT Press, 1993), 281; Speiser, *Genesis*, 299; R. Davidson, *Genesis 12-50*. Cambridge Bible Commentary. (Cambridge: Cambridge University Press, 1979) 224; B. Vawter, *On Genesis: A New Reading* (New York: Doubleday, 1977) 379.

2 S.D. Mathewson, 'An Exegetical Study of Genesis 38', *BSac* 146 (1989): 374 notes that chapters 39-45 of the Book of Jubilees moves straight from the events of Genesis 37 to those of Genesis 39, and then inserts the Judah-Tamar story (as Jubilees 41) after the events of Gen 41:1-49. Jubilees 42 continues the story of Joseph as recorded in Gen 41:53-57. Redford, *Biblical Story of Joseph*, 18 wrongly notes that the Book of Jubilees inserts the Judah-Tamar story between the events of Genesis 42 and 43.

3 G.A. Rendsburg, 'David and his Circle in Genesis XXXVIII', *VT* 36 (1986): 441 views it as referring more to David and his family that it does to Judah and his. J.A. Emerton, 'Some Problems in Genesis XXXVIII', *VT* 25 (1975): 345, 347, and 'Judah and Tamar', *VT* 29 (1979): 414-415 proposes that the details of the story suggest a setting in the time of the Judges, probably originating from Canaanite circles.

4 F. van Dijk-Hemmes, 'Tamar and the limits of patriarchy: Between Rape and Seduction', in *Anti-Covenant: Counter-Reading Women's Lives in the Hebrew Bible*. JSOTSup, 81, ed. M. Bal. (Sheffield: Almond Press, 1989), 146 describes the chapter

made by a redactor, but one which was purposefully and effectively woven into the final form of Genesis 37-50.[5] This study proposes that, irrespective of the pre-history of this text, in its present location it makes a significant contribution to the Joseph story.

Structure

The individual units of this chapter are easy to identify.[6] In verses 1-11, there is a focus on Judah establishing a family, with verses 1-6 being an exposition, and verses 7-11 containing the initial complications (the death of Er and Onan, and the perceived need to quarantine Tamar). In this unit, Tamar is passive. The second and major section is found in verses 12-26, in which Tamar takes the initiative. The movement in this section is from Tamar sidelined (verse 11) to Tamar vindicated (verse 26). It contains smaller scenes of Tamar's successful ploy (verses 12-19), an interlude (verses 20-23), and Tamar's public accusation and vindication (= resolution, verses 24-26). The third section has to do with the birth of

---

as "a carefully thought out departure". See also Seybold, 'Paradox and Symmetry', 61; Sailhamer, 'Genesis', 231; Baldwin, *The Message of Genesis 12-50*, 162; Mathewson, 'An Exegetical Study', 375, 385, 387, 392.

5 It is often placed elsewhere because of some chronological difficulties as outlined in G. Bush, *Notes on Genesis*. 2 vols. (New York: Ivison, Phinney & Co, 1860) 2:238; R.S. Candlish, *The Book of Genesis Expounded in a Series of Discourses*. 2 vols. (Edinburgh: Adam and Charles Black, 1868) 2:129. U. Cassuto, 'The Story of Judah and Tamar', in *Biblical and Oriental Studies*. trans. I. Abrahams. (Jerusalem: Magnes, 1973), 39, suggests that the chronology is tight but possible.

6 M. O'Callaghan, 'The Structure and Meaning of Genesis 38: Judah and Tamar', *Proceedings of the Irish Biblical Association* 5 (1981): 73 notes there are clearly three parts which he outlines as follows: 1. Judah's family building (verses 1-11); 2. Tamar's story (verses 12-26); 3. an account of Perez and Zerah (verses 27-30). H. Schüngel-Straumann, 'Tamar', *BK* 39 (1984): 150 also see three parts: verses 1-11 (Vorgeschichte), verses 12-26 (Hauptteil) and verses 27-30 (Folgen). J.W.H. Bos, 'Out of the Shadows: Genesis 38; Judges 4:17-22; Ruth 3', *Semeia* 42 (1988): 40 sees five parts in the story: verses 1-11 (Introduction and description); verses 12-19 (Scene 1); verses 20-23 (Interlude); verses 24-26 (Scene 2); verses 27-30 (Scene 3). However, she also writes of the first and second parts of the introduction (verses 1-6 and 7-11). Wenham, *Genesis 16-50*, 363 sees six clear scenes in the chapter - verses 1-5; 6-11; 12-19; 20-23; 24-26; 27-30. These are simply grouped into three larger units in the above analysis. Although Wenham inserts a break between verses 5 and 6, it is proposed to treat verse 6 as part of the exposition. A.J. Lambe, 'Genesis 38: Structure and Literary Design', in *The World of Genesis: Persons, Places, Perspectives* JSOTSup, 257, eds. P.R. Davies and D.J.A. Clines (Sheffield: Sheffield Academic Press, 1998), 103-104 views verses 1-6 ('equilibrium') as a unit, balancing verses 27-30.

Tamar's twins (verses 27-30).[7]

Genesis 38:1-11 - Judah Establishes a Family

Verses 1-6 redirect the reader's attention to the separate development of Judah and the establishment of his family. Beginning with ויהי בעת ההוא ('it happened at that time'),[8] a vague time reference, it describes how Judah descends from the heights of the family home at Hebron to the Canaanite city of Adullam (Josh 12:15).[9] The reader is not told why Judah leaves his brothers. If Judah's departure is related to the events of chapter 37, then no attention is drawn to that in the text. He 'settled near', or perhaps 'joined with', Hirah the Adullamite.[10]

The remaining events are quickly telescoped - his marriage, the birth of three sons and the marriage of the eldest son to Tamar. Several aspects of verses 1-6 are worth highlighting. Firstly, the concern with descendants connects this chapter with the wider context of the patriarchal narratives in Genesis, where progeny appears to be the crucial issue. Secondly, Judah's wife is unnamed yet the name of Er's wife is supplied. This suggests that Tamar will be a key character in the story.[11]

Thirdly, there appears to be no anti-Canaanite element in the story.[12]

---

7   E.M. Menn, *Judah and Tamar (Genesis 38) in Ancient Jewish Exegesis: Studies in Literary Form and Hermeneutics.* Supplements to the Journal for the Study of Judaism, 51. (Leiden: E.J. Brill, 1997) 18 notes that a trebling motif appears quite often in the chapter, joining the various sections together: Judah has 3 sons; 3 times Tamar is paired with a sexual partner (Er, Onan, Judah); there are 3 items given in pledge; there are 3 references to Judah withholding Shelah (verses 11, 14, 26); and the birth of twins in verses 27-30 restores the number of sons to 3.

8   This phrase occurs only three times in the Old Testament – here, Gen 21:22 and 1 Kgs 11:29. R. Alter, *The Art of Biblical Narrative.* (New York: Basic, 1981) 5 calls it an ambiguous formulaic time indication.

9   Wenham, *Genesis 16-50,* 366; Westermann, *Genesis 37-50,* 51; Emerton, 'Some Problems', 343.

10 Soggin, 'Judah and Tamar', 281 suggests that the root נטה, which usually means 'to open a tent', here may have more to do with a business arrangement. He proposes a second root [נטה II] meaning something like 'to join (in business)'.

11 M.E. Andrew, 'Moving from Death to Life. Verbs of Motion in the Story of Judah and Tamar in Gen 38', *ZAW* 105 (1993): 263. G.W. Coats, 'Widow's Rights: A Crux in the Plot of Genesis 38', *CBQ* 34 (1972): 461, however, regards Shua as the name of Judah's wife, not his father in law.

12 Gibson, *Genesis,* 244. *Contra* Mathewson, 'An Exegetical Study', 391, who suggests that Genesis 38 establishes that if the chosen people were to remain in the land, there is the danger that they would intermarry and lose their distinctive identity. Mathewson's argument is not very compelling. In chapter 38 there is no hint of the

Hirah is neutrally described (verse 1), while Judah's marriage to a Canaanite (verse 2) is neither explicitly criticised nor picked up later in the chapter. Tamar, although she is apparently a Canaanite,[13] is not even described as such, as if that was not important to the rest of the story. The final form thus shows no antipathy towards Canaanites, and the heroine Tamar is endorsed in verse 26 as being more righteous than Judah. This absence of anti-Canaanite polemic is suggestive of a more international or universal focus, perhaps anticipating the positive attitude to Egypt in chapters 39-41.

Verse 7 introduces the complication, but without much detail. The reader is only told that Er was wicked in God's sight and that the Lord slew him. Coats rightly points out that the "exact nature of his violation, the act that angered Yahweh, is not set out. It is irrelevant for the developing plot. The only purpose of this stage is to explain that Tamar became a widow."[14] The only unnecessary (and therefore potentially important detail) is that Er is twice described (verses 6, 7) as Judah's first-born, which is ominous in light of the use of this motif in Genesis.[15]

Verses 8-10 focus on Onan, who refused the legal or cultural or social obligation of impregnating his dead brother's widow in the brother's name. Onan's offence is not so much the practice of *coitus interruptus*, nor the performing of an unnatural act, but rather that he is seeking to avoid his responsibility to father a child for his deceased brother.[16] Onan's actions may be motivated by a desire for financial gain, but they also threaten the covenant line of promise.[17] From Tamar's point of view, they involve

---

dangers of intermarriage leading to adopting pagan religions. In fact, it is the Canaanite woman who reminds Judah of his obligations.

13 So, S.R. Driver, *The Book of Genesis*. Westminster Commentaries, 12th edn. (London: Metheun, 1926) 326; J. Skinner, *A Critical and Exegetical Commentary on Genesis*. ICC, (Edinburgh: T. & T. Clark, 1910) 449, 451; von Rad, *Genesis*, 357; Speiser, *Genesis*, 300; Wenham, *Genesis 16-50*, 366; J.A. Emerton, 'An Examination of a Recent Structuralist Interpretation of Genesis XXXVIII', *VT* 26 (1976): 90-93. For the contrary view see Sailhamer, 'Genesis', 232.

14 Coats, 'Widow's Rights', 462. A. Wildavsky, 'Survival Must not be Gained through Sin: The Moral of the Joseph Stories Prefigured through Judah and Tamar', *JSOT* 62 (1994): 39 notes that the Jewish commentators give the reason for Er's death as an action contrary to God's law, that is, 'ploughing on the roof' [= having sexual relations anally and so avoiding conception].

15 For a study of the 'first-born motif' in Genesis, see Syrén, *The Forsaken First-Born*.

16 Soggin, 'Judah and Tamar', 282. Green, *What Profit for Us?*, 64.

17 Wenham, *Genesis 16-50*, 367. The suggestion that this may have been financially motivated has been raised by Wildavsky, 'Survival', 39; S. Niditch, 'Genesis', in *The Women's Bible Commentary*. eds. C.A. Newsom and S.H. Ringe. (London: SPCK, 1992), 22; and Garrett, *Rethinking Genesis*, 175.

repeated sexual exploitation,[18] the denial of offspring to her dead husband, and her being prevented from coming securely into Judah's family.[19] It is a matter of dispute whether Tamar is entitled to marry the *levir*, or simply conceive a child.[20] The focus of the story, however, is on Onan's and then Judah's failure to fulfil their obligation towards Tamar.

Judah's reluctance to give Shelah to Tamar indicates that he views the deaths of Er and Onan as coming from a similar cause, somehow tied up with Tamar, "a jinxed barren wife".[21] Irony emerges as the reader is aware that their deaths are not caused by Tamar, but are due solely to the wickedness of Judah's sons. In verse 11, the narrator reveals Judah's deep fear that Shelah would die like the others, thus ending his line of descendants. His words of future provision for Tamar therefore cannot be taken by the reader at face value. They are words of pretence, not of promise.[22] Tamar seemingly trusts the words of Judah, and returns to her father's house.

Genesis 38:12-26 - The Vindication of Tamar

38:12-19 - Tamar's Initiatives

In verses 12-14, Tamar is no longer a passive and submissive figure, but rather one who takes initiative to right an injustice committed against her and her deceased husband.[23] The details of verse 12 indicate the sexual vulnerability of Judah - his wife has died, and it is the festive time of sheepshearing.[24] The garment motif, already prominent in Genesis 37, here

---

18 S.P. Jeansonne, *The Women of Genesis* (Minneapolis: Fortress, 1990) 102. Hamilton, *Genesis Chapters 18-50*, 436 argues that the phrase אם־בא should be understood as a frequentative use of the perfect and translated 'whenever he went in'. אם plus the Qatal form having a frequentative sense is discussed in J.C.L. Gibson, *Davidson's Introductory Hebrew Grammar - Syntax*. 4th edn. (Edinburgh: T&T Clark, 1994) §121b. Other biblical examples include Num 21:9; Judg 6:3; Job 7:4.

19 S. Niditch, 'The Wronged Woman Righted: An Analysis of Genesis 38', *HTR* 72 (1979): 145.

20 Coats, 'Widow's Rights', 463, Westermann, *Genesis 37-50*, 52 and Hamilton, *Genesis Chapters 18-50*, 435 speak only of a right to conceive a child, while Wenham, *Genesis 16-50* 369 understands the relationship in marriage terms.

21 Bos, 'Out of the Shadows', 47.

22 Jeansonne, *The Women of Genesis*, 102; Gunkel, *Genesis*, 398.

23 Westermann, *Genesis 37-50*, 52; Alter, *The Art of Biblical Narrative*, 8.

24 P. Bird, 'The Harlot as Heroine: Narrative Art and Social Presupposition in Three Old Testament Texts', *Semeia* 46 (1989): 123. The festive nature of the sheepshearing festival is set out by M.C. Astour, 'Tamar the Hierodule. An Essay in

recurs. Tamar will trick Judah by taking off the clothes which characterise her actual status (the widow's garments), and putting on the clothes and veil of a prostitute.[25] She sits down invitingly at the entrance to Enaim, on Judah's route.[26] There is possibly an intertextual link between verse 14 and wisdom stationing herself outside the town in Prov 8:2-3.[27] The justification for this trickery is given in verse 14b - the passing of time had shown that Judah had no intention of entrusting Shelah to Tamar. Judah's lack of justice and care has led Tamar to take this initiative.[28]

Verse 15 tells us that the ruse is successful, while verses 16-18, the only extended dialogue in the story, focus on the interaction between the two key characters. While Tamar is motivated by duty, Judah is driven by his desires. As Jeansonne observes, "Judah appears indecisive and lustful whereas Tamar appears skillful and prudent."[29] In exacting such valuable and distinctive items, Tamar acts with shrewdness, even wisdom, while Judah's excessive pledge marks him out as a person of folly.[30]

Judah's crassness is seen in the absence of any preliminaries, since his opening line is a request for intercourse. The astute Tamar, however, negotiates for what she will need as proof. Through Judah's pledge of his signet, cord and staff, Tamar gains irrefutable evidence of the identity of the

---

the Method of Vestigial Motifs', *JBL* 85 (1966): 192-193. Menn, *Judah and Tamar*, 22 points out that the connection between sheep shearing and revelry is evident in 1 Samuel 25 and 2 Sam 13:23-29.

25 Tamar is called a זונה in verse 14 and a קדשה in verse 21. Menn, *Judah and Tamar*, 68 argues that "[t]here must be at least some semantic overlap between the two words, or Hirah's question would make no sense". At 72-73 she adds that the narrator in Genesis 38 never explicitly states that Tamar was, or pretended to be, a prostitute, but that it was certainly necessary for the plot. The view that Tamar was a 'hierodule' is argued by Astour, 'Tamar the Hierodule', 185-186. See also Bal, *Lethal Love*, 101, and Bird, 'The Harlot as Heroine', 125-126, who suggest that she was a common prostitute.

26 I. Robinson, 'bĕpetaḥ ʿênayim in Genesis 38:14', *JBL* 96 (1977): 569 explores the meaning of the phrase בפתח עינים in Genesis 38:14, and renders the relevant part of the verse as '[s]he sat, invitingly/at Enaim, which is by the way to Timna.' For a study of the various translations of 'gate of Enaim' in the versions, see Emerton, 'Some Problems', 341-343, in which he concludes that it is possibly a place name.

27 I owe this observation to one of my graduate students, Ross Nightingale. Note that, apart from a similar scenario, there is the use of both דרך and פתח in both passages.

28 Bird, 'The Harlot as Heroine', 123; Coats, 'Widow's Rights', 463; Menn, *Judah and Tamar*, 23. On the issue of Tamar lying see O.H. Prouser, 'The Truth about Women and Lying', *JSOT* 61 (1994):15-28, who argues that deception is a justifiable weapon to enable disadvantaged and less powerful people to gain justice.

29 Jeansonne, *The Women of Genesis*, 103.

30 The great value of the pledge is noticed by Niditch, 'Genesis', 22; Vawter, *On Genesis*, 398. Alter, *The Art of Biblical Narrative*, 9 describes what Judah leaves as "a kind of ancient Near Eastern equivalent of all a person's major credit cards."

father of her child.[31] The clothing exchanges of verse 14 are then reversed in verse 19. Outwardly, Tamar remains the same, dressed in her widow's garments,[32] but by this ruse, she has fallen pregnant and thus enabled the seed of Judah to continue.

38:20-23 - An Interlude

This small interlude reinforces how completely Judah has been duped, and how little he is in control of the events around him. The prostitute cannot be found, so Hirah is unable to redeem Judah's pledges. Judah expresses fear in verse 23 that he might be laughed at, but the irony is that this entire interlude serves to poke fun at him.[33]

38:24-26 - Judah and Tamar Contrasted

These verses, which provide the climax of the narrative, display a series of contrasts between Tamar and Judah. Firstly, there is the contrast between the way Judah had previously indulged his sexual desires (with a זונה, verse 15), and how strongly he condemns Tamar for her sexual transgression (זנונים/זנתה, verse 24).[34] This was a casual affair for Judah, but is a matter of life or death for Tamar. Secondly, Judah's apparent control of, and power in, the situation, is overturned by Tamar's strategy which gives her effective or actual power.[35] Tamar's astuteness in producing the signet, cord and staff, causes Judah's apparent power to crumble. Finally, there is the comparison between Judah and Tamar drawn out by Judah himself: 'she is more righteous than I' (צדקה ממני, verse 26).[36] Matthewson points out that

---

31 Westermann, *Genesis 37-50*, 53 observes that "[t]he signet ring or cylinder seal is used to sign contracts; the staff has markings carved on it which are peculiar to the owner. The seal was carried on a cord around the neck." N. Furman, 'His Story Versus Her Story: Male Genealogy and Female Strategy in the Jacob Cycle', *Semeia* 46 (1989): 145 comments that "the signet, cord, and staff ... are desirable only because they function as signatures, as evidence of the identity of the progenitor, as proof in a paternity suit."

32 Her resumption of her widow's garments is seen to reflect her desire to remain Er's widow: O'Callaghan, 'The Structure and Meaning', 84; Wildavsky, 'Survival', 40; Fretheim, 'The Book of Genesis', 605.

33 Bos, 'Out of the Shadows', 41.

34 Bird, 'The Harlot as Heroine', 124; Brueggemann, *Genesis*, 309; Wildavsky, 'Survival', 41; Bal, *Lethal Love*, 102.

35 Andrew, 'Moving from Death to Life', 266 notes that Judah was ineffectual in sending a kid to the prostitute (verses 20, 23); Tamar is effective when she sends (שלח in both cases) word to Judah in verse 25.

36 Menn, *Judah and Tamar*, 7 notes how this verse was interpreted in Jewish rabbinic exegesis (*Testament of Judah, Targum Neofiti, Genesis Rabbah*). There צדקה is

Judah's verdict here is "the normative (authoritative) viewpoint of the story."[37] Righteousness here appears not to be measured by some absolute moral standard, but rather fulfilling the demands of one's position or relationship with others.

Two other aspects of this section are worthy of comment. Firstly, the granting of justice to Tamar gives the implied reader hope that the enslaved Joseph in Egypt might yet receive justice. Since Tamar's injustice had been righted against such odds, then perhaps Joseph's unfair enslavement can also be remedied. Secondly, a striking absence in this chapter is any prayer or appeal to God. While God may be seen by the reader to be acting behind the scenes, the human actors are in the foreground. This is often regarded as a good indicator of a wisdom perspective.

Genesis 38:27-30 - The Birth of Twins

This chapter ends with a distinct section in which Tamar gives birth to twin boys.[38] While these births round off Tamar's ruse nicely,[39] the detail of verses 28-30 seems to take the story in a different direction. These verses reach their tentacles back to earlier patriarchal accounts, and forward into the Davidic traditions.[40] There are links with the 'first-born' motif, and the struggles between twins, both of which are prominent in the book of Genesis.[41] In its present context, the success of Perez over his older brother is suggestive and ominous for the remainder of the Joseph narrative, hinting at the rise to pre-eminence of the younger son.[42]

---

understood as Judah's verdict ('she is righteous') while מ (= 'it is from me') is attributed to God and viewed as God accepting responsibility for what happened. This is stimulating, but unlikely.

37 Mathewson, 'An Exegetical Study', 380.
38 Menn, *Judah and Tamar*, 33 comments, however, that Tamar is not portrayed as a central character in the birth scene, as she is neither described as giving birth nor naming the children. The focus is now on the future descendants.
39 J. Goldin, 'The Youngest Son or Where Does Genesis 38 Belong?', *JBL* 96 (1977): 30 and van Dijk-Hemmes, 'Tamar', 152 both point out that the birth of twins restores what was lost in the death of Er and Onan.
40 Menn, *Judah and Tamar*, 1-2 notes that the connection with the Davidic line is not directly reflected in the text, although it is made in Ruth 4:18-22 and 1 Chr 2:3-15.
41 Goldin, 'The Youngest Son', 30.
42 Wenham, *Genesis 16-50*, 364; Ross, *Creation and Blessing*, 612; Furman, 'His Story', 145.

Chapter 38 as Part of the Joseph Story

Given this reading of the story, what is the meaning and significance of chapter 38 in its present context? What does it contribute to Genesis 37-50, and what does it tell us about the concerns of the whole story?

A Purposeful Delay

At the very least, the narrative effect of this chapter being placed between chapters 37 and 39, is to create a delay in the reader finding out about Joseph's fate in Egypt. It prevents the story of Joseph from moving forward, thus slowing down the narrative pace.[43] The effect of this is to create suspense.[44] The narrative descriptions of the next generations of Judah's family also give the impression of time passing.[45] This delay and passing of time thus serves a clear narrative purpose, and chapter 38 is thus best seen as an intentional rather than accidental interlude.[46]

The Wider Family of Jacob?

However, this chapter clearly does more than simply delay the Joseph narrative and create suspense. A common justification for the inclusion of this chapter is to propose that Genesis 37-50 is the second part of the ongoing story of Jacob (Gen 37:2), and not simply the story of Joseph.[47] Since this is the family story of Jacob, Judah as one of his sons gets the focus for a while. On this view, chapter 38 also serves to remind the implied reader, who is becoming engrossed in the story of Joseph, that there is a larger context of Jacob's extended family.

Yet this view does not seem to account for the actual contents of chapter 38. This chapter is the story of only Judah and Tamar, with no mention of Jacob or any of the other brothers. Furthermore, neither Jacob, Judah, nor any of the other brothers are mentioned in the three important chapters that follow, Genesis 39-41. It is preferable, therefore, to regard Genesis 37-50 as the story of Joseph, but to see that his story is enmeshed in the wider

---

43 Blenkinsopp, *The Pentateuch*, 108; Humphreys, *Joseph and His Family*, 205; Mann, *The Book of the Torah*, 67.

44 Alter, *The Art of Biblical Narrative*, 3-4; Longacre, *Joseph: A Story of Divine Providence*, 26; Wenham, *Genesis, 16-50* 363.

45 Wenham, *Genesis 16-50*, 363; H.C. Leupold, *Exposition of Genesis*. Vol. 2. (Grand Rapids: Baker, 1953) 976.

46 Thompson, *The Origin Tradition*, 121; G.R.H. Wright, 'The Positioning of Genesis 38', *ZAW* 94 (1982): 523.

47 Wenham, *Genesis 16-50*, 364-365; Ross, *Creation and Blessing*, 611. Westermann, *Genesis 37-50*, 49 argues that it is like the inclusion of the account in chapter 34 about Simeon and Levi and the fragment about Reuben in 35:22-23.

context of the book of Genesis.[48]

Thus, it is more accurate to say that this chapter concerns, not the whole family of Jacob, but only Judah, and in particular the descendants of Judah. Since Judah's elder brothers seem to have disqualified themselves in Jacob's eyes (34:30; 35:22), and now that Joseph has 'disappeared', Judah is the most likely to be regarded as the heir.[49] The story of Judah, and especially his role as the bearer of the line of the Abrahamic promise, is a major sub-plot in Genesis 37-50.[50] Judah is a key player in chapter 37, is one of the two main characters in chapter 38, is the brother who persuades Jacob to send Benjamin (43:1-15), and is a noble spokesman for the brothers (44:18-34). Furthermore, Jacob's blessing in Gen 49:8-12 makes it clear that his descendants will gain prominence among the later twelve tribes. As the bearer of the line of promise, Judah's story is thus interwoven with that of Joseph in this concluding section of the book of Genesis.[51] Such a view explains the non-mention of the other brothers in this chapter, the background problem of childlessness, and the way in which this interlude concludes with the very detailed reports of Perez and his brother in verses 27-30. It also accounts for the unusually large number of parallels between this story and chapter 49.[52]

Chapter 38 as a Microcosm of the Joseph Cycle

Some indeed have suggested that chapter 38 serves in the final form of the text as a cameo or microcosm of the Joseph story as a whole. Wildavsky, for example, sees crucial parallels between the two, although he regards both Judah and Joseph as negative examples, those who did not trust God when he said that he would keep his promises to the patriarchs, preserving his covenant people. In other words, Joseph and (initially) Judah are those who seek survival through sin rather than obedience to the moral law.[53] On a different tack, Lockwood has suggested that Judah's transformation in the

---

48 Chapter 9 will explore the connections between the Joseph story and the wider book of Genesis.

49 Goldin, 'The Youngest Son', 43; Goldingay, 'The Patriarchs', 21.

50 Garrett, *Rethinking Genesis*, 173.

51 Wenham, *Genesis 16-50*, 366-367 notes that up to this point the word זֶרַע (seed/descendant) has been almost exclusively used for the descendants promised to Abraham who would become a great nation and possessors of the land. He suggests that it is likely that it retains this further meaning here. If so, then this carries forward the concern with the progeny of the Abrahamic promise.

52 On the verbal and other parallels between chapters 38 and 49, see Rendsburg, *The Redaction of Genesis*, 83-86.

53 Wildavsky, *Assimilation versus Separation*, 41.

story is a miniature version of the story as a whole.[54] Lockwood claims that the change that overcomes Judah in chapter 38, culminating in his confession of guilt and sin, is a pointer to what will happen in the wider Joseph cycle as the brothers have a change of heart and are reconciled to Joseph.[55] Yet, verses 25-26 place no emphasis on a change of heart in Judah, but are simply an acknowledgement that he has been caught out and cannot deny the evidence. Whether his heart is changed can only be determined by reading on.

It is, however, proposed that chapter 38 is a microcosm of the Joseph story is several other ways.

STRUCTURAL PARALLELS

Firstly, the structure of chapter 38 appears to mirror that of the whole Joseph story. Both begin by describing the wider family, and the tensions within it. The dilemma facing the main character is then overcome without the express help of God. This leads finally to the continuation of the family line, with a focus on the descendants. The structural parallels are evident in the following table

The Joseph Story	Judah/Tamar	Description
Chapter 37	38:1-11	The wider family picture
Chapters 39-47	38:12-26	The human initiatives of the main character (God behind the scenes) to right a wrong through the use of a shrewd plan
46:8-27 and chapters 48-50	38:27-30	A genealogical summary of subsequent descendants [amplified in Joseph's case to include the future destiny of his brothers]

LIFE EMERGING FROM DEATH

Secondly, both chapter 38 and the broader Joseph story revolve around issues of life and death. More precisely, there is a pattern of life emerging from a backdrop of death.[56] In the broader narrative, there is Joseph's 'death' (37:32-35), and the prospect of starving to death (42:2). In chapter

---

54 P.F. Lockwood, 'Tamar's Place in the Joseph Cycle', *Lutheran Theological Journal* 26 (1992): 37 suggests that "[i]t is the Joseph story in a nutshell. ... As Joseph is to his brothers, so Tamar is to Judah."

55 Lockwood, 'Tamar's Place', 42.

56 Andrew, 'Moving from Death to Life', 262.

38, there is the death of Judah's wife and first two sons (38:7, 10, 12), as well as Judah's decision to keep Shelah and Tamar separated.

Tamar's actions bring new lives into being (38:27-30), while Joseph also tells his brothers that God sent him ahead to preserve life (45:5, 7). In addition, both stories end with a list of descendants as a symbol of continuing life. In chapter 38, the line of Judah continues (38:27-30), while in the wider story, chapters 48 and 49 outline the future of Jacob's descendants. In each case life is preserved and promoted despite the real possibility of death. A beneficial outcome is implied in both accounts, injecting a note of optimism and possibility.

GOD VINDICATES THE WRONGED RIGHTEOUS PERSON

Furthermore, in both stories, against the odds, God vindicates the righteous person who has been dealt with unfairly.[57] In chapter 38, when Tamar hears of Judah's trip, she cleverly tricks him, gaining the evidence she needs to implicate Judah, and succeeds in falling pregnant. Here is a cameo in which justice wins out. This chapter clearly teaches the value of resourcefulness, and how even seemingly impossible situations can be redeemed and reversed. The text seems to focus on this principle that justice will be brought about, rather than on a moral command such as 'act justly!'.

O'Callaghan, however, has proposed that the key to the chapter is almost entirely found in verses 27-30. He suggests that the narrative is about "the *propagation* of the family, the prolongation of Judah's line, or, to use a single word, *progeny*."[58] Arguing against the view that the story is about Tamar's resourcefulness, he concludes that the single theme is "the propagation of the line of Judah."[59] This appears to be reductionistic, since the story - especially verses 12-26 - is also about the human resourcefulness of Tamar. The exegesis above has argued that the resolution of the story comes in verse 26, with a positive evaluation of the shrewd strategy of Tamar. It is better, therefore, to see the chapter as an interweaving of the motif of human shrewdness, perhaps even wisdom, and a concern with the future progeny of the Abrahamic line of promise through Judah.

Humphreys notes that the effect of Judah being exposed in chapter 38 is that the righteousness of Tamar is revealed to all.[60] Perhaps this gives a narrative expectation that right will also triumph over the wrongs of chapter 37, which may entail the restoration of Joseph. The links between chapters 37 and 38 thus highlight a key theme that will emerge in the remainder of

---

57 Humphreys, *Joseph and His Family*, 131; Wenham, *Genesis 16-50*, 364.
58 O'Callaghan, 'The Structure and Meaning' 74. At 73, he explores the repeated vocabulary of the chapter, and notes that it deals with terms of family and family history.
59 O'Callaghan, 'The Structure and Meaning', 74.
60 Humphreys, *Joseph and His Family*, 37-38.

the Joseph story - God's behind-the-scenes vindication of the wronged righteous person (45:5-8; 50:20).[61]

In a way suggestive of wisdom connections, God works in the background of both stories, while the human resourcefulness of the leading characters bring about the movement from death to life. As will be the case in the broader Joseph story of Joseph, God uses shrewd, resourceful human action to preserve the Abrahamic line of promise. Thus, if Joseph has some 'wisdom-like elements' in his character, then the characterisation of Tamar could also have 'wisdom echoes'.[62] This will be explored further in chapter 11.

THE DECEIVER, DECEIVED

The deception motif also binds together chapters 37 and 38, and in both chapters an article of clothing is used.[63] Just as the brothers deceived Jacob about Joseph's 'death' (37:32-35), Judah continues true to form in chapter 38 by withholding Shelah from Tamar while giving her the impression that it was only a matter of time (38:11). It is this deception, made apparent by the passing of the years (38:14), that leads Tamar to dress up as a prostitute and so deceive the 'deceiver'.[64] The links between the motif in the two chapters is made patent by the similar vocabulary in 37:32-33 and 38:25-26[65]

וישלחו ... ויאמרו.חכר־נא...ויכירה ויאמר...בני... (37:32-33)

שלחה ... ותאמר הכר־נא ...ויכר...ויאמר...בני... (38:25-26)

There is also a goat used in relation to each story (the blood of the עזים in 37:31, and the עזים offered as a pledge in 38:17).[66] Furthermore, in both

61 Menn, *Judah and Tamar*, 43-44 comments that "[p]erhaps, as in the larger Joseph story, God may be present despite his narrative absences in Genesis 38 ... Words similar to Joseph's in Gen 50:20 ... could be loosely applied to the characters of Genesis 38."
62 Green, *What Profit for Us?*, 77 notes that "Tamar's action ... receives the benison of success. Narratively speaking, she can hardly be construed as anything but admirable." The promise of success in one's plan is also emphasised in the Book of Proverbs (for example, Prov 16:3; 15:22).
63 Humphreys, *Joseph and His Family*, 37.
64 Lockwood, 'Tamar's Place', 36 comments: "in their chief representative and spokesperson, Judah, the deceivers soon receive a taste of their own medicine."
65 Cassuto, 'Judah and Tamar', 31.
66 Alter, *The Art of Biblical Narrative*, 11 notes that the *Bereshit Rabba* 84:11, 12 draws out this contrast. Alter suggests that while the reader may make this connection, there is no evidence that Judah himself was conscious of it. This gives rise to dramatic irony, as we the audience are privileged with information denied to Judah.

contexts there is the mention of grief (37:34-35; 38:12). Alter thus rightly concludes "Judah with Tamar after Judah with his brothers is an exemplary narrative instance of the deceiver deceived."[67] A strong notion of retribution - Judah's deceit being matched at so many points by his being deceived - is woven into the two stories when they are juxtaposed.

All of these parallels appear to indicate that many of the themes in the larger Joseph story are subtly anticipated in chapter 38.

A Useful Set of Contrasts

In addition to these thematic similarities, there are a number of clear links between chapter 38 and the chapters which surround, often emphasising contrasting characters or features. These are not simply connections proposed by modern literary critics, for most of them were noted by the early Rabbinic commentators.[68] The links fall into two main categories:

RESPONSES TO SEXUAL INVITATION

A number of features connect Judah's sexual gratification in 38:12-19 with Joseph's refusal to the offer by Potiphar's wife in 39:7-12. The use of the root יר ('to go down') in 38:1 and 39:1 appears to suggest that the chapters are to be read in the light of each other.[69] In each case a garment is involved (38:14, 19; 39:12, 13, 15, 18), and used by a woman to deceive a male.[70] Both of the women involved are apparently foreigners, not Israelites. In both stories, physical evidence (the signet, cord and staff; Joseph's garment) determines what happens to the accused person. The offer of sexual gratification, ostensibly without consequences, is made to both Judah and Joseph.

The effects of juxtaposing the two accounts is to highlight the contrasting responses of the two brothers.[71] Judah is pictured as failing this vital test, rejecting the path of sexual self-control. Chapter 38 thus serves to introduce the question of character, with Judah providing a foil for the focus on Joseph's character in chapter 39.[72]

---

67 Alter, *The Art of Biblical Narrative*, 10.
68 Goldin, 'The Youngest Son', 28-29 comments that Rabbi Lazar noted the 'descent' in 38:1 and 39:1; Rabbi Yohanan noted the 'recognition' statements of 37:33 and 38:25; Rabbi Samuel bar Nahman sees the link between the Tamar incident and that with Potiphar's wife in chapter 39.
69 Andrew, 'Moving from Death to Life', 262. Green, *What Profit for Us?*, 63 suggests that "[t]he narrator's choice of verb stems also makes manifest that Judah does voluntarily what Joseph endures."
70 Wildavsky, *Assimilation versus Separation*, 58.
71 Alter, *The Art of Biblical Narrative*, 10; Pink, *Gleanings in Genesis*, 366.
72 Lockwood, 'Tamar's Place', 36.

In addition, a fruitful contrast between Tamar and Potiphar's wife emerges when the two texts are read together. Tamar's sexual act was prompted by her desire to fulfil her responsibility to her (deceased) husband; Potiphar's wife sought to breach her responsibility to her (alive) husband.[73] This double comparison (Judah and Joseph; Tamar and Potiphar's wife) serves to highlight the contrasting responses to sexual invitation, a key theme in Proverbs 5-7.

THE NATURE OF RIGHTEOUSNESS

Westermann has suggested that verse 26, with its vindication of Tamar, is "the goal of the narrative."[74] While this is helpful, it is, perhaps, better to view this verse as the point of resolution of the chapter. This is the immediate goal, but there is a further goal in verses 27-30 of showing that the line of promise will continue. In verse 26, the issues raised in the narrative are resolved as Tamar is publicly cleared, and her future secured. From now on, the line of Judah will continue. Yet, more importantly than all these is the endorsement of Tamar's actions and character as righteous.

Some commentators have difficulty with the notions of Tamar's 'prostitution' being described as 'righteous'. They see her as only more righteous than Judah,[75] or that her transgressions were outweighed by the need to continue the family line,[76] or that she was within her rights.[77] While there is truth in these views, they do seem to avoid the clear thrust of the text in its endorsement of Tamar's righteousness. Indeed, this text raises in a vivid way the Hebrew concept of righteousness as a relational idea.[78] Tamar sought to fulfil the responsibilities she apparently had as a result of her relationship with her husband. Judah's action in withholding Shelah was blocking Tamar's opportunity to meet the obligations of her relationship, and needed to be overcome.

Viewing righteousness as honouring the demands of a relationship makes sense of the contrasts drawn in the context. Clearly Judah has not

---

73 S.A. West, 'Judah and Tamar - A Scriptural Enigma', *Dor le Dor* 12 (1984): 250; Wildavsky, 'Survival', 47. Brenner, *The Israelite Woman*, 106-114 has suggested that there is a wider contrast between the positive temptress as seen in Ruth and Tamar, and the negative temptress found in Potiphar's wife and the 'foreign woman' of Proverbs 1-9.

74 Westermann, *Genesis 37-50*, 54.

75 J.M. Boice, *Genesis: An Expositional Commentary Volume 3: Genesis 37:1-50:26*. (Grand Rapids: Zondervan, 1987) 46.

76 Wildavsky, 'Survival', 46.

77 Westermann, *Genesis 37-50*, 48: "she is within her rights rather than I."

78 B.C. Birch, *Let Justice Roll Down: The Old Testament, Ethics and Christian Life* (Louisville: Westminster/John Knox, 1991) 60; Andrew, 'Moving from Death to Life', 267; Janzen, *Genesis 12-50*, 154.

acted righteously in preventing Shelah from acting as *levir*. Yet Tamar is also contrasted with the brothers in chapter 37 who have failed to honour their obligations to Joseph or Jacob when they sold their brother into slavery. There may also be an implied contrast between Tamar's righteousness and the 'wickedness' of Potiphar's wife in 39:9, where she proposed an action that would breach her relationship with her husband, as well as Joseph's relationship to both God and Potiphar. Thus, it appears that this crucial verse is foregrounding the issue of righteousness in relationships that will be significant for the broader story. This chapter "presents the reader with a question: can Tamar be blamed for what she did or not?" and provides the answer that Tamar is righteous, for she seeks to honour the obligations of her relationships.[79]

In the broader Joseph narrative, the ruptured family relationships are overcome by Joseph's testing of his brothers in chapters 42-44. It will be argued that Joseph does not opt for 'instant forgiveness', but rather creates a shrewd ruse to discern if the character of the brothers can change or has changed. In chapter 44, they are presented with another opportunity to leave their favoured younger brother. However, the impassioned speech of Judah (44:18-34) reveals that they have become committed to the welfare of their father and brother. Once they disclose their commitment to these relationships, Joseph makes himself known to them in relational terms (45:4). The outcome of Joseph's test is to effect a lasting restoration of family relationships, even after Jacob's death (50:15-21). Judah, then, is not righteous in chapter 38, for he does not fulfil the obligations of his relationships. By way of contrast, Joseph and Tamar both make opportunities to restore family harmony and unity.

The further issue of whether or not Tamar is to be regarded as a wisdom figure (in contrast to the folly of Judah) will be explored in chapter 11. However, it is already clear that the effect of the inclusion of her story is to raise the question of righteousness of character at an early stage in the Joseph narrative.

Summary

It has been argued that Genesis 38 discloses its full treasures only to those who refuse to read it as a literary orphan. When it is read as part of the Joseph narrative, this chapter is pregnant with meaning. As Menn comments, "[r]egardless of this narrative's prehistory, the final redaction of Genesis 38 in its present context is intentional and artful."[80] It draws

79 H.A. Brongers, 'The Literature of the Old Testament', in *The World of the Old Testament*. trans. S. Woudstra, ed. A.S. van der Woude. (Grand Rapids: Eerdmans, 1989), 138.

80 Menn, *Judah and Tamar*, 75.

attention to, and anticipates, several vital themes and motifs in the wider Joseph story. Reading chapter 38 as part of Genesis 37-50 in important not only for the light that it sheds on the tale of Judah and Tamar, but also for its illumination of the Joseph narrative itself. The implications of this for the integration of wisdom and covenant will also be drawn out in chapter 11, where the character and role of Tamar will be examined further.

CHAPTER 6

Genesis 39-41

The Structure of Genesis 39-41

The final form of Genesis 39-41 moves from Joseph being a mere slave (39:1) to his becoming second in command in Egypt, the one to whom all the world is coming to preserve their lives (41:57). Clearly therefore, this section has a neat narrative closure and the broad sweep of these chapters is that they outline the rise of Joseph.

It is important to view this account of the rise of Joseph as a cohesive section, for the tension introduced by Joseph's enslavement is not resolved until chapter 41. By way of contrast, if the analysis were to be of chapter 39 alone, then a commonly observed feature is that the chapter begins and ends with the reminder that God was with Joseph (verses 2-3, 21-23). This motif, it has been suggested, brackets the remaining material, and gives the theme for the chapter.[1]

However, if chapters 39-41 are regarded as one unit not three independent sections, this will result in a structure slightly different from the traditional chapter divisions. A number of scholars have pointed out that, if all of Genesis 39-41 is the literary unit, then it is best divided as follows: 39:1-20; 39:21-40:23; and 41:1-57.[2] Coats points out that the first two scenes (Joseph with Potiphar's wife; Joseph in prison) offer no resolution of the tension. Instead, the tension that is introduced in the first scene is transferred through the second and into the third (Joseph before the Pharaoh). Thus, neither the first nor second scenes can stand in isolation,

---

1   Westermann, *Genesis 37-50*, 60-61; Skinner, *Genesis* 457-460; Brueggemann, *Genesis*, 319-320; Fretheim, 'The Book of Genesis', 609; Kselman, 'Genesis', 115.

2   So, for example, Wenham, *Genesis 16-50*, 372; Humphreys, *Joseph and His Family*, 58-61. Similarly, G.W. Coats, *Genesis, With an Introduction to Narrative Literature*. FOTL, 1. (Grand Rapids: Eerdmans, 1983) 276-277, although he makes the first division between 39:20a and 39:20b. Gunkel, *Genesis*, 380 also inserts the break between verse 20a and verse 20b, on source critical grounds, while Scharbert, *Genesis 12-50*, 247-249 places the break after verse 21.

but must be read as part of chapters 39-41 as a whole.[3] Of course, after this third scene, there are no more dreams, there is no further rise of Joseph to a position of public power, nor is Joseph dealt with unfairly at any subsequent stage.

On this division, the first two units move from the promising start of God being with Joseph (who prospers and has his hopes raised), to his hopes being unfairly dashed (imprisoned; forgotten by the cupbearer). The third and climactic scene speaks again of the rise of Joseph, yet one that is sustained beyond his expectations, this time without any disappointment at the end. Thus, the pattern evident here reflects the common Hebrew practice of telling stories in three episodes or scenes, the first two of which are typically alike, with the third surprising the reader by its differences.[4]

This proposed structure also raises the motif that 'Yahweh was with Joseph' to greater prominence. If this motif serves only as an inclusio for chapter 39, then the concept may not be present in chapters 40-41. Yet, if the three scenes are read together, then the rise of Joseph is pictured in the first two cases as a prospering due to Yahweh being with him. In the third scene there is no need to state this explicitly, since it is already established from scenes one and two. This means, of course, that Joseph's administrative skill in chapter 41 is pictured as a result of God being with him, and presumably also when it recurs in 47:13-26. In other words, his administration is endorsed in the book, against the contemporary tendency to point out that it involved enslaving the Egyptians. Chapter 41 thus testifies to the fact that Joseph's careful planning and administration leads to life (41:57, in the light of 42:2).

Another way in which chapter 39 can be seen as a scene in the wider unit is that the testing of his character both precedes and justifies his being subsequently entrusted with power and administrative responsibilities. In other words, before Joseph can become a wise administrator, he must first have his moral fibre and character tested by an encounter with a persistent 'adulteress'. This progression reflects the way that the canonical form of the book of Proverbs is structured. In order to understand and apply the sentence sayings of Proverbs 10-29, the implied reader is invited to pass through the gate of Proverbs 1-9.[5] These early chapters focus on the fear of the Lord (1:7; 1:29; 2:5; 8:13; 9:10), the development of godly character (for example, 1:2-6; 2:1-11; 3:1-10; 4:1-13), the rejection of the 'adulteress'

---

3   Coats, *Genesis*, 279.
4   Wenham, *Genesis 16-50*, 372, citing Gen 14:1-16; Leviticus 8-10; Numbers 22-24.
5   See, for example, B.S. Childs, *Introduction to the Old Testament as Scripture* (London: SCM, 1979) 552-555, 557-558; R.N. Whybray, *The Composition of the Book of Proverbs*. JSOTSup, 168. (Sheffield: Sheffield Academic Press, 1994) 60-61; C.V. Camp, *Wisdom and the Feminine in the Book of Proverbs*. Bible and Literature Series, 11. (Sheffield: Almond Press, 1985) 191-208.

or loose woman (2:16; 5:3-23; 6:23-35; 7:1-27; 9:13-18), and the foundational choice of the way of wisdom over that of folly (1:20-33; 3:13-18; 9:1-6, 13-18). In light of the parallels with the Book of Proverbs, the testing of Joseph by Potiphar's wife assumes a greater significance in the rise of Joseph. It is not simply an obstacle to be overcome, but rather a necessary stage in the rise of Joseph. Joseph must show his 'fear of God', a tested moral character, by his choice of the way of wisdom, before he is entrusted with greater power and opportunity.

Genesis 39:1-20

Structure

Verse 1 is best viewed as outside the structure of this unit, as it hinges chapters 37 and 39 together. By recapitulating the situation at the end of chapter 37 (37:36), this verse returns the reader's focus to Joseph and smoothes the narrative transition between chapters 37 and 39.[6] Gen 39:1 is the first mention of Egypt since the last verse of chapter 37, and Potiphar is named in these two verses and nowhere else in the story. Furthermore, he is described as פוטיפר סריס פרעה שׂר הטבחים in both these verses and nowhere else. Finally, the link between the two chapters is established by the balancing of 'they sold him' (37:36 - מכר) with 'he bought/acquired him' (39:1 - קנה).[7]

If, then, the first section of the chapter proper (exposition) begins at verse 2, it ends after either verse 6a or 6b. While verses 2-6a deal with Joseph's prospering in the household of Potiphar, verse 6b should probably also be included because it fits better with 'exposition' than with the subsequent action.[8] Furthermore, verse 7 begins with an indefinite time clause (ויהי אחר הדברים האלה)[9] that appears to mark the start of the

---

6   Wenham, *Genesis 16-50*, 373 calls it a 'recapitulation of Joseph's sale'; Humphreys, *Joseph and His Family*, 58 labels it a 'transition'. Both see the verse as outside the structure of the rest of the chapter. Coats, *Genesis*, 276 regards verse 1 as part of the exposition, calling it a 'statement of location'.

7   Westermann, *Genesis 37-50*, 61.

8   Coats, *Genesis*, 279 suggests that verse 6b belongs to the exposition in that it discloses an essential fact about Joseph, which will be the foundation for the principal tension in verses 7-20. Humphreys, *Joseph and His Family*, 58 includes verse 6b with the section from verses 7-12, but separates it as a 'notice of Joseph's appearance' from the attempted seduction of verses 7-12.

9   E.I. Lowenthal, *The Joseph Narrative in Genesis*. (New York: KTAV, 1973) 35 suggests that this is a phrase which, in Genesis, always introduces a turning point (22:1, 20; 40:1; 48:1).

interaction between Joseph and Potiphar's wife, while verse 6b simply provides the background data. Longacre also sees verse 6b as a closure to verses 1-6, but notes that its purpose is to link the exposition with what follows.[10]

The attempted seductions and interaction between Joseph and Potiphar's wife mark off the next section as verses 7-12.[11] Verses 7-10 constitute the first part of this unit, with a new time reference in verse 11 (ויהי כהיום הזה) focusing attention in verses 11-12 on a particular incident as the climax of the attempted seductions.

Verses 13-18 constitute the next section, which coheres around the reports about Joseph. In verses 13-15, Potiphar's wife complains to the household servants, and in verses 16-18, she complains to her husband. Wenham suggests that her denunciation of Joseph continues until the end of verse 20, but it seems better to follow Humphreys in viewing verses 19 and 20 as 'Potiphar's response', this being the final section of the unit.[12] Coats puts verse 20b into the following scene on the basis that it is a statement of location, in parallel to verse 1, as well as anticipating the major development of chapter 40 in defining the prison as a place for the king's prisoners.[13] However, Longacre rightly points out that, in verse 20b, the clause ויהי־שם בבית הסהר (verse 20b) makes a good close to an episode, but that it is not an appropriate start to a new episode since, unlike verse 21, it lacks an explicit noun subject.[14]

39:1 - Hinge

As already indicated, verse 1 functions primarily to connect this chapter to chapter 37, most obviously in the parallels with 37:36. The variation in normal word order (placing the subject יוסף before the verb) represents a resumption of the focus on Joseph after the story of Judah and Tamar.

The description of Potiphar as שׂר הטבחים (literally 'chief of the butchers'),[15] with the additional reminder that he was איש מצרי would lead

10   Longacre, *Joseph: A Story of Divine Providence*, 32.
11   Following Humphreys, *Joseph and His Family*, 58-59. Wenham, *Genesis 16-50*, 373 separates verses 11 and 12 from verses 7-10, and regards them as the first part of Joseph's disgrace. Coats, *Genesis*, 276-277 regards verses 7-20a as the one scene, but this is to override the change in characters.
12   Wenham, *Genesis 16-50*, 373; Humphreys, *Joseph and His Family*, 59.
13   Coats, *Genesis*, 280. However, since verse 1 has been omitted in the structure of verses 2-20 outlined in this chapter, this obviates the need to find a parallel here to the earlier statement of location.
14   Longacre, *Joseph: A Story of Divine Providence*, 88.
15   Hamilton, *Genesis Chapters 18-50*, 458. He understands it to refer to the 'chief steward'. It seemingly means 'captain of the guards' as in 40:3. Skinner, *Genesis*, 457 suggests that perhaps it is those cooks and butchers who came to be the

the reader to suppose that Joseph should expect no favours from him. While Potiphar is connected to Pharaoh, and apparently has a high social standing, there does not yet seem to be any glimmer of hope for Joseph.

39:2-6 - Joseph Prospers

The exposition contained in these verses concentrates heavily on amplifying the motif that 'Yahweh was with Joseph'. This is asserted twice (verses 2, 3) and explained in the surrounding verses.

In verse 2, the statement that Yahweh was with Joseph seems to be connected with observation that he became איש מצליח, a prosperous or successful man.[16] Indeed, the Hebrew can bear the meaning that the result of Yahweh being with Joseph was that Joseph prospered.[17] In many translations, the last clause of verse 2 (ויהי בבית אדניו המצרי) hangs limply as an afterthought. However, the two contrasting areas of Potiphar's work are set out in verse 5 - in the house and in the field. In an Egyptian setting, working indoors rather than out in the fields would be viewed as a promotion. Thus, Joseph's working in the house seems to be an additional consequence of Yahweh being with him, and further evidence of his prospering.

In verse 3, his master saw that Yahweh was him and that Yahweh had caused all his deeds to prosper (מצליח, as in verse 2, implying that he succeeded because Yahweh caused him to succeed). The consequence of this was that Joseph found favour (חן) in the sight of Potiphar, and he personally attended (שרת) his master (verse 4).[18] Consequently, he was 'put in charge of' (פקד על) the household and all that Potiphar owned.[19]

---

bodyguard.

16 H. Tawil, 'Hebrew ḥṣlḥ/ṣlḥ, Akkadian ešēru/šūšuru: A Lexicographical Note', *JBL* 95 (1976), 407 notes that the semantic range of ṣālaḥ in verse 2 is "to proceed/pass/go (with speed) to advance progress prosper succeed".

17 B.K. Waltke and M. O'Connor, *An Introduction to Biblical Hebrew Syntax* (Winona Lake: Eisenbrauns, 1990) 548. The *waw* consecutive is thus being used to express a necessary consequence. See also Wenham, *Genesis 16-50*, 371.

18 Wenham, *Genesis 16-50*, 374 notes that שרת is close in meaning to עבד, but while the latter root can be used to describe menial jobs done by slaves (29:15, 18, 20), the former term "always implies personal service." (for example, Exod 24:13; Josh 1:1; 1 Kgs 19:21; 2 Sam 13:17). Wenham suggests that this means that he was appointed chief manager or steward of his household, officials (called *mer-per*) often mentioned in Egyptian texts. See J. Vergote, *Joseph en Égypte: Genèse 37-50 à la lumière des études égyptologiques récentes.* Orientalia et Biblica Lovaniensia, 3. (Louvain: Publications Universitaires, 1959), 25.

19 G. André, *Determining the Destiny: PQD in the Old Testament.* CBOTS, 16. (Uppsala: CWK Gleerup, 1980) 222-223 notes that the *hiphil* of פקד in verses 4, 5 means 'to appoint somebody or something in, over, or with somebody or

The new note in verse 5 is that of 'blessing' (ברך, both as a noun and a verb). While this may be recalling the use of ברך in the patriarchal promises, the main significance here appears to be that 'Yahweh blessing' is an explanation of what it means for Yahweh to be with Joseph.[20] Since Yahweh is with Joseph, the blessings flow to his master.

The extent of Potiphar's trust in Joseph is described in staggering terms in verse 6a

ויעזב כל־אשר־לו ביד־יוסף ולא־ידע אתו מאומה

This has been reinforced in the exposition by the fivefold use of כל (verses 3, 4, 5 [twice], 6). There is ample evidence here of Joseph's administrative skill being used for the benefit of others. The sole area which is not under Joseph's authority is הלחם אשר־הוא אוכל, which may refer to his food, or perhaps euphemistically (and ominously in the light of what follows) to his wife.[21]

Looking back over verses 2-6, two further questions need to be raised. Firstly, why is the name 'Yahweh' mentioned here (and in 39:21, 23), but rarely elsewhere in the Joseph narrative (only in 38:7, 10; 49:18)? Secondly, why does the narrator repeatedly point out that Joseph's rise was due to the fact that Yahweh was with him?

In relation to the first question, it is worth observing that the name Yahweh occurs only in the words of the narrator, and never on the lips of the characters.[22] The most likely explanation is that the name Yahweh appears here and at the opening of the next scene so that the implied reader will perceive that the rise of Joseph is the work of Yahweh, yet without Yahweh being foregrounded any more than is necessary. Indeed, this exposition seems to weave together the mention of Yahweh and the rise of Joseph.[23] What is more significant theologically is the glaring absence of the name 'Yahweh' elsewhere in the story, giving the impression of

---

something'. The phrase פקד על is used in the sense 'appoint over', 'entrust to', 'put in charge of' in Num 1:50; 2 Kgs 25:22.

20   'Bless' is a crucial word in Genesis, and is found twice in verse 5, though it is used rarely elsewhere in the Joseph narrative outside chapter 49. Wenham, *Genesis 16-50*, 374 and Hamilton, *Genesis Chapters 18-50*, 460 see this as a reference back to Gen 12:3.

21   Davidson, *Genesis 12-50*, 234 suggests that it refers to certain food taboos; Hamilton, *Genesis Chapters 18-50*, 461 and Lowenthal, *The Joseph Narrative*, 34, following *Genesis Rabbah* 86:6, argue that it is a euphemistic reference to Potiphar's wife. Ruppert, *Die Josephserzählung*, 45-46 suggests that it is more likely to be an idiom for 'his private affairs'. He is followed in this view by Wenham, *Genesis 16-50*, 374 and Westermann, *Genesis 37-50*, 64.

22   Westermann, *Genesis 37-50*, 62; Redford, *Biblical Story of Joseph*, 130.

23   So Fretheim, 'The Book of Genesis', 609.

Yahweh being present but behind the scenes.

It is also important to notice that it is not the mere mention of Yahweh that occurs, but the fact that Yahweh was with Joseph or blessing others because of Joseph. This leads us to the answer to the second question. Some have suggested that the narrator points out that Yahweh is with Joseph because this is the time when he is desperately alone, and most in need of the reminder of Yahweh's presence.[24] However, this psychological explanation is unlikely since the implied reader, not Joseph, is the one who is told that Yahweh is with Joseph. Yahweh does not appear, nor does he speak any word of comfort to Joseph.

Of course, this marks the Joseph narrative off from the previous patriarchal stories where Yahweh was with Isaac and Jacob (26:3, 24, 28; 28:15, 20; 31:3). In these earlier cases, Yahweh being with the patriarchs is coupled with his blessing them, as here in 39:2-6. Yet with Isaac and Jacob, Yahweh normally appeared visibly to the patriarchs, promising to be with them.[25] Here in chapter 39 there is neither the presence nor a promise of Yahweh, since he was operating behind the scenes. There is merely the narrator's observation that Yahweh was, in fact, with Joseph. Yahweh is introduced into the story to link Joseph's rise with Yahweh's behind-the-scenes care, but without distracting our attention from the person of Joseph.

The exposition ends with a physical description of Joseph, which leads neatly into the next section. It makes the observation about Joseph that he was יפה־תאר ויפה מראה (verse 6b), which is more likely to be a link between Joseph and his mother Rachel (described in identical terms in 29:17), than a negative comment on Joseph.[26]

---

24 For example, Hamilton, *Genesis Chapters 18-50*, 459; Fretheim, 'The Book of Genesis', 609.

25 The exception here is in 28:20, which is Jacob's request to God to be with him.

26 So Wenham, *Genesis 16-50*, 374, who notes that this double description is used only twice in the Old Testament - here and of Joseph's mother in 29:17. Thus, this comment simply serves as a trailer into the following incident. This is against the view expressed in the Midrash, referred to in Wildavsky, *Assimilation versus Separation*, 54; Leibowitz, *Studies in Bereshit*, 436; Lowenthal, *The Joseph Narrative*, 75. The Midrash blames Joseph for leading on his master's wife. J.L. Kugel, 'The Case Against Joseph', in *Lingering over Words: Studies in Ancient Near Eastern Literature in Honor of William L. Moran.* Harvard Semitic Studies, 37, eds. T. Abusch, J. Huchnergard and P. Steinkeller. (Atlanta: Scholars, 1990) 278-279, 283 is a modern exegete who suggests that the reference to Joseph's beauty, juxtaposed with his rise in Potiphar's house, indicates that after his rise he spent time making himself look handsome, and that this caused Potiphar's wife to notice him.

39:7-12 - The Attempted Seduction

Up to this point, there have only been general narrative descriptions of
Joseph. In this cameo, the narrator provides a specific set of incidents which
uncovers Joseph's true values and loyalties. Indeed, this section continues
the Joseph-centred perspective of verses 2-6, in which he was named six
times. Here Joseph is placed in the centre by defining the characters in
relation to him. Potiphar has already been called 'his [that is, Joseph's]
master' (אדניו, verses 2, 3) and is no longer called Potiphar after verse 1;
now the unnamed Mrs. Potiphar is called 'his master's wife' (אשת אדניו,
verses 7, 8). They are important to the story because they are linked to
Joseph. The non-naming of Potiphar's wife has the effect of her becoming a
stylised or stereotypical character in the story.[27] Her demand or invitation in
verse 7 is 'lie with me' (שכבה עמי). While some see this brevity as an
indication of the strength of her passion, it is more likely to be motivated by
the narrator's giving to her a stereotyped role.[28]

Joseph's lengthy answer (verses 8-9) is in stark contrast to both the few
words of Potiphar's wife and also the absence of Joseph's words when
wronged in chapter 37.[29] The reasons for his refusal of Mrs Potiphar's
overtures shed much light on what motivates Joseph and what he values.
Wenham sees three reasons here - it would be an abuse of the trust, an
offence against her husband, and a great sin against God.[30] Others suggest
that the abuse of trust in the act of adultery is what Joseph means by
'sinning against God'. Von Rad, for example, argues that there are not two
different offences in verse 9, but rather that "a wrong against the husband
would be a direct sin against God."[31] Coats notes that, if this is so, Joseph's

27 Kugel, 'The Case Against Joseph', 275; Kugel, *In Potiphar's House*, 31-32, 61
    notes that Potiphar's wife is not named here or in the Koran. In the post-Koranic
    sources, she is given the name Zulaika. Similarly, in the book of Job, Job's wife is
    not named, and performs the literary function of articulating a possibility for Job to
    consider and reject. For more positive, but unlikely readings of Potiphar's wife, see
    L.E. Donaldson, 'Cyborgs, Ciphers, and Sexuality: Re-Theorizing Literary and
    Biblical Character', *Semeia* 63 (1993): 85-93; A. Bach, 'Breaking Free of the
    Biblical Frame-Up: Uncovering the Woman in Genesis 39', in *A Feminist
    Companion to Genesis*. Feminist Companion to the Bible, 2, ed. A. Brenner.
    (Sheffield: Sheffield Academic Press, 1993), 318-342; A. Bach, *Women, Seduction
    and Betrayal in Biblical Narrative* (Cambridge: Cambridge University Press, 1997)
    34-61, 72-81.
28 Against, for example, Jeansonne, *The Women of Genesis*, 110, who suggests it
    implies that "the woman's passion is intense and lustful."
29 R. Alter, *Genesis: Translation and Commentary*. (New York: W.W. Norton, 1996)
    225 suggests that the contrast between her 2 words and Joseph's 35 is due to the use
    of contrastive dialogue as a way of accentuating character differences.
30 Wenham, *Genesis 16-50*, 375.
31 Von Rad, *Genesis*, 365.

response focuses on his wish to administer in a responsible way, the trust placed in him.[32] On this view he is portrayed as one who wisely uses power, a concern close to the heart of the sages.[33]

Perhaps in response to these suggestions of wisdom traces, it has been argued that the reason that Joseph gives in verse 9 (that it would be a sin against God) is a distinct reason and one different from the rationale given in the book of Proverbs (that adultery will lead to death, that it is not in your interests, that it is playing with fire etc.). Thus, some suggest that this incident is not like the warnings of Proverbs 5-7 (and hence not portraying Joseph as wise), but instead it may be like the Egyptian motif of the spurned or scorned wife.[34] She may indeed be both - the loose woman in verses 7-12, and the spurned wife in verses 13-18. However, in this section, at least, she emerges as one ready to betray her husband and seduce a handsome youth, and it is precisely in these verses that Joseph's wisdom emerges. Joseph's elaborate protestations give the reader an accurate guide to what is motivating Joseph.

The parallels between Joseph and wisdom ideas are clear from a closer reading of both Genesis and Proverbs. In Gen 39:8-9 (if 'sinning against God' is a distinct category) Joseph speaks first and at greater length about the trust his master has placed in him, the fact that she is the wife of another, that this is a wickedness. Only then does he describe it as 'a sin against God', perhaps as an attempted summary closure. Firstly, then, this is not the only reason, and the other reasons fit well into a wisdom perspective (for example, Prov 6:26, where sleeping with another man's wife is pictured as more dangerous than sleeping with a prostitute).

Secondly, and more significantly, the language of adultery as a sin against God is not absent from Proverbs. This is clearest in Prov 5:21-22, in the context of the first passage on the adulteress (5:1-23). While other reasons for rejecting the adulteress are given in the whole passage, verse 21 points out that human ways are seen by Yahweh, who examines their paths. Verse 22 then concludes that they are then ensnared by their iniquities and caught in their sin. The word for sin in verse 22 is חטאת, while the verb used by Joseph in Gen 39:9 is also from the חטא root.

The parallel passages in Proverbs also make much of the seductive speech of the adulteress (for example, Prov 2:16; 5:3; 6:24; 7:5, 13-21;

32   Coats, *From Canaan to Egypt*, 21.
33   Kugel, *In Potiphar's House*, 22; Brueggemann, *Genesis*, 315.
34   For example, Weeks, *Early Israelite Wisdom*, 96-98; Redford, *Biblical Story of Joseph*, 92. They are on much stronger ground in 39:13-18, but the link with the loose woman or adulteress of the book of Proverbs has already been made, as argued by Hamilton, *Genesis Chapters 18-50*, 463. Janzen, *Genesis 12-50*, 167 indicates that "Potiphar's wife embodies the enticing woman of Prov. 7:6-27 (even to the latter's Egyptian bed linens and her absent husband; vv. 16, 19)!"

9:15-17; 22:14). Verse 10 of this chapter notes that Potiphar's wife repeatedly (□י□ □י□) indulges in words that seek to persuade Joseph. Thus, when Joseph is present in verses 7-10, Potiphar's wife is portrayed as the stereotypical loose woman of Proverbs, not the spurned or scorned woman. Although verse 10 notes her many words, these are not recorded for the reader, for the focus does not appear to be on her reaction to Joseph's refusal, but rather on the reasons that Joseph gives in verses 8-9. The narrative focus in verses 7-10 is on the disciplined Joseph, not the rejected Egyptian mistress (as it would be in the spurned woman motif).[35]

One final clue that this incident has been included to draw attention to Joseph's character is what Kugel has called its 'gratuitous nature'. The story could have been eliminated entirely without undermining the narrative of Joseph's rise. All that would be necessary is that Joseph be gaoled for any offence. The amount of detail that is given in verses 7-18 suggests that the incident is recorded to draw attention to yet another injustice done to Joseph, and to his virtuous character as he resists temptation.[36]

Some writers have thought that this incident has been derived from the Egyptian Tale of Two Brothers (13th century BCE).[37] Most recent scholars have not been persuaded by such comparisons, and other closer parallels have been proposed.[38]

Verses 11 and 12 provide the climactic details to the attempted seduction. As Hamilton has pointed out, "Potiphar's wife now become insistent, not just inviting. She moves from seductress to aggressor."[39] On this particular day, Joseph finds Potiphar's wife alone in the house.

---

35   Along these lines Sarna, *JPS Torah Commentary*, 410 has commented "Scripture is silent about her fate, which is usually a prominent feature of the 'spurned wife' motif. The focus of the biblical narrative is Joseph's reaction to her coaxing".

36   Kugel, *In Potiphar's House*, 126.

37   Westermann, *Genesis 37-50*, 28; S.T. Hollis, 'The Woman in Ancient Examples of the Potiphar's Wife Motif, K 2111', in *Gender and Difference in Ancient Israel*. ed. P.L. Day. (Minneapolis: Fortress, 1989), 38. J.D. Yohannan, *Joseph and Potiphar's Wife in World Literature. An Anthology of the Story of the Chaste Youth and the Lustful Stepmother* (New York: New Directions, 1968) has explored the motif in world literature.

38   Wenham, *Genesis 16-50*, 374-375; N.M. Sarna, 'Joseph', in *Encyclopedia Judaica*. Vol. 10. (Jerusalem: Keter, 1972), 203. For a recent study of the parallels see H. Ringgren, 'Die Versuchung Josefs (Gen 39)', in *Die Väter Israels: Beitrage zur Theologie der Patriarchenüberlieferungen im Alten Testament*. Festschrift J. Scharbert zum 70, ed. M. Görg. (Stuttgart: Katholisches Bibelwerk, 1989), 267-270.

39   Hamilton, *Genesis Chapters 18-50*, 465. Some have suggested that Joseph had ulterior motives in entering the house on this day. However, A.M. Honeyman, 'The Occasion of Joseph's Temptation', *VT* 2 (1952): 85-87 rightly comments that since Joseph was going about his work as usual, he is thus blameless.

Scholars are divided over what garment was left behind, and the amount of clothing, if any, that covered the fleeing Joseph.[40] However, it is very clear that both Joseph and Potiphar's wife are now in an invidious position. Joseph has probably been seen to run, at least partially unclad, from his mistress's house, and has left behind a garment. Joseph's public flight means that Potiphar's wife faces the risk of being exposed to her husband, and she would be seen to have either initiated or consented to the incident unless she now raises her voice in protest.[41] She has resorted to a tactic that leaves her vulnerable and, now finally rejected, she seeks to cover her tracks. Potiphar's wife has habitually, and now climactically, shown the wrong way to use power and authority over others. To this extent, she is a foil to both Joseph's virtuous character and his later proper use of power and authority. Once again, Joseph is stripped of his robe, but the dream will continue.[42]

39:13-18 - The Versions of Potiphar's Wife

This section describes the two reports by Potiphar's wife. Dramatic irony emerges as the implied reader knows that the events have not been recounted accurately, but rather with an intention to deceive and shift the blame. The garment motif, so prominent in the previous two chapters, is present again, and is emphasised by its repetition (verses 13, 15, 16, 18).[43] The leaving behind of the garment and the fleeing outside are the two incontrovertible pieces of evidence that form the basis of the fabrication of the story.

---

40 Wenham, *Genesis 16-50*, 376 has proposed that the main clothing items of patriarchal times were mid-calf shorts and a tunic (that is, a kind of long T-shirt). Hamilton, *Genesis Chapters 18-50*, 465 notes that בֶּגֶד can refer in the Old Testament to both an outer garment (2 Kgs 7:15) and an inner garment (Ezek 26:16). G.C. Aalders, *Genesis Volume II*. Bible Student's Commentary, trans. W. Heynen. (Grand Rapids: Zondervan, 1981), 203 and Matthews, 'The Anthropology of Clothing', 32 suggest that it was probably the outer cloak or gown that hung over the shoulders and covered the tunic. Vawter, *On Genesis*, 403, and von Rad, *Genesis*, 366 suggest that this garment was doubtless the only one he had on, for he had come into the house to do his work, and men were not accustomed to wear a coat indoors. Thus he had to flee naked across the courtyard outside.

41 Thus M. Sternberg, *The Poetics of Biblical Narrative* (Bloomington: Indiana University Press, 1985) 424.

42 Matthews, 'The Anthropology of Clothing', 32; Brueggemann, *Genesis*, 315, astutely observes that "[t]he clothes do not make this man. It is the dream that makes this man and that the woman cannot take from him."

43 Jeansonne, *The Women of Genesis*, 111. Although da Silva, *La symbolique des rêves*, is otherwise a helpful study of the garment motif, she does not deal with this incident in any detail.

Potiphar's wife acts quickly and shrewdly to divert blame to Joseph. Her husband is the one who will need to be convinced, and what she says in verses 14-15 to the men of her household is intended as a preliminary to her words to Potiphar (verses 17-18). She must document her complaint, show the 'evidence', and give a contemporaneous account of the incident. She recounts the story to the household in such a way as to minimise her responsibility and to gain support from them.[44] Thus, when speaking to the household slaves, Potiphar's wife omits to mention that Joseph is a slave. While speaking to Potiphar, she describes Joseph as העבד העברי (verse 17), but he is simply called איש עברי when she addresses the slaves (verse 14). As an Egyptian, she appeals to the support of the Egyptian slaves, in reframing the incident from a mistress/slave exchange to an Egyptian/Hebrew one. This is highlighted by the use of the first person plural forms in verse 14

$$\text{ראו הביא לנו איש עברי לצחק בנו}$$

Potiphar's wife is implying that Joseph's 'attack' on her was an affront to, or mocking of,[45] all Egyptians (or all Egyptian woman), with whom she now identifies herself.[46] She places repeated emphasis on her cries for help (verses 14-15):[47] The repeated claim seems to have replaced the hard evidence she has in relation to the garment and Joseph's flight. Joseph's garment is now described as being left beside her (אצלי), rather than left in her hand (בידה, verse 12). This slight twist in the story changes Joseph from victim to seducer.[48]

Having apparently gained the support of the household, she keeps the

---

44 Wenham, *Genesis 16-50*, 376. Jeansonne, *The Women of Genesis*, 111 has pointed out that her manner of speech shows little respect for her husband before the slaves.

45 For the variety of ways in which the infinitive of צחק in verse 14 has been translated, see Hamilton, *Genesis* Chapters 18-50, 466. It includes 'insult', 'bring insult', 'mock', 'make a fool of', 'make a toy of', 'make a mockery of', 'sport with', 'make fun of someone', 'dally with', 'make love to', 'make sexual advances on', and 'play games with'. Hamilton translates it as 'sport in the presence of someone'. Von Rad, *Genesis*, 366 says that it is used of erotic play, as in Gen 26:8, where it appears to have the sense of 'fondling'.

46 Leibowitz, *Studies in Bereshit*, 418-419; Sternberg, *Poetics*, 425.

47 H. Jacobson, 'A Legal Note on Potiphar's Wife', *HTR* 69 (1976), 177 comments that her crying out aloud, or lifting her voice in verses 14, 15, 18 is important from a legal point of view. In a number of ancient societies a woman who claimed she had been raped had to show absence of complicity or consent by showing that she screamed at the time. Jacobson notes this is so in Israel (Deut 22:23-27) and some other societies, and so the reason for the detail of her crying out aloud may be that it gives her a legal defence.

48 Alter, *The Art of Biblical Narrative*, 110; Gunkel, *Genesis*, 409.

garment beside her (אֶצְלָהּ) until Potiphar returns (verse 16). Potiphar's wife has shrewdly marshalled the evidence, selectively reproduced and twisted it, so that it now appears convincing. However, while she has shown herself to be clever and daring, the implied reader must view her words and actions as an abuse of power and of speech, wrongly accusing an innocent man and backing her husband into a corner.[49] She is thus a real foil to Joseph's proper use of responsibility, power and words in verses 8-10. If Joseph in verses 8-9 is a model of wisdom, then Potiphar's wife in verses 13-18 is a warning about the abuse of authority.

39:19-20 - Potiphar's Response

This section focuses on Potiphar's response after a brief summary by the narrator of his wife's report. Now Potiphar becomes angry, although neither the object of, nor reason for, his anger is explicitly stated. A common view is that Potiphar believed his wife's carefully contrived story, and was angry at Joseph for his betrayal.[50] Others, however, have suggested that he was able to see through his wife's charade, and is therefore angry at her unfaithfulness, or at his need to save face due to her indiscretion, or even at his loss of Joseph's successful management of his estates.[51] It has been argued that the light sentence that Joseph receives for the 'attempted rape' (imprisonment rather than death) supports the view that Potiphar is not fully persuaded of Joseph's guilt.[52]

However, it could well be that narrative factors are at work here, for there are a number of glaring omissions in addition to the object of Potiphar's anger. There is no mention of any trial, the intended length of imprisonment, Joseph's words in his defence, or the fate of Potiphar's wife.[53] It is as if the attention of the implied reader is not to linger over such details. All that is necessary is to establish the injustice of the punishment, and Joseph's new location in the place where Pharaoh's prisoners were kept

---

49 Westermann, *Genesis 37-50*, 67.
50 For example, Skinner, *Genesis*, 459; Aalders, *Genesis*, 204.
51 J.P. Lange, *A Commentary on the Holy Scriptures: Genesis*. trans. T. Lewis and A. Gosman. (Edinburgh: T & T Clark, 1868) 597; Westermann, *Genesis 37-50*, 67 comments that "what or who is the object of his anger is an open question, and must remain so."
52 Lowenthal, *The Joseph Narrative*, 39; Gunkel, *Genesis*, 409; Redford, *Biblical Story of Joseph*, 92. W. Kornfeld, 'L'Adultère dans l'Orient antique', *RB* 57 (1950): 92-109 refers to the Instructions of Ani iii, 13 and Instructions of Onkhsheshonqy xxiii, 6f., which prescribe death for adultery.
53 Coats, *From Canaan to Egypt*, 21-22. Lange, *Genesis*, 597; Westermann, *Genesis 37-50*, 67; Jeansonne, *The Women of Genesis*, 113; Sarna, *JPS Torah Commentary*, 410.

(verse 20, אסורים המלך אשר־אסורי מקום).[54] Knowing the object of Potiphar's anger is not necessary, and there may well be a deliberate injection of ambiguity here.

As this story draws to a close, the setting for the next scene (39:21-40:23) is established. What is significant about the new setting is that, despite the downward movement into prison, it will be a place of greater opportunity in the longer term. Joseph needed to descend as a preliminary to his ultimate ascent.

Wisdom-like Elements

It is clear that 'wisdom-like elements' are prominent in this section of the rise of Joseph. While von Rad probably claimed too much in arguing that the temptation story of Joseph and Potiphar's wife was "a direct illustration of the warning against loose women" in the book of Proverbs,[55] there is a genuine narrative focus on Joseph's reasons for his refusal. In chapter 37, the reader gets no insight into how Joseph is reacting, but in 39:8-9 his thoughts and motives are described at length.[56] He is purposefully depicted as a person of integrity, one who refuses to abuse responsibility entrusted to him and who shows himself faithful in times of adversity and injustice.[57] He thus shows exemplary wisdom, in contrast to the stereotypical folly of Potiphar's wife.[58] One element of the seduction story that is generally not highlighted is that Potiphar's wife is an example of the wrong way to use power and position. As such she is, of course, a perfect foil for Joseph who will later model how to use power in the court (for the welfare of others) and over his brothers (to bring about a lasting reconciliation). It is telling that some of those who have most trenchantly criticised von Rad's view have conceded that there is wisdom editing in the narrator's comments in chapter 39.[59]

Furthermore, Joseph's administration of Potiphar's affairs (verses 2-6) also betrays 'wisdom-like elements'. There is the reminder of God's

---

54 Skinner, *Genesis*, 459. See Vergote, *Joseph en Égypte*, 25-28 for a useful discussion of the term בית הסהר (found only in this section of Genesis) in verse 20. Wenham, *Genesis 16-50*, 377 suggests that it was a fortress that also served as a prison, several of which are known in Egypt.
55 Von Rad, 'The Story of Joseph', 25. He referred specifically to Prov 23:27-28.
56 Berlin, *Poetics and Interpretation*, 76.
57 Sailhamer, 'Genesis', 235; White, *Narration and Discourse* 255-256; Niditch, *Underdogs and Tricksters*, 110. For an analysis of how this story was used in post-biblical texts (like 1 Maccabees 2:53, 4 Maccabees 2:1-4, the Book of Jubilees, the Testaments of the Twelve Patriarchs, the Wisdom of Solomon 10:13-14, the Koran and post-Koranic texts), see Kugel, *In Potiphar's House*, chapters 1-2.
58 Niditch, 'Genesis', 25; Wenham, *Genesis 16-50*, 378.
59 For example, Redford, *Biblical Story of Joseph*, 104-105.

behind-the-scenes activity in the repeated comment by the narrator that
Yahweh was with Joseph (verses 2-3), and also in the report that Yahweh
blessed Potiphar on account of Joseph (verse 5). That Joseph succeeded or
prospered in his administration fits well with the wisdom doctrine of
retribution, according to which righteousness of character is rewarded.
Potiphar is blessed not by God's direct intervention, but through the human
actions of Joseph[60] - a familiar wisdom theme, but one not common in the
preceding patriarchal accounts.

Genesis 39:21-40:23

Structure

The structural analyses of many scholars are of limited use here, since quite
a few regard only chapter 40 as the unit. Westermann, for example,
proposes a chiastic structure of chapter 40:[61]

```
1-4                    Meeting
      5-8                   Inquiry
            9-11, 12-13          Dream Explanation
                        14-15              Request
            16-17, 18-19        Dream Explanation
      20-22                 Fulfilment
23                    Forgetting
```

Ross adopts Westermann's structure and comments that it shows that
verses 14-15 express "the predominant idea in the episode".[62] However, a
closer look suggests that the text is not as neatly chiastic as this. For
example, the dream explanation is not one section but two. Both officials
tells their dreams then Joseph interprets each dream, but in the wrong order
for a chiasm. More significantly, the parallel is not between meeting (verses
1-4) and forgetting (verse 23), but between the request to be remembered
(verses 14-15) and being forgotten (verse 23).

Indeed, as has been argued above, 39:21-23 belong to this unit rather
than the preceding one, and must therefore be factored into the structure.[63]

---

60 Thus Fretheim, 'The Book of Genesis', 612.
61 Westermann, *Genesis 37-50*, 72.
62 Ross, *Creation and Blessing*, 631.
63 Humphreys, Coats and Wenham all attempt to analyse the structure of 39:21-40:23.
    Humphreys, *Joseph and His Family*, 59 identifies Joseph's plea in verses 14-15 as a
    distinctive feature of the cupbearer's dream, but does not link it with verse 23;

Wenham has rightly pointed out that there is a parallel structure between 39:1-20 and 39:21-40:23, which he sets out as follows[64]

39:2-6	Divine blessing of Joseph	39:21-23
39:7-19	Human maltreatment of Joseph	40:1-22
39:20	Joseph left in prison	40:23

This could be nuanced even further by the following, more elaborate parallel

39:2-6	Exposition: God blessing Joseph	39:21-23
39:7-10	Joseph and the dreaming officials/scheming wife	40:1-4
39:11-12	A precipitating incident	40:5-8
39:13-18	Verbal reports	40:9-19
39:19-20	The outcome	40:20-23

While such parallels can be sustained in general terms, they tend to obscure the new element that appears in 40:9-23. There is a narrative focus in chapter 40 on Joseph's request to be remembered (40:14-15), and the fact of his not being remembered (40:23), a focus not evident in chapter 39. In 39:1-20, no plea of Joseph is recorded, but in 40:14-15, Joseph seizes the opportunity to ask for his vindication. This bold step will anticipate his more elaborate initiative in 41:33-36. This would suggest the following outline

```
21-23  Exposition: Joseph's rise in prison
   1-8   Joseph and the dreaming officials
       9-11   Dream recounted
          12-13   Dream Explanation
                  [Expectation of dream fulfilled]
                       14-15   Remember me!
      16-17   Dream recounted
          18-19   Dream Explanation
              20-22   Dreams Fulfilled
                   23   Forgotten/not remembered
```

This structure highlights the theme of remembering and forgetting. In

Coats, *Genesis*, 277 sets out his proposed structure, which notices a request in verses 14-15 and the failure of the request in verse 23, but does not parallel them; Wenham, *Genesis 16-50*, 380 does not draw out the connection in his structural analysis.
64   Wenham, *Genesis 16-50*, 380.

relation to verses 14-15, their central position and the contrast with verse 23 show that they contain a key idea in the episode. They also prepare the reader for Joseph's later being remembered (41:9).[65]

39:21-23 - Joseph's Rise in Prison

The narrative thrust of this section is very much dependent on the pattern established in 39:1-20.[66] As in 39:2-6, there is the steady rise of Joseph, against the backdrop of adversity, with the intermediate result that whatever Joseph did, prospered (verse 23; see verses 3, 5), and that Joseph rose to a position of authority in his new setting (verse 22; see verses 5-6). Again Yahweh is mentioned (verses 21, 23 [twice], as in verses 2, 3, 5, yet not in 39:7-19 or 40:1-22), but without being foregrounded, and without any face-to-face encounter between Joseph and his God. Seybold has even suggested that Joseph's position in both Potiphar's house and the prison is similar to his situation at the beginning of chapter 37 - he is a favourite of the head of the household, set in a position of dominance over others like himself.[67] If so, the rise of Joseph in chapter 41 will raise the likelihood of Joseph's dreams of chapter 37 also being fulfilled.

The initial success of Joseph in chapter 39 was, however, a false start, for unfounded accusations took him from power to prison.[68] However, this imprisonment is immediately followed by the narrator's comment that the dreams will not be frustrated, for Yahweh was with Joseph (39:21). This is manifested in verse 21 by God extending kindness (חסד) to Joseph, and giving him favour (חן) in the gaoler's eyes.[69] This suggests that the earlier reference to Joseph finding favour (חן) in the eyes of Potiphar (39:4) was presumably also due to the Lord. While verses 22-23 specify Joseph's new responsibilities, verse 21 makes the prior assertion that this prospering is ultimately from the hand of Yahweh, the expression of his חסד, who moves behind the scenes to bring about the rise of Joseph. Now Joseph is in the place where Pharaoh's prisoners are kept, which brings him potentially even closer to the source of power. Kidner suggests that the symmetry of verses 1-6 and verses 19-23 "perfectly expresses God's quiet control and

---

65 It is instructive that Westermann, *Genesis 37-50*, 72, despite his chiasm, notes this link between verses 14-15 and verse 23.

66 Jeansonne, *The Women of Genesis*, 112.

67 Seybold, 'Paradox and Symmetry', 62.

68 Humphreys, *Joseph and His Family*, 38.

69 Wenham, *Genesis 16-50*, 381 observes that נטה is used with חסד only here in the Old Testament. He suggests that it hints at Joseph's prayers, but there is little evidence in the text to suggest to the implied reader that this connection should be made. On the translation of חסד in 39:21, see H.F. Peacock, 'Translating "Mercy", "Steadfast love", in the book of Genesis', *The Bible Translator* 31 (1980): 206.

the man of faith's quiet victory."[70] However, if 39:21-23 is seen as the introduction to chapter 40, then it rather portrays the same promising but stifled start in each case.

40:1-4 - The Setting

Verses 1-4 of chapter 40 serve largely to introduce Pharaoh's two officials. The fact that they are unnamed, and introduced by their role, is reminiscent of the way that Potiphar's wife was treated in the previous chapter. Like Potiphar's wife, these two are introduced not for them to be described or focused on, but in order to show what Joseph is like. The exact nature of the work of the two officials is not entirely clear, yet what is sufficient for the reader is to realise that they were officials in the "powerful but precarious position" of having access to Pharaoh.[71] The double mention in verse 1 of the phrase מלך־מצרים reminds the reader that these officials formerly had connections with the key person who had the power to reverse Joseph's circumstances.

The imprisonment of the cupbearer and baker occurs an indefinite time after Joseph had been incarcerated (ויהי אחר הדברים האלה - verse 1). In 39:20 Joseph is put where the *king's* prisoners are kept; in 40:1-3 the cupbearer and baker of the *king* of Egypt are put into prison, identified in verse 3 as the place where Joseph was bound. The reader expects them to meet, and this narrative expectation is fulfilled in verse 4.

Neither the narrator nor the characters disclose the nature of the offence (if any) that the cupbearer and baker were accused of, or whether these men were unjustly, perhaps even arbitrarily imprisoned. The nature of their supposed wrongdoing is not the focus of the narrative,[72] and the reader is not even told such details at the end. Wenham suggests that the repetition of the חטא root in 40:1 - previously used of Joseph's refusal to sin in 39:9 - implies a contrast between Joseph and these two officials, requiring that these two men actually committed the offence suggested.[73] While the parallel is rightly noticed, the text itself does not demand that the officials offended as charged, though it may well be the case.[74] Indeed, the repetition of על before each official leaves open both differing levels of guilt of, and a

---

70   Kidner, *Genesis*, 189.
71   Wildavsky, *Assimilation versus Separation*, 83. Vergote, *Joseph en Égypte*, 37 notes that there were 38 different cakes and 57 varieties of bread attested in Egypt, which gives a significant role to the chief baker. See also S. Bar, *A Letter That Has Not Been Read: Dreams in the Hebrew Bible* (Cincinnati: Hebrew Union College Press, 2001) 51-52.
72   Green, *What Profit for Us?*, 95.
73   Wenham, *Genesis 16-50*, 381-382.
74   Kidner, *Genesis*, 192 translates verse 1 as 'offended against', implying that there were grounds for Pharaoh's wrath.

separate fate for, the two men.[75]

Verse 3 supplies a lot of unnecessary detail that presumably serves a narrative purpose. The officials are placed in custody (במשמר), connecting them with Joseph who was earlier put into מקום אשר־אסורי המלך אסורים (39:20). The officials were put in the house of שר הטבחים, a designation used in 39:1 to describe Potiphar. Perhaps this has a literary function of linking the officials with Potiphar and thus with Joseph. A final link with Joseph is forged by the description that the officials were placed in the בית הסהר, which is an unusual expression for prison used only in Gen 39:20-40:5. This connection is made explicit by the last clause of verse 3, מקום אשר יוסף אסור שם. Joseph and the officials are in the same place.

Moreover, verse 4 narrates how Joseph was not merely in the same building, but entrusted with their care. Some have suggested that Joseph's service of these two officials is a menial task and contradicts the picture of Joseph in authority in 39:22-23.[76] However, the root used in 40:4 (שרת) is the same as that used in 39:4 to describe his waiting on Potiphar, and the description of 39:4-6 implies that Joseph exercised there a position of important responsibility.[77]

The other significant element of verse 4 is the time reference - that Joseph is with these two officials ימים במשמר. The plural form can signify a few days or a longer period.[78] This note serves the dual purpose of enabling Joseph to have ongoing access to the officials, but also reminds the alert reader that Joseph's unfair imprisonment is still lingering on.

40:5-8 - Joseph, the Officials and the Dreams

The time reference in verse 5 (בלילה אחד) indicates the beginning of the precipitating incident in which each official has a dream. The phrase found in verse 5 (איש כפתרון חלמו) is best understood as stating that the two

---

75 See Lowenthal, *The Joseph Narrative*, 41. B. Jacob, *The First Book of the Bible Genesis*. eds. E.I. Jacob and W. Jacob. (New York: KTAV, 1974) 269 suggests that they may have failed in their respective offices, which would imply a different 'offence' for each official.

76 Von Rad, *Genesis*, 369; Herbert, *Genesis 12-50*, 131; Skinner, *Genesis*, 460, Speiser, *Genesis*, 308. However, chapter 40 does not demand this reading, and 39:21-23 appears to preclude it.

77 Hamilton, *Genesis Chapters 18-50*, 475; Coats, *From Canaan to Egypt*, 23. Gibson, *Genesis*, 254 regards the cupbearer and baker as being delivered into Potiphar's custody, detained pending investigation in some part of Potiphar's house, not in the actual prison. On this reading Joseph was [temporarily] taken out of prison to attend them.

78 Hamilton, *Genesis Chapters 18-50*, 474 referring to E. Kautzsch, *Gesenius' Hebrew Grammar*. rev. and trans. A.E. Cowley. (Oxford: Clarendon, 1910) § 139h (hereafter *GKC*).

dreams had distinct meanings.[79] Their complaint about the absence of an interpreter in verse 8 (ופתר אין אתו) reinforces this reading, and suggests that, when these officials are confronted with such ominous dreams,[80] their being placed in custody prevents them having access to the interpreters available at the court.[81]

In the earlier, and parallel, precipitating incident (39:11-12), Joseph's character was displayed, and some writers have suggested that this focus is present here as well. Certainly, verses 6-7 give the impression of Joseph as "the alert caregiver",[82] who not only notices that the officials are troubled, but also takes initiative to enquire about the problem. Furthermore, in verse 8 Joseph shows a proper dependence on God as the source of the interpretations,[83] as well as human initiative in asking the officials to tell their dreams to him.

However, up to this point in the story there has been no identification of the wise with dream interpretation. This does not come until chapter 41, and Joseph's brothers and father (37:5-11) are the only ones who have been shown to interpret dreams in the narrative so far. An explicit link with wisdom could easily have been made at this point, but is not. It is better to conclude that Joseph's actions are consistent with his being portrayed as wise, but the text does not demand it. Yet, Joseph's willingness to interpret the dreams of the baker and cupbearer, demonstrates that he still believes that God can speak through dreams, and thus presumably that he believes in the message behind his own dreams.[84]

A few final comments are worth making about the literary features of the unit. After verse 5, the implied reader would expect to be told the content of the two dreams. Instead, verse 6 and especially verse 7 is full of repetition and otiose detail, mostly previously given. If one assumes that this is purposeful rather than poor narrative technique, then the retarding of the narrative pace has the effect of focusing the reader's attention on this

---

79 *Contra* Wildavsky, *Assimilation versus Separation*, 83 who suggests that they not only told the dream but also its meaning. Hamilton, *Genesis Chapters 18-50*, 476 observes that פתר = 'to interpret' occurs nine times in the Old Testament, all in Genesis 40-41 (40:8, 16, 22; 41:8, 12 [twice], 13, 15 [twice]).

80 The dreams are ominous in the sense that they appear to contain information about their future. See Vergote, *Joseph en Égypte*, 48 on the significance of dreams in Egypt.

81 Davidson, *Genesis 12-50*, 239; von Rad, *Genesis*, 371; Gibson, *Genesis*, 255; Wenham, *Genesis 16-50*, 382.

82 Fretheim, 'The Book of Genesis', 614. Similarly, see Wenham, *Genesis 16-50*, 382; Leupold, *Genesis*, 1009; Westermann, *Genesis 37-50*, 74-75; von Rad, *Genesis*, 370.

83 Hamilton, *Genesis Chapters 18-50*, 476 points out that each time Joseph interprets a dream, he expresses a conviction about God's control (40:8; 41:16, 25, 28, 32).

84 Brueggemann, *Genesis*, 322.

incident which is so suggestive of Joseph's character. Furthermore, this is the first occurrence of dialogue in the chapter, and dialogue was used with great effect in revealing Joseph's moral character in 39:8-9. This suggests that this unit has a contribution to make to the characterisation of Joseph, and that it might well contribute to a picture of Joseph as wise.

Another interesting aspect of verse 8 is what is not stated. You might expect 'interpretations belong to God. Tell the dream to *God*.' Instead it reads 'tell it to *me*.' The implicit and unexpressed premise is that Joseph will be God's spokesman, the authorised interpreter of dreams. Chapter 39 revealed that God was with Joseph. Now Joseph is starting to take charge.

40:9-11 - The First Dream Recounted[85]

The chief cupbearer tells his dream to Joseph in verses 9-11. This is, in itself, amazing for it means that the high Egyptian official has discerned that Joseph is trustworthy, either from his words or his actions during the time that he was in prison. This, however, is left tantalisingly unexplored in the narrative as the dream is narrated. The dream is not transparent in meaning like those in chapter 37, although the image of the vine fits well with his role as cupbearer. It appears to have a positive import in that, at the end of the dream, the cupbearer is placing the cup in Pharaoh's hand as before.[86] In the light of verse 8, the implied reader is not expected to understand the dream fully, but rather to look to Joseph to interpret it.

40:12-13 - The First Dream Explained

The familiarity of present day readers with this story can often lead them to conclude that the interpretation of this dream was self-evident. In fact, however, Joseph's skill is shown is "taking the decisive elements and passing over the unimportant and insignificant parts",[87] and in determining what parts are to be understood allegorically (three branches are three days), and what elements are to have their natural meaning (serving Pharaoh's cup).[88]

---

85   A full discussion of the dreams of chapter 40 is beyond the scope of this study. Many of the details are explored in such older monographs as E.L. Ehrlich, *Der Traum im Alten Testament*. BZAW, 73. (Berlin: Töpelmann, 1953) 65-73 and A. Resch, *Der Traum im Heilsplan Gottes* (Freiburg: Herder, 1964) 87-96. A useful modern study of these dreams is da Silva, *La symbolique des rêves*, 91-107, while J.-M. Husser, *Le songe et la parole: Etude sur le rêve et sa fonction dans l'ancien Israël*. BZAW 210. (Berlin: Walter de Gruyter, 1994) 231-248 explores the issue of wisdom elements in the dreams in chapters 40-41.

86   Weeks, 'Joseph, Dreams and Wisdom', 20-21.

87   Von Rad, *Genesis*, 371.

88   J.M.A. Janssen, 'Egyptological Remarks on the Story of Joseph in Genesis',

The interpretation begins in verse 12 in a very matter-of-fact way - Joseph stating with confidence what the dream meant.[89] There is no record of God revealing the dream, or of Joseph turning to God in prayer.[90] Joseph describes the positive outcome for the cupbearer in three ways in verse 13. Firstly, he will be pardoned (יִשָּׂא פַרְעֹה אֶת־רֹאשֶׁךָ).[91] Secondly, he will be restored to his former position (וַהֲשִׁיבְךָ עַל־כַּנֶּךָ), and finally, he will again put the cup in Pharaoh's hand. All of these involve Joseph being released from his presumably unjust imprisonment - yet Joseph remains unjustly incarcerated. In the light of the story as a whole this may operate as an anticipation of what will happen on a grander scale in the life of Joseph.

40:14-15 - Remember me!

What is absent in verse 14 is any comment by the narrator evaluating Joseph. Instead, Joseph continues to speak and takes initiative in the situation by asking to be remembered by the cupbearer once this official is reinstated.[92] This not only shows great confidence in his interpretation

---

Jaarbericht van het Vooraziatisch-Egyptische Genootschap: Ex Oriente Lux 14 (1956): 65 suggests that there were two kinds of dreams in Egypt, the 'theorematic' and the 'allegoric'. The meaning of a theorematic dream is obvious and needs no interpretation, while the allegoric dreams need an interpretation. On his classification, the dreams of chapter 40 are theorematic with an allegoric element. The allegoric element is the significance of the number 3. See also A. Caquot, 'Les songes et leur interprétation selon Canaan et Israel', in *Les songes et leur interprétation*. Sources Orientales, 2, eds. A.-M. Esnoul, P. Garelli, Y. Hervouet, M. Leibovici, S. Sauneron and J. Yoyotte. (Paris: Éditions du Seuil, 1959), 113; Weeks, 'Joseph, Dreams and Wisdom', 20.

89   J. Calvin, *A Commentary on Genesis*. trans. and ed. J. King. (London: Banner of Truth, 1965, reprint of 1847 translation, originally in Latin 1554) 309.

90   Hamilton, *Genesis Chapters 18-50*, 479.

91   Ruppert, *Die Josephserzählung*, 64 reads 'lift up the head' in verse 13 as meaning 'to pardon'. Von Rad, *Genesis*, 372 comments that "[t]his expression goes back ultimately to an actual custom in an audience: the petitioner stands or kneels with bowed head while the one on the throne takes him under the chin and raises his head (cf. II Kings 25.27; etc.)". Wenham, *Genesis 16-50*, 383 argues that here and in 2 Kgs 25:27/Jer 52:31 'lifting up the head' has the sense of 'deal kindly with', equivalent to the Akkadian *našū rēša* 'call someone into the presence of the king'. D. Marcus, ''Lifting up the Head': On the Trail of a Word Play in Genesis 40', *Prooftexts* 10 (1990): 21-22 sees four main uses of the expression נָשָׂא רֹאשׁ in the Hebrew Bible and suggests that the context indicates it refers to 'reviewing the case of a prisoner', without necessarily indicate the outcome of the review. Hamilton, *Genesis Chapters 18-50*, 480 argues that the phrase may only mean 'summon'. Even if this is the case, the other two expressions of verse 13 clearly imply the cupbearer's restoration.

92   White, *Narration and Discourse*, 257.

coming true, but also reveals his shrewd perception that an appropriate word here might enable the reversal of his unjust imprisonment. In so doing, Joseph appears to act wisely.

This action must be read (or perhaps 're-read') in the light of the chapter that follows, for the call to 'remember me' (זכרתני, verse 14; also והזכרתני) begins a trail that surfaces again in verse 23 (where the request is apparently frustrated - ולא־זכר שר־המשקים את־יוסף), and finally in 41:9, when the cupbearer does remember Joseph (את־חטאי אני מזכיר היום). In this last instance, the official's act of remembering precipitates the reversal of Joseph's circumstances. Thus, Joseph's forthright request in verses 14-15 will contribute to his own advancement.[93] This pattern of moving on in his words beyond the dream interpretation, will also recur in 41:33-36, when his carefully-chosen words lead to his promotion to a position of power.

The manner of Joseph's request in verses 14-15 is suitably deferential and astutely worded.[94] He asks for חסד not a reward, even though the syntax of verse 14 (beginning with כי־אם) may suggest that a reward had been offered.[95] He narrates being sold into slavery in Egypt in terms of being stolen or kidnapped (גנב גנבתי, verse 15), without mentioning the potentially damaging detail that he was handed over by his own brothers. The implied reader will also notice that the word for prison in verse 15 (בור) is the same as that for the pit in 37:24, which gives to the reader a further reminder of Joseph having being unfairly treated.

40:16-17 - The Second Dream Recounted

The chief baker observes either that the interpretation was favourable, or that Joseph interpreted well (the phrase טוב פתר can bear either meaning, or possibly even suggest both). On either reading, he would be inclined to tell his dream to Joseph, especially in light of some similarities between his dream and that of the cupbearer (the number three, and bread for the baker paralleling wine for the cupbearer).[96] In beginning his words to Joseph with אף־אני, he seems to be telling his dream with anticipation rather than dread, expecting that his dream too will have a favourable meaning.

What the baker fails to notice is that several of the differences are quite ominous. The cupbearer acts in his dream; the baker does not (the birds do).

---

93 So Fretheim, 'The Book of Genesis', 615. *Contra* White, *Narration and Discourse*, 257-258 who fails to take into account the longer term consequences.

94 Adar, *The Book of Genesis*, 145.

95 Nowhere else does כי־אם (= 'except') introduce a sentence in scripture. *GKC* §163d regards it as elliptical for 'I desire nothing else except'. Lowenthal, *The Joseph Narrative*, 44 and Westermann, *Genesis 37-50*, 76 agree that it presupposes the offer of a reward.

96 Fretheim, 'The Book of Genesis', 614-615.

Pharaoh is successfully served in the first dream but the baker is impeded in the second. Even more ominously, the baker's recounting of his dream ends with his being unable to drive off the birds.[97]

40:18-19 - The Second Dream Explained

Joseph's interpretation of the first dream will be sufficient to establish his credentials as a background to chapter 41. However, the unfavourable interpretation that he gives to the baker makes it clear that Joseph is not just given to flattery, telling important officials what they want to hear. He is as certain about this interpretation as he was about the one given to the cupbearer.[98]

Yet, even as he conveys the message of disaster, Joseph shows rhetorical skill in a clever play on words, and in keeping the bad news till last.[99] The baker, like the cupbearer will have his head lifted up, but the addition of מעליך transforms the nature of the action from pardoning to hanging.[100] Indeed, Joseph makes it clear that he will not only be hanged, but also impaled and his body publicly exposed.[101]

A significant feature of the narrative is that after verse 15, and again after verse 19 we have no response from either official.[102] There is no reaction, no promise, no speech. Instead the scene changes, and leads on to the fulfilment of the dreams. The narrative effect of these omissions is that the implied reader focuses not on these officials but rather on what this passage reveals about Joseph. Such a focus makes this a very Joseph-centred passage, providing an important background to chapter 41.

40:20-22 - The Dreams Fulfilled

The fulfilment of the two dreams is cleverly recounted. There is initially some unnecessary detail - such as the mention of Pharaoh's birthday[103] -

---

97   Fretheim, 'The Book of Genesis', 615; Skinner, *Genesis*, 463; Leupold, *Genesis*, 1015. Weeks, 'Joseph, Dreams and Wisdom', 21.
98   Lowenthal, *The Joseph Narrative*, 45. Wenham, *Genesis 16-50*, 384.
99   Wenham, *Genesis 16-50*, 384.
100 Marcus, 'Lifting up the Head', 18. Marcus notes that 'lift up your head from off you' in verse 19 has often been taken to mean decapitation. However, the usual phrase for decapitation is להסיר את הראש (1 Sam 17:46), so it is likely that it is simply hanging (as it is in verse 22) followed by impalement.
101 Wenham, *Genesis 16-50*, 384.
102 Westermann, *Genesis 37-50*, 78; Gibson, *Genesis*, 259-260. Hamilton, *Genesis Chapters 18-50*, 483.
103 Schmitt, *Die Nichtpriesterliche Josephsgeschichte*, 138-139 notes that amnesties were more commonly granted on the anniversary of a Pharaoh's accession, and it could be that this anniversary, rather than Pharaoh's birthday, is intended here.

which serves to build suspense. The play on the meaning of נשׂא את־ראשׁ is continued, with a single verb (וישׂא) having the heads of the two officials as its object. This means that the phrase either means merely 'summoned' to the feast, or that the one verb is being used to cover the two senses of verses 13 and 19. Yet, verses 21-22 make it very clear that the two officials receive the differing outcomes of restoration and hanging respectively.

The point of this unit is evident from the narrator's not recording any response from either official, but simply stating the outcome in language strongly reminiscent of Joseph's interpretations (compare verses 13, 19 and verses 20-22). The conclusion at the end of verse 22 is that these events happened 'as Joseph had interpreted to them' (כאשׁר פתר להם יוסף). The thrust of the narrative is thus that Joseph's interpretation proved reliable. Of course, the narrator could have added 'as God revealed to Joseph' or 'as God ordained through Joseph' or even 'as God determined', but the focus of the narrative's closure is simply on Joseph's interpretation proving true.

Significantly, there is no theologizing at the end of this chapter, nor any reference to God after the initial response of verse 8. Even when Joseph gives an unfavourable interpretation, he does not seek to hide behind the truth of verse 8. Once the theological point has been established, the distinctive thrust of the narrative can be developed. God is backgrounded as Joseph's ability is foregrounded.[104]

40:23 - Joseph Forgotten

Now that the dreams have been fulfilled, the narrative comes quickly to a close. There remains only the twist in the tail that the cupbearer did not remember Joseph. This ending continues the pattern of 39:1-20, with Joseph in both cases being unjustly left in prison.[105] The apparent hopelessness and manifest unfairness of Joseph's situation is emphasised by the narrator stating that the cupbearer did not remember (ולא־זכר) Joseph, but instead forgot him (וישׁכחהו).

Reading Genesis 39:21-40:23 as a Part of the Whole Story

There is value is looking both backwards and forwards into the broader Joseph narrative from the vantage point of this section. Looking back to chapter 37 - so dominated by Joseph's dreams of a rise to prominence - the fulfilment of the officials' dreams in this chapter is ominous. If this chapter establishes that dreams come true, then there is the narrative expectation

---

104 Longacre, *Joseph: A Story of Divine Providence*, 34; Fretheim, 'The Book of Genesis', 616.
105 Brueggemann, *Genesis*, 320.

that other dreams will also be efficacious.[106] Thus, there is a shift from 'will Joseph rise to prominence?' to 'how and when will he do so?'. Hence, this chapter calls back to mind Joseph's dreams of chapter 37, and moves the reader into chapter 41 expecting some kind of fulfilment.

Of course, there have been examples in 39:2-6, 21-23 of an amelioration of Joseph's circumstances in his setting, but now the rise of the cupbearer from prison to Pharaoh's court suggests a further tantalising possibility. If such a rise were possible for this official, might it not also be possible for the one who has received the dreams of chapter 37, the one who prospers because God is with him?[107]

Is there, however, any reflection on Joseph's character in 39:21-40:23? Several elements have been suggested, one of which is crucial. In 40:8, Joseph says 'Do not interpretations belong to God?' He then immediately says 'Tell me your dreams'. He shows a dependence on God, not a self-reliance, but also a confidence that God will speak to and through him. Perhaps this incidental information is dropped to give the reader an interpreted perspective on Joseph. It may also be that Joseph's inquiry after the officials in 40:7 reveals a genuine sympathy he had towards them.[108]

While Joseph interprets dreams in this chapter, there appears to be no hint that this pictures him as 'wise'. It is not until 41:8 that the reader is informed about the role of the wise in interpreting dreams. In this chapter, Joseph's ability to interpret dreams more likely provides the necessary background for chapter 41.

However, one key element of Joseph's character does emerge in this chapter. The structural analysis has shown that Joseph's taking of initiative in verses 14-15 is a crucial narrative highpoint in the unit. As he will with great success in 41:33-36, Joseph takes the initiative in securing his own advancement when given an opportunity to do so. This will be discussed more fully in the study of Genesis 41.

Finally, this chapter provides an important background for the events of the following one. In both there are two dreams, all interpreted rightly by Joseph; in both Joseph takes initiative to give more than merely the dream interpretation. Joseph's correct interpretation of the dreams in this chapter is the basis on which he is made known to Pharaoh in 41:9-13. Furthermore, after chapter 40, the reader expects that Joseph will be able to interpret the dreams of Pharaoh. Thus, these events raise the expectations of the reader as they move on to the following chapter.

---

106 So Seybold, 'Paradox and Symmetry', 65.

107 Longacre, *Joseph: A Story of Divine Providence*, 47-48 notes the contrast in chapter 40 between the above-the-story viewpoint of the reader and narrator and the within-the-story viewpoint of Joseph and the other characters. This enables the reader to connect the dreams in the different chapters.

108 So Wenham, *Genesis 16-50*, 385.

Genesis 41

Structure

At first glance, there appears to be a division in the chapter between Pharaoh's dreams (verses 1-36) and Joseph's rise to power (verses 37-57).[109] However, structuring the chapter in this way obscures an important pattern in the text. This study proposes the following structure for the passage[110]

1. Solving the problem of the dreams (verses 1-46)
  A   The dreams recounted (verses 1-7)
     B   The problem - the dreams uninterpreted (verse 8)
        C   A proposed solution (verses 9-13)
           D   The initial rise of Joseph (verses 14-16)
  A' The dreams recounted (verses 17-24)
     B'   The problem - the dreams interpreted (verses 25-32)
        C'   A proposed solution (verses 33-36)
           D'   The rise of Joseph (verses 37-46)

2. The dreams fulfilled and the solution tested (verses 47-57)
                       E   The years of plenty (verses 47-53)
                       E'   The years of famine (verses 54-57)

In this structure, some sections are quite clearly demarcated. Verses 1-7 open with a time reference, then outline Pharaoh's two dreams (verses 1-4 and 5-7). The distinctiveness of this section is indicated by the occurrence of הנה in verses 1, 2, 3, 5, 6, 7 and not again until verse 17. There is the mention of חלם at the beginning of each part of the dream (verses 1, 5) and as a summary at the end (verse 7), while at the conclusion of the dream, Pharaoh awakens. The number seven is also vital in each part. While the dream could be regarded as either one or two units, the common patterns and the use of הנה suggest one unit with two subsections.

The dream does not present a problem in itself, but the failure to find one who can interpret the dream (verse 8) creates the problem needing to be

109 So, for example, Westermann, *Genesis 37-50*, 85-86. Westermann divides the chapter into the following smaller units: verses 1-7, 8-13, 14-16, 17-24, 25-32, 33-36, 37-46, 47-57.

110 For a similar structure - though it differs on some of the details - see Wenham, *Genesis 16-50*, 389. He recognises some parallels between verses 1-16 and verses 17-46, and sees verses 47-57 as the fulfilment of the dream interpretation. His structure, however, does not draw attention to the two proposed solutions in verses 1-46.

solved in the first part of the narrative.

Verses 9-13, linking the passage with chapter 40, reintroduce the cupbearer who serves the narrative purpose of proposing a solution to the problem of the uninterpreted dream.

This is followed, from verse 14 onwards, by the initial rise of Joseph from imprisonment to the presence of Pharaoh. The precise extent of this section is disputable,[111] but several reasons can be given for seeing verses 14-16 as the appropriate unit. Firstly, that would make the next unit verses 17-24, which is a natural section involving Pharaoh's account of his dream, paralleling verses 1-7. Secondly, including verses 15-16 with verse 14 links the rise of Joseph with the activity of God. This linkage has already been seen in 39:1-6 and 39:21-23, and will be repeated in 41:37-46 (especially verses 38-39). Thirdly, in the parallel rise of Joseph later in this chapter, there is not merely a description of Joseph's rise, but also a reflection on his character. The cameo in verses 15-16 similarly gives an insight into Joseph's character.

The next sections are fairly clear. If verses 15-16 belong to the previous unit, then verses 17-24 recount Pharaoh's dream. While verses 25-32 can be described as the interpretation of the dream, it is important to see that the interpretation which is given creates for Pharaoh the further problem of how to deal with the coming crisis. In the context of the narrative, therefore, the dream interpretation outlines the problem that needs to be resolved. Thus, there is a parallel between the problem of the dream uninterpreted (verse 8) and now the problem of the dream interpreted (verses 25-32).

Verses 33-36 have frequently been regarded as a continuation of the dream interpretation of verses 25-32. However, if verses 25-32 outline the problem, it is best to regard verses 33-36 as a distinct section proposing to Pharaoh a possible solution. This is again in parallel with the earlier part of the chapter (verses 9-13). As previously, the adoption of the proposed solution leads to the rise of Joseph (verses 37-46, compare verses 14-16).While verse 46 is sometimes viewed as introducing the subsequent section, it functions well as a rounding-off summary to the story of Joseph's rise.[112] However, the phrase אֶרֶץ מִצְרַיִם (verse 46) also links verses 1-46 to what follows in verses 47-57, where the phrase appears in verses 48, 53, 54, 55 and 56.

On this outline of verses 1-46, there is a twin parallel structure, moving through the recounting of the dream, the problem (of the dream uninterpreted or interpreted), a proposed solution, and climaxing in rise of

---

111 Some see verse 14 rounding off verses 8/9-14; others propose that the verse stands alone; still others that verses 14-16 are merely the narrative setting for the retelling of Pharaoh's dreams.

112 *Contra* Ross, *Creation and Blessing*, 639; Longacre, *Joseph: A Story of Divine Providence*, 34; Aalders, *Genesis*, 216; Brueggemann, *Genesis*, 326.

Joseph. This structure suggests that the narrative thrust of the chapter is on the rise of Joseph, which is achieved through the behind-the-scenes working of God as well as through Joseph's own proposed solution.

The remainder of the chapter (verses 47-57) focuses on the fulfilment of the dream, and the testing of Joseph's solution. It neatly divides into two sections. Verses 47-53 concern the seven years of plenty, with verses 47-49 describing the gathering of grain during the years of plenty, the fulfilment of the first part of Pharaoh's dream. Verse 53 rounds off the description of the years of plenty. What is inserted in between (verses 50-52) is the interpreted account of the birth of two sons to Joseph. While this adds interesting details, this section locates his own fruitfulness in the time of plenty, a fact reinforced by the unnecessary and therefore significant interpretation of the names (especially Ephraim, verse 52). Not only does the account of his sons precede verse 53, but verse 50 explicitly mentions that his sons were born before the arrival of the years of famine. Thus, verse 53 is not the introduction to the following section, but rather a verse which rounds off the first seven years, thus tying Joseph's sons into the years of plenty.[113] This is reinforced by the use of כל twice in each verse in verses 54-57, but not in verse 53.[114]

Finally, verses 54-57 describe the seven years of famine. The cohesive subject matter is also reflected in the following almost-chiastic structure, and the recurring mention of the famine[115]

54		seven years of *famine* [רעב] begins
		famine [רעב] in all lands
		bread in Egypt
	55	land of Egypt *famished* [ותרעב]
		people went to Pharaoh, and sent to Joseph
	56a	*famine* [רעב] over all the earth
	56b	Joseph sold them the stored grain
		famine [רעב] severe in Egypt
57		other nations buying corn from Egypt
		famine [רעב] in all the earth

---

113 *Contra* Wenham, *Genesis 16-50*, 389; Ross, *Creation and Blessing*, 639. Longacre, *Joseph: A Story of Divine Providence*, 254 divides the unit after verse 54a, but that is unlikely in the light of the frequent use of רעב in verses 54-57 as well as verse 54a.

114 Hamilton, *Genesis Chapters 18-50*, 513.

115 For a similar chiastic structure of verses 54b-57, see Longacre, *Joseph: A Story of Divine Providence*, 36.

41:1-7 - The Dreams Recounted

The chapter begins with the observation that two years had passed. This reminds the reader that Joseph has endured another two years of unfair imprisonment.

The first part of the dream is given a setting by the Nile, which in Egypt was not just a river but a symbol of the life and fertility of the empire.[116] One group of healthy and plump cows is eaten up by seven thin and ugly cows. The dream echoes some features of Egyptian dreams. The seven cows reflect the detail of the Book of the Dead, while cows were seen as a symbol of Egypt.[117] The fantastic and unnatural detail of cows eating other cows appears ominous. Thinness (דקות, verses 3-4) prevails over fatness (בריאת, verses 2, 4), implying a threat to Pharaoh's Egypt.[118]

While the image changes in the second part of the dream (verses 5-7), again it is the thin (דקות, verses 6-7) ears of grain that consume the healthy (בריאות, verses 5, 7) ones. The repetition of דקות and בריאות/בריאת, in relation to both cows and ears of grain, ties the dreams together even before the interpretation is given.

The dream is ominous in that both livestock and agriculture appear to be under threat. In addition, even the mighty Nile does not seem enough to ensure life. The second part of the dream also mentions the east wind (קדים, verse 6), which may be a reference from a Palestinian viewpoint to the destructive *Ḥamsim* wind, a potential cause of disaster.[119]

41:8 - The Problem: the Dreams Uninterpreted

It is no wonder, then, that Pharaoh's spirit is troubled (ותפעם רוחו, verse 8). The apparently all-powerful Pharaoh is addressed by a twofold dream that is both ominous and potentially more powerful than him.[120] In calling for all the Egyptian court magicians (כל־חרטמי מצרים)[121] and wise men

---

116 Brueggemann, *Genesis*, 327.

117 J. Murtagh, 'The Egyptian Colouring of Genesis and Exodus', *Irish Ecclesiastical Record* 107 (1967): 254 and Janssen, 'Egyptological Remarks', 66: make the connection between the seven cows and the Book of the Dead. Wenham, *Genesis 16-50*, 390 notes that cows "symbolized Egypt, the primordial ocean, and one of the gods, Isis".

118 Westermann, *Genesis 37-50*, 87; Wildavsky, *Assimilation versus Separation*, 85; Alter, *Genesis*, 234.

119 D.C. Hopkins, *The Highlands of Canaan*. Social World of Biblical Antiquity, 3. (Sheffield: Almond Press, 1985) 81. The withering effects of the east wind can be seen in Ezek 12:10 and 19:12. For comments on the Palestinian perspective see Wenham, *Genesis 16-50*, 391; Janssen, 'Egyptological Remarks', 66.

120 Westermann, *Genesis 37-50*, 88; Hamilton, *Genesis Chapters 18-50*, 488.

121 Kidner, *Genesis*, 195 suggests that חרטמם refers to "those who were expert in handling the ritual books of priestcraft and magic." Similarly, Wenham, *Genesis*

(כל־חכמיה), he is calling on the learned in his court to enable him to regain control over events. Even more significantly, this means that it is the task of the 'wise' to interpret the dream in this narrative. They are expected to do so, and fail to do so, either because they are unable or perhaps unwilling to be the bearer of bad news.[122] The text seems to suggest that it was their inability, since they appear not to have discerned that the two 'dreams' were in fact one. Pharaoh shared with the magicians his dream (חלמו), but the narrator then records the problem that there was no one to interpret *them* (ואין־פותר אותם). The plural suffix suggests that "to the pharaoh it was one dream. But to his dream interpreters it was two dreams; they can neither interpret nor count correctly."[123] On either reading, however, one who could interpret the dreams convincingly would be regarded as 'wise'.

While Joseph will better the Egyptian sages at their own game, the focus of the chapter seems to be elsewhere. Although *all* the Egyptian wise men (כל־חכמיה) are decisively upstaged in the story, very little is made of their failure.[124] No explicit comparison is drawn between the power of Yahweh and that of the Egyptian gods, unlike the situation in Exodus 7-9 (for example, Exod 7:10-12, 20-22; 8:18-19; 9:11). Verse 8 could have made much of the humiliation of the 'heathen magicians' by the representative of God's people, but the tone of this chapter is vastly different from that of Exodus 7-9. The focus is simply on the fact that Joseph is doing what the 'wise' were expected to be able to do.

41:9-13 - A Proposed Solution

This section is repetitive for the implied reader, who knows the fuller version given in chapter 40. The repetition appears to serve several purposes. While it clearly slows the narrative pace and thus builds suspense, it also reminds the reader of the ominous fact that Joseph can interpret dreams. This creates anticipation that Joseph will do so with Pharaoh's dream. The cupbearer announces that את־חטאי אני מזכיר היום. In light of the immediate context (verse 10), 'my faults' (חטאי) seems to refer to the 'offence' for which Pharaoh had imprisoned him (40:1-3).[125]

16-50, 391.

122 Westermann, *Genesis 37-50*, 88; Wildavsky, *Assimilation versus Separation*, 85.

123 Hamilton, *Genesis Chapters 18-50*, 485. Hamilton notes that it is not yet called a dream in verse 4 when Pharaoh awakes, only when he awakes in verse 7, and there it is called a חלום (singular). Sternberg, *Poetics*, 398 had earlier made a similar observation. While this may have been only the narrator's perception, Pharaoh in verses 17, 22 refers to 'in my dream' (בחלמי; also חלום in verse 15), and Joseph in verse 25 explicitly says that 'the dream of Pharaoh is one' (חלום פרעה אחד).

124 Fretheim, 'The Book of Genesis', 620.

125 Calvin, *A Commentary on Genesis*, 321; Gibson, *Genesis*, 260; Longacre, *Joseph: A Story of Divine Providence*, 48.

However, the use of the root זכר in 40:14, 23 and now in 41:9 suggests that the cupbearer may also have had in mind his ungrateful forgetting of Joseph.[126] At least the reader will make this connection, especially since the cupbearer proceeds in verses 10-13 to summarise the events of chapter 40. The stage is thus set for Joseph to come before Pharaoh as the proposed solution to the problem of the uninterpreted dream.

While this passage provides a delay, it also provides a fuller description of the Egyptian setting. It gives more of the court atmosphere or ambience, as well as incidentally providing a model of the tactful speech of a courtier.[127]

Most importantly, the cupbearer's words also bring Joseph's dreams closer to fruition by bringing Joseph himself to Pharaoh's attention, and they begin to describe what he has to offer. The active working of God in the background can be seen in the overruling of the cupbearer's forgetfulness, so that he is remembered at an even more opportune time.[128]

This means that Joseph's wisdom is already displayed to Pharaoh through the cupbearer's telling of the incident in prison, even before Pharaoh has a chance to meet Joseph. In the cupbearer's account, Joseph is doing what the narrator has said the wise men were expected to do, but could not. Thus, when Pharaoh speaks of Joseph as נבון וחכם in verse 39, it is not only on the basis of his interpretation of Pharaoh's dream, but also because of this account in verses 9-13 and, perhaps as well, Joseph's self-effacing response in verse 16.

41:14-16 - The Initial Rise of Joseph

The impression in this section is one of haste and action. After many years of apparently fruitless waiting, Humphreys observes that "it takes but one verse (41:14) and a burst of verbs - send, call, bring, hurry, shave, clothe, come - to bring Joseph to his audience with the king of Egypt."[129] Here, then, is the initial rise of Joseph.

The symbolism of Joseph's change of appearance and clothing signal that this is a decisive event. Davidson observes that "[i]t marks the metamorphosis of Joseph. The life of the slave is now at an end; the new

---

126 So W.G. Plaut, 'Genesis', in *The Torah: A Modern Commentary*. (New York: Union of American Hebrew Congregations, 1981) 264; Wildavsky, *Assimilation versus Separation*, 85; Green, *What Profit for Us?*, 100; Wenham, *Genesis 16-50*, 391.

127 Hamilton, *Genesis Chapters 18-50*, 490; Green, *What Profit for Us?*, 100 describe the selective and strategic nature of the description.

128 Sailhamer, 'Genesis', 240.

129 Humphreys, *Joseph and His Family*, 40. Also Wessels, 'The Joseph story', 45 and Westermann, *Genesis 37-50*, 88.

life of prestige and power is about to begin".[130] In terms of shaving or hair-cutting,[131] this involves not only tidying Joseph up, but also a transition from a bearded Semite to a clean-shaven man fit for the Egyptian court.[132]

Da Silva sees that Joseph being given a change of clothes symbolically prepares for the social elevation of Joseph and the accomplishing of his dreams.[133] This is particularly likely in light of the garment motif which unifies chapters 37-41. Thus, Joseph's coat in chapter 37 is a sign of pre-eminence, and later as a witness of death. In chapter 38, Tamar takes off her widow's clothes and puts on those of a prostitute. In chapter 39, Joseph's garment used as evidence against him by Potiphar's wife. Now in chapter 41, new clothes are given to him at the time of his initial ascent (verse 14) and his investiture as a high official (verse 42).

Verses 15-16 are strictly unnecessary, and therefore are potentially a significant source of clues for interpreting what follows. Unfortunately, verse 16 is textually and syntactically difficult, with בלעדי [= 'It is not I', NRSV] not having precisely this sense elsewhere. The only possible exception is in Gen 14:24,[134] where it means 'not for me', in the sense that Abram declines to share in the booty offered by the King of Sodom, lest others say that they had made Abraham rich. Thus, it reflects Abram's desire to show his dependence on God. In Genesis 41:16, it also appears to indicate a desire, this time on Joseph's part, to show a dependence on God.[135]

The wider context of the story also suggests that it is not so much a denial of his ability, but rather an outworking of his reliance on God. Firstly, such a view is in keeping with his words to the courtiers in 40:8b and to Potiphar's wife in 39:9. In each conversation with an Egyptian he expresses an attitude of submission to God as his foundational belief. Secondly, when he refers to God in 40:8, and here again in 41:25, 28, and 32, Joseph actually proceeds to interpret dreams, as if there is no conflict in his thinking between God making the interpretations known and his using

---

130 Davidson, *Genesis 12-50*, 245.

131 Wenham, *Genesis 16-50*, 392 notes that נלח can refer to cutting the beard (2 Sam 10:4), or one's hair (Num 6:9) or both (Lev 14:9). It probably means both here.

132 K.A. Kitchen, *Ancient Orient and Old Testament* (London: Tyndale, 1966) 167 notes that "[i]n Egypt, white linen dress and clean-shaven face are customary in the tomb- and temple-scenes and are presupposed in Genesis 41:14, 42; while in Western Asia the Semitic and other peoples appreciated fine beards and often multi-coloured garments." Similarly, Murtagh, 'The Egyptian Colouring', 255.

133 Da Silva, *La symbolique des rêves*, 109-110; also Kselman, 'Genesis', 119.

134 Clines, *Dictionary Volume II*, 181.

135 Weeks, *Early Israelite Wisdom*, 102-103 has a useful discussion of the grammar of Gen 41:16, and notes that if the MT is retained it should be translated as 'besides me' or 'not just I but', with Joseph simply affirming the basis of his interpretation, and not denying he has any part in it.

Joseph's skill. Thirdly, Pharaoh does not appear to have understood Joseph's words as a denial, since in verse 17 he proceeds to tell Joseph his dream. Finally, the subject אלהים is placed before the verb in verse 16, as if to emphasise God, and perhaps suggest a contrast with Joseph - it is not so much me but moreso God. Joseph is able to do what he does only because God is working through him. Joseph is not denying his ability or skill, but is showing himself to be self-effacing, not seeking to supplant or minimise the role of God.[136] In so doing, he nicely fuses the overarching purposes of God in the background, and the tasks of human beings in the foreground.

41:17-24 - The Dreams Recounted

The lengthy repetition of Pharaoh's dream again serves to delay the narrative pace, as well as build suspense and expectation. There are a number of minor differences between verses 1-7 and verses 17-24, especially in verses 19 and 21.[137] However, what is significant is that the retelling of the dream in a more negative way suggests a growing anxiety in Pharaoh.[138]

41:25-32 - The Problem: the Dreams Interpreted

This speech, continuing until the end of verse 36, is the first lengthy discourse in the Joseph story.[139] Some discern in this speech a fine example of the art of courtly rhetoric,[140] but the initial section is much plainer than that. It is, however, clear, confident and authoritative.[141] There is no mention of how Joseph comes to know these things, nor is there any indication of a supernatural communication with or revelation to Joseph.[142] Yet, Joseph is able to state that the two parts of Pharaoh's dream have the same message. His skill is evident in his ability to explain the basic thrust of the dream, made clear by the threefold refrain that God is showing Pharaoh what he is about to do (verses 25, 28, 32).[143] It is also reflected in his knowing what

---

136 Fretheim, 'The Book of Genesis', 624 suggests that these disclaimers present Joseph as an ideal figure. On the other hand, Wildavsky, *Assimilation versus Separation*, 86 views Joseph as only appearing to be self-effacing.

137 Fretheim, 'The Book of Genesis', 621 points to the exaggeration and additional bizarre detail at the end of these verses, and the omissions in verse 19. See also Sailhamer, 'Genesis', 24.

138 Wenham, *Genesis 16-50*, 392; Hamilton, *Genesis Chapters 18-50*, 494.

139 Longacre, *Joseph: A Story of Divine Providence*, 34 notes that it is the second longest speech of the whole story.

140 Adar, *The Book of Genesis*, 145.

141 Lowenthal, *The Joseph Narrative*, 52.

142 Coats, *From Canaan to Egypt*, 27.

143 G. Savran, 'The Character as Narrator in Biblical Narrative', *Prooftexts* 5 (1985):

elements of the dream are significant and what are secondary.[144]

Verse 25 makes the foundational assertion about the identity of the two parts of the dream, then reveals its essential content. This leads naturally into the key to the significant symbols (cows, ears of grain) in verses 26-27. The second stage begins in verse 28 with a recapitulation - for the sake of emphasis - of verse 25, followed in verses 29-31 by the explanation of the realities behind the symbols in the years of plenty and famine. Joseph here places much more emphasis on the years of famine rather than the years of plenty. Thus, for example, he gives a more elaborate description of the negative symbols in verse 27 than of the positive ones in verse 26. In addition, he sums up the plenty in one sentence in verse 29, while providing much more detail about famine in verses 30-31.[145] Famine is not, however, seen as the judgement of God, but merely a future event that requires planning and forethought.[146] The final verse in this section (verse 32) makes the additional claim that the doubling of the dream is further evidence of the agency of God, and that God will do it soon. The implied reader will find this ominous in the light of Joseph's own doubled dream of his rise in chapter 37.[147]

This unit, then, poses a problem by virtue of Joseph's ability to interpret Pharaoh's dream. There is now an impending famine that needs to be planned for, a dilemma that requires a solution. That is the task of Joseph's continuing words in verses 33-36.

41:33-36 - A Proposed Solution

This section, beginning with the disjunctive וְעַתָּה, does not appear to have been part of the revelation of the dream.[148] Joseph now goes on to give wise counsel about how to respond in the light of the ominous events that he has just outlined.

It is commonplace for writers to indicate that Joseph's advice in verses 33-36 is a model speech for an aspiring courtier.[149] Indeed, there are aspects of the text that give some indication of a courtly wisdom connection.

---

12 observes that "it is not the interpretation that is the most significant, but rather the realization that God stands behind these predictions". Leibowitz, *Studies in Bereshit*, 441 comments that "[t]he name of God thus occurs in these three verses and is even inserted twice in the last verse against all the rules of syntax, in order to emphasise the central role of Divine Providence."

144 Jacob, *Genesis*, 276.

145 Hamilton, *Genesis Chapters 18-50*, 496-497; Westermann, *Genesis 37-50*, 91; Fretheim, 'The Book of Genesis', 621; Wenham, *Genesis 16-50*, 393.

146 Fretheim, 'The Book of Genesis', 621; Kidner, *Genesis*, 195-196.

147 Wenham, *Genesis 16-50*, 394.

148 *Contra* von Rad, *Genesis*, 376.

149 For example, Humphreys, *Joseph and His Family*, 147-148, 150.

Firstly, Longacre has observed that verses 33-36 follow the pattern of a hortatory discourse, but the unit has been modified by a shift from second to third person (and the consequent use of the jussive not imperative), so that it has become a 'deferential hortatory discourse', which is well suited to the setting of a commoner addressing royalty.[150] Thus, the way in which Joseph speaks is certainly consistent with wisdom speech.[151]

Secondly, Joseph has dealt with the interpretation of the dream in a manner that reflects familiarity with established protocol.[152] While he proceeds in verses 33-36 to give additional counsel, he is able to be heard because of his fine balance of boldness and deference.

Thirdly, Joseph's plan involves the choice of a person who is נבון וחכם (verse 33). This appears significant in that the word חכם is used in the book of Genesis only in this chapter (verses 8, 33, 39). Furthermore, the archetypal wise ruler Solomon is described as חכם ונבון in 1 Kgs 3:12, while the חכם root is linked with נבון also in Prov 10:13; 14:33 and 16:21.[153]

It has been objected, of course, that Joseph is seeking to promote himself at this point.[154] There is no clue in the text that discloses Joseph's motive, but what is evident later in the narrative is that all Pharaoh's officials approved the wisdom of his proposal (verse 37), and presumably also concur with Pharaoh's description of Joseph as נבון וחכם in verse 39. Joseph's motivation is concealed by the narrator, who apparently wishes the reader to observe that such a description fits Joseph well.

Another feature of this broader section is that it combines God's behind-the-scenes ordering of events (verses 25, 28, 32) with the need for decisive human action (verses 33-35). As von Rad comments, "[t]he fact that God has determined the matter, that God hastens to bring it to pass, is precisely the reason for responsible leaders to take measures!"[155] This emphasis on

---

150 Longacre, *Joseph: A Story of Divine Providence*, 119-136. Verses 33-36 are dealt with at 132-135.

151 Humphreys, *Joseph and His Family*, 143 notes that this is clearly seen in the advice which Joseph gives to deal with the danger. See also von Rad, *Genesis*, 376; Davidson, *Genesis 12-50*, 244-245; Adar, *The Book of Genesis*, 145.

152 Humphreys, *Joseph and His Family*, 74. The protocol in dream interpretation is set out in A.L. Oppenheim, 'The Interpretation of Dreams in the Ancient Near East', *Transactions of the American Philosophical Society* 46 (1956): 204-205 and Ehrlich, *Der Traum*, 78.

153 Hamilton, *Genesis Chapters 18-50*, 500. They also appear together in in Deut 4:6; Hos 14:10 (9E). In relation to the reference in Hosea, G.T. Sheppard, *Wisdom as a Hermeneutical Construct: A Study in the Sapientializing of the Old Testament*. BZAW, 151. (Berlin: Walter de Gruyter, 1980) 129-136 has argued that this is an editorial wisdom addition to the book. But see Westermann, *Genesis 37-50*, 92.

154 For example, Fretheim, 'The Book of Genesis', 621. For the contrary view, see Leupold, *Genesis*, 1032 and Brueggemann, *Genesis*, 332.

155 Von Rad, *Genesis*, 376. See also Brueggemann, *Genesis*, 331 and Savran, 'The

human initiative is potentially important since this is sometimes seen to be prominent in wisdom circles.[156] Certainly, the effect of Joseph's words is that he gains the initiative and determines the future direction of events.

Joseph's plan was to make provision during the years of plenty for the future years of famine, and it is this proposal that gives a richer insight into Joseph's character and abilities. While it has a superficial similarity to wisdom teaching on storing up food for the future (for example, Prov 6:6-11; 10:4-5), in Joseph's case it is more the taking of decisive action in the light of an impending crisis (the seven years of certain famine).[157]

The nature of his proposal is variously understood. Many see the word חמש in verse 34 to be a reference to taking one fifth of the produce during the prosperous years. This would anticipate 47:24, 26, where Joseph does take a fifth of the produce in tax, and would be consistent with the use of numerals as verbs elsewhere.[158]

Speiser notes that the *qal* passive participle of the root חמש means 'armed, equipped, prepared' in Exod 13:18; Josh 1:14; 4:12; Judg 7:11, leading him to translate the verb here as 'organize'.[159] In the context Wenham, too, prefers the meaning 'to organize', commenting that this is more consistent with the fairly general suggestions made in the following two verses.[160] This translation is also suggested by the phrase כל־אכל in verse 35.

While this latter reading has much to commend it, either possibility involves the storage of vast amounts of grain to be used during the future famine.[161] The plan appears to involve the appointment of one chief official (verse 33) who would need to be supported by a vast number of officials under him (verse 34). The ultimate goal of Joseph's proposal is the welfare of the land of his Egyptian hosts (ולא־תכרת הארץ ברעב, verse 36).

Character as Narrator', 8.

156 The classic statement of this is set out in Brueggemann, *In Man We Trust*.

157 The taking of initiative is best illustrated in the book of Proverbs by the ideal wife (perhaps wisdom personified) in Prov 31:13-22, 24, 27. Her wise actions will avert many possible dangers that may confront her or her family. See also Prov 21:5; 22:3; 27:23-24.

158 Hamilton, *Genesis Chapters 18-50*, 498, however, suggests that it could be translated as either 'take the fifth part of the land' or 'divide into five districts'. He notes that roots related to numerals can mean 'divide into three parts' (Deut 19:3) and 'divide into six parts' (Ezek 45:13). See Waltke and O'Connor, *Syntax*, 414.

159 Speiser, *Genesis*, 313.

160 Wenham, *Genesis 16-50*, 394. At 388, citing Longacre, *Joseph: A Story of Divine Providence*, 133, Wenham argues that the change from the jussive to the *waw* + perfect gives a resultative sense, leading to the translation 'so that he may organize'. At 134, Longacre gives more detailed argumentation for this view.

161 Aalders, *Genesis*, 214 points out that even one fifth of the grain produced in Egypt would be an enormous amount.

41:37-46 - The Rise of Joseph

This new section opens by observing that Joseph's plan or proposal (הדבר), not his ability to interpret dreams, was looked on with favour by Pharaoh and his servants.[162] While he may have spoken well, this gets no mention here and it is the wisdom of Joseph's plan that is valued.

The description of Joseph as איש אשר רוח אלהים בו (verse 38) is initially puzzling, but its general thrust is made clear by the epexegetical comment in verse 39 that Joseph is one who is נבון וחכם. The story clearly demonstrates that those who can propose and implement wise plans are valued greatly by those in power.[163] As will be seen, once Joseph gets the opportunity to speak, or to implement his plans, he does so wisely. In the book as a whole, he may well be a counterpart to Adam, whose rule as God's vice-regent was unsuccessful.[164]

The precise nature of Joseph's office in Egypt is not clear. Some argue that the reference to the phrase על-ביתי implies that he becomes vizier,[165] while others discern here a reference to a different high official in Egypt.[166] A promising mediating position has been proposed by de Vaux, who notes that in Israel the 'master of the palace' (for example, 1 Kgs 16:9; Isa 22:15, 19-20) was a much more important figure than in Egypt, indeed his powers were similar to those of the Egyptian vizier.[167] On this view, Joseph's Egyptian position is described by a title able to be understood by later Israelite readers.[168]

However, on any of these views it is clear that Joseph has been raised to

---

162 Skinner, *Genesis*, 468-469; Green, *What Profit for Us?*, 103; Hamilton, *Genesis Chapters 18-50*, 503.

163 Coats, *From Canaan to Egypt*, 27-28. Yet, W.J.P. Boyd, 'Notes on the Secondary Meanings of אחר', *JTS* New Series 12 (1961): 54 argues that the construct form (אחרי) is used in a causal sense = 'because'; implying that he selects Joseph because God has revealed to him the course of future events. See also Weeks, *Early Israelite Wisdom*, 104.

164 Sailhamer, 'Genesis', 242.

165 Vergote, *Joseph en Égypte*, 102-114; K.A. Kitchen, 'Joseph', in *Illustrated Bible Dictionary*. 3 vols. eds. J.D. Douglas and N. Hillyer. (Leicester: Intervarsity Press, 1980), 2:815.

166 Janssen, 'Egyptological Remarks', 66-67; C.F. Aling, *Egypt and Bible History* (Grand Rapids: Baker, 1981) 48; W.A. Ward, 'The Egyptian Office of Joseph', *JSS* 5 (1960): 144-150.

167 R. de Vaux, *Ancient Israel: Its Life and Institutions*. trans. J. McHugh. (New York: McGraw-Hill, 1961) 129-131. However, see the contrary argument by S.C. Layton, 'The Steward in Ancient Israel: A Study of Hebrew (ʾăšer) ʿal-habbayit in its Near Eastern Setting', *JBL* 109 (1990): 634-635.

168 Thus, Wenham, *Genesis 16-50*, 395. Even Layton, 'The Steward', 635 concedes that this is possible.

a position of prominence.[169] It is likely, then, that Pharaoh is designating Joseph in general terms as a person of authority, rather than outlining his particular duties.[170]

This is also evident in the detail of the rest of verse 40. While a variety of explanations have been offered for the phrase ועל־פיך ישק כל־עמי, it is generally agreed that it implies Joseph's authority.[171] The final phrase of the verse - רק הכסא אגדל ממך - also clearly announces Joseph's pre-eminence in Egypt, extended in verse 41 to be over all the land of Egypt. The giving of the signet ring, the garments of fine linen, and the gold chain are mentioned because of what they symbolise.[172] The ring, most likely with Pharaoh's seal upon it, signifies that power and authority to act has been delegated to Joseph.[173] The בגדי־שש is probably an Egyptian loan word that referred to court dress.[174] In the light of the garment motif earlier in the Joseph story, these garments appear to symbolise pre-eminence in much the same way as Joseph's coat did in chapter 37.[175] The gold chain was commonly associated with royal officials in Egypt,[176] while the second chariot appears to be further evidence of installation into high office. The call אברך (verse 43) is of disputed meaning, but appears to be either a pronouncement of Joseph's status or a call to pay homage to him.[177] On either reading, it is consonant with the exalted status of Joseph in the other details of the story.

The picture of the rise of Joseph in verses 40-44 provides a useful clue for understanding Joseph's re-naming and marriage in verse 45. Some see an implied rebuke for Joseph, arguing that he has denied his Hebrew

169 Vergote, *Joseph en Égypte*, 99; Ward, 'Office of Joseph', 150.

170 J.M. Cohen, 'An Unrecognized Connotation of *NŠQ PEH* with Special Reference to Three Biblical Occurrences', *VT* 32 (1982): 420.

171 K.A. Kitchen, 'The Term *Nsq* in Genesis XLI, 40', *ExpTim* 69 (1957): 30; Vergote, *Joseph en Égypte*, 96-97. The difficulty here is that ישק, from the root נשק, means literally 'kiss'. Instead of נשק the LXX suggests a different root קשב in the *hiphil*, meaning 'give heed, obey'. The Pesshita seems based on שפט (= 'shall be judged); the Targums reflect זון (= 'be supported, managed'). See also S.D. Sperling, 'Genesis 41:40: A New Interpretation', *The Journal of the Ancient Near Eastern Society of Columbia University* 10 (1978): 118.

172 Redford, *Biblical Story of Joseph*, 208.

173 Vergote, *Joseph en Égypte*, 116.

174 Kidner, *Genesis*, 196; da Silva, *La symbolique des rêves*, 142.

175 Da Silva, *La symbolique des rêves*, 21; R.B. Coote and D.R. Ord, *The Bible's First History* (Philadelphia: Fortress, 1989) 185. Wildavsky, *Assimilation versus Separation*, 120 perceives a more sinister symbolism but his proposal seems unlikely.

176 Redford, *Biblical Story of Joseph*, 208-213.

177 See, for example, W.W. Hallo, 'The First Purim', *BA* 46/1 (1983): 20, 25; J.S. Croatto, ''Abrek „Intendant" dans Gén. XLI, 41, 43', *VT* 16 (1966): 113-114.

heritage and has become thoroughly Egyptianised.[178] Certainly it speaks of
Joseph being integrated into the highest Egyptian circles,[179] but there does
not appear to be any negative inference drawn. This is striking in the light
of earlier attitudes to intermarriage in the book of Genesis (for example,
Gen 24:3-4), but would sit well with the greater openness to other nations in
wisdom circles.[180] In the context of verses 40-44 then, the renaming and
intermarriage appears to be further evidence of Joseph prospering in Egypt.
Thus, although Joseph is given a new name, this name is not interpreted for
the reader.[181] Similarly, even marriage into one of the highest Egyptian
religious families is included without rebuke, and indeed is followed by a
summarising comment about how Joseph was thus in authority over all the
land of Egypt

וַיֵּצֵא יוֹסֵף עַל־אֶרֶץ מִצְרָיִם

Verse 46 reveals that Joseph is now thirty years old. This gives some
perspective to the readers, who might recall that he was seventeen when he
came down to Egypt (Gen 37:2).[182] Thirteen long years had thus elapsed, a
fact not evident from the compressed narrative. The timing of this detail is
significant. At the very time that it becomes clear that Joseph has been
unfairly treated for such a long time, the reader is also being told of
Joseph's ultimate vindication and rise to power. Even the thirteen years can
be incorporated into God's ordering of events.[183]

This section ends with Joseph passing through all Egypt, taking
possession as it were, of the land over which he has now been granted
authority.[184]

41:47-53 - The Years of Plenty

The remainder of the chapter gives details about the fulfilling of Pharaoh's

---

178 Wildavsky, *Assimilation versus Separation*, 122, 125.
179 Humphreys, *Joseph and His Family*, 70; von Rad, *Genesis*, 378.
180 So Herbert, *Genesis 12-50*, 134; von Rad, *Genesis*, 378. Of course, a Solomonic
    setting would have reflected great sympathy for intermarriage with a high-ranking
    Egyptian woman, as can be seen in 1 Kgs 9:15-25. It is significant that the much
    later story of *Joseph and Asenath* describes how Joseph's wife converted to
    Yahwism, as if the story as it stands was unpalatable to at some forms of later
    Judaism.
181 Hamilton, *Genesis Chapters 18-50*, 508; Redford, *Biblical Story of Joseph*, 231.
    When Joseph names his own sons in verses 51-52, he gives them Hebrew names, a
    fact consistent with his not having renounced his Hebrew heritage.
182 Kidner, *Genesis*, 197.
183 Calvin, *A Commentary on Genesis*, 330-331.
184 Westermann, *Genesis 37-50*, 94, 96, citing a parallel in Gen 13:17.

dream, and the successful testing of Joseph's solution. Verses 47-49 describe the produce of the years of plenty in superlative terms, a more than ample fulfilment of the dream. The explicit mention of Joseph in verse 49 seems to indicate his successful administration of the task of storing up the grain.[185] Coats has observed that, in this chapter, Joseph does not emerge as a model of how to rise to power, but rather he illustrates how to use power, once one has already risen.[186] There also appears to be an allusion to the Abrahamic covenant promise in verse 49, where the phrase כחול הים echoes the earlier promises to Abraham (22:17) and Jacob (32:13[12E]). Wenham also observes that "[h]ere it immediately precedes the mention of the birth of Joseph's sons, a further fulfilment of those promises."[187] This suggests that, alongside the wisdom-like elements that appear in this chapter, the concerns of the Abrahamic covenant promise are present as well.

At first sight, the reference to the birth of Joseph's two sons seems out of place. However, it appears carefully bracketed between two time references in verses 50a and 53

$$\text{בטרם תבוא שנת הרעב (verse 50a)}$$
$$\text{ותכלינה שבע שני השבע (verse 53)}$$

This suggests that Joseph's sons are being purposefully placed in a setting of fruitfulness, again endorsing Joseph's marriage to Asenath (despite her being described as בת־פוטיפרע כהן און).

It also implies that the naming of the sons will be viewed positively and not reflect badly on Joseph. Others have used verse 51 to ask why Joseph did not make contact with his father.[188] This study suggests that neither name has a negative connotation. Joseph's explanation of Manasseh is that *God* has made him forget his hard toil and his father's house. Indeed, Joseph's reference in verse 51 to אבי את־כל־עמלי ואת כל־בית may well be a hendiadys meaning 'my suffering in my father's home' and thus the mistreatment he had received back in Canaan.[189] In the light of the story as a whole, Joseph surely refers to God having given him contentment despite his past suffering and losses.[190] The name given to Joseph by Pharaoh in

185 *Contra* the views of Coote and Ord, *The Bible's First History*, 185, who complain that it was the basis of enslavement and oppression and that "[p]lans like Joseph's cause famines."

186 Coats, *Genesis*, 284; Weeks, 'Joseph, Dreams and Wisdom', 7.

187 Wenham, *Genesis 16-50*, 397.

188 For example, Calvin, *A Commentary on Genesis*, 332. Similarly, Plaut, 'Genesis', 271; Gibson, *Genesis*, 264; and most recently, Wildavsky, *Assimilation versus Separation*, 123 and A. Ages, 'Why Didn't Joseph Call Home?', *Bible Review* 9 (1993): 42-46.

189 Hamilton, *Genesis Chapters 18-50*, 512. Also Sarna, *JPS Torah Commentary*, 269.

190 Baldwin, *The Message of Genesis 12-50*, 176-177; Brueggemann, *Genesis*, 329;

verse 45 was not interpreted, as if that was not of any great significance for the thrust of the passage. By contrast in verses 51-52, the names of Joseph's children are interpreted, as if they are of significance. Both presuppose hardship - עמלי (verse 51), and בארץ עניי (verse 52) - yet speak of how God has acted to reverse Joseph's circumstances, and lead to fruitfulness and peace. The naming of the two children thus suggests a positive movement in Joseph's life - having been enabled by God to forget his past losses, he now has begun to experience great fruitfulness in his new land.[191] Both names express gratitude to God.[192]

41:54-57 - The Years of Famine

This section leads nicely into chapters 42-43 by describing the severity of the famine.[193] Several aspects of the description are striking. Firstly, the universality of the famine is indicated by the word כל being used eight times in verses 54-57, twice in each verse.[194] Indeed, the phrase וכל־הארץ (verse 57) not only indicates the extent of the famine but also leads into the famine in the promised land that forms the backdrop to chapter 42.

Secondly, the description of the famine is very Joseph-centred. In verse 54, the years of famine began to come כאשר אמר יוסף. Pharaoh's instructions to the people are לכו אל־יוסף (verse 55) and it is Joseph who opens the granaries to the people (verse 56). The climax comes in verse 57 when

וכל־הארץ באו מצרימ הלשבר אל־יוסף

Thus, at the end of the chapter, verse 57 provides the logical conclusion to the story of the rise of Joseph. It is a nice inclusio with 39:1, and serves to bind this unit together.

Interim Observations

Chapter 41 is clearly crucial for this study. Joseph has risen to pre-eminence in partial fulfilment of his own dream in chapter 37,[195] and God's

---

and von Rad, *Genesis*, 379.

191 Kselman, 'Genesis', 119; Brueggemann, *Genesis*, 329.

192 Wenham, *Genesis 16-50*, 398; Westermann, *Genesis 37-50*, 97.

193 Westermann, *Genesis 37-50*, 98. Leupold, *Genesis*, 1038-1039 notes that this famine would have required a failure of rain in both the Syro-Palestine region as well as the catchment areas of the Nile. See the recent theory of C.J. Humphreys and R.S. White, 'The Eruption of Santorini and the Date and Historicity of Joseph', *Science & Christian Belief* 7 (1995): 151-162.

194 Hamilton, *Genesis Chapters 18-50*, 513.

195 Brueggemann, *Genesis*, 326.

behind-the-scenes activity is clearly evident. Joseph continues to be in the right place at the right time.

In addition, however, this chapter has testified to Joseph's rise to prominence being effected through Joseph's own decisive plans and action. This is not to say that there is a conflict between God's controlling activity and Joseph's initiatives, for while "[t]he sovereignty of God is the underlying theme of this chapter ... God had determined that his wise servant would be the means of delivering Egypt."[196] The twofold division of the chapter into verses 1-46 and verses 47-57 draws attention to the fact that Joseph rises to power through forthrightly proposing a solution to the problem raised in Pharaoh's dream. This solution is tested successfully in verses 47-57. Thus, Joseph is pictured as one who has acted wisely in the public arena.[197]

196 Ross, *Creation and Blessing*, 637.
197 Sailhamer, 'Genesis', 237.

CHAPTER 7

Genesis 42-45

Genesis 42-45 as a Whole Unit

It is clear to most writers that chapter 42 begins a new and distinct unit within the Joseph story. The chapter starts by reintroducing the patriarch Jacob (וירא יעקב), and then his sons, hinting that the narrative is now to move in a different direction.

The nature of this decisive change is, however, not always clearly explained by the commentators. A revealing indicator of this new thrust is the comparative absence of references to פרעה (Pharaoh) in chapters 42-44. The word פרעה is used 86 times in Genesis 37-50, including 12 times in chapter 40 and 32 times in chapter 41.[1] By way of contrast, פרעה appears only twice in chapter 42 (incidentally, as a conventional oath formula in verses 15 and 16), not at all in chapter 43, and only once in chapter 44 (as court flattery in verse 18). In particular, Pharaoh does not actively perform any action in chapters 42-44, despite the fact that the setting of most of these chapters is still in Egypt (42:5-25; 43:15-44:34). While reference to פרעה is made 6 times in chapter 45, this occurs only after Joseph has made himself known to his brothers (45:1). Furthermore, Pharaoh responds and speaks (45:16, 17) only after Joseph announces that he bears no grudge (45:5-11), and brothers are enabled to talk with Joseph (45:15, in contrast to not being able to talk to him לשלם in 37:4).

Pharaoh is the symbol of the Egyptian court, and his absence as a character from chapters 42-44, together with his reappearance in chapter 45

---

1   The word פרעה is found once in chapter 37 (37:36); not in chapter 38; once in chapter 39 (39:1); 12 times in chapter 40 (40:2, 7, 11 [x 3], 13 [x 2], 14, 17, 19, 20, 21); 32 times in chapter 41 (41:1, 4, 7, 8 [x 2], 9, 10, 14 [x 2], 15, 16, 17, 25 [x 3], 28 [x 2], 32, 33, 34, 35, 37, 38, 39, 41, 42, 44 [x 2], 45, 46 [x 2], 55); twice in chapter 42 (42:15, 16); not in chapter 43; once in chapter 44 (44:18); 6 times in chapter 45 (45:2, 8, 16 [x 2], 17, 21); 3 times in chapter 46 (46:5, 31, 33); 24 times in chapter 47 (47:1, 2, 3 [x 2], 4, 5, 7 [x 2], 8, 9, 10 [x 2], 11, 14, 19, 20 [x 2], 22 [x 2], 23, 24, 25, 26 [x 2]); not in chapters 48 or 49; 4 times in chapter 50 (50:4 [x 2], 6, 7).

after the apparent family reconciliation, strongly suggests that the focus has shifted from the Egyptian court to the family of Joseph.[2] This backgrounding of Pharaoh is matched by the foregrounding of the brothers, and their forced interactions with Joseph.

There are also other factors which suggest that chapters 42-45 are a distinct and coherent unit. Firstly, there is the inclusio between 42:2 and 45:26. In 42:2, Jacob sees that they need grain in order to live and not die (ונחיה ולא נמות); in 45:26, the last verse of the chapter, Jacob accepts that Joseph is alive (חי) and he wishes to see him before he dies (אמות). The theme of life and death is a recurring theme throughout these chapters,[3] and this also brackets this narrative section.

Secondly, there is the movement within chapters 42-45 from division within the family to apparent reconciliation. At the beginning of chapter 42, Joseph is separated geographically from his father and brothers. Then, the ten brothers are separated from Jacob and Benjamin (42:3, 4) by their journey to Egypt. Once in Egypt, divisions appear among the brothers (42:22), and Simeon alone remains in prison (42:24) while the other nine return to Canaan. Even at the banquet with Joseph, there is not only physical separation between Joseph and his brothers (43:32), but also Benjamin being treated differently to the others (43:34). When the silver cup is found, the brothers are invited to separate themselves from Benjamin (44:17). While some see these chapters as revealing information rather than bringing about change,[4] the process of seeming reconciliation in chapter 45 appears to have effected significant change within the family. This process of change gives coherence to chapters 42-45.

Thirdly, there are a number of structural parallels between chapter 42 and chapters 43-44, suggesting that they are meaningfully placed side by side. In some ways, chapter 43 shows a similar outline to chapter 42, though with a contrasting outcome - the reception of the brothers instead of their accusation.[5] However, the similarity of pattern is even more pronounced between the entirety of chapters 43-44 and chapter 42. This is usefully outlined in the following table[6]

---

2   Humphreys, *Joseph and His Family*, 177; Brueggemann, *Genesis*, 335.
3   See 42:18, 20, 36-38; 43:7, 8, 14, 27, 28; 44:9, 20, 22, 28-29, 30, 31; 45:5, 7, 26.
4   Thus, for example, Savage, 'Literary Criticism', 94-95.
5   Ross, *Creation and Blessing*, 657.
6   The table is a slight modification of that of Humphreys, *Joseph and His Family*, 97, with the addition of 'Brothers given food'. In a similar vein, Adar, *The Book of Genesis*, 150.

Initiation:		
Sent by Jacob	42:1-2	43:1-2, 11-12
Benjamin excepted/sent	42:4	43:3-10, 13-14
Journey by ten brothers	42:3, 5	43:15
First audience with Joseph	42:6-16	43:15c-16a
Interlude: Prison/welcome	42:17	43:16b-25
Second audience with Joseph	42:18-22	43:26-34
Joseph's private reaction	42:23-24	43:30-31
Brothers given food	42:25-26	43:32-34
Interlude: Homecoming	42:27-28	44:1-13 (aborted)
Third audience with Joseph	42:29-34 (anticipated)	44:14-34

Fretheim makes the interesting suggestion that the two journeys of chapters 42-44 mirror the doubled dreams of the previous chapters.[7] Certainly the doubling motif has been prominent in the Joseph story thus far,[8] with doubled dreams being followed either by a complication (chapter 37) or resolution (chapters 40 and 41). In this section, the doubled journeys of chapters 42-44 are resolved by the family reconciliation in chapter 45. The previous pattern appears to be followed here, giving integrity to chapters 42-45 as a unit.

However, there are still a variety of readings of these chapters. Some see Joseph depicted here as a tyrant administering a cruel test; others see him as the archetypal wise man.[9] The narrator has not seen fit to include a long speech from Joseph which might make his motivation clear, and so a closer exegetical study of the text is needed.

The reading strategy proposed here is that chapters 42-45 should be read as part of the Joseph story as a whole. Of course, this means that regardless of any likely prehistory, the implied reader of the final form is invited to read them after, and in the light of, the preceding chapters 37-41. It has

---

7   Fretheim, 'The Book of Genesis', 627. Also Humphreys, *Joseph and His Family*, 41.

8   Wildavsky, *Assimilation versus Separation*, 99.

9   For the negative reading of Joseph's character here, see Miscall, 'Analogies', 34; Wildavsky, *Assimilation versus Separation*, 103. Wildavsky incorrectly attributes a similar view to Humphreys, but the quotation in question is, in fact from Redford, *Biblical Story of Joseph*, 103, where he identifies Joseph as "stubborn, bullying ... this brow-beating tyrant who plays with his victims like a cat with a mouse". In fact, Humphreys, *Joseph and His Family*, 180 looks at Redford's reading of chapters 42-45 and wonders if this is the Joseph that is in the text. For a positive reading of Joseph as wise in these chapters, see von Rad, 'Ancient Wisdom', 292-300; Longacre, *Joseph: A Story of Divine Providence*, 50-51; Garrett, *Rethinking Genesis*, 171.

been argued in the previous sections of this book that Joseph has been portrayed quite positively, in terms of his tested character (chapter 39), his care for others (chapter 40) and his wise planning (chapter 41). Furthermore, the narrator of chapter 38 has seemingly endorsed the use of 'deception' in order to bring about a righteous outcome, while the dreams of chapter 37 suggest the rise of Joseph as being central to the narrative as a whole.

The net result of reading chapters 42-45 through the filter of the preceding parts of the Joseph narrative is that, at the very least, the implied reader is invited to view the character and actions of Joseph sympathetically, perhaps even generously. This heuristic assumption may need to be challenged by the text of chapters 42-45, but it seems to be the fairest starting point.

In fact, such a sympathetic approach is also suggested by the presence of dramatic irony in chapters 42-45.[10] The implied reader shares with Joseph knowledge of Joseph's identity that is denied to the brothers, and is thus invited to collude with Joseph. Events are seen from Joseph's perspective (in contrast, say, to 37:12-36), and the implied reader is placed on Joseph's side of the divided family.[11] Joseph's previous actions appear to entitle him to the benefit of the doubt when his motives are not stated.

Genesis 42

Structure

The component parts of the chapter appear to be as follows: the ten brothers sent to Egypt (verses 1-4); the arrival in Egypt (verse 5); the first audience (verses 6-16); the brothers put in prison (verse 17); the second audience (verses 18-24a); Simeon imprisoned (verse 24b); the brothers supplied with grain and they depart (verses 25-26); the journey stop (verses 27-28); and the remaining brothers back with Jacob (verses 29-38). While there are a variety of ways of clustering these segments,[12] this study proposes to see the

---

10   Gibson, *Genesis*, 265; Alter, *The Art of Biblical Narrative*, 164.

11   Thus, Humphreys, *Joseph and His Family*, 105, 106.

12   Humphreys, *Joseph and His Family*, 61-62 sees six sections in the chapter; Wenham, *Genesis 16-50*, 404 has five scenes; Coats, *Genesis*, 284-285 sees a transition in verse 1a, followed by 4 sections or panels, each marked by a change in location; Ross, *Creation and Blessing*, 648-649 sees three sections in the chapter; C. Westermann, *Joseph: Studies of the Joseph Stories in Genesis*. trans. O. Kaste. (Edinburgh: T & T Clark, 1996) 63-64 sees three sections. He omits verses 27-28, 38, as these are often assigned source critically to J whereas the rest is regarded as E. Other scholars who place more weight on source criticism tend not to be

smaller units belonging to, and rounding off, the preceding larger sections.

Thus, verses 1-5 constitute the first section, in which the command to go to Egypt is completed by their arrival in Egypt. The second section comprises verses 6-17, outlining the first meeting with Joseph and completed by the ten being put in prison. The third section more contentiously covers verses 18-26, which includes not only the second meeting but also the outcome of this meeting in the imprisoning of Simeon, supplying the brothers with grain and their departure. There is a smaller fourth section in verses 27-28, which covers the finding of the money at the journey stop and which is finished by the brothers' rhetorical question. The fifth and final section is verses 29-38 - the interaction between Jacob and the brothers - which finishes with Jacob's decision not to send Benjamin down to Egypt, a complication that links chapter 42 with the following chapter.

42:1-5 - Joseph's Brothers Sent to Egypt

This section not only leads into the meeting of Joseph and his brothers, but also introduces several crucial threads that will be woven into the narrative tapestry.

At the outset, there is the re-introduction of Jacob, who has been absent since chapter 37. This is highlighted by the unnecessary double use of the word 'Jacob' in verse 1 (obscured in many English translations), a literary device which serves to highlight the centrality of a character.[13] Although Jacob will not meet Joseph in chapters 42-45, he hangs over the chapters by being as firmly based in Canaan as Joseph is in Egypt. Jacob's authority is also evident in the text of verses 1-2. He formulates the plan to buy grain, and the ten are sent off at his command. There may even be a hint in verse 1 that the brothers are standing around looking at each other because they are unable to fix the crisis in which they find themselves.[14] The seriousness of the famine is such that, in verse 2, it has become a matter of life and death (ונחיה ולא נמות).[15] The lack of action by the brothers is in contrast to the

---

concerned with the structure of the final form.

13   Wenham, *Genesis 16-50*, 405, relying on the text-linguistic work of Longacre, *Joseph: A Story of Divine Providence*, 144. The second occurrence of Jacob is replaced by 'he' in the RSV, NRSV, NIV, NEB, although it is present in the KJV, and it is included in a footnote in the NJPS.

14   A. Dillmann, *Genesis Critically and Exegetically Expounded*. trans. W.B. Stevenson, Vol. 2. (Edinburgh: T & T Clark, 1897) 381; Driver, *The Book of Genesis*, 348.

15   Speiser, *Genesis*, 321 comments that the verb שבר (procure/buy) together with the noun בר (grain) gives a sense of 'get us an emergency supply of grain' (42:3). Similarly, Sarna, *JPS Torah Commentary*, 291. Egypt was, of course, the natural place to find food during a famine (Herbert, *Genesis 12-50*, 135; von Rad, *Genesis*,

picture of Joseph in chapter 41, who moved decisively to preserve the lives of many.

The motif of life and not death is also foregrounded in this chapter, introduced in verse 2. Sailhamer has argued that "[a]s is frequently the case in biblical narratives, the words spoken at the beginning of a story foreshadow the final outcome."[16] This alerts the implied reader to the importance of the theme of life and not death in these chapters.[17] In fact, there is life in Egypt, because Joseph is in Egypt. This accounts for the anomalous reversal of the prospect of death in the promised land, but the hope of life outside.

Jacob is thinking of physical survival, but the death of Jacob's family would also put into question the promises to the patriarchs that have been so crucial since Genesis 12, when an earlier famine caused Abraham to leave the promised land for Egypt (Gen 12:10).[18] In the Joseph story, the death of Jacob's family would also preclude the fulfilment of Joseph's dreams.

In many ways, the narrative in chapter 42 begins in a way which mirrors the events of 37:12-14. There Jacob used his authority to send Joseph off to a distant place where, without Jacob's knowledge, *the ten brothers* could exercise power over Joseph. Here in chapter 42, Jacob uses his authority to send the ten off to a distant land where, again without Jacob's knowledge, *Joseph* could exercise power over the ten.[19]

Furthermore, the significance of Jacob sending the ten sons (verse 3) is made clear in verse 4 by specifying that Jacob did not send the now-adult Benjamin, just as he had not sent out Joseph in 37:12. It seems that Jacob is showing Joseph's brother the same kind of favouritism that he showed to Joseph.[20] His motive, expressed in verse 4, is that he was afraid that harm may now come to Benjamin (פֶּן־יִקְרָאֶנּוּ אָסוֹן). It is possible that Jacob has in mind what happened to Joseph when he was entrusted to the ten, or he may simply be apprehensive in the light of the loss of both Joseph and Rachel on journeys.[21] However, even if he did not suspect the ten, there are still two

---

382), especially since famine in Canaan was due to a lack of rainfall, whereas in Egypt the crops were dependent on the flooding of the Nile.

16   Sailhamer, 'Genesis', 244.
17   Fretheim, 'The Book of Genesis', 627. See footnote 3 for the biblical references.
18   See D.J.A. Clines, *The Theme of the Pentateuch*. JSOTSup, 10, 2nd ed. (Sheffield: Sheffield Academic Press, 1997) 48-49.
19   Adar, *The Book of Genesis*, 148; Sarna, *JPS Torah Commentary*, 291; Fretheim, 'The Book of Genesis', 627.
20   R. Alter, 'Joseph and his Brothers', *Commentary* 70 (1980): 62; Hamilton, *Genesis Chapters 18-50*, 516; Green, *What Profit for Us?*, 118.
21   Sarna, *JPS Torah Commentary*, 292; Leupold, *Genesis*, 1044. In relation to the word אָסוֹן Wenham, *Genesis 16-50*, 405 comments that "Jacob is using what may be a vague term to describe a fate like Joseph's befalling Benjamin".

interesting implications. Firstly, if harm might befall Benjamin, then it might also befall the others. Yet he sends them as if they are dispensable, not as precious as Benjamin. Secondly, Jacob, apparently knowing nothing of the events of chapter 41, is afraid that harm may befall his sons. For the implied reader who knows of the foreshadowed rise of Joseph to power, there is a heightening of the tension as the brothers' situation is much more precarious than Jacob realises.

Finally, in the light of Joseph's storing of grain in chapter 41, verses 1-5 of this chapter engender a narrative expectation that Joseph and the ten brothers will meet. This likelihood is increased by the theme of God's behind-the-scenes control of events that has been prominent in the Joseph story thus far. There are also some indications in the text that are suggestive to an alert reader. In verse 1, the ten are described by reference to Jacob - they are בניו. In verse 3, after they are commanded to go to Egypt, they are described as אחי־יוסף עשרה, and they are usually described as 'brothers' in the rest of the chapter. As Hamilton points out, "[t]his shift in designation prepares us for the eventual meeting of long separated brothers."[22]

42:6-17 - The First Audience with Joseph

As the narrator begins to outline the first meeting between Joseph and his brothers, a few important details are provided by way of reminder. In particular, the narrator recalls that Joseph was in charge of all the land, and of the sale of the grain. It is a picture of Joseph having risen to a position of prominence and power, as was foreshadowed in the dream of chapter 37.

In response to this, the brothers come and bow down before him,[23] with the disparity in status emphasised further by the addition of the word ארצה, 'to the ground'. The verb used of bowing down (וישתחוו) is that found in the dreams in 37:7, 10. The linking of the dreams and the brothers' bowing down is even more strongly suggested by the explicit mention in verse 9 that Joseph remembered the dreams that he had dreamed about the brothers. The implied reader would therefore make a connection between Joseph's rise to power - and the exercise of it in the following chapters - and the dream of chapter 37.[24]

Wenham also suggests that verses 7 and 8 echo chapter 37 because of the repetition of the root נכר (used in 37:32), as well as התנכר ('he pretended')

---

22   Hamilton, *Genesis Chapters 18-50*, 515; see also Alter, 'Joseph and his Brothers', 61.

23   J.S. Ackerman, 'Joseph, Judah and Jacob', in *Literary Interpretations of Biblical Narratives II*. ed. K.R.R. Gros Louis. (Nashville: Abingdon, 1982), 86 and Fretheim, 'The Book of Genesis', 628 view this as fulfilling Joseph's first dream.

24   Ackerman, 'Joseph, Judah and Jacob', 87.

being a play on words with התנכל ('they plotted') in 37:18.[25] The use of these echoes, he suggests, indicates that Joseph's seemingly strong treatment of his brothers is simply a matter or mirroring their earlier actions towards him.[26] At the very least these echoes of chapter 37 picture Joseph reacting as one unjustly wronged, not a petty tyrant.

This may also shed light of the meaning of וידבר אתם קשות (verse 7), often translated as 'he spoke harshly' or 'roughly'. In the light of the preceding phrase (ויתנכר אליהם, as well as verse 8 which follows) the thrust appears to be that he did not treat them as one would treat a brother, but simply played the role of an Egyptian official.[27] He treated them as if the second in charge of Egypt was speaking to men he did not know from another land. In fact, the content of 'speaking harshly' appears to be the words he addresses to them in verses 9-16. This makes verse 7 an anticipatory summary of the rest of this section.[28]

Thus the biggest issue in the chapter is why Joseph sets up the test he does, and whether he is justified in doing so. Is he seeking vengeance, reconciliation, punishment, or something else? The absence of an explicitly stated motive necessitates exploring the various possibilities.[29]

Some have proposed that Joseph is acting vindictively here, seeking to exact revenge on his brothers.[30] This seems to be supported by the unfounded accusations and imprisonment of the brothers, but does not appear to account for all of the text.[31] Verse 9, for example, begins not with Joseph recalling their wrongful treatment of him, but rather remembering his dreams.[32] In the Joseph narrative the narrator does not often provide the

---

25 Wenham, *Genesis 16-50*, 406.
26 Ackerman, 'Joseph, Judah and Jacob', 89-90.
27 Hamilton, *Genesis Chapters 18-50*, 134 comments: "Joseph did speak to his brothers "roughly," but no more roughly than God spoke to Adam and Eve in Eden. And God's ultimate design in Eden is to restore these two. Rough words are redemptive words." Wenham, *Genesis 16-50*, 406 makes the interesting proposal that by not filling out what he means by 'spoke harshly' "the narrator leaves the reader to surmise and fill the gap himself, and this allows the creation of a multidimensional image of Joseph."
28 Thus C.F. Keil and F. Delitzsch, *Biblical Commentary on the Old Testament, Volume 1: The Pentateuch*. trans. J. Martin. (Grand Rapids: Eerdmans, 1951) 355.
29 White, *Narration and Discourse*, 259; Humphreys, *Joseph and His Family*, 44. Sternberg, *Poetics*, 286 sets out the four possibilities as "punishing, testing, teaching, and dream fulfillment".
30 For example, Wildavsky, *Assimilation versus Separation*, 103; Redford, *Biblical Story of Joseph*, 103; Miscall, 'Analogies', 34.
31 Kidner, *Genesis*, 199, for example, refers to 42:16-19, 24 and 44:9-10. S. Schimmel, 'Joseph and his Brothers: A Paradigm for Repentance', *Judaism* 37 (1988): 61.
32 Ackerman, 'Joseph, Judah and Jacob', 87 sees that 42:9 is a crucial verse, linking

reader with insight into Joseph's mind, so it is significant when it is found. In addition, a motive of revenge does not explain the language of 'testing' (verses 15-16), or Joseph's letting nine of the brothers go free (verses 19-20). Nor would it account for the command to bring the innocent Benjamin (verse 20), knowing that the pain it would bring to Jacob, or even Joseph's own tears in these chapters.[33] In the broader context, Genesis 50:15-21 makes it clear that Joseph had an ideal opportunity for taking revenge but gave theological reasons why he would not do so. A re-reading of this chapter in the light of 50:15-21 would seem to preclude vengeance being the driving motive for Joseph.

More feasible is the view that he is seeking to punish or discipline his brothers or even to teach them a lesson, prior to forgiving them. This is commonly seen as constituting only part of Joseph's motives.[34] The involvement of the innocent Benjamin, and Joseph's failure to stop after the brothers confess their guilt (verse 21), establish that this is not the sole or even dominant motive.

A third suggestion is that Joseph acts in such a way as to to bring Benjamin into his presence.[35] This might be designed to fulfil the second part of the dream,[36] or to see if they had disposed of Benjamin as they had done with Joseph himself,[37] or simply because he longed to be reunited with his only full brother. However, this view does not account for the test continuing past Gen 43:16, for the subsequent ruse is then superfluous. Furthermore, in chapter 45, Joseph weeps not only with Benjamin (verse 14), but also with all his brothers (verse 15).

Many, therefore, suggest that this is a genuine test, but not of whether the brothers are telling the truth, but rather of whether they have changed. Will they trade in a brother to save their own skins? It is noteworthy that sending back either one or nine is inconsistent with the charge of spying which Joseph makes against them. To allow any of them to return would have permitted the fulfilment of their mission as spies. As von Rad puts it,

---

everything that follows with his dreams. Similarly, Sailhamer, 'Genesis', 245.

33   Fretheim, 'The Book of Genesis', 630. Turner, *Announcements of Plot*, 155-156.

34   G. Lawson, *Lectures on the History of Joseph*. (London: Banner of Truth, 1972, originally 1807) 136; von Rad, *Genesis*, 383; Vawter, *On Genesis*, 418; Turner, *Announcements of Plot*, 163-164.

35   Coats, *From Canaan to Egypt*, 34; von Rad, *Genesis*, 382; Hamilton, *Genesis Chapters 18-50*, 522; Calvin, *A Commentary on Genesis*, 338.

36   Turner, *Announcements of Plot*, 160.

37   Turner, *Announcements of Plot*, 157, however, wonders why Joseph would think they would treat Benjamin badly, since the reasons they treated him badly were Jacob's favouritism (information given to the reader only in 43:28) and Joseph's boasting, neither of which applied to Benjamin. Yet, Joseph would know that the reason Jacob favoured him would surely now apply to Benjamin, and thus would have good grounds for his suspicions.

"[h]e does not test whether they are spies. He knows that they are not. He tests whether they are the same old brothers or whether perhaps an inner change has occurred in them."[38] As shall be seen in the study of the text, this involves an elaborate reconstruction of the scenario of chapter 37.[39] The brothers will also be faced with the reconstruction of the same temptation in order to establish whether or not they had changed.[40] Turner, however, notes this is possible but is reading between the lines. He distinguishes whether this was the *aim* or just the *result* of Joseph's ploy,[41] and thinks that the story as a whole does not picture this as Joseph's intention. While the distinction between aim and result is difficult to establish in the absence of an expressed motive, the high level of Joseph's planning, both in chapter 41 and chapters 42-44, makes it more likely that the resolution of chapter 45 was the intended outcome.

Closely related to this is the view that Joseph's motive was to achieve a lasting reconciliation within the family. Turner objects to this view, urging that the confession of the brothers in 42:21-22 would have told Joseph that they had reformed, yet all Joseph does is weep (verse 24). He concludes "that the narrative provides no support for the view that Joseph treated his brothers harshly in order to ascertain or provoke their repentance."[42] Turner draws out the contrast between Joseph and Esau in Gen 33:4, who demanded no test or trial before reconciliation with his brother, and suggests that this does not reflect well on Joseph.

The contrast with Genesis 33 is interesting, but it need not be understood as Turner suggests. While it does appear to show free forgiveness on Esau's part, there appears to be no restoration of family unity, as Jacob does not wish to travel with Esau (verses 12-15), and they choose to dwell apart

---

38   Von Rad, 'The Story of Joseph' 30. Redford, *Biblical Story of Joseph*, 150 sees a fourfold test of their integrity in the areas of loyalty to each other and to Benjamin, their honesty, and their present attitude to their youngest brother.

39   F.B. Meyer, *Joseph: Beloved - Hated - Exalted* (London: Lakeland, 1975) 72-73 cites an interesting parallel in English literature. In Shakespeare's *Hamlet*, Hamlet's uncle murdered his brother, the King of Denmark (Hamlet's father). The deed was done secretly, but Hamlet finds out about it and instructs a group of dramatic performers to re-enact the murder scene before the royal pair. As they do so, the king rises hastily from his seat and says, 'Oh, my offence is rank, it smells to Heaven ... ' (Act 3, Scene 3).

40   Schimmel, 'A Paradigm for Repentance', 62; Leibowitz, *Studies in Bereshit*, 460-461; Alter, 'Joseph and his Brothers', 63; Niditch, *Underdogs and Tricksters*, 119-120; Fretheim, 'The Book of Genesis', 628, 630; Sarna, *JPS Torah Commentary*, 293; Longacre, *Joseph: A Story of Divine Providence*, 50-51; Garrett, *Rethinking Genesis*, 171.

41   Turner, *Announcements of Plot*, 157. However, see Green, *What Profit for Us?*, 121.

42   Turner, *Announcements of Plot*, 158-159.

from each other (verses 15-20). In chapter 42, the narrator appears to suggest that a 'cheap forgiveness' at this point would not have enabled the brothers to change and thus would not have brought about a lasting reconciliation.[43] In order to achieve this, the brothers needed to have their memories and guilt brought to the surface, and dealt with, which happens not only in 42:21-22, but also in 42:28; 44:16; 50:16-17. A family *truce* may have been possible at 42:21-22, but it appears that Joseph sets his sights higher than this.

The legitimacy or otherwise of the test is a crucial issue in the characterisation of Joseph. Significantly, the patriarchal accounts also include the testing of Abraham in Genesis 22. Here God himself tests Abraham in order to clarify his faith and to strengthen his relationship with the God of promise. This testing appears to be endorsed, though not explained, both by the narrator (for example, Gen 22:14, 15-18) and by the broader canon (for example, Heb 11:17-19). Testing appears not only to be legitimate, but can also bring about change. In Joseph's case, his "piety resides in this - he would rather see his enemies purified of their sinfulness than punish them for it."[44]

This may also have ramifications for the presence of 'wisdom-like elements' in chapters 42-45. While most of the wisdom corpus is poetic in form, it is significant that one of the few examples of wisdom narrative is the prologue to Job. Again God both institutes a test, and does not seek to justify it. Indeed, through this test Job's understanding of God's purposes and plans are expanded (Job 38-41; 42:3, 5) and his stance before God is refined (42:6). This testing, in the context of a wisdom narrative, served to clarify and change the nature of Job's faith. What is perhaps significant is that this wisdom book focuses much attention (chapters 3-31) of the process of the testing, and the detailed account of how the changes came about. While this is not confined to wisdom narrative (see Genesis 22), its absence in Genesis 33 and presence in chapters 42-45 is perhaps suggestive of wisdom-like concerns.

This is further reinforced by another Hebrew narrative that is seeking to describe the wisdom of a key character - 1 Kings 3.[45] After Solomon has

43   Westermann, *Joseph*, 66; E.M. McGuire, 'The Joseph Story: A Tale of Son and Father', in *Images of Man and God: Old Testament Short Stories in Literary Focus*. Bible and Literature Series, 1, ed. B.O. Long. (Sheffield: Almond Press, 1981), 14; Longacre, *Joseph: A Story of Divine Providence*, 50; Fretheim, 'The Book of Genesis', 630.

44   Schimmel, 'A Paradigm for Repentance', 63.

45   Kebekus, *Die Joseferzählung*, 248-249 notes the connection between Joseph's description in chapter 41 as 'wise and discerning' and 1 Kgs 3:4-15, but does not extend the link to the rest of 1 Kings 3. This text is generally regarded as a key part of the Deuteronomistic History, and may not have arisen in wisdom circles. Yet, it is sufficient for the purposes of this study that the narrative revolves around

been granted wisdom to rule, this is immediately tested in verses 16-27. Solomon's test of proposing to cut a baby in half, in isolation from the rest of the narrative, is hardly 'wise'. Yet, it is precisely such a test that shrewdly discerns the presence of true maternal feelings (verse 26a) and, therefore, the people regarded Solomon's test as evidence of both his wisdom and his fitness to rule (verse 28).

Thus, the detailed account of the testing of the brothers in chapters 42-44, which shrewdly brings about both lasting reconciliation and change in the brothers, is at least suggestive of the presence of wisdom-like concerns in narrative form. The testing that Joseph uses here certainly does not preclude his being characterised as wise.[46]

It is therefore the working hypothesis of this study that Joseph's motive in testing the brothers was to bring about a lasting reconciliation within the family through confronting them with their past wrongs, and enabling them to make a choice that was different to the pattern of chapter 37.

In this light, the allegation that they were spies made good sense. Egypt's north-eastern frontier was its weakest defence point,[47] a reality graphically picked up in the phrase 'nakedness of the land' (אֶת־עֶרְוַת הָאָרֶץ, verse 9).[48] The accusation of spying is a serious one that enables Joseph to take decisive action, as well as exert strong psychological pressure on the brothers.[49] The accusation of being spies may also cause the brothers to recall that, in the events of chapter 37, they virtually accused Joseph of spying on them, aiming to bring another 'bad report' to Jacob.

The helplessness of the brothers is emphasised in several ways in the section. Firstly, there is the need to bow down before 'the man' (verse 6). This difference in status at the court is reinforced by the use of characteristic courtly terms like 'my lord' (אֲדֹנִי, verse 10) and 'your servant(s)' (עֲבָדֶיךָ, verses 10, 11, 13).[50]

Solomon asking for, and being given wisdom to govern (1 Kgs 3:9-14).

46 So Garrett, *Rethinking Genesis*, 171 writes: "Joseph's deception of his brothers in Egypt would have been regarded by the ancients as an act of wisdom, not unwisdom." *Contra* Turner, *Announcements of Plot*, 154-155; Coats, *From Canaan to Egypt*, 38.

47 Vergote, *Joseph en Égypte*, 160; von Rad, *Genesis*, 382; Driver, *The Book of Genesis*, 349.

48 R.M. Schwartz, 'Joseph's Bones and the Resurrection of the Text: Remembering in the Bible', in *The Book and the Text*. ed. R.M. Schwartz. (Oxford: Basil Blackwell, 1990), 50 observes that: "[t]his term for 'nakedness' … refers not to nudity but to the sight of something that should remain hidden, something that it is illicit to see." Kidner, *Genesis*, 199 suggests that it is "a forceful way of saying 'to pry into all our private affairs'."

49 Sarna, *JPS Torah Commentary*, 293.

50 Vergote, *Joseph en Égypte*, 162. Wenham, *Genesis 16-50*, 407 notes that the deferential use of these terms is also good Hebrew etiquette (1 Sam 3:9; 16:16;

Secondly, the brothers' lack of control in the situation is reflected in their constant volunteering of unsolicited information, much of which Joseph wanted to find out.[51] In particular, he discovers the fact that both Jacob and Benjamin are still alive, despite being absent from this journey. The brothers appear to be caught off-guard, lurching from one line of defence to another.[52] Thus, when they add information such as there being twelve brothers (verse 13), they have to explain why only ten are present, which undercuts the force of their previous argument that no man would send all ten sons on a spying mission. Since they are not all of the brothers of one man, even if they all die, his family line still continues. So it is logical for Joseph to come back as he does in verse 14 and allege that they are spies. The mention of the younger brother discloses something previously kept hidden, and makes their story less credible (though the implied reader knows it is true).

Thirdly, their helplessness is accentuated by the dramatic irony that emerges from the implied reader sharing with Joseph knowledge of his identity, a vital fact of which the brothers are ignorant. This irony is highlighted even more by the *double entendre* of verse 11 when they say כלנו בני איש־אחד, with Joseph and the implied reader knowing it also includes the man they stand before.[53] There is further dramatic irony in verse 13, when the brothers wrongly suggest that והאחד איננו ('one is no more'), in the presence of Joseph himself.[54] In the same verse, the appeal by the brothers to family solidarity must be understood ironically by the reader who knows of the events of chapter 37.[55]

The presence of dramatic irony may also account for Joseph swearing an oath in the name of Pharaoh (חי פרעה, verses 15, 16). Many see here a clear example of Joseph being untrue to his God,[56] although there are other possible explanations.[57] The implied reader, however, knows that Joseph

22:15; 27:5).

51 G.W. Savran, *Telling and Retelling: Quotation in Biblical Narrative* (Bloomington: Indiana University Press, 1988) 44; Sarna, *JPS Torah Commentary*, 293.
52 Driver, *The Book of Genesis*, 349; Coats, *Genesis*, 286.
53 Ackerman, 'Joseph, Judah and Jacob', 88-89.
54 Alter, 'Joseph and his Brothers', 63.
55 Fretheim, 'The Book of Genesis', 628. Ackerman, 'Joseph, Judah and Jacob', 88-89 has also suggested that there is dramatic irony in verses 15-16.
56 Calvin, *A Commentary on Genesis*, 342; Lawson, *History of Joseph*, 141; Wildavsky, *Assimilation versus Separation*, 96.
57 Westermann, *Genesis 37-50*, 109 notes that "it corresponds to the Israelite oath by the life of the king, as in 2 Sam. 15:21". So also Sarna, *JPS Torah Commentary*, 294. Humphreys, *Joseph and His Family*, 182 view this as "a conscious attempt to give an Egyptian coloration to the narrative", as does Janssen, 'Egyptological Remarks', 68. Alter, *Genesis*, 247 quite reasonably observes that verse 23 indicates that Joseph was speaking Egyptian.

worships not Pharaoh but the same God as the brothers (for example, Gen 41:16, 25, 28), so that this appears to be simply another part of projecting a facade of a distant Egyptian official.

It is important to notice that the test, although a test of their words, is ultimately a test of whether there is אמת in the brothers.[58] They may have understood this to mean 'truth', but it appears to have a wider connotation of 'faithfulness' here. The real test is of their character, and this is the very issue that will be tested by Joseph's scheme.

The first test is preparatory to the final release of all except Simeon.[59] The use of the word משמר for confinement or custody - the same word used in 40:3, 4, 7 - may suggest that the brothers are required to experience something of what Joseph had undergone as a result of their actions years before.[60] It may also have enabled Joseph to plan his next move as he observed their reaction.[61]

42:18-26 - The Second Audience with Joseph

In the account of the second meeting, the motif of life recurs (verse 18). The syntax of the Hebrew (a sequence of two imperatives, זאת עשו וחיו) implies that life depends on fulfilling the condition of doing what Joseph had commanded.[62]

The basis on which Joseph claims that he can be trusted is that he 'fears God' (את־האלהים אני ירא, verse 18). Of course, the 'fear of the LORD/God' is a foundational wisdom concept,[63] which might lead to the suggestion of

---

58 For the range of meaning of אמת, see D.J.A. Clines, ed., *The Dictionary of Classical Hebrew Volume I* (Sheffield: Sheffield Academic Press, 1993) 328-332. It can refer to reliability or trustworthiness of character, stable conditions, truth of words and sincerity of motives.

59 Ross, *Creation and Blessing*, 648.

60 Alter, 'Joseph and his Brothers', 64; Ackerman, 'Joseph, Judah and Jacob', 91; Fretheim, 'The Book of Genesis', 628. Wenham, *Genesis 16-50*, 408. Sternberg, *Poetics*, 290 makes the suggestion that the three days' arrest corresponded to Joseph's three years in prison.

61 M. Dods, *The Book of Genesis*. The Expositor's Bible. (London: Hodder & Stoughton, 1896) 384.

62 *GKC* § 110f, cited in Wenham, *Genesis 16-50*, 402, points out that the sequence of two imperatives "serves to express the distinct assurance or promise that an action or state will ensue as the certain consequence of a previous action".

63 For example, Prov 1:7, 29; 2:4-5; 3:7; 8:13; 9:10; 14:26-27; 15:16, 33; 16:6; 19:23; 22:4; 23:17; 24:21; 31:30; Ecc 3:14; 5:7 [6]; 7:18; 8:12-13; 12:13; Job 1:1, 8, 9; 2:3; 4:6; 6:14; 15:4; 22:4; 28:28; 37:24. See L. Wilson, 'The Book of Job and the Fear of God', *TynBul* 46 (1995): 59-79 and the literature cited in footnote 1 of that article. This argues that the 'fear of God' need not be the same as the 'fear of the LORD', but is so in the wisdom books of Job and Ecclesiastes.

wisdom influence here. However, 'fear of God' can have a more restricted sense of "a standard of moral conduct known and accepted by men in general",[64] a meaning it appears to have in Gen 20:11 and, in an Egyptian setting, in Exod 1:17, 21. In these latter cases, it signifies 'a sense of right and wrong' or 'a basic respect for life', and the brothers would probably have understood his words in this way.[65]

Verse 19 indicates a change in Joseph's plan. Now only one brother needs to stay behind, leaving the rest to carry back the much-needed grain. Joseph has thus provided a way that will bring life back to Jacob and his family in Canaan, and yet will still test the brothers. Being forced to leave one brother behind may have been intended by Joseph to remind his brothers of the earlier situation in which they chose to sell an innocent brother.[66] In verse 21 this connection is certainly drawn, where it is emphasised by the wordplay between the distress (צרת נפשו) that they saw in Joseph, and the distress (הצרה) that had now come on them.[67] The brothers' 'confession' (אשמים אנחנו על־אחינו) is somewhat ambiguous as אשמים could refer either to their 'guilt' or their 'punishment'.[68] The text, however, does make clear that Joseph's plan has as its larger goal to ensure that Benjamin is brought down to Egypt[69]

ואת־אחיכם הקטן תביאו אלי (verse 20)

Verses 21-24a are narrative asides that do not advance the action, yet enable the reader to gain perspective. These verses disclose something of the thoughts of the brothers, as well as the emotions of Joseph, sending signals to the implied reader about how they should regard the various characters.[70]

In relation to the brothers, their present predicament as powerless victims is balanced by a reminder that they are the ones who sold their brother into slavery. This is further heightened by the inclusion of information not given

64   R.N. Whybray, *Wisdom in Proverbs*. SBT, 45. (London: SCM, 1965) 96. *Contra* Brongers, 'La Crainte du Seigneur', 163 who argues that the two terms 'fear of the LORD' and 'fear of God' must always mean the same thing, as in Lev 25:17.
65   Weeks, *Early Israelite Wisdom*, 100-101.
66   Dods, *The Book of Genesis*, 385; Wenham, *Genesis 16-50*, 408; Sternberg, *Poetics*, 296; Coats, *From Canaan to Egypt*, 37.
67   Ross, *Creation and Blessing*, 653; Sarna, *JPS Torah Commentary*, 295; Driver, *The Book of Genesis*, 350.
68   Calvin, *A Commentary on Genesis*, 344. Fretheim, 'The Book of Genesis', 629 suggests that it means both.
69   E.F. Roop, *Genesis*. Believers Church Bible Commentary. (Scottdale: Herald, 1987) 266-267.
70   Wenham, *Genesis 16-50*, 408.

in chapter 37 of Joseph's great anguish.[71] The effect of including this is to convey to the reader the utter helplessness of Joseph in the earlier situation and, by implication, the cold-heartedness of the brothers. Yet, their recognition of their fault in that situation is one that gives hope of change in the brothers and thus the possibility of reconciliation in the family.

Reuben's response in verse 22 serves both to highlight the disunity among the brothers as well as provide Joseph with more unsolicited information.[72] As the conversation abruptly ends, the reader is given a taste for what was going on among the brothers, but that part of the story is left dangling as a loose thread.

The mention of an interpreter in verse 23 is a puzzling feature.[73] Perhaps its major contribution is to explain why the brothers dared to speak so freely in verses 21-22.[74] Alter notes that the interpreter's presence has been withheld until this point, allowing the earlier conversations with the brothers to have an air of intimacy that an interpreter would spoil.[75]

Verse 24a, when Joseph turns away to weep, also reveals something of the inner turmoil that Joseph is undergoing, and implies that he still has a real affection for his brothers.[76] If this verse were not present, Joseph could easily appear cold-hearted, even icy, but his tears prevent Joseph from being seen in such a light. He has to turn aside lest he give the game away. The mention of Joseph weeping is thus both a means of conveying Joseph's inner turmoil, and a tension breaker that gives further hope for reconciliation, in view of the brothers' earlier expression of remorse.[77]

The action resumes in verse 24b with binding of Simeon. No reason is offered in the text as to why Simeon was chosen,[78] but the binding of one brother before their eyes would be a vivid reminder for the nine as they return to Canaan.

---

71   Hamilton, *Genesis Chapters 18-50*, 52; Alter, 'Joseph and his Brothers', 64.

72   Coats, *From Canaan to Egypt*, 35.

73   One intriguing aspect is why the brothers spoke as freely as they did in the presence of the interpreter. Lowenthal, *The Joseph Narrative*, 71 suggests that the interpreter may have been dismissed at this stage. Vergote, *Joseph en Égypte*, 168 comments that they may not have been an interpreter in the modern sense, given the Egyptian view that foreigners were inferior.

74   Lawson, *History of Joseph*, 162.

75   Alter, *The Art of Biblical Narrative*, 167-168.

76   White, *Narration and Discourse*, 259 comments that what distinguishes this story from earlier accounts of 'deception' is that we see the emotional effects of this deception on Joseph and his private thoughts and struggles (42:8, 9, 23, 24; 43:30, 31; 45:1, 2).

77   Fretheim, 'The Book of Genesis', 630; Janzen, *Genesis 12-50*, 168.

78   Sternberg, *Poetics*, 291 suggests that "[a]s Leah's second son, Simeon makes the perfect hostage for Benjamin, Rachel's second." See also Wenham, *Genesis 16-50*, 409.

As the brothers are sent home with their grain bags replenished, Joseph also (secretly) commands each one's money to be returned (verse 25). Some see this as a sign of Joseph's love and concern,[79] while others discern here a desire to make the brothers' lot more difficult.[80] Joseph's action certainly has the effect both of providing for his family in time of famine, as well as making the brothers appear for a second time before Jacob minus one brother but with money instead.[81]

42:27-28 - The Journey Home

These verses are a small unit that first recount the ominous finding of the money, as well as outlining the brothers' reaction. They take place in neither Canaan nor Egypt, but rather in a resting place (מָלוֹן) on the road home.[82] As one of the brothers attempts to feed his donkey, he finds his money, possibly at the top of a bag inside his sack.[83]

This discovery has significance for several reasons. Firstly, it leaves them open to the charge that, even if not spies, they are not fully honest, and appear to be thieves.[84] Secondly, their reaction (verse 28) is the focus of the unit (מַה־זֹּאת עָשָׂה אֱלֹהִים לָנוּ), highlighting the activity of God.

This has several interesting ramifications. Importantly, what the reader knows to be the actions of Joseph, are seen by the brothers as the actions of God.[85] This reinforces the view of chapters 39-41 that Joseph does what he does because God is with him. In other words, God is acting not directly, by means of mighty acts, but instead through the actions of humans like

79   Calvin, *A Commentary on Genesis*, 346; Boice, *Genesis*, 150. Von Rad, *Genesis*, 384. Baldwin, *The Message of Genesis 12-50*, 179 notes that ten asses would be able to carry about half a ton of grain, which would be a significant amount.

80   Gunkel, *Genesis*, 422; Lowenthal, *The Joseph Narrative*, 74; Davidson, *Genesis 12-50*, 256; Vawter, *On Genesis*, 421. Westermann, *Genesis 37-50*, 111.

81   Ackerman, 'Joseph, Judah and Jacob', 92; Wildavsky, *Assimilation versus Separation*, 97; Humphreys, *Joseph and His Family*, 44; White, *Narration and Discourse*, 263; Hamilton, *Genesis Chapters 18-50*, 535.

82   Keil and Delitzsch, *The Pentateuch*, 358 note that "מָלוֹן, camping-place for the night, is merely a resting-place, not an inn, both here and in Ex. iv. 24". The NRSV translates מלון as 'lodging place'; the NJPS as 'night encampment'. Westermann, *Genesis 37-50*, 111 suggests 'stopping place'.

83   Sarna, *JPS Torah Commentary*, 296 notes that the word אמתחת is used fifteen times in this story, but nowhere else in the Bible. בפי ('at the mouth of') is used only with אמתחת and never with שׂק (sack). Thus, he suggests that the 'pack' or bag (אמתחת) must have been inside a sack.

84   Westermann, *Genesis 37-50*, 112.

85   Green, *What Profit for Us?*, 125. The brothers see God doing what humans have in fact done. At one level they are simply mistaken; at a deeper level, however, they are quite accurate.

Joseph. There is also a strong notion here that God rewards the righteous and punishes the wicked. The outcome is that they are confused, again not knowing what to think or how to make sense of these developments.[86]

42:29-38 - The Brothers Report to Jacob

The final section is set in the land of Canaan, and commences with the brothers' version of what happened in Egypt (verses 29-34). This is significant not for any new information it conveys, but rather for what the brothers choose to omit. They do not mention that they were all imprisoned, that one of them found the money on the return trip, or that 'the man' spoke to them in terms of life or death.[87] Instead, they give a positive gloss to the trip by ending with 'the man's' permission to trade in the land if they return with Benjamin, a fact only implied in earlier account.[88] Three times they focus on the issue of being 'honest men', which they hope will convince Jacob since he too knows that they are not spies. In other words, when they did deviate from the earlier account, they did so to make it more likely for Jacob to let Benjamin go.[89] It is perhaps significant that the pattern here of arrival, report and Jacob's lament echoes the earlier sequence of chapter 37.[90]

The discovery of the money in verse 35 is difficult to square with the earlier account of verse 27,[91] but this obviously discordant note is not explained. Instead, attention is drawn to Jacob's reaction of anticipated grief, and the inability of Reuben to persuade Jacob.[92] Jacob reacts to the discovery of the money in the same way as his sons, viewing it as bad news and the cause of trouble and dismay.

---

86   In relation to the phrase וַיֵּצֵא לִבָּם Wenham, *Genesis 16-50*, 409 comments that "[t]he expression is used only here, so its meaning is uncertain." Literally it means 'their hearts went out of them', translated by the NRSV as 'they lost heart'. Wenham cites Jacob, *Genesis*, 774 who suggests that the sense might be that of 'confusion' here, that is 'they did not know what to think'.

87   Sternberg, *Poetics*, 297; Savran, *Telling and Retelling*, 43-44; Lowenthal, *The Joseph Narrative*, 76; Alter, 'Joseph and his Brothers', 66.

88   Fretheim, 'The Book of Genesis', 629.

89   Leibowitz, *Studies in Bereshit*, 470-472; Wenham, *Genesis 16-50*, 412.

90   Westermann, *Genesis 37-50*, 112.

91   Sarna, *JPS Torah Commentary*, 296 and Sternberg, *Poetics*, 298 make some unlikely suggestions. Westermann, *Genesis 37-50*, 113 argues not unreasonably that the matter should be solved text critically.

92   White, *Narration and Discourse*, 260-261 suggests that Jacob comes close to charging them directly with the murder of Joseph, since the term 'bereaved' (שָׁכַל) in the *piel* characteristically refers to the murder of a child or person (Gen 27:45; 1 Sam 15:33; Ezek 14:15; Jer 15:7).

Reuben's proposal to offer his sons as surety is quickly rejected,[93] and perhaps Reuben himself is impliedly rejected as the spokesman for the brothers. Even more revealing is Jacob's implication that only Benjamin is precious to him, and that life would scarcely be worth living if Benjamin were to die. Benjamin is clearly another favourite like Joseph.[94] In chapter 37 Jacob sent the favourite son and lost him; this time he does not entrust the favourite to his other sons.

Genesis 43

Structure

The geographical settings are significant indicators of the structure of this chapter. The first fourteen verses are set in Canaan while verses 16-34 take place in Egypt. Verse 15 is a hinge or transitionary verse in which the first part concerns the departure from Canaan and the second the arrival in Egypt.[95] It is thus proposed to see the major divide in the chapter between verses 1-15a and 15b-34.

The second section should probably also be divided further into verses 15b-25, where the brothers deal with Joseph's steward, and verses 26-34, where the brothers share a meal with Joseph.[96]

43:1-15a - The Brothers Persuade Jacob to Send Benjamin

At the end of chapter 42 there appeared to be an obstacle to Joseph's plan, climaxing in verse 38 with Jacob refusing to allow Benjamin to go down to Egypt with his brothers. The initial section of this chapter concerns the overcoming of this complication, which enables Joseph's plan to proceed to

93 As Humphreys, *Joseph and His Family*, 45 points out, "can dead grandsons in any conceivable way make up for lost sons?" Similarly, Wildavsky, *Assimilation versus Separation*, 98 observes that a "vow to kill a man's grandchildren is not likely to appeal to him."

94 Jacob, *Genesis*, 289 concludes that "Benjamin is a second Joseph."

95 The allocation of verse 15 is difficult. Humphreys, *Joseph and His Family*, 62 and Coats, *Genesis*, 289 view it as a section on its own, on a par with verses 16-25 and 26-34. Fretheim, 'The Book of Genesis', 633 links it with verses 1-14 while Wenham, *Genesis 16-50*, 418, Westermann, *Joseph*, 75 and Longacre, *Joseph: A Story of Divine Providence*, 278-279 link it with the verses that follow.

96 Scholars such as Fretheim, 'The Book of Genesis', 633; Wenham, *Genesis 16-50*, 418; Humphreys, *Joseph and His Family*, 62-63 and Coats, *Genesis*, 288-289 have a two-fold division of vv.15/16-34, while Westermann, *Joseph*, 75; Sarna, *JPS Torah Commentary*, 297-302 prefer to retain these verses as one section.

the next stage. Thus, while Joseph is not present until verse 26 (except for verses 15b-16, when he does not meet with the brothers), he is portrayed as having a powerful influence on the events of this narrative. As Hamilton notes, "[t]he man in Egypt is in control. The game will have to be played by his rules."[97] He is, in verses 1-10, the man who has set the conditions for gaining more food, and who thus determines that Benjamin must travel to Egypt. In verses 11-14, he is the one who must be appeased.

Famine in the land of Canaan is mentioned emphatically at the beginning of verse 1 (והרעב כבד בארץ).[98] It is this irresistible fact - which was part of Joseph's interpretation of Pharaoh's dream - that will ensure that the immovable Jacob will change his mind. A reasonable time must have passed, since they have consumed all the grain which they brought from Egypt,[99] and are thus left with no choice but to return.

A key function of verses 3-10 is that they foreground Judah as the spokesman for the brothers, rather than the first-born Reuben.[100] In verse 2, Jacob tells the brothers to go, but in verse 3 it is Judah who replies on behalf of his brothers. Furthermore, this section gives a positive impression of Judah. Jacob appears to be pretending that the brothers could go down without Benjamin, and initially he does not give permission for him to go. Judah draws his father back to the hard facts, reminding Jacob that they were warned sternly not to return without their younger brother.[101] Yet, Judah also treats his father with due respect, for in verses 4-5 he defers to Jacob, saying that he will only take Benjamin to Egypt if his father sends him.[102] Judah firmly states the condition for another trip to Egypt (since, without Benjamin, it is both pointless and suicidal), but leaves the decision with Jacob.[103]

---

97 Hamilton, *Genesis Chapters 18-50*, 540. See also Savran, *Telling and Retelling*, 86, who argues that the repetition of Joseph's demand to see Benjamin (43:3, 5, 7) result in this being pictured as controlling what happens to Jacob's family.

98 Leupold, *Genesis*, 1060. Hamilton, *Genesis Chapters 18-50*, 539 points out that ארץ must refer here to Canaan.

99 In relation to the verb כלו, there may be a reference back to its previous use in Genesis 41:30 to speak of the famine consuming the land. So Hamilton, *Genesis Chapters 18-50*, 539.

100 Fretheim, 'The Book of Genesis', 633; Westermann, *Genesis 37-50*, 121; Sarna, *JPS Torah Commentary*, 297.

101 The use of the infinitive absolute intensifies the expression here: *GKC* § 113n. Sarna, *JPS Torah Commentary*, 298 notes that the phrase העד העד "expresses a solemn admonition tantamount to a threat". Westermann, *Genesis 37-50*, 121 suggests that it is used in the same sense of 'warn' in Exod 19:21, 23.

102 Hamilton, *Genesis Chapters 18-50*, 540.

103 Some commentators note that the exact words ascribed in verse 5 to Joseph do not appear in the previous narrative. Thus, for example, Savran, *Telling and Retelling*, 35. It appears, however, to be a fair and legitimate summary of what Joseph has

When Jacob (now called Israel) starts to level accusations against the brothers (verse 6, the plural form הרעתם is used), as a group they seek to justify themselves (verse 7, the plural ויאמרו). Judah alone is not sidetracked by Jacob (verse 8 - ויאמר יהודה), for he reasserts the central issue of the need to go in order to obtain grain. Judah sees that the present crisis is a matter of life and death (ונחיה ולא נמות),[104] as Jacob himself had previously said (42:2). He urges action (שלחה הנער אתי ונקומה ונלכה), introduces the new element of the survival of the children (גם־טפנו),[105] and reminds him that delay is costly (verse 10). Furthermore, his offer to be a surety responsible for Benjamin (הנער, verse 8)[106] is more balanced and sensible than the rash words of Reuben, who offered the death of his two sons in 42:37. What is recorded in verses 3-5, 8-10, is a respectful, well-argued speech.[107] In other words, Judah is being pictured quite positively as an effective spokesman for the brothers. This is an anticipation for the implied reader of the role that he will perform in chapter 44.[108] He appears to be a different Judah from the one who suggested selling Joseph to the Ishmaelites, and who in chapter 38 was afraid to allow his third son to continue the family seed.

When Jacob grudgingly agrees to send Benjamin, he still shows himself to be a strategist by sending along with his sons, an offering of choice fruits, nuts and other produce.[109] In verse 12, he orders them to take with them double the amount of money, apparently to return the money from the last trip.[110]

---

said, and no negative inference about Judah's reliability seems to be implied.

104 Sailhamer, 'Genesis', 250.

105 Leibowitz, *Studies in Bereshit*, 474. Wenham, *Genesis 16-50*, 421 notes that טף refers to younger ones who are dependent and vulnerable, and thus requiring the protection of their parents.

106 Hamilton, *Genesis Chapters 18-50*, 541-542 notes the apparent anomaly of referring to Benjamin as הנער, since he would be in his 30s, and suggests that it is due to his unmarried status. It is more likely, however, to be used for the literary reason of connecting Benjamin with the description of Joseph in 37:2, perhaps to make the parallel between the two favoured sons.

107 Fretheim, 'The Book of Genesis', 634. *Contra* Davidson, *Genesis 12-50*, 260.

108 Adar, *The Book of Genesis*, 150.

109 So Driver, *The Book of Genesis*, 353; Sarna, *JPS Torah Commentary*, 299.

110 H.M. Morris, *The Genesis Record: A Scientific and Devotional Commentary on the Book of Beginnings*. (Grand Rapids, Baker, 1976) 606 proposes that, in addition to the 10 bundles of the previous trip, they now take 10 more, giving 20 bundles of money. He suggests that the brothers may have noticed the ironical connection between there 20 bundles and the earlier 20 pieces of silver/money for which they sold Joseph (37:28). However, a. the brothers did not yet know it was Joseph, so no irony would have arisen; b. the money is never described as 20, so it is unlikely that even the reader would discern the irony or contrast. In fact, it may not have been 20 but 19 [omitting Benjamin] or 30 - double plus the original 10.

After he has planned, Jacob prays a prayer of blessing, committing them to the God (שַׁדָּי אֵל) who will superintend their travels (verse 14). Even in his prayer, Jacob singles out Benjamin by naming him, whereas he does not name the other brother. There is also dramatic irony for the implied reader, who knows that there are two 'other brothers' alive in Egypt.[111] There is no word from Benjamin, so the implied reader's focus is forced elsewhere. [112]

The import of Jacob's final words (וַאֲנִי כַּאֲשֶׁר שָׁכֹלְתִּי שָׁכָלְתִּי, verse 14) is difficult to assess. In its setting, it does not appear to be a trusting submission to the will of God, but more wallowing in self-pity.[113]

The trip to Egypt takes place quickly from a narrative point of view - in a single verse.[114] Ominously, the brothers are now simply described as הָאֲנָשִׁים, and this abandoning of relational or kinship terms lasts to the end of this chapter (verses 17, 18, 24), and largely continues until Joseph reveals himself in chapter 45.[115]

43:15b-25 - The Brothers Brought to Joseph's House

Now that the brothers stand before Joseph, the reader expects the pace of the action to increase. However, it is slowed down by a long section in which the brothers are taken to Joseph's house by his steward. This is ominous, for such extensive preliminaries to the meeting with Joseph did not take place on the first journey. Thus, a sense of anticipation and suspense is built up.[116]

On the previous journey, the brothers came without any apparent sense of anxiety. This time, although they expect accusation over the returned money, there are no charges of either spying or theft. They clearly wondered how this unpredictable official would arbitrarily use his position of power (verse 18).[117] Irony emerges as the very actions that they fear in verse 18 - being overpowered, their possessions seized and being sold into slavery - are virtually the same as the way they treated Joseph in chapter 37.[118]

Instead they are warmly received, invited to a meal and enquiries are

111 Fretheim, 'The Book of Genesis', 634; Roop, *Genesis*, 269.
112 Fretheim, 'The Book of Genesis', 635; Humphreys, *Joseph and His Family*, 70-71; Green, *What Profit for Us?*, 141.
113 However, Candlish, *The Book of Genesis*, 202 and Fretheim, 'The Book of Genesis', 635 view Jacob's words quite positively.
114 Von Rad, *Genesis*, 388; Westermann, *Genesis 37-50*, 123.
115 Longacre, *Joseph: A Story of Divine Providence*, 148, 149; Hamilton, *Genesis Chapters 18-50*, 548. The change in terminology also serves to heighten the impact for the reader of Benjamin being described as a brother of Joseph in verses 29-30.
116 Von Rad, *Genesis*, 38; Wenham, *Genesis 16-50*, 422.
117 Westermann, *Genesis 37-50*, 124; von Rad, *Genesis*, 388.
118 Hamilton, *Genesis Chapters 18-50*, 549.

made of their family. Their mind is set at rest by two events in verse 23. Firstly, the steward assured them the money had been paid, and then Simeon is released into their company. While the actions of Joseph in having the money returned are ascribed by the steward to the actions of their God, the implied reader will note that this has in fact been ordered by Joseph. For the reader, then, God is pictured as working through the actions of Joseph.[119] Events are attributed to God, but accomplished by Joseph's initiatives.

It is possible that there is a hint of dramatic irony in the steward's greeting (שלום לכם) in verse 23. This verse reintroduces the theme of שלום (begun in 37:4) and this will be picked up again in verses 27-28. Joseph's actions will finally restore שלום to the family of his brothers, and there is an implication here that this is what is needed.[120] In verse 24, further kindnesses - outward symbols of שלום - are extended to them in the provision (in a famine setting) of fodder for their donkeys as well as water to wash their feet.

The brothers wish to establish their innocence.[121] Their initiative in raising the issue of the money with the steward (verses 19-22) makes it seem that they pass the testing of their honesty, but it may also be consistent with returning the money out of fear or because Jacob makes them return it. The charge of spying is not mentioned again.

Yet, neither charge is of interest to the narrator, who focuses instead on the preparations for the meal. The brothers wash in anticipation of the meal (verse 24), and they prepare their gift or tribute for when Joseph will return home (verse 25).

43:26-34 - The Shared Meal

This final section is one where the pace of the action slows down still further. Within the flow of chapters 42-45 as a whole, this is an interlude. As such it serves several purposes, mainly preparing for subsequent events.

Firstly, it provides another occasion for the brothers, this time including Benjamin, to bow down before him. The action of bowing down is recorded twice (verses 26, 28), although on this occasion there is no explicit mention of the dream being fulfilled. Presumably, that connection has been sufficiently forged for the reader by 42:6, 9.

Secondly, it confirms that Joseph is concerned for the welfare of his brothers. It is rather astounding in verse 27 that Joseph first inquires about

---

119 Alter, 'Joseph and his Brothers', 67; Wenham, *Genesis 16-50*, 422.
120 Of course, Westermann, *Joseph*, 77 rightly notes that this "is the usual form of greeting for meeting people or receiving guests." It appears, however, to have a deeper, more suggestive meaning here as well.
121 Hamilton, *Genesis Chapters 18-50*, 549.

the שָׁלוֹם of his brothers, and only then about his father.[122] However, it is true that Joseph's concern for his half-brothers is eclipsed by his affection for his full brother, Benjamin. This is indicated by the idiom וישא עיניו (verse 29), which often implies that the object seen is of special significance.[123] He blesses Benjamin (verse 29) and is so overcome with emotion for his brother(s)[124] that he has to withdraw and weep (verse 30). There are powerful emotions welling up inside Joseph, but he knows that he has to control them in public, and release them in private, in order to continue the test. His character is seen not in him being emotionless, but in being able to show self-control in the face of strong emotions. The idiom נכמרו רחמיו ('his mercies were heated up') is elsewhere only found in 1 Kgs 3:26, where it describes a mother moved with love for her child.[125]

Thirdly, it gives a picture of apparent שָׁלוֹם, a foretaste of what is to come, and a backdrop or ideal by which to judge reality. This is suggested by the threefold use of שָׁלוֹם in verses 27 and 28,[126] and the shared meal in which they drink freely (verse 34). In the words of Humphreys "they are now lulled into trust."[127] It is, of course, not the full-orbed reality of שָׁלוֹם, but it is a glimpse of what could be if relationships can be restored.

Fourthly, it builds up suspense for both the characters and the implied reader as hints are dropped about a wider agenda, while at the same time conveying information about the Egyptian cultural setting. The separate seating arrangements are explained in verse 32, revealing a curiosity about Egyptian customs.[128] For the implied reader, the threefold division into Hebrews, Egyptians and Joseph may raise the question of where Joseph belongs. The seating of the brothers according to their age is ominous, and might alert them to realise that 'the man' knows more about them than they

---

122 *Contra* Turner, *Announcements of Plot*, 162 who argues that Joseph's first words to them are about his father's well-being (43:27), as if his plot to ensure Jacob also came down may have backfired. This argument is both too subtle, and also omits noticing that his first words follow his enquiry about the brothers and not his father.

123 So Wenham, *Genesis 16-50*, 423 citing Gen 13:10; 18:2; 22:4, 13; 33:1, 5; 37:25.

124 Sternberg, *Poetics*, 301 notes that the consonantal Hebrew text could mean either 'his brother' or 'his brothers'. However, the context surely supports the Masoretic pointing, indicating at this point Joseph's feelings for Benjamin.

125 Sarna, *JPS Torah Commentary*, 302; Davidson, *Genesis 12-50*, 263. Brueggemann, *Genesis*, 340 notes that the same root is used of God's passion for Israel in Hos 11:8.

126 Humphreys, *Joseph and His Family*, 95 describes this as "a veritable burst of šalôms."

127 Humphreys, *Joseph and His Family*, 114.

128 For the rationale behind eating separately see Sarna, *JPS Torah Commentary*, 302; Vergote, *Joseph en Égypte*, 188-189. There is no implied condemnation of the Egyptian practice.

have told him.[129] Of course, this section builds up suspense for the reader who recalls the earlier occasion on which the brothers ate in Joseph's presence (Gen 37:25).[130]

Finally, it begins to test how the brothers will react when favouritism is shown towards Benjamin.[131] In verse 34 Benjamin, the cherished younger child, is publicly given extra portions of food as a sign of special favour. The extra food here operates as an equivalent sign to the coat given to Joseph in chapter 37, but this time there is no reaction by the brothers.

Outwardly, all seems well at the end of this chapter, but it is clear to the implied reader that the matter is not yet finished.

Genesis 44

Structure

In many ways, chapter 44 is a continuation and climax of the preceding one, both thematically and structurally.[132] Fretheim sees three sections on the basis of location: verses 1-5 (in Egypt); verses 6-13 (along the way between Egypt and Canaan); verses 14-34 (again in Egypt, at Joseph's house).[133] However, this time the geographical marker does not seem to be very significant, as verse 4 emphasises that they had not gone far. Verses 1-13 seem rather to be part of one ill-fated journey.

Verses 14-34 could be treated as one section, but Judah's extensive speech (verses 18-34) seems sufficiently different from the to-and-fro conversation of verses 14-17 to justify it being treated as a separate unit.

---

129 Keil and Delitzsch, *The Pentateuch*, 362; Candlish, *The Book of Genesis*, 209. Ross, *Creation and Blessing*, 661 describes this as being, from the viewpoint of the brothers, "a troubling display of apparent divine intervention". Morris, *The Genesis Record*, 610 calculates that the odds of seating eleven people in order of age by chance was 39,917,000 to 1.

130 Sarna, *JPS Torah Commentary*, 302. Hamilton, *Genesis Chapters 18-50*, 555.

131 Lawson, *History of Joseph*, 223 proposes that Joseph's was testing "whether the superior honours given to Benjamin would kindle up envy in their breasts against him." Similarly, Ross, *Creation and Blessing*, 661; Morris, *The Genesis Record*, 610; Meyer, *Joseph: Beloved - Hated - Exalted*, 95; Fretheim, 'The Book of Genesis', 635; Sarna, *JPS Torah Commentary*, 302; Leupold, *Genesis*, 1076.

132 Von Rad, *Genesis*, 391.

133 For other views on structure see Fretheim, 'The Book of Genesis', 638; Hamilton, *Genesis Chapters 18-50*, 556-570; Ross, *Creation and Blessing*, 663; Humphreys, *Joseph and His Family*, 63; Coats, *Genesis*, 289-290 and Wenham, *Genesis 16-50*, 418-419.

Judah's speech, the longest oration recorded in Genesis,[134] seems to begin with a lengthy recapitulation of the past (verses 18-29) in which an opening request (verse 18) is followed by two reports of previous conversations (verses 19-23 and 24-29). Next comes a description of the consequences for Jacob if they return without Benjamin (verses 30-31). The section is rounded off by verses 32-34, which pivot around Judah's plea and proposal (verse 33). This central plea is bracketed by two reasons for the request, one in verse 32 and one in verse 34 (each introduced by כִּי).[135]

44:1-13 - An Ill-fated Journey

This section covers the aborted departure from Egypt, and the discovery of the cup in Benjamin's baggage. The events of verses 1-13 set up a scenario in which the brothers are faced with the temptation to leave their favoured younger brother behind, and return to their father. In other words, the choice they made in chapter 37 is now being forced upon them once more.[136] This is the climax of Joseph's scheme to see if the brothers had changed.[137] The central question is, as Speiser puts it, "Would the brothers revert to type, and welcome the opportunity to leave Benjamin, this time with a genuine excuse?"[138]

As in 42:25, Joseph commands that the brothers' bags be filled with grain, and each man's money be placed there also. A variety of reasons might be proposed for the return of the money, but this is a detail not picked up in the rest of the chapter.[139] It is not even clear whether the brothers know about the returned money, whether it is simply the extra money they brought with them that is returned, or if the food was given to them as a gift. The return of the money serves, however, a narrative purpose of making this intended return parallel to the safe journey home in chapter 42, which raises the expectations of the reader.

These hopeful expectations, however, are shattered in verse 2 by the command to place Joseph's silver cup in the bag of Benjamin (who is

---

134 Leibowitz, *Studies in Bereshit*, 483.
135 So M.A. O'Brien, 'The Contribution of Judah's Speech, Genesis 44:18-34, to the Characterization of Joseph', *CBQ* 59 (1997): 432; Coats, *Genesis*, 290. Wenham, *Genesis 16-50*, 426 has a similar structure but regards verses 30-32 as a description of the consequences for Jacob, while only verses 33-34 are allocated to Judah's plea. O'Brien's analysis appears to pay more careful attention to the syntax of verses 32-34.
136 Ackerman, 'Joseph, Judah and Jacob', 98; Westermann, *Joseph*, 86.
137 Westermann, *Joseph*, 90; Sternberg, *Poetics*, 302.
138 Speiser, *Genesis*, 335. Similarly, Lawson, *History of Joseph*, 226.
139 Lawson, *History of Joseph*, 228 suggests that the money was put into all the sacks so that the brothers would have no reason to suspect that Benjamin really was a thief. This seems to be the most likely option.

described as הקטן). The expectation is now that this cup will be discovered, but no reason is given at this stage for the action.

The reason for hiding the cup is revealed in Joseph's words of verses 4-5. His words focus on the specialness of the cup (he drinks from it and uses it for divination), but also on the theme of good and evil. [140] Joseph's first question is, in fact, למה שלמתם רעה תחת טובה (verse 4), as if the principle on view here is the supplanting of טובה by רעה. [141] His words conclude with the summary statement that the brothers have done wrong (הרעתם, the *hiphil* of רעע, verse 5). The brothers are thus charged with having done evil, and with repaying evil for good. The reader of the whole of the Joseph story can discern that this is precisely what the brothers did in chapter 37. Thus, their conscience is being pricked one more time before they have to choose whether or not to abandon Benjamin. this section is also an anticipation of the key motif in Gen 50:20, where both טבה and רעה recur, together with the idea of reversal.

Once, however, it is evident that the brothers are to be charged with stealing the cup, the information given in verse 2 becomes of paramount importance. The cup was to be hidden in Benjamin's sack. This climactic scheme has the effect of separating Benjamin from the brothers, and making him vulnerable. [142]

Dramatic irony emerges as the implied reader shares this knowledge with Joseph and his steward. This renders the brothers' protestations as both foolish and fatal. [143] While the reader knows where the cup is hidden, the brothers make the offer that the thief be put to death (the life/death motif again) and the rest will become slaves (verse 9). The steward, however, asks only that the thief will become a slave, while the rest of the brothers can depart freely (verse 10). [144] Even before the search, the reader knows that the brothers have thus agreed for Benjamin to be enslaved, while they go free. The test is finally in place, and has been so carefully crafted by Joseph to discern if the brothers had changed. [145] While many see Joseph's actions

---

140 The mention of the silver cup is omitted in the MT of verse 4, but it is present in the LXX, Syriac and Vulgate. Either the MT is defective at this point, or the cup as the subject must be implied by the subsequent questions in verse 5. The effect of its omission is to place even greater emphasis on the mention of 'good' and 'evil'. On the theological issues about Joseph possessing a cup for divination, see Von Rad, *Genesis*, 392; Westermann, *Genesis 37-50*, 132.

141 Sailhamer, 'Genesis', 253.

142 Wenham, *Genesis 16-50*, 424

143 Coats, *From Canaan to Egypt*, 42; Hamilton, *Genesis Chapters 18-50*, 562; Lowenthal, *The Joseph Narrative*, 92.

144 In other words, as Driver, *The Book of Genesis*, 358 points out, the steward is demanding much less than they are offering.

145 Keil and Delitzsch, *The Pentateuch*, 364. Some parallels between the brothers here and Joseph in chapter 37 are pointed out by Wenham, *Genesis 16-50*, 424 and

as despotic and cruel,[146] this study argues that this is not so when this chapter is viewed as part of the Joseph story as a whole, rather than as an isolated unit.

The search of the sacks comes to its inevitable end in verses 11 and 12, but it is verse 13 that is particularly suggestive. The brothers appear to show genuine grief as they tear their clothes (ויקרעו שמלתם),[147] an expression last used of Jacob's sorrow over the loss of Joseph in 37:34. The reappearance of the clothing motif is also significant in that Joseph's robe symbolised the message of the dream, and the motif re-emerges here as Joseph's plan is coming to a climax.

The genuineness of the brothers' grief is also supported by the fact that they do not go off home but return to Joseph's house in solidarity with Benjamin. They reaffirm their intention to stay with Benjamin, despite being told that they may depart as free men (verse 10). Their actions indicate a change in character, which leads in the remainder of the chapter to a focus on their words.

44:14-17 - The Brothers Return to Joseph's House

This brief section crystallises the choice for the brothers, and closes with Joseph repeating to them the same offer that the steward had made in verse 10.

There is a progressive narrowing of the narrative focus on to Judah. Having left as האנשים (verse 3), they return to Joseph's house as יהודה ואחיו (verse 14), and it is Judah who becomes their spokesman (ויאמר יהודה, verse 16; ויגש אליו יהודה ויאמר, verse 18).[148] This section thus leads nicely into Judah's speech in verses 18-34.

When the brothers appear before Joseph they fall to the ground (verse 14). This further fulfilment of Joseph's dreams[149] is neatly wedged between the clothing motif in verse 13, and the mention in verse 15 of Joseph divining, which casts the reader's minds back to Joseph's earlier role as the dreamer and interpreter of dreams. There thus appears to be a strong narrative hint that all these strange happenings are an outworking of the

Fretheim, 'The Book of Genesis', 639.
146 For example, Coats, *From Canaan to Egypt*, 83 suggests that "Joseph displays a despotic unconcern for his prey". See also Fritsch, 'God Was With Him', 27-28; M. Maher, *Genesis*. Old Testament Message, 2. (Wilmington: Glazier, 1982) 244; von Rad, *Genesis*, 391.
147 Wenham, *Genesis 16-50*, 425 regards this as "the first clear sign of fraternal solidarity".
148 Sternberg, *Poetics*, 305. Alter, *Genesis*, 262 notes that this grammatical device implies that Judah is the principal agent and the "thematically focused subject of the verb."
149 Hamilton, *Genesis Chapters 18-50*, 565. Turner, *Announcements of Plot*, 160.

dream of chapter 37.

It is along these lines that verse 15 should be interpreted. The focus there is not or whether it was right or wrong for Joseph to suggest that he divined, or whether or not he did so, or if he was unwisely boasting here.[150] Rather, the verse serves the narrative purpose of recalling the message of Joseph's dream.

Verse 16 is puzzling for the reader, who sees Judah confessing their guilt, (את־עון) but knows that the brothers were innocent of the theft of the cup (verse 2). If the brothers were not guilty in relation to the cup, the reader's mind is cast backwards to see if there is another event in view. It seemingly must refer to their corporate guilt in relation to the betrayal of Joseph, their deceit of Jacob, or a combination of the two.[151] Alternatively, as Westermann suggests, עון may take on the sense of punishment rather than guilt,[152] although this is not a natural way to read מצא in the expression האלהים מצא את־עון.[153]

Interestingly, this apparent confession is pushed aside, as Joseph offers the brothers a way to escape from any unjust punishment, if they are willing to leave their younger brother behind (verse 10). The question is sharply put to the brothers - will they leave behind one whom they know is innocent, in order to save and even advance themselves? Kidner makes an apt comparison when he comments that, "[l]ike the judgment of Solomon, the sudden threat to Benjamin was a thrust to the heart: in a moment the brothers stood revealed."[154] Here is a test that reaches the very core of the issue at stake.[155] The alternative that is offered to them is that they return to Jacob 'in peace' (לשלום).[156] Of course, Joseph has so far been guided by the

---

150 *Contra* Weeks, *Early Israelite Wisdom*, 95 who argues that Joseph is boasting here.

151 Sailhamer, 'Genesis', 254; Ackerman, 'Joseph, Judah and Jacob', 89; Wenham, *Genesis 16-50*, 425. Fretheim, 'The Book of Genesis', 640 makes the interesting connection that verse 16 is the only verse in the chapter that mentions God, and it is here that their guilt is faced.

152 Westermann, *Genesis 37-50*, 133-134.

153 See, for example, the combination of מצא and עון in Ps 36:3 [36:2E]; and Hos 12:9 [12:8E], where it clearly means guilt or wickedness, not punishment. Ross, *Creation and Blessing*, 664 notes that מצא occurs eight times in the narrative (verses 8, 9, 10, 12, twice in verses 16, and once more in verses 17 and 34). Thus it builds up to a peak in verse 16.

154 Kidner, *Genesis*, 204-205.

155 Von Rad, *Genesis*, 393; Sarna, *JPS Torah Commentary*, 223; Kendall, *God meant it for good*, 172-173; Lockwood, 'Tamar's Place', 40; Sternberg, *Poetics*, 303, 306; Ross, *Creation and Blessing*, 663; Fretheim, 'The Book of Genesis', 639.

156 Davidson, *Genesis 12-50*, 268 suggests that 'in peace' in its context must mean something like 'unharmed' or 'safe and sound'. While this is conceivably how the brothers would have understood Joseph's words, they would have a fuller meaning for the implied reader.

view that a lasting שלום can only be achieved by reconciliation in the family.[157] The brothers have previously tried to obtain שלום by removing a brother. Joseph is thus testing whether the brothers are seeking an escape from their troubles or a fuller שלום. The implied reader awaits the response from the brothers with anticipation.

44:18-34 - Judah's Speech

Judah's speech is anomalous in that the longest speech in such a Joseph-centred story is given to Judah rather than to Joseph. Of course, the very length of the speech has the important literary effects of retarding the narrative pace and building suspense, but it may serve other functions as well.

One recent suggestion would, if sustained, undermine the view of Joseph's character that is argued for in this book. O'Brien has proposed that Judah's speech "provides a subtle but effective exposure of *Joseph* [emphasis mine] as a person with a deeply flawed character like his brothers."[158] He proposes this on the basis of differences between Judah's reports in verses 19-23 and 24-29, and the earlier accounts in chapter 42 and 43. O'Brien objects to the usual 'benign' characterisation of Joseph, suggesting that Joseph's desire for power over his brothers (44:23) and his desire to have Benjamin, blinded him to the effect this had on his father. Furthermore, there was no need to test the brothers since chapter 42 already tells us that they were changed men.[159] The 'flawed' Joseph is only transformed in chapter 45, when he reveals himself to be "someone who has been prepared to place his father in mortal danger for his own advantage."[160]

This study has argued for a different reading of these events. Of course, it is difficult to discern precisely when the brothers did change, but the change was clearly not established until Judah's speech in chapter 44. The events of chapter 42 only show that they were innocent in this case of putting a favoured younger brother at risk, in that they did not mention Benjamin's existence maliciously. It does not show that they would not sacrifice a younger brother if they could gain advancement through doing

---

157 Baldwin, *The Message of Genesis 12-50*, 186 points out that their return without Benjamin would not, in fact, bring about an effective reconciliation.

158 O'Brien, 'The Contribution of Judah's Speech', 430.

159 O'Brien, 'The Contribution of Judah's Speech', 436, 439. O'Brien's evidence that the brothers had changed is that 43:7, and the detail of chapter 42 show that it was not from any evil motive that they divulged the existence of Benjamin; and that they showed no hostility toward a favoured younger brother in contrast to their attitude in 37:20.

160 O'Brien, 'The Contribution of Judah's Speech', 445.

so. This is still untested until chapter 44. Indeed, O'Brien's view of the brothers is arguably too benign.

In relation to Joseph testing his brothers, Joseph's strong expressions of emotion (42:24; 43:30; 45:1), and his expression of concern for their father's well-being (43:7, 27; 45:3), seem to reveal his internal anguish over the pain which was necessarily caused in the test.[161] Yet, it has been argued that Joseph's test was justified by a need to bring about lasting reconciliation to a strife-torn family. Thus, despite many insightful features of O'Brien's article, his essential thesis is not persuasive.

Judah's speech instead serves four positive functions within the Joseph story as a whole. Firstly, it cleverly summarises the story for the reader immediately prior to the climax in chapter 45.[162] There is a detailed review of past events in verses 19-29, followed by Judah's explanation of the consequences (introduced by ועתה, verse 30)[163] and his plea to be enslaved in place of his brother (verse 33). This recapitulation of the story serves to provide a panoramic perspective for the reader, and directs attention to Judah's climactic request.[164]

Secondly, as it retells the story from the viewpoint of the brothers, it provides Joseph - and perhaps also the reader - with some important further information. The very fact that Judah speaks (as earlier in verse 16) indicates that he is effectively pre-eminent among the brothers, and now their destiny hangs on his words.[165] This provides Joseph with insight about the dynamics among the brothers.

While Joseph would have been familiar with the details narrated in verses 19-24, he could not have known about the events in Canaan. In relation to Jacob, Joseph learns that his father believes him to be torn to pieces (verse 28), and that Benjamin now has a special place in Jacob's affections (verses 30-31). In addition, Joseph discovers that Judah has offered himself as a surety (ערב) for the boy (verse 32), and is prepared to honour that obligation by offering to remain in his place (verse 33). Joseph also learns about the danger to Jacob's life if Benjamin does not return (verses 29, 31, 34), and of Judah's concern for his father's life (verse 34).[166]

Thirdly, Judah's speech contains features common in the addresses of

---

161 *Contra* O'Brien, 'The Contribution of Judah's Speech', 441 who speaks of "Joseph's seeming disregard for his father in 44:23."

162 Westermann, *Genesis 37-50*, 137 sees the narrator presenting "the whole story in a nutshell in the argumentation underlying Judah's request."

163 Westermann, *Genesis 37-50*, 136.

164 Von Rad, *Genesis*, 394 and Westermann, *Joseph*, 88-89 outline how the material in verses 19-29 is carefully chosen for its value in grounding the request of verse 33.

165 Calvin, *A Commentary on Genesis*, 370.

166 Savran, 'The Character as Narrator', 9; Savran, *Telling and Retelling*, 87. Westermann, *Genesis 37-50*, 136 comments that "Joseph now hears for the first time what happened at home when the brothers came back without him."

wise courtiers, several of which are prominent. There is, for example, much deferential language such as אדון and עבד. In the opening verse of the speech (verse 18), this tone is set by the double use of both אדני and עבדך, as well as the comparison with Pharaoh (כי כמוך כפרעה). Such deferential language is commonly used by courtiers in addressing superiors, and this is consistent with the view that part of the role of this speech is to give a model to aspiring courtiers, a common theme in wisdom books like Proverbs.[167] Even Niditch, who calls Judah's discourse "a plodding, Polonius-like speech"[168], highlights that it is a speech at home in a court setting.

The events are also shrewdly and selectively narrated in order to advance the brother's cause. He omits certain key events, threats or accusations that might make Joseph defensive and therefore unsympathetic. There is, for example, no mention of the accusation of spying (42:9, 14, 30), Simeon's arrest (42:19, 33), the days they spent in custody (42:17), the threat of being put to death (42:18, 20), the finding of the money (42:28, 35), the theft of the silver cup (44:4, 12) or Benjamin's innocence (44:2).[169] As Hamilton summarises, "Judah thoughtfully recalls only the portions of previous conversations that will be helpful in gaining Benjamin's release."[170]

There is also in the speech a fine balance of submission and initiative. Judah's submissiveness is shown in his deferential language, in his omission of certain events, and in his willingness to accept that one person must be enslaved. He does not plead for mercy, or forgiveness, nor does he protest that Benjamin is innocent.[171] Yet his words exhibit great boldness as he requests this powerful Egyptian official to change his decision, without seeming defiant or rebellious.[172] Unlike the earlier panic-filled words of the brothers (42:10-11, 13; 43:20-22; 44:7-9), the words of Judah are pro-active not reactive. Judah moves from details known by Joseph, to information about Jacob that Joseph could not know. This is likely to be court etiquette, as Judah lays the groundwork for his request at the end, a request that cannot be simply stated baldly. Since 'the man' had earlier asked about their father (43:27), Judah targets the deleterious effect of Joseph's action on Jacob.[173] It is a speech designed to persuade Joseph, to enable him to change his decision and not lose face. He will still enslave someone for the

167 Humphreys, *Joseph and His Family*, 178 suggests that "Genesis 44:16-34 is an extended model of how one should address a superior in correct court style."
168 Niditch, *Underdogs and Tricksters*, 89.
169 Wenham, *Genesis 16-50*, 425, 426; Sarna, *JPS Torah Commentary*, 306; Westermann, *Genesis 37-50*, 135; Savran, *Telling and Retelling*, 59.
170 Hamilton, *Genesis Chapters 18-50*, 569.
171 Savran, 'The Character as Narrator', 7 notes that Judah's request is basically that he be permitted to fulfil the pledge he made to Jacob.
172 Sarna, *JPS Torah Commentary*, 306; von Rad, *Genesis*, 394; Gibson, *Genesis*, 287.
173 Savran, 'The Character as Narrator', 7; Wenham, *Genesis 16-50*, 425.

theft of the cup, but he will in addition have been magnanimous towards the aging Jacob. If Joseph rejects Judah's plea, the implication is that Joseph will be responsible for Jacob's demise.[174]

Thus, in many ways, Judah is presented here as having become quite similar to Joseph who, in chapter 41, was able to seize the opportunity and speak persuasively in a court setting. Judah has thus learned to acquire some wisdom-like traits,[175] and displays them in this argued presentation. This gives a hint to the implied reader that Judah, as well as Joseph, will be prominent in what follows.[176] It also reinforces the wisdom-like traits already shown by Joseph, since Judah is portrayed more positively precisely at the point where he changes to be more like Joseph.

The fourth function served by this speech is to depict the apparent change in character of the brothers, as represented by Judah. Coats, however, has argued that there is not a character change in Judah, but only a decision to act differently towards his brother in the midst of a crisis. He suggests that Judah speaks as he does, simply because of his surety oath and a fear for his father's life.[177] In other words, they are only dependent on circumstances, rather than representing a transformed moral nature.

However, Judah's willingness to offer himself as surety itself indicates a substantial change,[178] while his concern for his father's life contrasts strongly with the lack of concern shown by the brothers at the end of chapter 37.[179] This concern for his father seems to be a genuine concern, not merely a rhetorical tool, since Judah's heightened emotions lead him to omit the deferential language used up to this point.[180]

The logic of the narrative also supports the notion that the brothers have changed, since Joseph in chapters 42-44 has deliberately recreated a scenario similar to that of chapter 37, in order to see how the brothers will respond.[181] The fact that Judah now refuses to leave behind the favoured younger brother surely implies a significant character change.[182] This is also supported by the length and evident passion of Judah's speech. While Judah has become a skilful orator, he is portrayed in the narrative as genuinely

174 Savran, *Telling and Retelling*, 61.
175 Adar, *The Book of Genesis*, 151-152.
176 Longacre, *Joseph: A Story of Divine Providence*, 55-56.
177 Coats, *From Canaan to Egypt*, 43.
178 So, for example, Hamilton, *Genesis Chapters 18-50*, 570.
179 Alter, *The Art of Biblical Narrative*, 175; Sternberg, *Poetics*, 308.
180 Lowenthal, *The Joseph Narrative*, 101; Humphreys, *Joseph and His Family*, 48, who both note that Judah no longer describes himself as עבדך in verse 34.
181 Thus Westermann, *Genesis 37-50*, 137; Alter, 'Joseph and his Brothers', 68; Alter, *The Art of Biblical Narrative*, 174; Hamilton, *Genesis Chapters 18-50*, 570.
182 Von Rad, *Genesis*, 395; Herbert, *Genesis 12-50*, 139; Speiser, *Genesis*, 33; Humphreys, *Joseph and His Family*, 48-49; Savran, *Telling and Retelling*, 60.

repentant.[183] Since Judah was the key playmaker in the betrayal of Joseph, so he is the one who takes the initiative to sacrifice himself for the favoured younger brother. This is, thus, a significant turning point in the whole narrative, and will lead naturally to Joseph's revealing of himself in the next scene.

Genesis 45

Structure

While this chapter continues on closely from chapter 44,[184] there are several distinct sections within it. The first scene appears to be the self-revealing of Joseph in verses 1-15, a section nicely marked off by the motif of weeping used as an inclusio in verses 1-2 and 14-15.[185] An indication of the significance of this unit is the fact that Humphreys labels it the 'resolution'.[186] It is composed of four sub-sections: Joseph's self-disclosure (verses 1-4); Joseph's reassurance of his brothers (verses 5-8); Joseph's arrangements for his family (verses 9-13); and the apparent reconciliation (verses 14-15).[187]

It is not clear whether the next section, beginning at verse 16, should end with verse 20 or verse 24.[188] However, verses 21-24 read most naturally as

---

183 Indeed, Wenham, *Genesis 16-50*, 431 suggests that "[n]o more moving example of true contrition and repentance is to be found in Scripture, unless it be the parable of the prodigal son".

184 As is pointed out by Westermann, *Genesis 37-50*, 141, who rightly notes that verses 1-8 are the answer to Judah's request in 44:18-34; also Wenham, *Genesis 16-50*, 419.

185 Fretheim, 'The Book of Genesis', 643.

186 Humphreys, *Joseph and His Family*, 64. Similarly, Wenham, *Genesis 16-50*, 418; Brueggemann, *Genesis*, 343. Longacre, 'Who Sold Joseph into Egypt?', 81.

187 Some commentators (such as Humphreys, *Joseph and His Family*, 64; Sarna, *JPS Torah Commentary*, 308-309) divide verses 1-8 into verses 1-3 and 4-8. However, it appears better to read verse 4 as continuing and amplifying the disclosure begun in verses 1 and 3. In verse 4 Joseph adds אֲחִיכֶם to his previous self-description in verse 3. Verse 5 then begins the new unit of reassurance, starting with וְעַתָּה. Westermann, *Genesis 37-50*, 142 suggests that verses 1-8 is divided between verses 1-2 and 3-8. This is to miss the inclusio between verses 1-2 and 14-15.

188 Brueggemann, *Genesis*, 343; Candlish, *The Book of Genesis*, 219; and Sarna, *JPS Torah Commentary*, 310-311 make a division after verse 20. Those who opt for verse 24 as the end of this section include Longacre, *Joseph: A Story of Divine Providence*, 304-305; Wenham, *Genesis 16-50*, 419; Coats, *Genesis*, 290; Humphreys, *Joseph and His Family*, 64.

the implementing of the instructions of Pharaoh as evident in verse 21

ויתן להם יוסף עגלות על־פי פרעה

Furthermore, Joseph, the implementer of Pharaoh's will, is the subject of most of the verbs in verses 21-24, and they are, therefore, best regarded as part of verses 16-24.

The remaining section, comprising verses 25-28, centres on Jacob in Canaan and his response to the news of Joseph's new situation.

The three sections thus focus on the key characters of Joseph (verses 1-15), Pharaoh (verses 16-20, and to a lesser extent in verses 21-24) and Jacob (verses 25-28).[189] This sets out quite neatly the structure of the chapter.

45:1-15 - Joseph Reveals his Identity

As this section is the climax of chapters 42-45, it may well provide further insight into Joseph's motives in testing his brothers. It will certainly be a vital unit for determining the thrust of the story as a whole.

VERSES 1-4 - JOSEPH'S SELF-DISCLOSURE

What emerges strongly here is that Joseph releases powerful emotions.[190] Although he had earlier controlled the public showing of his tears (42:24; 43:30), there is no longer any need to continue his ruse. Von Rad had proposed that Joseph's self-control, reminiscent of the book of Proverbs, contributed to picturing him as a wisdom figure.[191] Crenshaw rightly pointed out that, in this section, Joseph is hardly in control of his emotions.[192] Weeks has also responded that the root אפק, used here in the *hithpael* with the sense of 'self-control', is nowhere used in the wisdom corpus.[193]

However, this debate appears to have missed the reason for the mention of Joseph's tears. The reference to Joseph's strong emotions at this point neither confirms nor precludes Joseph being identified as a wisdom figure. Rather, it provides the implied reader with some insight into Joseph's

---

189 This was pointed out by Candlish, *The Book of Genesis*, 219, although he divided the last two sections differently, seeing Jacob's piety in verses 21-28.

190 Hamilton, *Genesis Chapters 18-50*, 571 translates not as 'could no longer control himself' [NRSV] but that Joseph was 'unable to give vent to his emotions'. He wants to express his emotions, not control them. In this Hamilton is following R. Gordis, *The Word and the Book* (New York: KTAV, 1976) 188-189.

191 Von Rad, 'Ancient Wisdom', 295-296.

192 Crenshaw, 'Method', 137.

193 Weeks, *Early Israelite Wisdom*, 94.

motives in perpetuating his disguise. Immediately after the narration of Judah's speech giving evidence of the character change in the brothers, Joseph releases the powerful emotions that he has had to keep in check.[194] At first, it may not be clear to the readers (it was not clear to the brothers - verse 3b) whether the emotions would turn out to be anger or affection, but whichever it will be certainly provides crucial insight into what has motivated Joseph to act as he has done. Joseph's exhortation for the brothers to come closer (verse 4) shows that his attitude is one of invitation, not condemnation, and his words of reassurance (verses 5-8) make it clear that Joseph welcomes the brothers with acceptance and forgiveness.[195]

This release of emotion therefore serves a key literary function of clarifying the motivation of Joseph as one of affection rather than revenge.[196] The hyperbolic descriptions of the result clauses in verse 2 narrate that his weeping was so strong that it was heard by מצרים (without qualification, as if it refers to all Egypt) and by בית פרעה, even though all Joseph's attendants had been required to leave the room.

Thus, the role of the opening two verses of this unit is to eliminate for the implied reader the possibility that Joseph acted to secure vengeance against those who had wronged him. Rather than preclude him from being a wisdom figure because of his lack of self-control, it enhances the positive characterisation of Joseph.

This unit also functions to emphasise Joseph's self-disclosure. This is hinted at in the anticipatory summary in verse 1 (בהתודע יוסף אל־אחיו), and is developed in verses 3 and 4. Joseph's revelation is initially very brief (אני יוסף, verse 3), and filled out with more detail in verse 4

אני יוסף אחיכם אשר־מכרתם אתי מצרימה

Both disclosures reveal something about Joseph. Joseph's words in verse 3 highlight how important Jacob was to Joseph.[197] After a very brief identification of himself, there is no call for any apology.[198] Instead, Joseph immediately asks about the welfare of his father (אני יוסף העוד אבי חי). Joseph longs to know if his father is still alive, which will lead in verse 9 to Joseph's call to Jacob to come down to him in Egypt. The picture is one of Joseph as a dutiful and loyal son.

---

194 Maher, *Genesis*, 249.
195 Westermann, *Genesis 37-50*, 148.
196 Sailhamer, 'Genesis', 256.
197 Savran, *Telling and Retelling*, 63. Lowenthal, *The Joseph Narrative*, 103 suggests that Joseph asks a question that he has already asked in order to 'break the ice', and give the brothers a chance to say something, but more appears to be happening than this alone.
198 So Redford, *Biblical Story of Joseph*, 170.

The shock appears to be too much for the brothers, who know that they have betrayed and enslaved the one who now has power over them. As Joseph was silent in chapter 37, they are now speechless and unable to answer (verse 3) as the tables have been turned. Indeed, they are not recorded as saying anything until they are back with Jacob in 45:26 (although it is mentioned in 45:15 that they talked with him). They are 'dismayed' (נבהלו), perhaps because of what they have done, or perhaps that their deeds will now be made known to Jacob.[199]

Joseph's second self-disclosure is also telling. He does not describe himself as 'your lord' but as 'your brother' (אחיכם, verse 4). Joseph reveals that he still regards them as brothers, not strangers.

The mention of their having sold him into Egypt - which is added only after he has described himself as their brother - does not appear, in this context of reconciliation, to be an instance of tightening the screws still further.[200] Rather, it contributes to the story in two ways. Firstly, it discloses to the brothers some information which only Joseph could have known since, for obvious reasons, they had not mentioned enslaving their brother in their earlier addresses.[201] Secondly, it leads nicely into the thematic or theological analysis of the sale as God working behind-the-scenes (verses 5-8).[202]

Finally, the setting of the reconciliation scene is significant. This part of the story climaxes not in the court (unlike chapters 39-41), but in the family.[203] Joseph is still in his house (44:14) not in a public or official location. Moreover, he sends his attendants, as symbols perhaps of the Egyptian court, out of his presence (verse 1).[204] Joseph is alone with his brothers and it is in this family context that reconciliation begins to take place. Chapters 42-45 thus seem to involve the attempted restoration of שלום in the family, with the court only in the background.

VERSES 5-8 - JOSEPH'S REASSURANCE OF THE BROTHERS

This section serves as a stable platform from which the implied reader can look back over the Joseph story and gain some perspective. Joseph is reflecting, as their brother and as a reliable character, on the events of the past, and his understandings have the ring of truth about them. Verse 6

---

199 White, *Narration and Discourse*, 268.

200 Candlish, *The Book of Genesis*, 219-220; Lawson, *History of Joseph*, 259.

201 Lowenthal, *The Joseph Narrative*, 103 rightly points out that "[o]nly by showing that he knows their secret does he prove his identity beyond doubt."

202 Von Rad, *Genesis*, 398.

203 Westermann, *Genesis 37-50*, 142.

204 Calvin, *A Commentary on Genesis*, 376 also proposes that he dismisses his attendants because he does not want to broadcast his brothers' crimes. If so, this appears secondary to the effect of focusing on the family, not the court.

functions partly to remind the reader that his interpretation of Pharaoh's dream is being fulfilled. If Joseph was correct is his assertion of what God was doing in the years of plenty and famine (41:25, 28, 32), he is entitled to be trusted in his analysis of God's purpose in bringing Jacob's family down to Egypt.[205] Joseph's description of his current status (verse 8b) also provides tangible corroborative evidence of this being a purposeful relocation.

What, then, emerges from Joseph's analysis of the situation? The primary theme is that God has sent Joseph, which is found in verses 5, 7, and 8

כי למחיה שלחני אלהים לפניכם (verse 5)
וישלחני אלהים לפניכם (verse 7)
לא־אתם שלחתם אתי הנה כי האלהים (verse 8)

The significance of this theme of God sending Joseph arises from the fact that the narrator has not previously drawn attention to this, but instead has explained the descents to slavery, to Egypt and to prison being caused by human agents. Now Joseph is asserting that the active but hidden hand of God was at work, even though all the actions could be accounted for in human terms. Although God has not appeared to Joseph, he has been busily working behind the scenes to bring about those events foretold in the dreams of chapters 37, 40 and 41.

There is some dispute as to whether this constitutes a concept of providence, and, furthermore, whether it is an example of a 'wisdom-like element'. Westermann concedes that "this story is all about … God's rule over human activity, God's guidance of destinies which can totally transform human plans and make out of them something which corresponds to God's plan".[206] Yet, he argues that this is wrongly understood as God's providence, and that, in any event, the use of the *qatal* form in verse 5

205 Hamilton, *Genesis Chapters 18-50*, 575 rightly notes that "[t]he concepts expressed in v. 5 are not those of the narrator, but of Joseph." However, the implications of this are moot. Miscall, 'Analogies', 31 argues that neither the narrator nor God endorses Joseph's view. D.J.A. Clines, 'God in the Pentateuch: Reading against the Grain', in *Interested Parties: The Ideology of Writers and Readers of the Hebrew Bible*. JSOTSup, 205; Gender, Culture, Theory, 1. (Sheffield: Sheffield Academic Press, 1995), 195 comments in passing on Gen 45:8 and 50:20, observing that these words of Joseph's do not necessarily represent the narrator's point of view. This is argued in a more sustained way by Fung, *Victim and Victimizer*. However, the effect of including this view of Joseph in the climactic scene surely implies that it is endorsed by the narrator. It is also nowhere denied by God or the narrator, and Joseph's previously reliable words engender a narrative expectation that these words can be trusted.

206 Westermann, *Joseph*, 96.

would preclude any idea of God's ongoing providential activity.[207] The grammatical point is hardly decisive, for it could simply refer to the single clearest example of God being providentially at work. Whether one wishes to label the phenomenon as providence is more of a technical point, but in a general sense it appears to be a patent example of God's behind-the-scenes activity. Instead of God himself intervening, or appearing to others to make them act in certain ways, all that is seen in the story thus far are the apparently unprompted actions of a wide range of human beings - his brothers and father, a shepherd, traders, gaolers, his master's wife, court officials, Pharaoh and so on. Yet, both the good and the bad combine together to further God's ultimate purposes.[208] This is a distinctive feature of the Joseph cycle that differentiates it from the other patriarchal stories that precede it.[209]

More difficult is the question of whether this concept of God working behind-the-scenes has a wisdom affinity.[210] While similar ideas are reflected in the book of Proverbs (for example, 16:4, 7; 9; 19:21; 20:24), a fuller discussion of this issue will be undertaken in chapter 10.

Another key theme that emerges from verses 5-8 is that of 'life' in the sense of survival. The goal of Joseph being sent ahead was לְמִחְיָה (verse 5) and, more elaborately, in verse 7

$$\text{לשום לכם שארית בארץ ולהחיות לכם לפליטה גדלה}$$

The current and continuing famine of verse 6 is a real threat to life. This theme of life is picked up later in the chapter in verses 26 and 28. Again there is considerable debate over whether the wisdom dichotomy of life and death is in view, or whether the concern is rather the patriarchal motif of keeping alive the promised Abrahamic line in the face of threats.[211] In the context of the Genesis 37-50, the two foci merge, as Joseph brings life to both the line of promise, and to much of the Ancient Near East. It is thus possible that both are envisaged, particularly since the text does not

207 Westermann, *Genesis 37-50*, 143.
208 Dillmann, *Genesis*, 402; Morris, *The Genesis Record*, 626 comments that a "multiplicity of seemingly accidental and unrelated events - events which seemed to be ugly and difficult at the time - is gradually woven together by an unseen divine hand into a glorious tapestry in which every portion is ideally situated in its proper and unique place."
209 Gibson, *Genesis*, 291-292; Skinner, *Genesis*, 487.
210 Those who see a wisdom affinity here include von Rad, *Genesis*, 400 and Humphreys, *Joseph and His Family*, 179. Those who see no wisdom affinity include Westermann, *Genesis 37-50*, 143 and Weeks, *Early Israelite Wisdom*, 108.
211 V.P. Hamilton, *Handbook on the Pentateuch* (Grand Rapids: Baker, 1982) 135 argues that it is primarily the patriarchal motif which is represented. However, Fretheim, 'The Book of Genesis', 644-645 suggests that both might be in view.

preclude either so as to make the choice clear for the implied reader.[212]

Some have argued that the use in verse 7 of the word 'remnant' (שארית) - a key concept in the Hebrew Bible for the survival of the covenant line - implies that only the covenant promises are in view in verses 5-8.[213] While the word שארית occurs only here in the Pentateuch,[214] the idea is clearly evident in the Noah story, where God's concern is for all humanity.[215]

The significance of verses 5-8 should not be under-estimated. They are, in many ways, like a junction where key themes, motifs and strands intersect. Thus, the two themes that are prominent here are common to both wisdom and non-wisdom interests. There is the theme of 'life', and that of 'God's overarching control'. If this is a viewing platform for the Joseph narrative, this may well be significant in explaining how the 'wisdom-like elements' are connected to the covenant promise strand. It is here that the two intersect because they have ideas in common. However, in the remainder of the story each strand is free to develop its own distinctiveness and leave the other behind. It has been suggested that 'wisdom-like elements' have been prominent in chapters 39-41 and probably also chapters 42-44. The covenant promise idea will become progressively more visible in the rest of the Joseph story, as the book of Genesis comes to an end.

The point that is not explicitly made in verses 5-8 is that Joseph's wise human actions have brought about the situation in which they now find themselves. This is, perhaps, because so much weight has been placed here in these earlier chapters, so that it is now time to balance the picture with other emphases.

Of course, if one were to take the view that wisdom elements are entirely absent in verses 5-8, it would still be significant that these covenant promise ideas are very close to similar concepts in the wisdom tradition. Thus, they may be seen as a summary of what the Joseph story contributes to the book of Genesis or Pentateuch as a whole. It could still be argued that Joseph's 'wisdom-like' actions in chapters 39-44 were the means God used to bring about his purpose of preserving life.

While the above-mentioned issues are clearly the most crucial in this

---

212 Westermann, *Genesis 37-50*, 144.

213 For example, Hamilton, *Genesis Chapters 18-50*, 576; Coats, *From Canaan to Egypt*, 46; Davidson, *Genesis 12-50*, 272; Keil and Delitzsch, *The Pentateuch*, 366; Vawter, *On Genesis*, 435.

214 Westermann, *Genesis 37-50*, 144; J.J. Scullion, *Genesis: A Commentary for Students, Teachers, and Preachers*. Old Testament Studies, 6. (Collegeville: Liturgical Press, 1992) 323.

215 See G.F. Hasel, *The Remnant: The History and Theology of the Remnant Idea from Genesis to Isaiah*. 3rd edn. (Berrien Springs: Andrews University Press, 1980) 135-147 where the remnant idea is traced back to Noah. Lowenthal, *The Joseph Narrative*, 104 also notes some connections with the story of Noah.

section, a number of other minor matters also emerge. Firstly, Joseph's attitude to his brothers remains, as in verses 1-4, one of acceptance not condemnation. Although he refers to their selling of him, this fades into the background when Joseph foregrounds the active working of God to achieve his purposes. The force of verse 5 is that the brothers should stop being distressed or angry at themselves

ועתה אל־תעצבו ואל־יחר בעיניכם

There is nothing in the text to imply that a full reconciliation between Joseph and his brothers has not taken place.[216] While the later incident of 50:15-21 suggests that the brothers may not be fully sure of Joseph's forgiveness, there is no hint in the rest of the Joseph story that Joseph is not, for his part, fully reconciled to the brothers who have wronged him.

Secondly, it has already been argued that verse 6 serves to secure the implied reader's bearings in time. However, the mention that there are five more years of famine signals to the reader that Jacob is not likely to remain in Canaan. His family has already been severely affected by the famine (42:2; 43:1-2), although only two years have passed.

Thirdly, Joseph's high position in Egypt, outlined in verse 8, means that Jacob can safely come down to this foreign land. The phrase אב לפרעה has been explained by Vergote as most likely a transposition of the Egyptian title *it ntr* ('father of God'), but which has been modified quite naturally by the Hebrew author to avoid any blasphemous sense that it might otherwise have had.[217] In any event, the balance of verse 8 makes it clear that Joseph is powerful since he is not only אדון over Pharaoh's house, but also 'ruler over all the land of Egypt' (משל בכל־ארץ מצרים). There is not even any mention of his being second in command.

VERSES 9-13 - JOSEPH'S ARRANGEMENTS FOR THE FAMILY

As a unit, this is neatly bracketed by verses 9 and 13. In both verses, there is a call to 'make haste' (מהר); in both, a concern for אבי; in both, a reference to Jacob coming down (ירד); and in both, there is an emphasis of Joseph's exalted position in Egypt (verse 9, אדון לכל־מצרים; verse 13, כל־כבודי במצרים). In terms of content, the section comprises Joseph's message to be given to Jacob (verses 9-11), and Joseph's exhortation to his brothers.

Joseph is sketched in these verses as one who plans well,[218] and as one who will act to secure the future of the covenant line. As in verse 8

---

216 *Contra* Fretheim, 'The Book of Genesis', 643.

217 Vergote, *Joseph en Égypte*, 114.

218 Adar, *The Book of Genesis*, 153 views them as "words of wisdom in the same vein as were his statements to Pharaoh in chapter 41."

(directed to the brothers), he now assures his father that he is able to provide abundantly since he is Lord over all Egypt (verse 9). He explains his plan to settle them near him in the fertile region of Goshen (verse 10).[219] Of course, this could be understood as a further fulfilment of the dream of chapter 37, for his father and brothers will now be under Joseph's beneficial rule in this foreign land.

An interesting feature to notice in verses 9 and 13 is that Joseph displays a delight in the splendour of Egypt. This is not very common in the biblical accounts, where there is much more often a focus on the idolatry or depravity of foreign countries. Yet it is again a feature of the wisdom strand to have a more international focus and a willingness to explore other cultures.

The need for them to migrate to Egypt is outlined in verse 11 as there are still five more years of famine. Indeed, verse 11 speaks not only of Jacob's descendants being kept alive (the least that was necessary), but also that Joseph would provide for them (וכלכלתי אתך) so that they will not even be impoverished (תורש).

An interesting question posed by these verses is whether they reveal anything of Joseph's attitude to his brothers. Hamilton proposes that Joseph distances himself from his brothers in verses 9-10, calling Jacob אבי but describing his brothers to Jacob as בניך not 'my brothers'.[220] However, no distancing is necessarily implied here since this is more likely to be explained by a tendency to define people by reference to the patriarch. Thus, he describes himself to Jacob as בנך in verse 9. He has already called himself their brother in verse 4, and the picture in verse 15 is one of reconciliation.

VERSES 14-15 - APPARENT RECONCILIATION

Joseph's attitude to his brothers is clarified in verses 14 and 15, where the narrator records two facts. Firstly, Benjamin appears to have a special place in Joseph's affection, since he is singled out in verse 14, when Joseph and Benjamin embrace each other. Benjamin is, of course, Joseph's only full brother, and the issue here is not favouritism, but special affection.

Secondly, Joseph takes initiative to show strong affection to his other brothers in verse 15. The same verb (וינשק) is used of Joseph's expression of affection for both Benjamin and his brothers, with the addition that he kissed his brothers as well. The response of the brothers seems to express apparent reconciliation with Joseph. Whereas in 37:4 they were not able to

---

219 Goshen is a name not attested in Egyptian sources, but 47:11 records that in later times it bore the name 'the land of Rameses'. Kidner, *Genesis*, 207 regards it as being "in the eastern part of the Nile delta, near Tanis, the seat of the Hyksos kings of the seventeenth century and of the Ramessides of the thirteenth century".

220 Hamilton, *Genesis Chapters 18-50*, 580.

speak peaceably with him, the narrator now mentions that דברו אחיו אתו (verse 15b).[221]

45:16-24 - Pharaoh's Provision for Joseph's Family

This section serves to reinforce Joseph's claims (verses 8-11, 13) that he is able to provide liberally for his family from Canaan. Egypt is pictured very positively here, with an outline of the gracious provision by Pharaoh without strings attached. While Joseph's words may have had the appearance of boasting, they are now vindicated by the reaction of Pharaoh and his courtiers.[222] Pharaoh's words of generosity - although in the more formal language of a royal edict - confirm that Joseph's latest plan also pleases Pharaoh.[223] Thus Joseph's plans, like all wise planning, are able to be implemented. Pharaoh firstly gives commands to Joseph (verses 17-20),[224] which Joseph then puts into action (verses 21-23). The repetition involved in Joseph carrying out Pharaoh's decrees highlights how Pharaoh and Joseph are echoing each other.

The provision is abundant. The brothers are to be given grain to take back to Canaan to meet the family's immediate needs (verse 17). Against the background of famine, they are to be given the good produce of the land (את־טוב ארץ),[225] which is described as being את־חלב הארץ. In a culture where goods were carried by people and animals, they are offered carts or wagons (עגלות, verse 19).[226] The force of ועינכם אל־תחס על־כליכם (verse 20) is not that they *cannot* bring their possessions but rather that they will not *need to* do so.

Verse 22 sees the reappearance of the clothing motif, as Joseph provides garments (חלפות שמלת) for all his brothers.[227] This adds a nice note of

---

221 Coats, *Genesis*, 293; Hamilton, *Genesis Chapters 18-50*, 581-582. Wenham, *Genesis 16-50*, 429. Even Wildavsky, *Assimilation versus Separation*, 110 concedes that "[f]amily conversation, if not family peace, is at long last established."

222 Wenham, *Genesis 16-50*, 429 notes that Pharaoh's courtiers also approved.

223 Hamilton, *Genesis Chapters 18-50*, 583-584; Westermann, *Genesis 37-50*, 147; Humphreys, *Joseph and His Family*, 53.

224 This explicit in verse 17. Davidson, *Genesis 12-50*, 274 also points out that the personal pronoun 'you' in verse 19 is singular. It is a command from Pharaoh to Joseph, rather than to the brothers. The balance of verse 19, in the plural, is the content of what Joseph is commanded to say to his brothers.

225 Keil and Delitzsch, *The Pentateuch*, 367 rightly point out that "טוב, "the good," is not the best part, but the good things (produce) of the land, as in vers. 20, 23, xxiv. 10, 2 Kings viii. 9."

226 Boice, *Genesis*, 192.

227 Keil and Delitzsch, *The Pentateuch*, 368 identify them as "dress clothes which were worn on special occasions". Also Leupold, *Genesis*, 1100.

closure to the family reconciliation, as clothing had previously been used to divide the brothers (37:3), and to deceive their father (37:32-33).[228]

However, a puzzling note is struck in this verse by the reference to Benjamin being given 300 pieces of silver, and five garments. On a first reading, this might suggest that the favouritism of 37:3 has resurfaced. While there is undeniably special consideration here for Benjamin, it is not as clear, in the absence of a comment by the narrator, whether or not this is to be read negatively.

Several factors mitigate against a negative reading. Firstly, in 37:3-4 the special gift of clothing was followed by the comment that the brothers hated Joseph. No such comment is made here. Secondly, there appears to be a singling out of Benjamin for Joseph's special affection in verses 14-15, while at the same time affirming his affection for the rest of his brothers. This might suggest that the special consideration given here to Benjamin does not imply a rejection of the others. Thirdly, there is a sense in which it was appropriate to recompense Benjamin more than the ten. They were being tested by Joseph in chapters 42-44 because of their past transgressions. Benjamin, on the other hand, had to be included in the accusation despite his previous innocence. Perhaps this extra gift was intended to compensate him in some way. Lastly, the fact that the extra garments were given after the reconciliation seems to imply that they were not intended to provoke the brothers to jealousy. However, the text does not clarify the reason for this disparity, but instead moves on.

One final matter which emerges in verse 24 is whether or not Joseph has become paternalistic towards his brothers

וישלח את־אחיו וילכו ויאמר אלהם אל־תרגזו בדרך

The root רגז has a range of meanings. Janzen notes that it can mean 'be agitated, quiver, shake, be excited, perturbed or quarrel'.[229] While some understand Joseph giving parting words of reassurance, it seems more likely that Joseph is giving them a gentle warning, being realistic enough to know that their characters have not been entirely transformed.[230] The explanation to Jacob, and the absence of Joseph, may have led to recriminations, justifications and accusations which Joseph wished to prevent.[231]

---

228 Wenham, *Genesis 16-50*, 429; Sarna, *JPS Torah Commentary*, 311; Fretheim, 'The Book of Genesis', 645.

229 Janzen, *Genesis 12-50*, 175. He sees it as having a dual force: "he offers them a wry word of caution (don't fall to squabbling again) and reassurance (don't be agitated by what you don't fully understand)."

230 Coats, *From Canaan to Egypt*, 48; Humphreys, *Joseph and His Family*, 85.

231 Kidner, *Genesis*, 208; Davidson, *Genesis 12-50*, 274. Speiser, *Genesis*, 337, 339

45:25-28 - *Jacob Learns that Joseph is Alive*

This brief section serves to close off the story of family reconciliation by describing the reaction of Jacob to the news about Joseph. Jacob, who had previously been so willing to accept bad news (37:23), now finds it difficult to believe his sons (verse 26). However, the words of Joseph, and the provisions carried in the carts (verse 27) compel belief.[232]

The theme of 'life' reappears as the brothers return to Jacob. Thy tell Jacob that Joseph is still alive (חי, verse 26); when he accepts their words, Jacob's spirit is revived (ותחי, verse 27); Jacob announces that Joseph is alive (חי, verse 28) and wishes to go to him before his death (אמות, verse 28, the antonym of life). This linking of Joseph and life is prominent in the story, and the connection has already been implied by Jacob himself (42:2).

Finally, the focus on restoration of family relationships is emphasised by Jacob's words in verse 28. Jacob does not mention the provision of food, or even the glory of Egypt. He simply wishes to see Joseph (ואראנו). This forms a neat transition to the descent of Jacob and his family in chapter 46.[233]

---

and Lowenthal, *The Joseph Narrative*, 109 both translate as 'do not be fretful on the way'.

232 Longacre, *Joseph: A Story of Divine Providence*, 39 discerns a chiasm here that centres on Joseph words and gifts in verse 27.

233 Westermann, *Genesis 37-50*, 148.

CHAPTER 8

Genesis 46-50

A quick glance at the contents of the final five chapters of Genesis does not reveal many 'wisdom-like elements'. Apart from Joseph's advice to his brothers (46:31-34), his administration in Egypt (47:13-26), and the final resolution with the brothers (50:15-21), the remaining chapters seem to resemble more closely the other patriarchal narratives. In particular, they deal with the Abrahamic promises, complete the life of Jacob, round off the book of Genesis, and lead into the book of Exodus that follows.[1] Westermann understands this as a dovetailing of the Joseph narrative (in a narrow sense) with the broader Jacob story.[2]

Considerations of space prohibit as detailed an analysis of this remaining section. However, the contents of these chapters are important to this study, and require some examination. It is here that the elements of the Abrahamic promise are seen most clearly, and it will be crucial to explore how they intersect with the 'wisdom-like elements' in the rest of Genesis 37-50.

Furthermore, these chapters are important for concluding the story of Joseph, as they outline events like the reunion between Jacob and Joseph, the agricultural reforms of Joseph, the settlement of the brothers in Egypt, the final removal of uncertainty in fraternal relations, and ultimately the death of both Jacob and Joseph. A literary reading of the Joseph story cannot ignore such important components of the narrative.[3]

Genesis 46-47

Structure

While many commentators discern a new section beginning at 47:28,

---

1   Wenham, *Genesis 16-50*, 491-492; Westermann, *Joseph*, 101. Humphreys, *Joseph and His Family*, 196-197 points out that units like 50:24-25; 46:1-4 and chapters 48 and 49 in particular link the Joseph story to its larger context.

2   Westermann, *Genesis 37-50*, 192, 213.

3   *Contra* Scullion, *Genesis*, 326.

chapter 48 commences with a time marker (ויהי אחרי הדברים האלה) which makes it more natural to see a break at this later point.[4] This is reinforced by Wenham's observation that the two previous journeys to Egypt both end with Jacob mentioning his death (42:38; 45:28), as he does in 47:29-31.[5] The similarity with the prior journeys thus suggests that the closing verses of chapter 47 round off the unit rather than begin the following section.

While the two chapters contain a variety of material, it is proposed to divide them into the following sections

46:1-7 - Jacob's vision and the journey to Egypt
46:8-27 - the list of travellers
46:28-30 - Jacob and Joseph reunited
46:31-47:6 - Joseph's instructions given and implemented
47:7-10 - Jacob meets and blesses Pharaoh
47:11-26 - Joseph provides for his family and for Egypt
47:27-31 - the preparations for Jacob's death

46:1-7 - Jacob's Vision and the Journey to Egypt

This passage is strikingly different from the preceding Joseph story, and is very reminiscent of the earlier patriarchal accounts. The explicit mention of sacrifice, as well as God's appearance and his direct communication with the patriarch, are typical of the previous narratives, yet tellingly absent from the Joseph story.[6] Indeed, these events produce such a jarring effect that they draw attention to the distinctiveness of the Joseph narrative. The only time in the Joseph narrative that God speaks directly to anyone is here, when he speaks to Jacob, not Joseph. It reminds the implied reader that Joseph never shares the not-uncommon patriarchal experience of hearing or meeting God.[7]

In this section, there are several obvious echoes of the patriarchal stories. Beer-sheba is a place with strong patriarchal connections (Gen 21:32-33; 22:19; 26:32-33; 28:10), and the narrator specifically observes that the

---

4   Wenham, *Genesis 16-50*, 438. Gunkel, *Genesis*, 445 also agrees that chapter 48 marks a new beginning, although his argument is largely on source critical grounds.
5   Wenham, *Genesis 16-50*, 437 explores the similarities and differences between this journey and those of chapters 42 and 43.
6   Scullion, *Genesis*, 326-327; Westermann, *Genesis 37-50*, 155; Redford, *Biblical Story of Joseph*, 18-19; Brueggemann, *Genesis*, 353 suggests that, "[t]his narrative is placed here to assert that the old promises of Genesis 12-36 are still operative.".
7   While the Hebrew expression for vision is plural in form, it appears to be singular in meaning, as in Ezek 8:3; 40:2 (so Westermann, *Genesis 37-50*, 152, 155 and Wenham, *Genesis 16-50*, 436). Lowenthal, *The Joseph Narrative*, 112 and Sarna, *JPS Torah Commentary*, 313 (also *GKC* § 124e) suggest an 'intensive plural', expressing grandeur and importance.

sacrifices were offered to the God of his father Isaac (לאלהי אביו יצחק),
who in Gen 26:2 was prohibited from going down to Egypt.[8] The double
call to Jacob in verse 2 (יעקב יעקב), and his response (הנני) are also
reminiscent of God's dealings with Abraham in Gen 22:11.[9] Even more
clearly, the promise of verse 3 that, in Egypt, God will make a גוי גדול out
of Jacob, recalls the initial promise to Abraham in Gen 12:2.[10] The link with
the exodus in verse 4 is also significant in that the book of Exodus connects
God's deliverance of his people from Egypt with his remembering his
covenant with the patriarchs (Exod 2:24, 25).[11] Thus White rightly observes
that Jacob's vision "stitches the Joseph narrative to the previous unifying
theme of the history of the promise."[12] This also accounts for the
elaboration of his offspring in verses 5-7,[13] and in more detail in verses 8-
27.

However, despite this dominant note of patriarchal promise, the journey
to Egypt is also pictured by the narrator in personal terms. It is a journey to
Joseph, for he will die in Joseph's presence (ויוסף ישית ידו על-עיניך, verse
4).[14] Even such a strong emphasis on the promises does not exclude Joseph
from the narrative, for the two are woven together.

The literary effect of including this and the following section is very
revealing. While the implied reader would expect Joseph and Jacob to be
reunited quickly after 45:28, the journey (and the travellers) are described
in great detail. This inevitably alerts the reader to the twin function of
Jacob's descent to Egypt. On a family plane, it enables the reuniting of a
fractured family. However, the detail and patriarchal overtones of 46:1-27
also serves to recall the broader context of the Abrahamic promises before
Joseph meets Jacob. As the story comes to a conclusion, both the resolution
of the family conflict and the partial fulfilment of the broader promises are
coming to a climax.

---

8   Weeks, *Early Israelite Wisdom*, 105 thus suggests that this cancels the earlier
    prohibition against travelling to Egypt found in 26:1-5.
9   Lowenthal, *The Joseph Narrative*, 188. Alter, *Genesis*, 273.
10 Westermann, *Genesis 37-50*, 156; Alter, *Genesis*, 273; Brueggemann, *Genesis*, 353.
    It also links in with Exod 1:7, which states that this is exactly what happened.
11 Coats, *From Canaan to Egypt*, 89; Westermann, *Genesis 37-50*, 156; von Rad,
    Genesis, 402; Vawter, *On Genesis*, 441.
12 White, *Narration and Discourse*, 237.
13 Wenham, *Genesis 16-50*, 442 notes that the word used twice for descendants in
    verses 6 and 7 is זרע (seed), used elsewhere in the patriarchal stories of the
    promised offspring.
14 Westermann, *Genesis 37-50*, 157 rightly observes that the detail about Joseph
    closing Jacob's eyes does not relate to the tradition of the promises to the
    patriarchs.

46:8-27 - The List of Travellers

These verses amplify the general information given in verses 6-7, and thus do not serve to advance the storyline at all. They are, however, significant in that they force the implied reader to pause. Indeed, the extent of the apparently unnecessary detail suggests that the reader is urged to ask the question 'why is all this included, and why here?'.

The number 'seventy' appears to be symbolic. Though they are counted as sixty-six (verse 26),[15] it appears that it was important to the final editor to claim that there were seventy - "a large round number, ten times sacred seven".[16] It suggests, at the very least, that the chosen family line is now reasonably certain to continue. While not yet a great nation (Gen 12:2), a family group of this number is unlikely to be totally destroyed, and thus the covenant promise is at least partially fulfilled.[17] Despite the threats during the patriarchal accounts, God is portrayed as having been faithful to his word.

This is supported by noticing that the opening words of verse 8 are repeated exactly in Exod 1:1 (ואלה שמות בני־ישראל הבאים מצרימה).[18] The final form of the Pentateuch sees a continuity between the seventy of Gen 46:8-27 and the multitude of Israelites in Exod 1:1-7. This list of travellers to Egypt thus has important implications for the subsequent history of covenant community of Israel.

The more intriguing issue is why this information is included at this point of the story. The fact that it immediately follows verses 1-7, which were bursting with echoes of the patriarchal promises, suggest that this element in the narrative is being reinforced. The implied reader has been immersed in Joseph's rise to power, and wise use of it, coupled with his scheme to achieve reconciliation with his brothers. Now the editor is drawing back from this specific focus in order to show the larger picture of God's purposes for the world through his covenant people. The need to do this implies that chapters 42-45 (and even more clearly chapters 39-41) are not simply a story of God preserving his covenant line, but have a more particular purpose - to show the shrewd and successful initiative of Joseph.

What is now asserted, however, is that the events of the previous chapters *also* serve to further the fulfilment of the patriarchal promises,

---

15 Sarna, *JPS Torah Commentary*, 317 comments that "since this [66] is not a typological or symbolic number in the Bible, it must therefore represent a genuine calculation based on the data just recorded."

16 Alter, *Genesis*, 276; Vawter, *On Genesis*, 444. Sailhamer, 'Genesis', 261 suggests links with the "seventy nations" of Genesis 10. However, there is no explicit mention of seventy in Genesis 10, which probably makes the connection unlikely.

17 Clines, *The Theme of the Pentateuch* (1997), 48-49; Keil and Delitzsch, *The Pentateuch*, 369.

18 This is pointed out by Westermann, *Genesis 37-50*, 159.

which has been the crucial theme from Genesis 12 onwards. The wisdom of Joseph (which will be again be evident in 46:31-34 and 47:13-26) is now to be reframed, and harnessed to the cause of the chosen line becoming a great nation.

This passage may also be a preliminary to the meetings with Pharaoh in chapter 47. The list of Jacob's descendants reminds the reader that Jacob is patriarchal head of an extended family, a position respected in the Ancient Near East, which may justify him offering a blessing to Pharaoh (47:7, 10). However, the disparity between a clan of seventy and the numbers of mighty Egypt would also be patent.

In preparing for the meetings with Pharaoh, the emphasis on the patriarchal promises makes it clear that more is at stake than simply the fate of a wandering family. God's ongoing purposes for his covenant people will be affected by the outcome of the subsequent encounters between Jacob's family and the Egyptian court.

46:28-30 - Jacob and Joseph Reunited

While these three verses ostensibly record only the meeting of Jacob and Joseph, they also provide several important hints for the implied reader. Firstly, the land of Goshen, which appears to be a fertile region in the eastern part of the Nile delta, is mentioned three times in verses 28-29, as if this location will be significant for the future story. This will become explicit in 46:34 and 47:4, 6.

Secondly, Judah is unexpectedly foregrounded in this narrative. Although he is the direct object of the verb שלח, Judah is placed first in the sentence, presumably for emphasis.[19] In the light of Judah's emerging leadership (43:8-10; 44:14, 18-34), and in view of the projection of future leadership in 49:8-12, this appears to be another hint of Judah's special role as leader.[20]

In verse 29, Joseph's eagerness to be reunited with his father is also evident. Having been reconciled to his brothers in chapter 45, he is now restored to Jacob, thus accomplishing the full family reunion. Joseph does not rest on his authority in Egypt, but harnesses his chariot, goes up to meet his father, and shows affection for him in a manner similar to his love for Benjamin in 45:14.[21]

---

19   Hamilton, *Genesis Chapters 18-50*, 601. Judah is a direct object of the verb.

20   Longacre, *Joseph: A Story of Divine Providence*, 56; Janzen, *Genesis 12-50*, 17; Sailhamer, 'Genesis', 263.

21   Sarna, *JPS Torah Commentary*, 318 In relation to making his chariot ready, the *qal* form of the root אסר is used, which normally has an active sense of 'he harnessed' not 'he caused to be harnessed'. Given his position in Egypt, it is unlikely that he harnessed the chariot himself, but the use of the *qal* form gives the impression of

Davidson has suggested that the narrator shows restraint in his description of this reunion, since verse 30 records Jacob's words and not Joseph's.[22] However, Joseph has already revealed his eagerness, and weeps on his father's neck in verse 29. The literary function of verse 30 is to focus attention on Jacob and his words, and thus to see the reunion from his point of view. While he displays clear affection for Joseph, the surrounding context of the patriarchal promises may also imply that Jacob is confident that the covenant will continue.

46:31-47:6 - Joseph's Instructions Given and Implemented

Verses 31-34 are, strictly speaking, unnecessary since they advance the action no further.[23] They are included for another purpose, of which the most likely is to draw attention to the character of the person giving the instructions. If, as will be argued, the advice given by Joseph leads to success for the brothers, this cameo contributes to the picture of Joseph as a shrewd counsellor.

The passage is often misunderstood, and needs to be read carefully. Some commentators suggest that Joseph is telling his brothers to say to Pharaoh that they are 'keepers of livestock' (אנשׁי מקנה), not 'shepherds' (רעה צאן), but the brothers ignore Joseph's instructions, say they are 'shepherds' (רעה צאן), yet succeed anyway.[24]

Certainly they do succeed in getting permission to settle in the fertile border region of Goshen (47:6), just as Joseph had planned (46:34). However, the text is read more naturally as claiming that the brothers carry out the essence of Joseph's instructions. In 46:32, Joseph outlines what he intends to say to Pharaoh. Of the brothers (described as האנשׁים), Joseph says that they are 'shepherds' (רעי צאן), immediately following this with a כי clause that appears to function epexegetically of the men being 'shepherds' (כי־אנשׁי מקנה היו). מקנה is often a general term for livestock of a variety of kinds,[25] and it is filled out in the rest of this verse by reference to their flocks (צאנם) and their herds (בקרם). The description of the brothers as רעי צאן in not in contrast with their being אנשׁי מקנה, but rather appears

---

his being very keen to reach his father.

22   Davidson, *Genesis 12-50*, 283.

23   Westermann, *Genesis 37-50*, 167.

24   So, Brueggemann, *Genesis*, 356-357; Coats, *From Canaan to Egypt*, 52; Roop, *Genesis*, 280.

25   F. Brown, S.R. Driver and C.A. Briggs, *A Hebrew and English Lexicon of the Old Testament* (Oxford: Clarendon, 1906) 889 understands מקנה to mean cattle in general, including cows, sheep, horses, asses, even camels. It is a category for purchasable domestic animals. Sarna, *JPS Torah Commentary*, 318 observes that the term אנשׁי מקנה is not used elsewhere in the Old Testament apart from 46:32, 34.

to be another way of giving a similar description.[26] When Joseph comes before Pharaoh, he is not trying to make a fine distinction between 'shepherds' and 'keepers of livestock' more generally, for he simply mentions their flocks and their herds (צאנם ובקרם, 47:1). The brothers say that they are רעה צאן, but in 47:6 Pharaoh offers to put them in charge of his מקנה.[27] In the light of all this, the more natural reading of 46:34 is that, when they are describing themselves as אנשי מקנה, they mean that they look after both sheep and cattle, flocks and herds.

The apparent difficulty of this view is why Joseph mentions in 46:34 that all shepherds are 'abhorrent to the Egyptians' (כי-תועבת מצרים). The best solution is to regard this clause as the reason to mention their occupation, rather than as the reason to avoid mention of it. Since the Egyptians will be wary of semi-nomadic shepherds,[28] there will be less trouble if they are kept away from the capital, even if it means that they must stay in what was a sensitive border region.[29] Since other Egyptians may have viewed them suspiciously, Pharaoh may be more inclined to keep them separate, and not move them from their current location in Goshen (47:1). Such a reading of verse 34 seems to be consistent with the details of the rest of 46:31-47:6.

On this reading Joseph correctly anticipates Pharaoh's question to the brothers (מה-מעשיכם, 46:33/47:3), which was essential to the success of his plan. Furthermore, the brothers are to be seen in 47:4 as acting in accordance with Joseph's instructions.[30] Joseph's carefully prepared plan secures his goal of enabling the brothers to live in Goshen, use its rich land, and keep a degree of separateness from the Egyptians.[31]

Indeed, the fact that Pharaoh gives instructions to Joseph (47:5-6), rather than answer the brothers' request, reminds the implied reader that Joseph is a powerful administrator with great authority in the land. There appears to be a focus in this passage on yet another of Joseph's wise plans coming to a successful fruition.[32] Of course, this also makes this section lead nicely into

---

26 *Contra* Lowenthal, *The Joseph Narrative*, 120.
27 Sarna, *JPS Torah Commentary*, 319 notes that Egyptian kings possessed vast herds of cattle. Rameses III, for example, is said to have employed 3,264 mainly foreign men to take care of his cattle.
28 Vergote, *Joseph en Égypte*, 188 notes that it is not hatred of shepherds as such but rather the nomadic shepherds. See also Westermann, *Genesis 37-50*, 168; Maher, *Genesis*, 254.
29 Davidson, *Genesis 12-50*, 283; B.A. McKenzie, 'Jacob's Blessing on Pharaoh: An Interpretation of Gen 46:31-47:26', *WTJ* 45 (1983): 390.
30 So, for example, Fretheim, 'The Book of Genesis', 653; Wenham, *Genesis 16-50*, 446; Kidner, *Genesis*, 210; Adar, *The Book of Genesis*, 154. For some possible supplementary reasons, see Wenham, *Genesis 16-50*, 445; Westermann, *Genesis 37-50*, 168.
31 Herbert, *Genesis 12-50*, 145; Keil and Delitzsch, *The Pentateuch*, 374-375.
32 Adar, *The Book of Genesis*, 154 sees this as an example of Joseph's practical

the description of Joseph's administration in 47:13-26.

47:7-10 - Jacob Meets and Blesses Pharaoh

When Jacob meets with Pharaoh, this event is described by the narrator as a distinct encounter, something apparently separate from that of 47:1-6. It is, perhaps, as if this meeting is told in order to make some other (or additional) point, now that the family's future has been secured.

McKenzie has noted that "two points are emphasized in this passage, namely Jacob's age (since it occupies over half the passage and is found at its center) and the fact that Jacob *brk* Pharaoh (since it appears twice)."[33] Jacob's comments about his age draw another link with the broader patriarchal narratives, a comparison made explicit in verse 9.[34] This connection with the earlier chapters in Genesis is also echoed in use of the root ברך (verses 7, 10), which probably in the context has the sense of Jacob 'blessing', not merely 'greeting', Pharaoh.[35] It is significant that Joseph is not recorded as making any plans in relation to the meeting between Pharaoh and Jacob. The theology undergirding this audience is that of the patriarchal narratives, where the patriarch is the channel of God's blessing, a blessing which finally extends to all the families of the earth (Gen 12:3).[36]

Thus, this section reintroduces the link with the patriarchal promises. Having focused on Joseph's astute planning in 46:31-47:6, the story now reverts to that motif introduced in 46:1-27 - that of the Abrahamic promises being fulfilled. In other words, the separate meetings that Pharaoh conducts with Jacob and with five of the brothers, serve to emphasise, and wedge together, Joseph's wisdom and the fulfilment of the promises.

47:11-26 - Joseph Provides for his Family and for Egypt

This unit has two unequal parts. Verses 11-12 outline, in summary terms, how Joseph provides for his family who are now settled in Egypt. Verses

---

wisdom.

33 McKenzie, 'Jacob's Blessing', 391.
34 McKenzie, 'Jacob's Blessing', 394.
35 McKenzie, 'Jacob's Blessing', 393 McKenzie notes that ברך can mean either 'bless' or 'greet' and thus ought to be translated 'to greet with a blessing' or 'to bless in greeting'. Lowenthal, *The Joseph Narrative*, 123 proposes that 'blessed' seems more preferable to 'greeted', since if Jacob prayed for long life for Pharaoh, that would account for the question of 47:8. However, quite a number of scholars try to empty verses 7 and 10 of any note of blessing: Sarna, *JPS Torah Commentary*, 320; R. de Vaux, *La Genèse* (Paris: Éditions du Cerfs, 1953) 204; Vawter, *On Genesis*, 446.
36 Alter, *Genesis*, 280; Sailhamer, 'Genesis', 264; Westermann, *Genesis 37-50*, 171.

13-26 then describe, in a more extensive way, Joseph's successful administration of the land.

Verse 11 recounts how Joseph carries out Pharaoh's command (given in verse 6), settling his family in what is called, from the perspective of the later narrator, the 'land of Rameses'.[37] The focus is again on Joseph's provision, doing first for his own family, what he will soon do for all Egypt. He secures life in the setting of famine.[38] Indeed, Joseph provides for them לְפִי הַטָּף (47:12),[39] even for the very young ones who are most vulnerable in times of famine.

Verses 13-26 outline some important changes that Joseph makes in the course of his administration of the land.[40] Scholars, however, differ over whether Joseph's policies are portrayed in the narrative as evidence of his wisdom, or of his folly, or even sin.

Those who view this passage negatively argue that Joseph's actions here are anything but wise.[41] Indeed, what flows from his administration is that the Pharaoh gets all the land, the Egyptians become slaves, and possibly are even relocated.[42] There is the danger that this is reading modern sensibilities into an ancient text,[43] especially when no negative implication is drawn in the passage, nor is any explicit connection made with Israel's later slavery in Egypt. Alternatively, Weeks has argued that all the steps that Joseph

---

37 Vergote, *Joseph en Égypte*, 186 and Vawter, *On Genesis*, 447 view this as anachronistic, since Rameses II belonged to the nineteenth Egyptian dynasty (13th century BCE). However, see K.A. Kitchen, 'Review. Joseph en Égypte: Genèse chap. 37-50 à la lumière des études égyptologiques récentes by J. Vergote', *JEA* 47 (1961): 161.

38 Sarna, *JPS Torah Commentary*, 320; Westermann, *Genesis 37-50*, 171.

39 Sarna, *JPS Torah Commentary*, 320 notes that this phrase "should normally mean "by the mouth of/according to the children." Sarna translates 'down to the little ones', noting the LXX understands it to mean 'per person', and Hizkuni 'as much as children can eat' that is, 'liberally'. Keil and Delitzsch, *The Pentateuch*, 376 propose the translation 'according to the necessities of each family'.

40 V.A. Hurowitz, 'Joseph's Enslavement of the Egyptians (Genesis 47:13-26) in the Light of Famine Texts from Mesopotamia', *RB* 101 (1994): 356 sees three scenes of unequal length in 47:13-26: verses 13-14; 15-17 and 18-25, with an aetiological comment in verse 26. McKenzie, 'Jacob's Blessing', 395 sees four sections, each of which describes one aspect of the blessing.

41 Coats, *Genesis*, 299; Wildavsky, 'Survival', 48; I. Caine, 'Numbers in the Joseph Narrative', *Jewish Civilization: Essays and Studies* 1 (1979): 9-10; Fung, *Victim and Victimizer*, 35-39.

42 The MT of verse 21 reads הֶעֱבִיר אֹתוֹ לֶעָרִים, but the Samaritan Pentateuch and the LXX reflect an alternative reading [הֶעֱבִיד אֹתוֹ לַעֲבָדִים] which would not involve any reference to deportation to the cities. See Lowenthal, *The Joseph Narrative*, 127. Many of the modern English versions, such as the NRSV and NIV, opt for the reading proposed by the Samaritan Pentateuch and LXX.

43 As Wenham, *Genesis 16-50*, 449, 452 points out.

takes are suggested by the Egyptians themselves, not by Joseph.[44] Such scholars also point out that the 'pagan' Egyptian priesthood is not affected by this reform, due to allowances paid by Pharaoh (verses 22, 26), and such an exemption is an offence to Yahwistic faith. A truly wise ruler, they say, ought not to promote other faiths.[45]

However, it is significant that verses 13-26 are unnecessary for the forward movement of the story, concern neither Joseph's relationship with his brothers, nor the survival of the covenant line. Indeed, the brothers are strikingly absent. Just as they were not mentioned in chapters 39-41, they are again not referred to in 47:13-26. This is particularly important in view of the number of references to the brothers in virtually all other parts of Genesis 37-50.[46]

One likely implication of this is that 47:13-26 continues where chapter 41 left off, and it does so in two ways.[47] Firstly, it demonstrates to the reader the severity of the famine, just as Joseph had said (41:30-31).[48] Joseph's words have proved true and therefore Joseph has been trustworthy. Secondly, if, as has been argued above, chapter 41 has pictured Joseph as a wise administrator, then this passage in chapter 47 would *prima facie* continue that same portrayal unless clear clues were to be found in the text. The reader who makes the connection with chapter 41 would start with the assumption that this unit gives more detail about Joseph's wise administration in practice.[49] Furthermore, if Joseph provides food for his brothers in verses 11-12 - and that is described positively - there is the narrative expectation that providing food for others is also viewed

---

44   Weeks, *Early Israelite Wisdom*, 99-100.

45   Wildavsky, *Assimilation versus Separation*, 141. Kitchen, 'Review', 161 rightly points out that "the text does not state that the priests paid no taxes but only that they were exempt from Joseph's 20 per cent levy."

46   The word אֵת appears in various forms in 82 verses in Genesis 37-50, but not at all in chapters 39-41. It is also not found in the record of Joseph's administration in 47:13-26, but appears in every other chapter: 37:2, 4, 5, 8-14, 16, 17, 23, 26, 27, 30; 38:1, 8, 9, 11, 29, 30 [while אֵת usually refers to Judah's sons, the wider family is in view]; 42:3, 4, 6-8, 13, 15, 16, 19-21, 28, 32-34, 38; 43:3-7, 13, 14, 29, 30; 44:14, 19, 20, 23, 26, 33; 45:1, 3, 4, 12, 14-17, 24; 46:31 [however, Joseph's brothers are described verses 5-7 as Jacob's sons or seed, while verses 8-27 outline the brothers and their descendants in great detail]; 47:1-3, 5, 6, 11, 12; 48:6, 19, 22 [אֵת in verses 6 and 19 refer to Manasseh and Ephraim, but the concern of the whole passage is with the future destiny of these tribes]; 49:5, 8, 26 [this chapter is entirely about the brothers, but they are usually named, rather than described as a group]; 50:8, 14, 15, 17, 18, 24.

47   Vawter, *On Genesis*, 449; Gunkel, *Genesis*, 442.

48   Wenham, *Genesis 16-50*, 447; Keil and Delitzsch, *The Pentateuch*, 377. Alter, *Genesis*, 283.

49   Fretheim, 'The Book of Genesis', 653-654.

positively.

Indeed, this appears to be the primary function of the passage.[50] Chapter 41 has already a connection between Joseph's administration and his wisdom, and this passage appears to provide further data that reinforces this characterisation of Joseph. As in chapter 41, there is the absence of any indication of a negative attitude towards Egypt.[51] This universal, non-polemical perspective is elsewhere seen as a feature of the wisdom movement.

Joseph has engineered a scenario in which he is able to secure for Pharaoh control over the land and its people, perhaps regaining them from the Egyptian nobility.[52] The task of a courtier is to advance the interests of his master, and Joseph has certainly accomplished that.[53] This is especially important when, as here, the survival of the people was at stake. While the process could have been narrated with an emphasis on loss of freedom, that is not the narrative which is found in chapter 47.

Indeed, a number of details serve to produce a more positive picture of Joseph's reforms. For example, the Egyptians themselves make the offer to become slaves (verses 19, 25), and Joseph responds to their request (verses 20-21).[54] Joseph also gives them something of value in exchange for what they trade - grain for money (verse 14), grain for livestock (verses 16-17), grain for land (verse 19), and, when they become slaves, he provides them with land to work on and seed to sow (verse 23).[55] The language of slavery is commonly associated with concepts like 'take', but a key idea in this passage is one of exchange.[56] They are allowed to keep the generous amount of eighty per cent of their crop (verse 24).[57] This positive impression of Joseph's reforms is reinforced by the verdict of the Egyptians (החיתנו = 'you have preserved our lives', verse 25), where they focus on what they have gained (life), not what they have lost.[58] Their verdict is

---

50 *Contra* those who regard its function as simply a 'tax etiology', such as Westermann, *Genesis 37-50*, 176; Scullion, *Genesis*, 329.

51 Niditch, *Underdogs and Tricksters*, 122.

52 Herbert, *Genesis 12-50*, 146-147.

53 Humphreys, *Joseph and His Family*, 147; Sarna, *JPS Torah Commentary*, 321; von Rad, *Genesis*, 410; Adar, *The Book of Genesis*, 156; Roop, *Genesis*, 280.

54 Sarna, *JPS Torah Commentary*, 322.

55 Hamilton, *Genesis Chapters 18-50*, 618 notes that "[e]ach time the citizenry gives Joseph something of theirs, he gives something back of value.

56 The preposition ב seems to have this force in verses 16, 17 [five times], 19.

57 In relation to the rate of taxation not being exorbitant, Davidson, *Genesis 12-50*, 288 points out that 1 Macc 10:30 mentions a tax of one third of their grain and one half of their fruit.

58 Alter, *Genesis*, 283; Adar, *The Book of Genesis*, 155. Hurowitz, 'Joseph's Enslavement', at 355-360 explores the language against the background of Mesopotamian legal texts concerning people sold into slavery in order to enable

meant to shape our reading. They appear grateful, and seem to embrace quite willingly the kind of slavery to Pharaoh that will give them enough to live on.[59]

In its present context, then, there are good grounds to believe that the acquisition of all the land is a way of bringing it all under the wise administration of Joseph, whose assigned task is to make his master prosper and keep Egypt alive. There is no negative implication about slavery - rather it is the means of the people of Egypt being kept alive. Instead of death without Joseph's intervention, they find life through Joseph's wise provision.

If such a reading of the section is to be adopted, it also suggests another reason for the inclusion of the passage at this point. It has been argued above that the patriarchal promises have resurfaced in chapter 46, and are the basis of Jacob's blessing of Pharaoh in 47:7-10.[60] Since part of the Abrahamic promise was to be a blessing to the nations (Gen 12:3), it is not surprising to have verses 13-26 now outline how Jacob's son Joseph, through his administration of the land, brought great blessing to Egypt in the face of famine. This cameo thus also serves to provide a snapshot of the partial fulfilment of the patriarchal promises.[61]

If so, then Joseph's wise actions become the means by which God begins to fulfil his covenant promises, unlike the book of Exodus where overt divine intervention is evident. Wisdom and covenant promise are thus woven together in these verses, as human wisdom is used by God to further his purposes.

47:27-31 - Preparations for Jacob's Death

Verse 27 is a hinge verse, which rounds off the previous section, while leading into verses 28-31. The focus is now back on Jacob and his family.[62] The observation that Israel was fruitful and multiplied greatly is resumptive of the patriarchal promise motif, which is appropriate as Jacob prepares for

---

them to eat.

59 Janssen, 'Egyptological Remarks', 70; Kitchen, 'Joseph' *IBD*, 815; and Sarna, *JPS Torah Commentary*, 322 observe that this is simply making the practice conform to the Egyptian theory that Pharaoh was the owner of all land anyway.

60 McKenzie, 'Jacob's Blessing', 395 argues that "Gen 47:13-26 should be interpreted as the fulfillment of the blessing on Pharaoh anticipated by both Gen 46:31-47:6 and 47:7-10. The absence of the term "blessing" in Gen 47:13-26 does not imply that the concept is also absent." At 399 he observes that there are further examples of blessing in 48:8-22 and 49:1-27.

61 Wenham, *Genesis 16-50*, 452; Keil and Delitzsch, *The Pentateuch*, 380; Fretheim, 'The Book of Genesis', 654.

62 Longacre, *Joseph: A Story of Divine Providence*, 29.

his burial with the patriarchs in the promised land (verse 30).[63]

This passage clearly moves the reader to a new time frame, some seventeen years later (verse 28; compare verse 9). The fact that Jacob has remained in Egypt well beyond the seven years of famine indicates that the descent to Egypt was not merely a temporary expediency, but rather an ongoing part of God's purposes. The mention of his lifespan of 147 years[64] leads quite naturally into a concern for his imminent death, an event which will hover over chapters 48 and 49.

Three striking features are present in verses 29-31. Firstly, there is Jacob's deferential tone towards Joseph (אִם־נָא מָצָאתִי חֵן בְּעֵינֶיךָ, verse 29). While there are other explanations, the most likely one is that this is one further indicator of Joseph's prominence in Egypt.[65] Secondly, it is not entirely clear why Jacob must make Joseph swear an oath. (verses 29, 31). At least it speaks of the strength of Jacob's desire, as the detail makes sure that Egypt is pictured as only a stage on the path back to the land of Canaan (verse 30).[66] Jacob's provision for his future removal is a powerful symbol that God's people will not be in Egypt forever.[67] Thirdly, it is significant that Joseph is singled out among the brothers. Only Joseph is summoned to Jacob's bedside (verse 29), and only Joseph swears the oath (verse 30).[68] While this is due perhaps to the fact that he is in a position of authority in Egypt, it also serves to highlight that Joseph's distinctive role is not ignored as the focus moves back to Jacob.

The final verse of this chapter is difficult, but it most likely refers neither to Jacob's death[69] nor his bowing down to Joseph in fulfilment of the dream.[70] It is most probably an expression of thankfulness that he has been

---

63 Wenham, *Genesis 16-50*, 449; Baldwin, *The Message of Genesis 12-50*, 197-198.

64 Sarna, *JPS Torah Commentary*, 324 suggests that there is number symbolism in the 147 years. See also J.G. Williams, 'Number Symbolism and Joseph as Symbol of Completion', *JBL* 98 (1979): 86-87.

65 However, see F. Steiner, 'Enslavement and the Early Hebrew Lineage System. An Explanation of Genesis 47:29-31; 48:1-16', in *Anthropological Approaches to the Old Testament*. Issues in Religion and Theology, 8, ed. B. Lang. (Philadelphia: Fortress, 1985), 22-23 who makes the suggestion that Joseph, being sold as a slave, is legally no longer Jacob's son.

66 Lowenthal, *The Joseph Narrative*, 133 and Sarna, *JPS Torah Commentary*, 324 propose that the existence of an oath would strengthen Joseph's hand when he would request Pharaoh's permission to leave Egypt to bury his father.

67 Westermann, *Genesis 37-50*, 183; Hamilton, *Genesis Chapters 18-50*, 625.

68 H. Seebass, 'The Joseph Story, Genesis 48 and the Canonical Process', *JSOT* 35 (1986): 33 notes that this constitutes a great honour for Joseph.

69 Wenham, *Genesis 16-50*, 449-450 argues that the parallels with 24:1-9 imply that this is not a proleptic summary of Jacob's death, but rather an anticipation of it.

70 *Contra* Ackerman, 'Joseph, Judah and Jacob', 108.

able to put his affairs in order.[71]

Genesis 48:1-49:28

Structure

Seebass has commented that "the contents of 48-49 stand out like relics from another world within the surrounding genre of novel(la)."[72] While this section may differ formally from the surrounding material, it picks up the theme from 47:28-31 that Jacob is preparing for his death. As such, it addresses the crucial question of the future of the patriarchal promises for the descendants of Jacob.[73] The Joseph story, which started with the breaking of peace in chapter 37, approaches a conclusion through the pronouncement of blessings.

The major divide in this section is between chapter 48, which concerns Jacob, Joseph and his two sons, and chapter 49:1-28, which deals with all twelve sons of Jacob. Chapter 48 can be further subdivided into verses 1-7, in which Jacob announces his intention to bless Ephraim and Manasseh; verses 8-20, in which the blessing takes place; and verses 21-22, where the focus returns to Joseph.[74] Chapter 49:1-28 could be further subdivided into twelve sections but will, for sake of convenience, be discussed as one unit.[75]

48:1-7 - Joseph's Sons Legitimated

The blessing of Joseph's sons in chapter 48 is an integral part of Jacob preparing for his imminent death. Joseph, however, is not marginalised, for in verse 1 the narrator only mentions that Joseph was told that his father was ill. Indeed, Jacob's first blessings are not addressed to all of his children, but only to Joseph's sons.

---

71 So Vawter, *On Genesis*, 451. The LXX reading - της ραβδου αυτου, 'his staff' - appears to be based on מַטֵּהוּ rather than הַמִּטָּה.

72 Seebass, 'Canonical Process', 36. Similarly, Weeks, *Early Israelite Wisdom*, 105. This study views them as an important part of the narrative as a whole.

73 Wenham, *Genesis 16-50*, 459; Seebass, 'Canonical Process', 32. Brueggemann, *Genesis*, 367 adds "[t]he first task of the dying father was to bind the coming heirs to the promise. This is the function of chapter 48 and, in a secondary way, the poem of chapter 49.

74 Ross, *Creation and Blessing*, 690, although he includes 47:28-31.

75 This would be based on an introduction in verses 1-2 plus 11 other sections. Ten of these would concern individual sons, while the final section deals with Simeon and Levi together. For a more detailed analysis of the structure of chapter 49, see M. O'Connor, *Hebrew Verse Structure* (Winona Lake: Eisenbrauns, 1980) 425-433.

In verses 3-4, Jacob reveals that his background theology is that of the covenant promises of descendants and land, reaffirmed to him at Luz (or Bethel, Gen 35:6, 9-12).[76] This whole chapter, then, is about the passing on of the blessings of the patriarchal promises.

Jacob announces his intention to make Ephraim and Manasseh his sons, just as Reuben and Simeon were (verse 5). Many have seen here, and in verses 8-20, an intra-family adoption.[77] While the technical language of adoption formulas may lie behind the text, the fact that Joseph's sons are adults,[78] and presumably remain living with Joseph, has led Westermann to propose that legitimation is in view here rather than adoption.[79] The effect of this is that "their position as tribal ancestors in Israel is traced back to the will of the dying patriarch."[80] Ominously, Jacob mentions the younger son Ephraim before his older brother in verse 5 (compare verse 1).[81] The reference to Rachel in verse 7 seems to imply that Jacob's action was at least partly motivated by his desire to honour the memory of his favourite wife by giving her more sons.[82]

48:8-20 - Ephraim Exalted over Manasseh

Jacob's question when he saw Joseph's sons (מִי־אֵלֶּה, verse 8) has engendered a variety of interpretations. Some discern a different source here,[83] while others suspect that Jacob's failing eyesight (verse 10) was the reason the sons had to be identified. However, a formal question like this would not be surprising in an adoption (or legitimation) ritual, and this probably accounts for it here.[84] Other evidence of such a formal ceremony

---

76   Brueggemann, *Genesis*, 359; Hamilton, *Genesis Chapters 18-50*, 628-629.
77   H. Rand, 'The Testament of Jacob, An Analysis of Gen. 49:18', *The Jewish Bible Quarterly/Dor le Dor* 18 (1989-1990): 103; Sarna, *JPS Torah Commentary*, 325; Alter, *Genesis*, 287.
78   Keil and Delitzsch, *The Pentateuch*, 381 rightly note that, since 17 years had passed (47:9, 28), Manasseh and Ephraim would be about 18 or 20 years old.
79   Westermann, *Genesis 37-50*, 185; Scullion, *Genesis*, 333.
80   Scullion, *Genesis*, 333.
81   Sarna, *JPS Torah Commentary*, 326; Wenham, *Genesis 16-50*, 463.
82   G. Tucker, 'Jacob's Terrible Burden: In the Shadow of the Text', *Bible Review* 10 (1994): 25-28 makes the interesting suggestion that Gen 48:7 should be rendered, in part, 'Rachel died on my account'. On this reading Jacob is unburdening himself to Joseph, confessing that his rash vow to Laban in Gen 31:32 actually condemned Rachel to death.
83   For example, Westermann, *Genesis 37-50*, 186.
84   Sarna, *JPS Torah Commentary*, 326-327 regards it as part of the formal interrogation which belonged to the second stage of the legal adoptive process. See also Alter, *Genesis*, 288. A similar kind of question occurs in Gen 27:18, where Jacob receives the blessing of the first-born from Isaac, though there, too, it may be

may be seen in the two sons being placed on or near Jacob's knees (verse 12), a "symbolic gesture that betokens acceptance and legitimation as son and heir."[85]

The literary function of the question in verse 8 is that it allows both Joseph and Jacob to give a theological interpretation of the events that have occurred. It is revealing that both Joseph and Jacob attribute the events that have happened to God - Joseph says that God has given him his sons (verse 9); Jacob asserts that God has enabled him to see Joseph's children (זרעך, verse 11). This has not been through overt intervention by God, for in the narrative both these events have come through human initiative. God has been working behind the scenes, with human actors as his instruments.

As Westermann observes, "vv. 13-20 are concerned with the precedence of Ephraim over Manasseh."[86] The elaborate detail of verses 13-14 draws the reader's attention to the fact that Jacob places the more significant right hand on the younger son, Ephraim. Joseph correctly positions his sons, but Jacob thwarts Joseph's intentions by crossing his hands. Although Joseph's two sons are blessed by the same words (verses 15-16, 20), the symbolism of crossing the hands is made clear by the explanation that the younger brother will be greater (verse 19) and by the narrator's summarising comment[87]

וישם את־אפרים לפני מנשה (verse 20)

Another important aspect of the blessings is that they are strongly focused on God,[88] who is explicitly identified as the God of the patriarchs (verse 15), and therefore of the covenant promises. Jacob here was no innovator; he was heir to the past. Jacob's wish that they grow into a teeming multitude is reminiscent of the Abrahamic promise of innumerable descendants.[89]

A final observation on this section is that, when Jacob blesses Ephraim and Manasseh, the narrator records ויברך את־יוסף (verse 15). Although Jacob's hands are on Joseph's sons, Joseph is the person who is said to be blessed. The LXX seeks to change the referent by reading αὐτούς ('them') here, but this is to miss the point developed in verses 21-22 that, in having

---

   due to the patriarch's failing eyesight. Modern parallels would include a minister asking, in a wedding service, 'who brings this woman to be married to this man?' or the request, in an infant baptism, to 'name this child'.

85   Sarna, *JPS Torah Commentary*, 327.
86   Westermann, *Genesis 37-50*, 182. See also Vawter, *On Genesis*, 455.
87   Brueggemann, *Genesis*, 364; Fretheim, 'The Book of Genesis', 660.
88   Brueggemann, *Genesis*, 361. He notes mention of God twice in verse 15; the angel (as an alternative way of referring to God) in verse 16, and another mention of God in verse 20.
89   Davidson, *Genesis 12-50*, 296. Sarna, *JPS Torah Commentary*, 328.

both his sons legitimated as Jacob's sons, Joseph is, in effect, gaining a double inheritance.[90]

48:21-22 - Joseph's Lot in Relation to his Brothers

This small section seems to resume the concerns of verses 1-7, with the reminder in verse 21 that Jacob is about to die, but that God will bring them to the land of their fathers. God's covenant promises will ultimately prevail. Though addressed to Joseph, the presence of the plural pronominal suffixes in verse 21 (והיה אלהים עמכם והשיב אתכם אל־ארץ אבתיכם) are a reminder that the patriarchal promises are for all of Israel.[91]

The precise translation of verse 22 is much disputed, with שכם אחד being variously understood as 'portion', 'mountain slope' or a reference to the area of Shechem.[92] If translated in any of these ways, it refers to an extra entitlement of land or even double portion received by Joseph. Alter, however, has argued that שכם אחד should not be regarded as the object of the verb נתן, but rather functions adverbially. He notes that its only other Old Testament occurrence is in Zeph 3:9, where it is used adverbially in the idiomatic sense of 'with one accord'. He thus translates 'I have given you with single intent over your brothers … '.[93] This is an attractive solution, and it is noteworthy that, on any of these readings, Joseph is being advantaged over his brothers.

Thus, before the narrator records the words addressed to all twelve tribes, chapter 48 has made it very clear that Joseph will be abundantly blessed.[94]

49:1-28 - The Testament of Jacob

This part of chapter 49 is a very complex text and a minefield for exegetes.[95] It is a mixture of longer oracles (verses 8-12; 22-26) and shorter

---

90 Sarna, *JPS Torah Commentary*, 328 also notes that the Vulgate departs from the Hebrew of its presumed *Vorlage* to read 'he blessed *the sons of* Joseph'.

91 Sarna, *JPS Torah Commentary*, 330.

92 See Wenham, *Genesis 16-50*, 466; Sarna, *JPS Torah Commentary*, 330.

93 Alter, *Genesis*, 291. It is, however, by no means clear that 'with single intent' is properly equivalent to 'with one accord'.

94 *Contra* Sailhamer, 'Genesis', 269 who proposes that "the blessing recorded in this chapter is largely subordinated and superseded by the blessing of Jacob that follows in chapter 49."

95 Sarna, *JPS Torah Commentary*, 331 comments that "there is much uncertainty of meaning, extreme allusiveness, and considerable double entendre. The chapter is the most difficult segment of the Book of Genesis." Similarly, E. Fox, *In the Beginning: A New English Rendering of the Book of Genesis* (New York: Schocken, 1983) 201.

sayings (verses 19, 20, 21, 27); blessings (especially on Judah and Joseph) and rebukes (verses 3-7 and more mildly in verses 14-15); reflections on the past (verses 4, 6) and predictions for the future (verses 8, 10, 13, 16-17). This has engendered a variety of views on their unity of composition,[96] and the dating of the various sections.[97] While verse 28 appears to imply that they are all blessings, it is perhaps better to regard them as the last testamentary words by the patriarch Jacob to his sons.[98]

The details of this section are of limited value for this study. There is no suggestion that any significant wisdom-like elements are present, not even in the almost-proverbial sayings (for example, verses 19-21, 27) or animal imagery (verses 9, 14, 17, 21, 27) used to describe some of the sons. The focus here is very much on Jacob and his sons, not Joseph and his brothers.[99]

However, it does appear to have a role within the Joseph narrative, especially when it is viewed in its broader canonical context. One important observation is that the movement of the passage is from a focus on the 'sons of Jacob' (verses 1-2, בני יעקב ... בניו), to the 'tribes of Israel' (verse 28, שבטי ישראל).[100] The section assumes the fulfilment of the patriarchal promises,[101] and envisages a time when the sons will have become tribes within Israel. This, of course, creates a natural bridge to the later books in

---

96 Thus, for example, H. Seebass, 'Die Stämmesprüche Gen 49:3-27', *ZAW* 96 (1984): 333-350 argues for the essential unity of the chapter, against H.-J. Zobel, *Stammessprüche und Geschichte: Die Angaben der Stammessprüche von Gen 49, Dtn 33 and Jdc 5 über die politischen und kultischen Zustände in damaligen "Israel"*. BZAW, 95. (Berlin: Walter de Gruyter, 1965) 4-26. Sarna, *JPS Torah Commentary*, 331 proposes a redactional structure.

97 J.D. Heck, 'A History of Interpretation of Genesis 49 and Deuteronomy 33', *BSac* 147 (1990): 26 argues for a setting in the time of the patriarch Jacob; D.N. Freedman, 'Who is like thee among the gods: the religion of early Israel', in *Ancient Israelite Religion: Essays in Honor of Frank Moore Cross*. eds. P.D. Miller, P.D. Hanson and S.D. McBride. (Philadelphia: Fortress, 1987), 321 believes that Genesis 49 has come from the early period of the tribal league; B. Vawter, 'The Canaanite Background of Genesis 49', *CBQ* 17 (1955): 18 regards the chapter as representing a very early stage of theological thinking in which Yahwism is refining the crude concepts of Canaan. J. Coppens, 'La Bénédiction de Jacob: Son cadre historique à la lumière des parallèles ougaritiques', in *Volume du Congrès: Strasbourg 1956*. VTSup 4. (Leiden: E.J. Brill, 1957), 113-114 argues that it should be dated in the time of the Judges, not in a post-exilic period. Scullion, *Genesis*, 338-339 dates it from the reign of David, but including many earlier elements.

98 Heck, 'Genesis 49 and Deuteronomy 33', 21. Speiser, *Genesis*, 370 notes that 'cursed' (ארור) is used in verse 7, and the first three sons are sternly rebuked, not blessed. Brueggemann, *Genesis*, 365 prefers to label it as a 'testimony'.

99 Sailhamer, 'Genesis', 265.

100 Heck, 'Genesis 49 and Deuteronomy 33', 21.

101 Sailhamer, 'Genesis', 274.

the canon, where this transition has taken place, and serves to make the Joseph narrative a forward-looking tale which connects Genesis with the rest of the Pentateuch.

Furthermore, the focus on particular tribes is important for the Joseph narrative. Reuben, literally the firstborn, shall no longer be prominent, because he had defiled his father's bed (verse 4), presumably a reference to his sleeping with Bilhah (Gen 35:22).[102] Simeon and Levi will be scattered and divided (verse 7) because they were united in killing men in anger, probably a reference to the revenge killings at Shechem (Gen 34:25).[103] The first three sons thus appear to have disqualified themselves from being regarded as the firstborn.

After the first three sons, the rest are only briefly described, with the exception of Judah and Joseph.[104] Even Benjamin is scarcely mentioned (verse 27).[105] The prominence of Judah and Joseph is most naturally explained by their leading roles in the Joseph narrative itself. In other words, the final form of the testament of Jacob functions as a comment on the preceding Joseph narrative, and draws out some implications for the future of Israel.[106]

Judah is highly exalted in verses 8-12, though some of the imagery is unclear.[107] His brothers will bow down to him and praise him (verse 8), and he is compared to a fearsome lion.[108] In verse 10, his future is described in

---

102 Sarna, *JPS Torah Commentary*, 332.

103 S. Gevirtz, 'Simeon and Levi in 'The Blessing of Jacob' (Gen 49:5-7)', *HUCA* 52 (1981): 93. Sarna, *JPS Torah Commentary*, 334. On the details, see C.M. Carmichael, 'Some Sayings in Genesis 49', *JBL* 88 (1969): 435; Vawter, 'The Canaanite Background', 4; A. Caquot, ''Siméon et Lévi sont frères' (Gn 49,5)', in *De la Tôrah au Messie*. eds. M. Carrez, J. Doré and P. Grelot. (Paris: Desclée, 1981), 113.

104 Isaachar and Dan are dealt with in greater detail than the others. Isaachar in verses 14-15 would prefer a life of ease and luxury to the hard work and freedom he could have. In the end he finds slavery, being prepared to trade liberty for the material things of life (so Vawter, *On Genesis*, 463-464). Dan, although small, would help his brothers to gain their rights against oppression (verses 16-17). The images in verse 17 explain this. As a snake can strike at the legs of a horse and overthrow the more powerful animal, so Dan would be able to exert itself as one of the tribes. Freedman, 'Who is like thee', 322-323 argues that verse 18 is probably not part of the Dan saying while Rand, 'The Testament of Jacob', 105 proposes that it is Jacob's prayer for forgiveness.

105 Indeed, Brueggemann, *Genesis*, 366 suggests that chapter 49 is a secondary addition in its context, not only because it deals with Joseph (not Ephraim and Manasseh) but also because it only barely mentions Benjamin, who is greatly valued in the Joseph story.

106 Longacre, *Joseph: A Story of Divine Providence*, 23.

107 So Maher, *Genesis*, 266.

108 P. Culbertson, 'Blessing Jacob's Sons, Inheriting Family Myths', *Sewanee*

royal terms of ruling over the peoples.[109] While this could be regarded as being fulfilled in an idealised picture of the Davidic-Solomonic era, some have discerned here a messianic reference.[110] Two pictures of the abundance of this time are given in verse 11 - that vines will be so plentiful that one can afford to tie a donkey to them, and wine is flowing so freely that it can be used to wash clothes.[111] The picture is one of the future pre-eminence of Judah.[112]

However, there is also a strong emphasis on the fruitfulness (verse 22) and blessings (verses 25-26) bestowed on Joseph.[113] Judah's future exaltation as ruler, does not preclude Joseph being abundantly blessed by God. The high concentration of divine names and titles in verses 24-25 asserts that God will help Joseph by being with him and blessing him.[114] Of course, this motif of God being with Joseph, leading to his prospering, has been a key element of the Joseph narrative up to this point. What appears to be taking place is that Joseph's present character is being projected into the future. The one who was 'set apart from his brothers' (נְזִיר אֶחָיו, verse 27) in chapter 37, and throughout the story, will be set apart from his brothers by the abundance of his future prosperity.[115]

The juxtaposition of blessing on both Judah and Joseph is potentially quite significant. Chapter 49 seems to imply Judah, as the firstborn, will be the bearer of the patriarchal promises and the successor of Jacob, and as such will prosper.[116] Yet this does not preclude Joseph, one set apart from

---

Theological Review 37 (1993): 69; E.M. Good, 'The 'Blessing' on Judah, Gen. 49:8-12', *JBL* 82 (1963): 428.

109 Culbertson, 'Blessing Jacob's Sons', 69; Sarna, *JPS Torah Commentary*, 335. Most of the translations of יָבֹא שִׁילֹה entail a very positive and powerful future role for Judah.

110 Maher, *Genesis*, 266 suggests that if verse 10 is translated 'until he comes to whom it belongs' this leaves open a messianic interpretation which, he claims, "is supported by the following verses which describe the reign of Judah in paradisiacal terms." Also R. Martin-Achard, 'A propos de la bénédiction de Juda en Genèse 49,8-12 (10)', in *De la Tôrah au Messie*. eds. M. Carrez, J. Doré and P. Grelot. (Paris: Desclée, 1981), 127.

111 Hamilton, *Genesis Chapters 18-50*, 662; von Rad, *Genesis*, 425; Vawter, *On Genesis*, 462; Alter, *Genesis*, 296.

112 Keil and Delitzsch, *The Pentateuch*, 398; Sailhamer, 'Genesis', 269.

113 Culbertson, 'Blessing Jacob's Sons', 73 notes that Joseph "receives the longest and most laudatory blessing". Similarly, Sarna, *JPS Torah Commentary*, 342.

114 Scullion, *Genesis*, 342. M. Sæbø, 'Divine names and epithets in Genesis 49:24b-25a: some methodological and traditio-historical remarks', in *History and Traditions of Early Israel: Studies Presented to Eduard Nielsen May 8th 1993*. eds. A. Lemaire and B. Otzen. (Leiden: E.J. Brill, 1993), 131.

115 Hamilton, *Genesis Chapters 18-50*, 686.

116 Garrett, *Rethinking Genesis*, 176 comments that Joseph is given a special bounty, but the position of first-born is given to Judah. *Contra* B.J. van der Merwe, 'Joseph

his brothers by his wisdom, also prospering due to God being with him in blessing. Chapter 49 affirms both, and does not need to read either one down in order to exalt the other.[117] Both the covenant promises and wisdom can be celebrated and furthered at the same time.

Genesis 49:29-50:26

Structure

The Joseph narrative concludes with a number of smaller pericopes which outline the deaths of Jacob and Joseph, and a final reconciliation between Joseph and his brothers, while looking forward in hope to the future of the people of God.[118] It is proposed to deal with this text in three sections

- Jacob's death and burial (49:29-50:14)
- Joseph and his brothers (50:15-21)
- Joseph's death (50:22-26)

In a sense 49:29-50:14 could be regarded as two units, outlining Jacob's charge to his sons and death in 49:29-50:1, and the burial in 50:2-14. However, the mention of Joseph and his reaction in 50:1 links the two together, and smoothes the transition from the charge addressing the twelve sons (49:29-32), to Joseph taking control of the funeral arrangements.

49:29-50:14 - Jacob's Death and Burial

This section, in many ways, resumes chapter 47. Jacob's commission for burial in Canaan, given to Joseph in 47:29-31, is now given in more detail to all the brothers (49:29-32). In his charge, Jacob outlines a number of events relating to the burial of the earlier patriarchs and their wives, which makes clear to the reader Jacob's understanding of the continuity between the patriarchs, and therefore the promises of the covenant. The burial place was where Abraham and Isaac were buried, the plot of land that was

---

as Successor of Jacob', in *Studia Biblica et Semitica*. eds. W.C. van Unnik and A.S. van der Woude. (Wageningen: Veenman & Zonen, 1966), 221-232 who suggests that Joseph, not Judah, is the one pictured as Jacob's successor.

117 As Janzen, *Genesis 12-50*, 190 points out, this tension is partially resolved through projecting Judah's leadership into the future. In this way it does not conflict with Joseph's dreams, and his leadership in Egypt. Vawter, *On Genesis*, 461-462 fails to see this distinction.

118 Westermann, *Genesis 37-50*, 210.

purchased by Abraham for Sarah's burial.[119] Its twofold significance is that it was in Canaan, the place of Israel's future, but it was also a symbol of the inheritance of the whole land. When Jacob's death finally comes, it is described in terms that explicitly set him in the context of his ancestors (ויאסף אל־עמיו, 49:33).

Once Jacob died, the focus is again on Joseph's reaction (50:1)[120] and initiatives (50:2-7), with the brothers not mentioned again until the funeral procession is already leaving (verse 8). Joseph, the man in authority as in chapter 41, orders the embalming of *his* father (אביו, verse 2). The absence of any mention of Egyptian religious practices implies that no negative inference should be drawn from Jacob being embalmed.[121] The embalming process is described as being carried out by Joseph's servants, the physicians (עבדיו את־הרפאים, verse 2). Of course, Joseph himself will later be embalmed (verse 26).

Since Joseph is probably still mourning, he asks officials in Pharaoh's household to speak to Pharaoh on his behalf.[122] It is a carefully worded request[123] addressed to Pharaoh that omits Jacob's twice-mentioned wish not to be buried in Egypt (47:29, 30), emphasises that he has sworn an oath to his father, and inserts the new detail that Jacob had prepared this grave for himself.[124] As in 41:37, Joseph's words meet with Pharaoh's approval

---

119 B. Gemser, 'Be'ēber hajjardēn: in Jordan's Borderland', *VT* 2 (1952): 349-355 has argued persuasively that the phrase בעבר הירדן (verse 10) which would usually be translated 'beyond the Jordan', can mean 'in the region of the Jordan', and probably does so here. More recently, A. Demsky, 'The route of Jacob's funeral cortege and the problem of eber hayyarden', in *Minhah le-Nahum: Biblical and Other Studies Presented to Nahum M. Sarna in Honour of his 70th Birthday*. JSOTSup, 154, eds. M. Brettler and M. Fishbane. (Sheffield: Sheffield Academic Press, 1993), 54-64 has argued that the phrase refers to a place between Gaza and Beer-sheba, near Tell-Gerar.

120 Roop, *Genesis*, 290.

121 Vawter, *On Genesis*, 471; Vergote, *Joseph en Égypte*, 199; Lowenthal, *The Joseph Narrative*, 147. Sarna, *JPS Torah Commentary*, 347 points out that while embalming is normally undertaken by priestly, here it is performed by the physicians. The embalming process is outlined in detail in Murtagh, 'The Egyptian Colouring', 257.

122 Herbert, *Genesis 12-50*, 159 reasonably suggests that "Joseph, in a state of ritual mourning, could not come personally into the presence of Pharaoh, but would need to have royal permission to leave the country." Similarly, Keil and Delitzsch, *The Pentateuch*, 410.

123 The rhetoric of Joseph's successful request is insightfully analysed by Savran, *Telling and Retelling*, 43.

124 Sarna, *JPS Torah Commentary*, 348 notes that כריתי from the root כרה would normally mean either 'I dug' or 'I purchased', but in 2 Chr 16:14 כרה appears to mean simply 'to prepare a grave in advance'. He therefore translates it as 'I made ready'.

(verse 6).

The funeral procession also emphasises the centrality and authority of Joseph. Verse 7 starts off with וַיַּעַל יוֹסֵף לִקְבֹּר אֶת־אָבִיו, and only then mentions the many others who accompanied him - Pharaoh's servants, the elders of his household and the land of Egypt, Joseph's household, and only then mentions the brothers and Jacob's (אָבִיו, *his* father's, verse 8) household. Even the chariots are explicitly described as going up with Joseph (עִמּוֹ, with *him*, verse 9), and Joseph is singled out as mourning for his father (וַיַּעַשׂ לְאָבִיו אֵבֶל, verse 10). At the end of the burial time, the narrator again draws attention to Joseph by observing that Joseph returned to Egypt - *he* and *his* brothers, and those who had gone up with *him* to bury *his* father (verse 14)

וַיָּשָׁב יוֹסֵף מִצְרַיְמָה הוּא וְאֶחָיו וְכָל־הָעֹלִים אִתּוֹ לִקְבֹּר אֶת־אָבִיו

Thus, although verse 12 records that Jacob's sons did for him what he had commanded them, the focus in the burial account is very much on how Joseph accomplished this delicate task, getting permission from Pharaoh to leave Egypt, and honouring him with a great procession and appropriate mourning.[125]

50:15-21 - Joseph's Brothers Finally Reconciled

Verse 15 raises the new threat of Joseph's attitude after Jacob's death, with Joseph no longer constrained by the presence of his father.[126] Here, then, is a final opportunity for the reader to observe the character of Joseph.

Verse 15 also clearly shows that the breakdown has not fully been resolved from the brother's point of view, for they still perceive that they need to ask for Joseph's forgiveness. This passage is therefore resumptive of chapter 45 where, as far as the first-time reader was concerned, the matter had already been settled. The fact that Joseph's stance does not change reveals that the matter had been settled from his viewpoint, and that the only uncertainty lay with the brothers. Joseph had already forgiven them after the testing of chapters 42-45, but the brothers still needed reassurance. For this reason, Joseph tells them not to be afraid (אַל־תִּירָאוּ, verses 19, 21).

In verses 16-17, the brothers convey to Joseph instructions[127] allegedly

---

125 Maher, *Genesis*, 271.

126 Vawter, *On Genesis*, 473; Wenham, *Genesis 16-50*, 493. Adar, *The Book of Genesis*, 158.

127 The MT reads וַיְצַוּוּ in verse 16, but the LXX renders it καὶ παρεγένοντο, 'and they came'. While צוה normally means 'command', it can mean 'to commission' (*BDB* 846), as here in the sense of sending someone else with these instructions to Joseph. This would be consistent with the brothers not coming to Joseph until verse 18

from Jacob to him, to forgive them for their wrongdoing. It is a moot point amongst commentators as to whether these instructions preserve otherwise unrecorded words of Jacob, or whether they were fabrications by the brothers.[128] The fact that Jacob was not privy to the discussions in chapter 45, and the way in which their dilemma is introduced in verse 15, makes it more likely that this story has been created by the brothers in response to their perceived crisis.

Joseph's response of 'weeping' (ויבך יוסף, verse 17) is ambiguous on its own,[129] but needs to be understood in the light of Joseph's subsequent words of explanation. His positive attitude towards his brothers, 'although you intended evil against me' (ואתם חשבתם עלי רעה, verse 20), makes it likely here that Joseph's tears were a result of his realising that his brothers still did not believe his goodwill towards them.[130]

Joseph's character is here displayed most patently. In a situation where he could take revenge without any apparent consequences, Joseph refuses to do so. He asks the rhetorical question (התחת אלהים אני, verse 19), showing that for him, this is a matter of character, not consequences.[131] The response portrays Joseph as one who is not vengeful, or seeking to pay others back. Now that he is in a position of power, he refuses to use that power for self-serving purposes. Joseph's words are used sparingly by the narrator in Genesis 37-50, often revealing what Joseph is like on the inside, or what motivates him. They are, thus, a very fruitful guide to his character. Here, his words confirm the 'wisdom-like elements' that have earlier been noted.[132]

Furthermore, if this pericope is resumptive of chapter 45, its theological undergirding is likely to continue that of the earlier reconciliation passage.[133] This makes unlikely Brueggemann's stimulating suggestion that

---

(reading וילכו there instead of the suggested emendation ויבכו, 'and they wept').

128 Those who do not view this as a fabrication include Keil and Delitzsch, *The Pentateuch*, 411-412; Lowenthal, *The Joseph Narrative*, 151-153 and von Rad, *Genesis*, 432. Hamilton, *Genesis Chapters 18-50*, 703 argues that this request is made up by the brother. W. Brueggemann, 'Genesis L 15-21: A Theological Exploration', in *Congress Volume Salamanca*. VTSup, 36, ed. J.A. Emerton. (Leiden: E.J. Brill, 1985), 44 suggests that the reader is meant to be unsure.

129 Brueggemann, 'Genesis L 15-21', 45.

130 *Contra* Lowenthal, *The Joseph Narrative*, 155, who suggests that Joseph is weeping as he realises the extent of his father's concern for the brothers.

131 Lowenthal, *The Joseph Narrative*, 156; Hamilton, *Genesis Chapters 18-50*, 705.

132 Vawter, *On Genesis*, 473; Adar, *The Book of Genesis*, 159. Although Brueggemann, *Genesis*, 375 wants to argue that Joseph is an expression of the psalmic lament tradition, he also concedes that "Joseph is here an embodiment of what is most honorable in the *wisdom tradition* of Proverbs."

133 *Contra* Fretheim, 'The Book of Genesis', 643 who argues that there are crucial differences between Gen 45:5-8 and 50:15-21.

this passage reflects a theology of lament reminiscent of the psalms, or Westermann's view that a salvation oracle is reflected in verses 19-21.[134] As in 45:5-8, this is an assertion that God has worked behind the scenes, in and despite human actions, to bring about his purposes of life and blessing.[135]

Of course, while this appears to reflect a 'wisdom-like' doctrine of providence, it is also significant to note that God's purpose was that many people might be kept alive (לְהַחֲיֹת עַם־רָב, verse 20). In particular, this includes the members of Jacob's family, the line of promise. In other words, God's working behind the scenes has enabled the partial fulfilment of the Abrahamic promise, both in keeping Jacob's family alive and bringing blessing to the Egyptians.[136] Furthermore, in verse 21, Joseph proceeds to reassure his brothers by undertaking that he will continue to provide for them. This makes explicit the idea of Joseph's wise administration enabling the continuance of the promised line. Wisdom and promise dovetail yet once more. Thus, Westermann is correct in viewing this section as the "true conclusion of the Joseph narrative".[137]

When the reader casts their mind back to the dream of chapter 37, it is apparent that God's purposes - effected through the rise and prospering of Joseph - have prevailed. It is, therefore, an appropriate touch in the narrative, to have the dream recalled as the brothers bow before Joseph (verse 18).[138]

50:22-26 - Joseph's Death

In this final section, the story of Joseph is quickly finished by a brief narration of his death and burial. He lives to the Egyptian ideal lifespan of 110 years, seeing his children of several generations (verse 23).

However, the story also finishes with a strong hint to the implied reader to look back to the patriarchal promises and forward to their fulfilment in the exodus.[139] Verse 24 refers explicitly to the land promised to the patriarchs - Abraham, Isaac and Jacob.[140] In verse 25, Joseph more allusively makes the Israelites swear to carry up his bones from Egypt 'when God surely visits you' (פָּקֹד יִפְקֹד אֱלֹהִים אֶתְכֶם). This is also hinted at

---

134 Brueggemann, 'Genesis L 15-21', 48; Westermann, *Joseph*, 108-109.
135 Humphreys, *Joseph and His Family*, 116; Roop, *Genesis*, 291; Sarna, *JPS Torah Commentary*, 350.
136 Westermann, *Genesis 37-50*, 205.
137 Westermann, *Joseph*, 107.
138 Gunkel, *Genesis*, 464. Roop, *Genesis*, 291; Brueggemann, *Genesis*, 370-371; Westermann, *Joseph*, 108. Scullion, *Genesis*, 346 comments that "[t]hey are again, and finally, prostrate before Joseph, this time knowing who he is."
139 Humphreys, *Joseph and His Family*, 108.
140 Brueggemann, *Genesis*, 379; Humphreys, *Joseph and His Family*, 196; Baldwin, *The Message of Genesis 12-50*, 220.

in verse 26, when the narrator records that Joseph is preserved by embalming, and placed in a coffin, not a grave or tomb.[141] The anticipation of the exodus is clear.[142]

While the Joseph story has a clear literary integrity, the text itself suggests that it is a story embedded in a much larger story.[143] In its broader canonical context, it both contributes to, and draws meaning from the stories and texts which surround it.

Genesis 46-50 as a Whole Unit

Narrative Focus in Chapters 46-50

The narrative focus of chapters 46-50 is a significant but often neglected factor. While some of this material appears extraneous, all of it seems to be tied into the story of Joseph, and there is a strong Joseph-centred perspective throughout.

These chapters are not simply narrative, yet even the non-narrative material is now embedded in narrative.[144] Jacob's journey to Egypt and his visions, narrated in 46:1-7, are governed by 45:28

עוד־יוסף בני חי אלכה ואראנו בטרם אמות

The reason for this journey, in its present narrative setting, is to 'see Joseph'. This journey is then amplified by verses 7-27, with verse 28 being resumptive of the journey *to Joseph*. This narrative thread then continues as far as 47:12. 47:13-26 is a narrative which explicitly relates to Joseph and

---

141 J.L. Magness, *Sense and Absence* (Atlanta: Scholars, 1986) 60 notes that a coffin is "not a final resting place but a means of conveyance." Similarly, Keil and Delitzsch, *The Pentateuch*, 413.

142 Magness, *Sense and Absence*, 58-59; Scullion, *Genesis*, 347; Herbert, *Genesis 12-50*, 160.

143 Humphreys, *Joseph and His Family*, 55; Gibson, *Genesis*, 318; H. Ausloos, 'The Deuteronomist and the Account of Joseph's Death (Gen 50,22-26)', *Studies in the Book of Genesis: Literature, Redaction and History*. Edited by A. Wénin. BETL 155. (Leuven: Leuven University Press, 2001) 381-395.

144 For an example of this, see B.G. Webb, *The Book of the Judges: An Integrated Reading*. JSOTSup, 46. (Sheffield: JSOT Press, 1987) 36. He argues there that the literary unit is a *narrative* text, and that non-narrative elements (such as the hymn of chapter 5) are embedded in the narrative by introductory words (for example, 5:1). Even theological statements ('Israel did what was evil in the sight of Yahweh') are narrated events - one character (Israel) did what another character (God) disapproved of.

his administration, the Joseph to whom Jacob has come. 47:12, 27 nicely bracket this cameo, so that verse 27 resumes the narrative. Two more narrative events happens in 47:29 and 48:1. In the first, the dialogue between Jacob and Joseph (47:29-31) thus becomes embedded in the narrative. Joseph alone of the brothers is summoned. The second narrative event (48:1) speaks of Joseph's initiative on hearing his father was ill. The blessings on Joseph's sons in the rest of the chapter is an unpacking of this new situation of the imminent death of Joseph's father. The Joseph-centred focus is reflected in the narrative introduction in verse 1, and the fact that the first blessings are addressed not to all Jacob's children, but only to Joseph's children.

Chapter 49 is less connected, but is essentially the ripple effect of the Joseph-centred events of chapter 48. Chapter 49 ends with a resumption of the narrative in verses 28-33, so that, in their present form, they too are embedded in the narrative story of Joseph. The sayings of chapter 49 give special prominence to two sons - Judah (verses 8-12) and Joseph (verses 22-26).

The death of Jacob is also recorded as part of the Joseph narrative. Ch. 50:1-2 immediately makes this clear by being Joseph-centred again. The other sons are backgrounded as Joseph is foregrounded. Although the broader narrative (50:12, 13) indicates that the brothers played a part in the burial of Jacob, they are in 50:1-7 excluded from our focus until all the arrangements are made and the journey begins. This narrative focus makes the brothers seem to be an appendage, while the reader's attention is focused on Joseph.

This is reinforced by Jacob being described as *Joseph's* father (50:5, 6, 7, 10, 14), never as as 'their' father (despite the presence of the brothers in verse 14). Only in verse 15 does the spotlight come around to the brothers, and Jacob is, for the first time in the chapter, called 'their' father. 50:15-21, however, does not sideline Joseph, for it portrays him as one with supreme power over his brothers. The book ends in 50:22-26, with a narrative description of the death of Joseph. The death of the other brothers is not mentioned. Thus, chapters 46-50 maintain throughout a narrative emphasis and focus on the person of Joseph. This perspective helps to bind these chapters into the literary unit of Genesis 37-50.

The significance of this narrative focus lies in the fact that Joseph is not left behind as the narrator's concern turns more and more to the continuation of the patriarchal promises.

Chapters 46-50 and the Themes of Chapters 37-45

This study has proposed that a number of key themes have emerged from chapters 37-45, such as the breakdown of relationships within the family, Joseph's programmatic dream, and the issue of the overarching, but behind-the-scenes activity of God. All of these are addressed, and brought to completion, in chapters 46-50.

Firstly, the breakdown in relationships within the family. This is not resolved in any substantial way until chapter 45 when, in 45:15, his brothers talk with him. Yet, the problem is not fully resolved. In chapters 46 and 47, Jacob and the brothers move to the land where Joseph is a powerful figure, which raises the possibility of Joseph using his power to gain revenge.[145] Chapters 48 and 49 serve to both remind the reader of the imminent death of Jacob (a fearful possibility in 50:15) and also to raise the problem of the future relationships between the families of each of the brothers (for example, 48:22; 49:7, 8, 10, 26). Finally, chapter 50 explicitly raises the new threat of Joseph's attitude after Jacob's death (50:15), with Joseph no longer constrained by the presence of his father. Verse 15 clearly shows that the breakdown has not fully been resolved from the perspective of the brothers, and they seek to deceive Joseph. Thus, the family relationships are only finally restored by Joseph's words of reassurance in 50:19-21.[146]

Joseph's dream is at least partially fulfilled by the end of chapter 45.[147] This is observed by the narrator several times in chapters 42-44 (42:6; 43:26; 44:14) and most significantly in the thoughts of Joseph himself (42:9). The 'second dream' cannot be fulfilled 'literally' in that Joseph's mother Rachel has already died (35:18-20). Yet, in a broader sense, the dream(s) speak of a rise to prominence of Joseph above all his family, and this theme, too, continues in chapters 46-50.[148] Thus, Joseph provides richly for his family in the land of Goshen (47:1-12, 27), and the entire chapter sets forth Joseph as a powerful administrator, on whom his family depend.

Joseph's prominence is also seen in chapters 48 and 49. The death-bed blessing of Joseph's two sons is recounted in chapter 48, both prior to, and in more detail than, the other descendants in chapter 49. Moreover, legitimating Joseph's two sons (48:8-20) leads him to have an advantage over the others. Jacob's charge to his sons to bury him is given first to Joseph (47:29-31) and only later to the others (49:29-32). This prominence continues in chapter 50, where Joseph's brothers acknowledge the powerful position of Joseph by their 'fabrication' of a message from their father (50:15-17). Thus, chapters 46-50 continue the portrayal of Joseph's rise to prominence and power.

---

145 Thus Coats, 'Redactional Unity', 15 sees 46:1-47:27 as the conclusion to the Joseph story proper.
146 White, 'The Joseph Story', 58; Niditch, *Underdogs and Tricksters*, 118.
147 Ackerman, 'Joseph, Judah and Jacob', 94-95.
148 Ackerman, 'Joseph, Judah and Jacob', 108 suggests that the second dream is fulfilled in 47:31 when Jacob bowed down on the head of the bed, with the object left ambiguously unstated. Ackerman's suggestion is unlikely, and has received little support.

Finally, chapters 46-50 also contribute to the theme of God's behind-the-scenes activity set forth clearly in 50:4-15. Certainly, the descent of Jacob and his sons to Egypt (46:1-7; 47:1-12, 27-28) is the narrative conclusion to Joseph's pivotal words, למחיה שלחני אלהים לפניכם (45:5). Joseph's success in his administration (47:13-26) is a continued outworking of 'the LORD was with Joseph' (39:2, 21, 23), the way in which God's hidden activity is described in chapter 39.

While chapters 48 and 49 do not advance this theme in any significant way, even here (and perhaps also in 46:8-27), the presupposition behind the blessings and listing of descendants is that God will continue to ensure the preservation of life. Chapter 50 proclaims the theme of God's hidden but powerful rule even more clearly than chapter 45. In 45:5, 7, the focus was on the preserving of life; in 50:20 there is the explicit statement of the principle that

ואתם חשבתם עלי רעה אלהים חשבה לטבה

It therefore seems appropriate to conclude with Humphreys that "[t]he tensions set forth in chapter 37 are not resolved until chapter 50".[149] The issues which displayed Joseph's wisdom in chapters 37-45, receive a fitting closure in chapters 46-50.

---

149 W.L. Humphreys, *Crisis and Story: Introduction to the Old Testament* (Palo Alto: Mayfield, 1979) 86.

PART 3

WISDOM AND COVENANT
IN THE JOSEPH STORY

CHAPTER 9

The Abrahamic Promises and Genesis 37-50

It has been common in some recent approaches to read a literary unit without regard to anything outside the text. This was especially the case in text-centred literary readings, such as the early work of the 'Sheffield school'.[1] A key principle here was the self-sufficiency of the text as a 'free-standing' entity, set loose not only from authorial intention, but also from its canonical context.[2] Such an approach can be implemented most fruitfully where the unit comprises a whole book (for example, Judges, Jonah).[3]

---

1   Examples of this would include D. Gunn, *The Story of King David: Genre and Interpretation.* JSOTSup, 6. (Sheffield: JSOT Press, 1978); D. Gunn, *The Fate of King Saul: An Interpretation of a Biblical Story.* JSOTSup 14. (Sheffield: JSOT Press, 1980); Webb, *The Book of the Judges.* D.J.A. Clines, *The Theme of the Pentateuch.* JSOTSup, 10. (Sheffield: JSOT Press, 1978) is an interesting example because of the overlap with the Joseph narrative. The index of biblical references, which includes 7 pages of references to the Pentateuch and only 14 individual references outside the Pentateuch, reveals that Clines' approach was to discern the theme of the Pentateuch almost without reference to the broader biblical context. The 'Sheffield school' appears to have moved on from such text-centred approaches. Thus, for example, D.J.A. Clines and J.C. Exum, 'The New Literary Criticism', in *The New Literary Criticism and the Hebrew Bible.* JSOTSup, 143. (Sheffield: Sheffield Academic Press, 1993), 12 redefine 'the new literary criticism' to exclude rhetorical criticism, structuralism and formalism, and to refer only to criticisms that are post-structuralist. Indeed, the shift can be seen clearly in the fact that Clines has in 1997 published a second edition of *The Theme of the Pentateuch*, in which he adds an afterword (pages 127-141) qualifying the conclusions of the first edition as a result of newer approaches.
2   T. Longman, *Literary Approaches to Biblical Interpretation.* Foundations of Contemporary Interpretation, 3. (Grand Rapids: Academie, 1987) 25-27 emphasises the role of the self-sufficiency of the text for the New Critics. Thus, M.H. Abrams, *A Glossary of Literary Terms.* 4th edn. (New York: Holt, Rinehart & Winston, 1981) 83 notes that those who argue for an 'intentional fallacy' hold the view that "meaning and value reside within the text of the finished, free-standing, and public work of literature itself."
3   Useful studies here include Webb, *The Book of the Judges*, and L.R. Klein, *The Triumph of Irony in the Book of Judges.* Bible and Literature Series 14. (Sheffield: Almond Press, 1989). P. Trible, *Rhetorical Criticism: Context, Method, and the Book*

However, sometimes the text of the literary unit suggests that it is part of a larger (con)text. A parallel example here is the recent debate on structure in, and the literary integrity of, the book of Numbers. Olson has argued that Numbers has a putative unity on its own, yet other writers have insisted that Num 1:1-10:10 also need to be understood in light of a broader Sinai unit that reaches from Exodus to Numbers.[4] Thus, for example, crucial ideas in the book of Numbers about the people of God, holiness, priesthood and worship all presuppose information given in the preceding books of Exodus and Leviticus. While Numbers arguably is a literary unit in its own right, there are clear links with its surrounding literary, or even canonical, context.

A similar duality exists with the Joseph narrative. This study has argued that Genesis 37-50 is a coherent unit with literary integrity. However, the detailed analysis of the text has also shown that these chapters point back to what precedes them in Genesis, and forward to what follows them in the rest of the Pentateuch. In other words, the text of Genesis 37-50 itself suggests that it is entwined in a broader literary context, since it presupposes something has gone before and hints that something will follow after. It is thus a unit that needs to be read in its own right, but also understood as a text that has been embedded canonically in the Pentateuch.

Fundamental to both the book of Genesis and the Pentateuch is the theme of covenant, or, more specifically, the patriarchal promises. Clines has found widespread support for his view that the theme of the Pentateuch as a whole is the partial fulfilment and partial non-fulfilment of the promises to the patriarchs.[5]

---

of Jonah. Guides to Biblical Scholarship, Old Testament Series. (Minneapolis: Fortress, 1994).

4 G.J. Wenham, *Numbers*. OTG. (Sheffield: Sheffield Academic Press, 1997) 13-25 provides a useful recent summary of this debate, sparked largely by D.T. Olson, *The Death of the Old and the Birth of the New: The Framework of the Book of Numbers and the Pentateuch*. Brown Judaic Studies, 71. (Chico: Scholars, 1985). While the precise details of structure are disputed, the general point of Numbers being both a book and part of a wider context, has been strongly argued by Olson.

5 D.J.A. Clines, 'Images of Yahweh: God in the Pentateuch', in *Studies in Old Testament Theology*. eds. R.L. Hubbard, R.K. Johnston and R.P. Meye. (Dallas: Word, 1992), 81 notes that he has moved from the position expressed in the first edition of *The Theme of the Pentateuch* (1978). He argues that "the Pentateuch is a novel in that it is a machine for generating interpretations ... There are so many complex strands in it, so many fragmentary glimpses of its personalities, that we cannot reduce it to a single coherent graspable unity that all readers will agree upon." In footnote 3 on page 96 he comments that some readers may ask how this view squares with his earlier book. He answers that "[i]t does not. I now think that there is more than one way of saying "what the Pentateuch is all about," though I still think that the theme of the fulfillment and non-fulfillment of the threefold promise is one

The present chapter proposes to draw together, and develop, some of the observations already made about the relationship of the Joseph story to this broader context. This will be attempted in two sections. Firstly, it is proposed to reconsider the Joseph story as part of the book of Genesis, exploring the connections and allusions that are present in the final form. Secondly, the broader links with the Pentateuch as a whole are developed.

The Joseph Story as Part of Genesis

There are two ways in which chapters 37-50 are connected with the book of Genesis as a whole. Firstly, there are occasions when the text of the Joseph narrative refers to previous incidents, people or events, giving a clear message to the implied reader that a broader context is being assumed. Secondly, and more substantially, a reading of the whole of the book of Genesis would make it clear that a number of themes, motifs, literary devices, structural markers and characters are shared between chapters 37-50 and the rest of the book.

Internal Clues of a Broader Context

Firstly, then, a reader studying Genesis 37-50 would be aware that there is an implied wider story of which the Joseph narrative is a part. This is particularly the case at the beginning and end of Genesis 37-50. The opening unit of 37:2-4, under the guise of providing the reader with necessary background information, actually assumes that certain knowledge is already understood. Birth narratives are often significant in biblical and epic stories, but Joseph is already seventeen, with his birth being recorded back in Gen 30:22-24. Jacob is mentioned in verse 2, but not introduced in any detail. Although Jacob will be vital for the unfolding story, the narrator does not even name all his wives, number his children, or mention that he is the bearer of the Abrahamic promises. Bilhah and Zilpah are mentioned (verse 2), but not Rachel and Leah. Neither do these verses indicate which of the wives is the mother of Joseph.

The order of the sons and the identity of the first-born are also integral to the story, not only in the power plays of chapter 37 and the sayings of chapter 49, but also in the rise to prominence of Joseph and Judah within chapters 37-50. A first-time reader would sense a gap in background information at this point that would render them confused or unclear. The story commences as if the implied reader is expected to know more than they are told. These gaps are not filled later in the story and therefore some prior information is presupposed.

---

fruitful way of talking about the Pentateuch."

Towards the end of the Joseph narrative, there are further hints of a wider tale. In Gen 50:24 there is an explicit reference to the covenant promise of land to Abraham, Isaac and Jacob. In Gen 46:1, God is described by the narrator as the God of Jacob's father Isaac, though neither Isaac's identity, nor the significance of this comment is explained to the reader. In addition, the previous importance of both Beer-sheba and earlier theophanies is not outlined. The narrator appears to assume that the reader already possesses the necessary information. There are also references to Jacob's ancestors in his burial charge (49:29-32), and in the description of the burial (50:13), including details of Abraham buying a cave as a burial site, and the mention of Sarah, Isaac, Rebekah and Leah.

Chapter 49 also assumes a prior story. The disqualification of Reuben, Simeon and Levi is necessary for the rise to prominence of Judah that is reflected in the Joseph story. In the wider book of Genesis this is explained by Reuben sleeping with Bilhah (35:22) and by Simeon and Levi's revenge attack on Shechem (34:25-31). These events are prior to the Joseph narrative, yet they are the events referred to in Jacob's testamentary words to his sons (49:3-7). The final form of chapter 49 thus presupposes knowledge of these earlier incidents.

Thus, the hints and implications contained in Genesis 37-50 suggest a broader context of the Joseph story. Once the reader follows the trajectories of these internal clues, an ever-widening context is found in the patriarchal narratives as a whole, the book of Genesis and the Pentateuch. This expanding context will be explored in the remainder of this chapter.

The Toledot Formula and Genealogies

The final form of the book of Genesis contains many clear links with the Joseph narrative, the most prominent of which is the adoption of the *toledot* formula in 37:2 and the use of genealogies (especially 46:8-27).[6] A number

6   A number of recent studies have considered the *toledot* formula and the genealogies of Genesis: M.D. Johnson, *The Purpose of the Biblical Genealogies With Special Reference to the Setting of the Genealogies of Jesus.* SNTSMS, 8. (Cambridge: Cambridge University Press, 1969); M.H. Woudstra, 'The *Toledot* of the Book of Genesis and their Redemptive-Historical Significance', *CTJ* 5 (1970): 184-189; J. Scharbert, 'Der Sinn der Toledot-Formel in der Priesterschrift', in *Wort - Gebot - Glaube: Beiträge zur Theologie des Alten Testaments. Walter Eichrodt zum 80. Geburtstag.* ATANT, 59, eds. H.J. Stoebe, J.J. Stamm and E. Jenni. (Zurich: Zwingli Verlag, 1970), 45-56; P. Weimar, 'Die Toledot-Formel in der priesterschriftlichen Geschichtsdarstellung', *BZ* 18 (1974): 65-93; R.R. Wilson, *Genealogy and History in the Biblical World* (New Haven: Yale, 1977); S. Tengström, *Die Toledotformel und die literarische Struktur der priesterlichen Erweiterungsschicht im Pentateuch.* CBOTS, 17. (Uppsala: Almqvist & Wiksell, 1981); R.B. Robinson, 'Literary Functions of the Genealogies of Genesis', *CBQ* 48 (1986): 595-608; D.L.

of studies have suggested that these devices provide the macrostructure for the book as a whole.[7] The *toledot* formula is used ten times in Genesis in crucial structural places. There are five occurrences in Gen 1:1-11:26 (2:4; 5:1; 6:9; 10:1; 11:10), matched by five in Gen 11:27-50:26 (11:27; 25:12; 25:19; 36:1/9; 37:2).[8] The second group of references begin the account of the offspring of Terah, Ishmael, Isaac, Esau and Jacob respectively,[9] making it evident that the formula is a prominent structural marker in the patriarchal narratives. Indeed, in both sections of the book of Genesis the *toledot* formula serves to indicate a turning point in the larger story.[10] In terms of the Joseph narrative, it marks a new stage where Joseph acts to preserve life and bring reconciliation to his family, but it also clearly links these last chapters of Genesis with the preceding ones.

Christensen, 'Biblical Genealogies and Eschatological Speculation', *Perspectives in Religious Studies* 14 (1987): 59-65; R.S. Hess, 'The Genealogies of Genesis 1-11 and Comparative Literature', *Bib* 70 (1989): 241-254; N. Steinberg, 'The Genealogical Framework of the Family Stories in Genesis', *Semeia* 46 (1989): 41-50; T.D. Alexander, 'From Adam to Judah: The Significance of the Family Tree in Genesis', *EvQ* 61 (1989): 5-19; K.F. Plum, 'Genealogy as Theology', *SJOT* 1 (1989): 66-92; B. Renaud, 'Les généalogies et la structure de l'histoire sacerdotale dans le livre de la Genèse', *RB* 97 (1990): 5-30; Garrett, *Rethinking Genesis*; T.D. Andersen, 'Genealogical Prominence and the Structure of Genesis', in *Biblical Hebrew and Discourse Linguistics*. ed. R.D. Bergen. (Dallas: Summer Institute of Linguistics, 1994), 242-266; N.A. Bailey, 'Some Literary and Grammatical Aspects of Genealogies in Genesis', in *Biblical Hebrew and Discourse Linguistics*. ed. R.D. Bergen. (Dallas: Summer Institute of Linguistics, 1994), 267-282; D.M. Carr, 'Βίβλος γενέσεως Revisited: A Synchronic Analysis of Patterns in Genesis as Part of the Torah (Part Two)', *ZAW* 110 (1998): 327-347.

7 Renaud, 'Les généalogies', 13; Coats, *Genesis*, 36 and Andersen, 'Genealogical Prominence', 252; T.W. Mann, '"All the Families of the Earth". The Theological Unity of Genesis', *Int* 45 (1991), 343; Garrett, *Rethinking Genesis* relies on the *toledot* sayings as structural markers.

8 Renaud, 'Les généalogies', 7; Childs, *Introduction*, 146. There are, strictly speaking, eleven occurrences, but 36:9 appears only to be resumptive of 36:1, for both concern the *toledot* of Esau. Renaud prefers to see verse 9 as original, since it begins the names of Esau's offspring. Weimar, 'Die Toledot-Formel', 88 argues that verse 1 is original and verse 9 is secondary. This does not give rise to any significant difference for the purpose of this study.

9 Woudstra, 'The *Toledot*', 187-188 points out that the *toledot* formula names the character who is the starting point, while the subsequent narrative or genealogy describe those who issue from this starting point. Similarly, E. Blum, *Die Komposition der Vätergeschichte*. WMANT, 57. (Neukirchen-Vluyn: Neukirchener Verlag, 1984), 434; Andersen, 'Genealogical Prominence', 253.

10 Scharbert, 'Der Sinn', 45-56. Weimar, 'Die Toledot-Formel', 65-93 suggests that the *toledot* formulas also imply divine blessing. Certainly, the command to multiply fruitfully (1:28), and the covenant promise of descendants (12:2-3) are both explicitly linked with blessing.

The genealogy of 46:8-27, without a *toledot* formula, also binds the Joseph story to the rest of Genesis where genealogies are prominent (5:1-32; 9:18-19; 11:10-32; 22:20-24; 25:12-18, 19; 36:1-43). Indeed, Robinson argues that, in the book of Genesis, "[t]he promise unfolds along the genealogical line."[11]

This pattern of *toledot* formulas and genealogies means that the Joseph narrative is an integral part of, at least, the final form of Genesis and thus the reader is invited to understand it in this larger context.[12]

The Joseph Narrative and the Other Patriarchal Accounts

It is clear that there are both substantial differences and striking similarities between the Joseph narrative and Genesis 12-36. The differences are important because they highlight for the reader some crucial themes of the Joseph story.[13] They also serve narrative functions such as the closure of the book, and the transition of Israel from Canaan to Egypt.

However, the echoes of the earlier patriarchal accounts can easily be overlooked in this focus on the differences. This section will examine some important connections between Genesis 12-36 and 37-50 in order to demonstrate that the final form of the Joseph narrative is understood more fully when read in its canonical setting of the patriarchal accounts.

The setting and pattern of the Joseph story are, for example, reminiscent of those of the earlier patriarchs. Of course, there are differences like the length of the Joseph narrative compared to the short episodes of the patriarchs,[14] and there is much less of a focus on the journeys and more on the interaction between the characters.[15] However, this movement towards longer stories is one that happens progressively through Genesis 12-50, so that the Jacob cycle contains longer stories than the Abraham cycle.[16] Indeed, Cohn has also argued that, throughout the patriarchal stories there is simultaneously an emphasis on God being progressively backgrounded, as

---

11 Robinson, 'Literary Functions', 604. Similarly, Steinberg, 'The Genealogical Framework', 41; Alexander, 'From Adam to Judah', 8.

12 B.P. Robinson, *Israel's Mysterious God* (Newcastle: Grevatt & Grevatt, 1986) 16; Robertson, *Literary Critic*, 7.

13 The differences between Genesis 12-36 and 37-50 will be explored, and their significance examined, in the next chapter.

14 Thus, for example, Redford, *Biblical Story of Joseph*, 68; White, 'The Joseph Story', 54; E. Fox, 'Can Genesis be Read as a Book?', *Semeia* 46 (1989), 33.

15 For example, J.G. Gammie, 'Theological Interpretation By Way of Literary and Tradition Analysis: Genesis 25-36', in *Encounter with the Text: Form and History in the Hebrew Bible*. ed. M.J. Buss. (Philadelphia: Fortress, 1979), 120; Niditch, *Underdogs and Tricksters*, 119.

16 R.L. Cohn, 'Narrative Structure and Canonical Perspective in Genesis', *JSOT* 25 (1983): 14.

well as human figures being delineated in a more sophisticated way.[17] He opines that the gradual withdrawal of God's presence allows for an increase in human freedom, climaxing in the initiatives of Joseph, so that the earlier parts of Genesis lead logically to the Joseph narrative. While Cohn's argument is probably putting it too highly, his article has indicated certain elements of continuity throughout the book of Genesis.

Westermann, in arguing that insufficient attention has been paid to the links between the Joseph story and the patriarchal traditions, makes several pertinent observations.[18] Firstly, all the main characters mentioned in chapters 37, 42-45 have been the subject of narratives in the previous patriarchal story. The roots of the Joseph story are, thus, embedded in the patriarchal traditions. Secondly, what is narrated about the daily lives of these people in chapters 37-45 agrees with what is revealed in chapters 12-36. Thus, the family is the established community structure, characters are referred to by their position in the family, and economic activities and concerns are the same (for example, shepherding flocks, life threatened by famine). Furthermore, in both the father is chief of the group, and the group does not wage war against others. Finally, the conflicts that punctuate both narratives are between members of families, especially between brothers. The father has a passive role in the rivalry.

Miscall has proposed that the Jacob and Joseph stories are analogous, since they possess common plot structure: "treachery between brothers, a twenty year separation, and a subsequent reunion."[19] Some, indeed, have argued that such parallels, and the ongoing presence of Jacob, suggest that the Joseph story is best understood as the second part of the Jacob narrative rather than an independent cycle.[20] Clearly such writers discern significant elements of continuity that are often overlooked.[21]

Williams has indicated some further connections between Joseph and the patriarchs.[22] For example, Joseph went down to Egypt, like Abraham (chapter 12) and Jacob (chapter 46), and, like Abraham, had an Egyptian wife (Gen 16:3; 41:45). Furthermore, as the favoured youngest son, his life at risk, as was the case with Isaac and Jacob (Genesis 22; 27:41-45; 32:25-32; 37:18-36).[23] In fact, the three main figures of Genesis - Abraham, Jacob

---

17 Cohn, 'Narrative Structure', 12-13.

18 Westermann, *Genesis 37-50*, 27. See also Dietrich, *Die Josephserzählung*, 45-52.

19 Miscall, 'Analogies', 28. See also the parallels noted by Carr, 'Synchronic Analysis', 338.

20 *Contra* Adar, *The Book of Genesis*, 138; Wenham, *Genesis 16-50*, 345; Goldingay, 'The Patriarchs', 20.

21 For example, Wenham, *Genesis 16-50*, 461 gives a long list of how the closing chapters (48-50) of the Joseph story contain references to earlier episodes in the book.

22 Williams, 'Number Symbolism', 86.

23 Williams, 'Number Symbolism', 86.

and Joseph - were all driven far from home, alienated and often in danger.[24]

In particular, certain distinctive ideas from the earlier patriarchal narratives resurface in the Joseph story. This can be seen in such motifs as that of brotherly strife, the favouring by the father of the younger son at the expense of the first-born, and the son's deceit of his father through the use of clothing. These are key concepts in the Joseph narrative that can only be understood fully in the light of the previous chapters of Genesis.

Coats rightly points out that "[t]he strife theme belongs to the complex of narrative motifs developed throughout the range of the Abraham saga and the Jacob saga."[25] Indeed, the theme of family strife - especially between brothers - is a recurring idea as far back as Cain and Abel (Genesis 4). This study has argued that the unresolved brotherly strife of previous generations is finally overcome by Joseph's ruse in chapters 42-45, and by his refusal to exact vengeance on his brothers after Jacob's death (50:15-21). This theme engenders a powerful tension in the Joseph narrative because of the failures to achieve reconciliation in the preceding patriarchal accounts. In other words, the literary force of this motif in Genesis 37-50 is accentuated by reading the Joseph story as part of the book of Genesis.

Related to the theme of brotherly strife is the motif of the father favouring the younger son instead of the first-born. In the Joseph story the brothers are presented as rivals for the status of first-born.[26] The three eldest brothers (Reuben, Simeon and Levi) are excluded because of their previous indiscretions (referred to in Gen 49:3-7),[27] although Reuben appears to attempt, on two occasions, to reassert his role as first-born (37:21-30; 42:37). Judah, who comes next, is on the ascendancy throughout the story (37:26; 38; 43:8-10; 44:14, 18-34; 46:28) and his future is extravagantly described (49:8-12). However, undergirding all these struggles is the present rise to prominence of Joseph, in fulfilment of his dream. Like Jacob before him, Joseph as the younger son is used by God to preserve the descendants of Abraham. As Niditch writes

> The recurrence of the underdog pattern in the heart of Genesis leads surely to Joseph. He is the next generation's Jacob, the successful younger son whose youngest son in turn will carry on his leadership. The Joseph tale is not an isolated work but through traditional patterning fully integrated into a larger tale of generations.[28]

---

24 Garrett, *Rethinking Genesis*, 122. Kselman, 'Genesis', 111 notes a common setting of famine in 12:10; 26:1 and 41:57.

25 Coats, 'Joseph, Son of Jacob', 977; Lowenthal, *The Joseph Narrative*, 2; Mann, *The Book of the Torah*, 67.

26 White, 'The Joseph Story', 57; White, *Narration and Discourse*, 238.

27 R.E. Friedman, 'Deception for Deception', *Bible Review* 2 (1986), 30.

28 Niditch, *Underdogs and Tricksters*, 78.

It is interesting that the motif of the younger brother, which is so prominent in Genesis, disappears after the Manasseh/Ephraim blessing (chapter 48) and remains submerged until the Davidic-Solomonic times.[29] Here is a motif that is, therefore, a distinctive and indeed exclusive feature of Genesis in the accounts of pre-monarchical Israel. It thus clearly locates the Joseph story as part of the wider book of Genesis.

The parallels between Jacob's deceiving his father through the use of clothing (Gen 27:15-29) and the Joseph story have already been highlighted. Jacob's sons deceive their father through the use of Joseph's robe (37:31-35), while Tamar deceives her father-in-law through taking off the garments of widowhood, and putting on those of a prostitute (38:12-19). The repetition alerts the reader to the retributive pattern that Jacob and Judah are treated in the same way that they treated their father.[30]

Clearly, there are some important connecting threads between the Joseph narrative and the preceding patriarchal accounts. Genesis 37-50 presupposes, and often alludes to, details that are established and motifs that are present in these earlier chapters. Such observations invite examination of whether the patriarchal promises are also significant in the Joseph story.

The Joseph Narrative and the Patriarchal Promises

Redford has argued that the absence of any mention of the promise or 'covenant' in the Joseph story results in a theological outlook that is different from that of the patriarchal narrator.[31] However, while Genesis 37-50 has its distinctive theological emphases, the patriarchal promises first given to Abraham are undoubtedly in the background of the Joseph narrative. In relation to Abraham, Isaac and Jacob, the promises are foregrounded because God confirms his covenant with each of these figures (for example, Gen 12:1-3; 15:1-21; 17:1-22; 22:15-18; 26:2-5, 24; 28:10-17; 35:9-12).[32] He does not do so with Joseph, or any of Joseph's brothers, but that is presumably a result of their not being included as patriarchs (for

---

29 It appears from Exod 7:7 that Moses is the younger son, but nothing is made of this in the Moses story. Indeed, in his birth narrative (Exod 2:1-10), Moses' conception appears to follow immediately on his parents' marriage (Exod 2:1-2) and Aaron's existence is not mentioned.

30 Friedman, 'Deception for Deception', 24.

31 Redford, *Biblical Story of Joseph*, 247. Similarly, R. Rendtorff, *The Problem of the Process of Transmission in the Pentateuch*. JSOTSup, 89, trans. J.J. Scullion. (Sheffield: Sheffield Academic Press, 1990) 56.

32 G.G. Nicol, 'Story-Patterning in Genesis', in *Text as Pretext. Essays in Honour of Robert Davidson*. JSOTSup, 138, ed. R.P. Carroll. (Sheffield: Sheffield Academic Press, 1992), 222.

example, Exod 2:24; 3:6, 15; 4:5).[33] It does not mean that they are not inheritors of the benefits and responsibilities of the Abrahamic covenant.

A detailed discussion of the Abrahamic promises is outside the scope of this study. However, a brief analysis of its content is necessary in order to assess their presence and influence in the Joseph narrative.

Zimmerli has proposed that "[l]ike a scarlet thread the promise runs through the whole subsequent history of the patriarchs ... and keeps the story moving."[34] VanGemeren puts it very colourfully: "If we describe the *toledot* formulas as the skeletal structure of Genesis, then we certainly have to designate God's promises to the forefathers as the circulatory system".[35] Even Westermann, who argues that it was not an original component of many of the narratives, concedes that the promise made to the fathers "is the most frequent motif in Genesis 12-50 and also beyond Genesis."[36] The Abrahamic promises are indispensable in understanding the patriarchal narratives.

More difficult is the question of how the promises can best be classified and counted, as well as which one is of the greatest significance. Clines discerns three constituent elements of the promise - descendants, relationship and land.[37] Blythin proposes a dual promise of land and descendants.[38] VanGemeren argues for a fourfold division, noting that these four elements are all outlined in four places (12:1-3, 7 and 22:17-18 - Abraham; 26:3-4 - Isaac and 28:13-15 - Jacob). He suggests that:

The four basic areas of promise are (1) a seed, or offspring; (2) a land, namely, the land of Canaan; (3) a blessing to the patriarchs, specifically, the presence of God in protection and guidance, and (4) a blessing to the nations through the patriarchs.[39]

---

33 Coats, 'Joseph, Son of Jacob', 976-981; Keil and Delitzsch, *The Pentateuch*, 334; Adar, *The Book of Genesis*, 137.

34 W. Zimmerli, *Man and his Hope in the Old Testament*. SBT, 20. (London: SCM, 1971) 50. See also W. Zimmerli, 'Promise and Fulfillment', trans. J. Wharton, in *Essays on Old Testament Interpretation*. ed. C. Westermann, English translation ed. J.L. Mays. (London: SCM, 1963), 111-112 and J.J. Scullion, 'The God of the Patriarchs', *Pacifica* 1 (1988), 148.

35 W.A. VanGemeren, *The Progress of Redemption: The Story of Salvation from Creation to the New Jerusalem* (Grand Rapids: Academie, 1988) 104.

36 C. Westermann, *The Promises to the Fathers*. trans. D.E. Green. (Philadelphia: Fortress, 1980) 119, 122-124. J. Hoftijzer, *Die Verheissungen an die drei Erzväter* (Leiden: E.J. Brill, 1956) 2-29, also argues that in most of the passages where a promise is made to any of the patriarchs, this promise is a later addition or interpolation. At 23 Hoftijzer argues that only in Gen 15 is the promise of posterity and land an original part of the text.

37 Clines, *The Theme of the Pentateuch* (1997), 31-47.

38 I. Blythin, 'The Patriarchs and the Promise', *SJT* 21 (1968): 56-73.

39 VanGemeren, *The Progress of Redemption*, 104.

Westermann sees a cluster of promises, with a variety of combinations. He refers to the promise of a son; the promise of the land; the promise of increase; the promise of blessing; the promise of aid or presence.[40] In particular, Westermann regards the promise of a son and the promise of increase as distinct promises. McComiskey also sees a wide range of promises, including the extra promise that kings would descend from Abraham.[41]

Since it is the content of the promises rather than their classification that concerns us, this study proposes to analyse the four areas set out by VanGemeren - land, offspring or descendants, blessing, and blessing to the nations - while acknowledging that the last two are closely linked (see Genesis 12:3).

The identity of the most central promise is a moot point. Blythin proposes that "[t]he promise of land is the more prominent aspect of the twofold promise."[42] Wolff, on the other hand, sees that the goal and climax of the Abrahamic promise (and its *Leitfrage*) is that "in the people of Abraham all humanity can gain blessing."[43] However, Clines has helpfully suggested that different aspects of the promises are emphasised in different books in the Pentateuch,[44] and it is therefore proposed to analyse each of the four elements to determine whether or not they are important to the Joseph narrative.

The promise of the land does not loom large in the Joseph narrative, since the story takes not only Joseph, but also Jacob and his other sons, out of Canaan and into Egypt. Westermann sees the promise of the land referred to in 48:4 and 50:24 in the Joseph narrative.[45] The first of these is a recital of the events and words of Genesis 35, where God appeared to Jacob at Bethel, and speaks of the future promise of possession of the land. In fact, there is, in the Joseph story, no rush to return to the land of Canaan by either Joseph or Jacob. For example, Jacob lived seventeen years in Egypt (47:28), though the famine only lasted seven.[46]

---

40 Westermann, *Promises*, 128-129. He notes that chapter 17 contains all of them except aid/presence.

41 T.E. McComiskey, *The Covenants of Promise. A Theology of the Old Testament Covenants* (Leicester: Inter-Varsity Press, 1985) 17.

42 Blythin, 'The Patriarchs and the Promise', 64.

43 H.W. Wolff, 'The Kerygma of the Yahwist', trans. W.A. Benware, in *The Vitality of Old Testament Traditions*. 2nd edn., eds. W. Brueggemann and H.W. Wolff. (Atlanta: John Knox, 1982), 47-49, 53. The quotation is from 49.

44 Clines, *The Theme of the Pentateuch* (1997), 30. By way of generalisation, he suggests that the posterity element is prominent in Genesis 12-50, the relationship element in Exodus and Leviticus, and the land element in Numbers and Deuteronomy.

45 Westermann, *Promises*, 143.

46 Turner, *Announcements of Plot*, 171.

The second occurrence of the promise (50:24) is much more significant, since it is found in the final unit of the Joseph story. Westermann rightly comments that

> In this sentence the Joseph story reaches its goal: the linking of the exodus narrative with the patriarchal narrative. Here is a direct statement that the promise of the land to the patriarchs has as its actual goal the deliverance of *Israel* from Egypt and the entrance of *Israel* into Canaan.[47]

It is worth noting that the promise of the land is, in the Joseph story, not assumed to be fulfilled in the present, but rather in some future generation. It is a future goal, not a present expectation.

Indeed, the promise of the land is also behind the burial of Jacob (47:29-31; 49:29-50:14) and the placing of Joseph's body in a coffin (50:26). Jacob's burial in the land of Canaan with the other patriarchs (49:31) is both a statement that this is where he belongs, as well as an anticipation that this is where his descendants will live. Joseph's being placed in a coffin is, in the light of 50:24-25, a powerful symbol that Egypt is not to be the permanent home for Jacob's offspring, since God will ultimately bring them back to the promised land. These burial practices thus serve to link the Joseph story with the remaining books of the Pentateuch and beyond (for example, Josh 24:32).

Scullion, following Westermann, has proposed that "[t]he promise of myriads of descendants is independent of the promise of a son."[48] However, Westermann concedes that the promise of descendants logically includes the promise of a son, that the two are linked together in Gen 15:1-6; 16:7-12; 21:12-13, and that "[t]he promise of a son is not found throughout Genesis 12-50; it is limited to the Abraham cycle".[49] While it appears that the promise of a son is only the first stage of the promise of descendants[50] (and hence confined to the Abraham story), it is sufficient for our purposes

---

47 Westermann, *Promises*, 21. Humphreys, *Joseph and His Family*, 196 views the reference in Gen 50:24-25 as a linking device.

48 Scullion, 'The God of the Patriarchs', 149. Westermann, *Promises*, 11 writes that "[t]he promise of a son is not identical with the promise of descendants (that is, the promise of many descendants), but represents an independent type." At 106 he notes the promise of a son (not many descendants) is the focus, for example, in Genesis 18.

49 Westermann, *Promises*, 132-133. The quotation is from page 133.

50 So McComiskey, *The Covenants of Promise*, 17 who sees the birth of Abraham's son Isaac (Gen 21:1-3) as an 'earnest' of the promise of offspring, not a separate promise. The promises of descendants sometimes speak of the increase of seed (21:12; 26:24; 16:10); that the seed will be like the stars (15:5; 26:4) or the dust and sand (13:16; 28:14; 32:13) or both (22:17). Sometimes there will be a great increase without mention of seed (17:2; 48:16). The rest refer to the making of a 'nation' or group of people (21:13; 12:2; 21:18; 46:3; 18:18; 17:4, 5, 6, 16, 20; 35:11; 28:3; 48:4).

to note that only the promise of descendants is a concern of the Joseph narrative.

Westermann notes that there are a large number of passages in Genesis that combine the promise of many descendants with blessing (17:16, 20; 22:17; 26:4, 24; 28:3-4; 32:12; 35:9-12; 48:3-4, 16), often explicitly leading to an increase.[51] In chapters 37-50, Westermann sees the promise of increase in 46:3; (47:27); 48:4, 16, 19.[52] It is undoubtedly here in the final chapters, and so the Joseph story is folded into the patriarchal promises.

However, the promise of descendants should not be construed so narrowly that it is only present when there is reference to a great nation or many peoples. If Clines is right in seeing the posterity element as dominant in Genesis 12-50,[53] then the promise of descendants also includes the birth of a son and heir, as well as the survival of the promised line despite dangers and threats. This is another reason why it is important to consider the Joseph narrative as part of the book of Genesis, for it is in the rest of the book that the meaning of the promise of descendants is found.

If the promise of descendants includes the survival of Jacob and his family, then the whole Joseph story is riddled with this theme, and not merely chapters 46-50. A key issue in chapter 37 is that brotherly strife is so strong that the brothers nearly kill the favoured son. This raises the question of how long such a family can survive. In the light of 49:8-12, Judah is destined for future greatness. Chapter 38 deals with Judah's progeny, reduced to one son who is denied marriage. Judah's line would have ended but for the wise scheming of Tamar.[54] It is not without significance that this chapter ends with further offspring for Judah (38:27-30).

In chapters 39-41, Jacob's family is backgrounded and thus there is no overt connection with the promise of descendants. However, Joseph's rise to power, and his ensuring supplies of grain for the years of famine, become important preliminaries for the events of chapters 42-45.

Chapter 42 is told against this setting of famine (41:56-57), which is a real threat to the survival of the promised line of Jacob and his family (42:2). This study has previously argued that chapters 42-45 outline both how Joseph enables the physical survival of his clan, as well as the more significant task of bringing about lasting reconciliation within the family. If the family is disintegrating in chapter 37, then at the end of chapter 45 (and restated in chapter 50) the brotherly strife has been faced and dealt with. Thus, chapters 42-45 depict the overcoming of two threats to the line of promise - the threat of famine, and the threat of brotherly hatred. This

---

51 Westermann, *Promises*, 19.
52 Westermann, *Promises*, 149.
53 Clines, *The Theme of the Pentateuch* (1997), 30.
54 Turner, *Announcements of Plot*, 170.

brotherly hatred is, of course, a common motif in the preceding patriarchal accounts (Isaac and Ishmael; Jacob and Esau), where it also imperils the promise of descendants.

Chapters 46-50 heighten the focus on the promise of descendants, beginning with the explicit mention of the promise in 46:3, followed by the genealogy of 46:8-27. In the midst of famine (47:13), Jacob and his family are amply provided for (47:12), and they multiply abundantly in Goshen (47:27). While Abraham's descendants are not yet a great nation, this seems reasonably likely by the end of the book.[55] This leads naturally into the blessing of Joseph's sons in chapter 48 (especially verses 4, 16, 20) and the testamentary words in chapter 49 about the future of Jacob's sons as heads of future tribes.

Thus it appears that the patriarchal promise of descendants is woven right through the Joseph story, and not merely added during the closing chapters. What is distinctive in chapters 38-45 is that the promise is preserved not through direct intervention by God, but through the human actions of Tamar and, more importantly, Joseph, who showed initiative in organising famine relief and shrewdness in accomplishing reconciliation within the family.

The Abrahamic promise of blessing or relationship is the third element, and the most difficult one to define. Clines comments that "sometimes the relationship is expressed as a blessing, sometimes as a 'being with' or guidance, sometimes as a continuance of God's relationship with former patriarchs."[56] VanGemeren also notices this breadth of meaning and comments that the head of blessing

> may seem to be a catchall for various expressions of God's relationship with the patriarchs, but within the diversity of language pertaining to blessing there is most certainly a unifying theme. The Lord has promised to be with the patriarchs, and this constant relationship may be expressed in terms of blessing (12:2b; 22:17; 26:3 28:3), presence (26:3; 28:15; 31:3; 46:4; 48:21), protection (15:1; 26:24; 28:15), or covenant (15:18; 17:7).[57]

Westermann observes that the promise of God's presence and help in found in 46:3-4; 48:21; 50:24, and perhaps in 48:15.[58] This would mean that

55 Turner, *Announcements of Plot*, 170-171. Clines, *The Theme of the Pentateuch* (1997), 40 notes that, by this time, "the family has become established, and, barring drastic misfortunes, is likely to survive", although the prospect of becoming a great nation is yet to be realised.
56 Clines, *The Theme of the Pentateuch* (1997), 36.
57 VanGemeren, *The Progress of Redemption*, 106.
58 Westermann, *Promises*, 140.

it is only found in the closing section of the Joseph story and thus is not of great significance for the narrative as a whole. Others have suggested that it is present in 39:2, 23 in the narrator's description of God 'being with' Joseph.

The difficulty of precise definition have caused some to limit the promise more narrowly. Vetter examines the use of the 'I will be with you' formula in the patriarchal narratives and notes that it occurs only in the setting of a journey.[59] Since the idea of God being with Joseph on a journey is absent from Genesis 37-50, Preuss has therefore argued that this formula is absent from the Joseph narrative.[60] Westermann thus proposes that the use of this formula as part of the patriarchal promises "must be distinguished from the use of the formula by others to confirm someone's success, wealth, or superiority, a use found clearly in Genesis only in the Joseph narrative (39:2; 39:23)."[61]

Clines, however, has replied that, while the promise of God 'being with' an individual often appears in connection with a movement or journey, it elsewhere is found in the context of settling down and staying at one place (for example, 26:3; 31:5).[62] This appears to be a minor usage of the phrase, but could cover the examples of 39:2 and 39:23. It might be better to see the context being one of presence in the midst of uncertainty, of which one example could be a journey.

The promise appears to be present in 46:4, 48:21 and 50:24. In each case, God is asked or promises to be with Jacob, Joseph and their descendants in the midst of future uncertainties. It may also be present in 39:2, 23, underlining God's protection of Joseph in Potiphar's house and in prison. However, if it is present, then the protective presence of God is described by the narrator for the reader's benefit. God does not appear to Joseph, nor is Joseph ever told that God is with him. If it is to be located in chapter 39, it is still not foregrounded. It would appear, therefore, that while traces of this promise occur in the Joseph narrative, the promise is not of great significance to the narrative as a whole.

The final aspect of the Abrahamic promise is that of blessing to the nations. While some have understood this to be a purely spiritual blessing,[63] it appears to be more holistic, including material prosperity as well. Wolff has argued strongly that the significant aspect of the promise was the blessing to the nations, and thus the promise is the attempt to retrieve God's

---

59 D. Vetter, *Jahwes mit-Sein als Ausdruck des Segens*. Arbeiten zur Theologie, 5. (Stuttgart: Calwer Verlag, 1971) 9.
60 H.D. Preuss, 'Ich will mit dir sein', *ZAW* 80 (1968): 152.
61 Westermann, *Promises*, 143.
62 Clines, *The Theme of the Pentateuch* (1997), 36.
63 For example, J.H. Walton, *Covenant: God's Purpose, God's Plan* (Grand Rapids: Zondervan, 1994) 60 describes it as God revealing himself.

universal purpose to do good to all which he had begun in creation.[64]

The theme of blessing to the nations is quite prominent in chapters 37-50, with Joseph being a blessing to all he meets - Potiphar's household (39:2-5), the chief gaoler (41:21-23), Pharaoh (41:46-49; 47:13-26), all Egypt (41:56) and even all the world (41:57), as well as to the promised line of Jacob (45:10-12; 47:11-12).[65] Jacob also plays a minor role in relation to the nations through the pronouncing of blessings on Pharaoh (47:7, 10).

Joseph thus does much more than merely keep alive the chosen descendants of Abraham.[66] It is largely Joseph's careful administration of the food supplies, and wise distribution, that results in blessing to the nations. Egypt and the nations around (41:57) depended on Joseph for their very survival. Wolff concludes that the Joseph story is "a capsule drama showing how, through the wisdom of one of the Patriarchs of Israel, blessing came even upon the powerful empire of Egypt."[67] Important for this study is his observation that "[t]he wisdom given to the Patriarch of Israel [i.e. Joseph] is here the means by which blessing is transmitted".[68]

In summary, then, the elements of land and relationship are present but not prominent in the Joseph narrative. However, the Abrahamic promise of descendants is found in and behind many parts of Genesis 37-50. When these chapters are read as part of the patriarchal accounts, it is evident that Joseph's actions ensure the partial fulfilment of this promise. They are not yet a great nation, but their survival has been largely secured.

In addition, the Joseph story begins to flesh out the least developed aspect of the Abrahamic promises - that of blessing to the nations. Joseph acts to keep many people alive, and causes his masters to prosper. This, of course, is only a foretaste of what it means to bless the nations - a theme carried through and beyond the Old Testament - but it is a very tangible earnest of what is to come.

The Joseph Narrative and Genesis 1-11

This study has so far argued for a connection between Genesis 37-50 and chapters 12-36. However, further support for the view that the Joseph narrative is understood best in the light of the book of Genesis is provided

---

64 Wolff, 'The Kerygma', 47-49. Similarly, VanGemeren, *The Progress of Redemption*, 107.

65 Turner, *Announcements of Plot*, 172.

66 *Contra* M.A. Beek, *A Journey Through The Old Testament*. trans. A.J. Pomerans. (London: Hodder & Stoughton, 1959) 55 who sees Joseph's works as confined to the promised line.

67 Wolff, 'The Kerygma', 59.

68 Wolff, 'The Kerygma', 60.

by its links with Genesis 1-11. Two links are particularly important.

Firstly, the patriarchal accounts to which the Joseph narrative is connected are themselves linked with Genesis 1-11. Clines has strongly argued that the recurring pattern in Genesis 1-11 of spread of sin-spread of grace leads to the view that 12:1-3 provides the missing grace element of the Babel cycle.[69] As such, the Abrahamic promises in Gen 12:1-3 are God's answer to the snowballing of human sin in chapters 1-11. God's purposes for the world and humanity are, thus, effected by the choosing of a particular people, the descendants of Abraham. As Goldingay comments, "[t]he blessing in Abraham is a re-statement of the blessing of creation."[70]

A significant thematic parallel between Genesis 1-11 and the Joseph story can be seen in this idea of blessing, since the ברך root is prominent right throughout the book of Genesis. One of the fundamental assertions of the creation account in Genesis 1:1-2:3 is that God blessed the sea creatures and birds (1:22), human beings (1:28; see also 5:2) and the seventh day (2:3). Even after the flood, God's purposes for humanity are blessing (9:1). Furthermore, there is the fivefold use of ברך in the promise to Abraham (12:2-3), as well as frequent mention in many other sections of the Abraham cycle (for example, 17:16, 20; 22:17; 24:1). The Jacob cycle revolves around the transfer of blessing from Isaac (chapter 27). The Joseph cycle outlines how God blesses Potiphar's house on account of Joseph, the narrative ends with Jacob blessing Pharaoh (47:7, 10), Joseph's two sons (48:9, 15, 16), and giving a kind of testamentary blessing on all his own sons (chapter 49, especially verses 25-26, 28).[71] The blessing theme thus links the Joseph story not only with the earlier patriarchal accounts but also with Genesis 1-11.[72]

Secondly, some parallels have been proposed between the figure of Joseph and certain characters in Genesis 1-11. Dahlberg suggested that Joseph is an antitype of Adam, and noted several connections. For example, he suggests that Joseph is an ideal administrator, whose wise dominion preserves the whole world (41:56-57). Adam, by way of contrast, was also given the role of administration over the earth (2:15, as the outworking of the dominion of 1:28), but brings death to the world (3:19). People come to Joseph to find life (42:2; 45:5, 7; 50:20) but the actions of Adam led to humanity being cut off from the tree of life (3:22-24).[73] Adam is tempted by

69 Clines, *The Theme of the Pentateuch* (1997), 84-86.
70 Goldingay, 'The Patriarchs', 27.
71 Fox, 'Read as a Book?' 34.
72 Fretheim, 'The Book of Genesis', 595. Another theme that could be used to illustrate this connection would be the brotherly strife motif, which is present in the patriarchal accounts and the Joseph story, but begins with Cain and Abel in Genesis 4.
73 B.T. Dahlberg, 'On Recognizing the Unity of Genesis', *TD* 24 (1976), 363-364. However, T.E. Fretheim, *The Pentateuch*. Interpreting Biblical Texts. (Nashville:

the prospect of becoming 'like God' (3:5), but Joseph refused to usurp God's authority and stand in his place (50:19).[74] The noun for Joseph's robe (כתנת פסים, 37:3) is used only once elsewhere in the book of Genesis. It is employed in 3:21 to describe the garments of skin (כתנות עור) with which God clothed Adam and Eve.[75] In summary, the distinctive parallels raise a reasonable possibility that a purposeful contrast is being drawn, with Joseph largely achieving what Adam failed to accomplish. Dahlberg also sees some connections between Joseph and Noah, but these appear to be more tenuous.[76]

Thus, Dahlberg concludes that "the story of Joseph, taken together with the primeval narratives that comprise chapters 1 through 11 in Genesis, forms with them, rhetorically, an *inclusio* for the whole of Genesis."[77]

This is a suggestive proposal, although perhaps a little over-argued. However, it at least shows evidence of some connection between the Joseph narrative and Genesis 1-11. At the level of the final form of the text, a reading of the Joseph story precluding its context in the book of Genesis, would sever connections like those noticed by Dahlberg, and result in an impoverished reading of the text.

The Joseph Story as Part of the Pentateuch

The Joseph Narrative and the Book of Exodus

It appears from the above material that the Joseph narrative is clearly embedded in the wider context of the book of Genesis. However, there are also several hints in Joseph story that more is to come, and that subsequent narratives are to be expected.

The clearest example of this is the way that the story ends with the explicit re-statement of the Abrahamic promise of land which was yet to be fulfilled (50:24). This assumes that there will be an account of a journey out of Egypt, and into the land of Canaan, which is precisely what follows in

Abingdon, 1996) 69 observes that no new Eden emerges in the Joseph narrative.

74 B.T. Dahlberg, 'The Unity of Genesis', in *Literary Interpretations of Biblical Narratives II*. ed. K.R.R. Gros Louis. (Nashville: Abingdon, 1982) 129 observes that the parallel here also includes the terms 'good' and 'evil' in 3:4-5 and 50:19-20.

75 Dahlberg, 'On Recognizing the Unity', 365.

76 Dahlberg, 'The Unity of Genesis', 130 notes that, in 41:57, the whole world came to Joseph to be preserved in a time of universal disaster, like the animals in Noah's time of universal flood. Furthermore, just as Joseph built storehouses; so Noah built the ark. In addition, the theme of gathering and release of produce is found in both.

77 Dahlberg, 'On Recognizing the Unity', 363.

Exodus - Deuteronomy, and even as far as the book of Joshua.[78] This future journey is also symbolised by the final two verses of the Joseph story (50:25-26), where Joseph makes the Israelites swear that when God 'visits' them (he uses an emphatic construction, פָּקֹד יִפְקֹד, as in verse 24, presumably to indicate its certainty), they will take his bones with them. It is apparently for this reason that Joseph is not buried in Egypt, but only placed in a coffin.[79] The book thus ends with a temporary arrangement that anticipates a more permanent solution in the form of burial in Canaan. Exod 13:19 records that Moses took Joseph's bones with him when the Israelites left Egypt,[80] and the burial of these bones is later narrated in Josh 24:32.

Thus, while the Joseph narrative is a coherent literary entity, with a sense of closure secured by Joseph's death, it is also a story that finishes with anticipation and openness. As Magness points out

> In spite of the rounding off which operates on several levels, a sense of openness remains. The Israelites are still in Egypt, still in exile, not in their homeland, the land of promise. ... But the muted note is not one that is likely to die out; it holds the reader in anticipation of the outburst of a full symphonic climax. For the ending turns our thoughts to another land, and to a future time.[81]

It is very significant that these threads are picked up immediately in Exodus 1-2. Exod 1:1-7 is clearly a transitional passage that gives a resumptive summary of Jacob and his sons coming to Egypt and dying (verses 1-6), followed by the new information that their descendants multiplied greatly in Egypt (verse 7). This increase in numbers is an apparent furthering of the Abrahamic promise of descendants, in view of the repetition of this promise to Jacob in Gen 46:3. The book of Exodus thus begins with a looking back both to the Joseph narrative, and to the Abrahamic promises.

Both of these connections are developed further. In Exod 1:8, there is the explicit mention of a new king in Egypt, אֲשֶׁר לֹא־יָדַע אֶת־יוֹסֵף. This implies that the Moses narratives need to be understood in the light of Joseph in Egypt.[82]

The relationship element of Abrahamic promises is reflected in Exod

78 E.A. Martens, *God's Design. A Focus on Old Testament Theology*. 3rd edn. (N. Richland Hills: Bibal, 1998) 32.
79 Magness, *Sense and Absence*, 60.
80 S.B. Frost, *Patriarchs and Prophets* (London: John Murray, 1963) 44.
81 Magness, *Sense and Absence*, 58.
82 A.W. Pink, *Gleanings in Genesis* (Chicago: Moody, 1922) 342. Lowenthal, *The Joseph Narrative*, 1 describes Joseph as "the link between Canaan and Egypt... the bridge between the Patriarchs and Moses".

2:23-25, where God's decision to help the Israelites is based on the covenant with the patriarchs (verse 24)

וַיִּשְׁמַע אֱלֹהִים אֶת־נַאֲקָתָם וַיִּזְכֹּר אֱלֹהִים אֶת־בְּרִיתוֹ אֶת־אַבְרָהָם
אֶת־יִצְחָק וְאֶת־יַעֲקֹב:

The subsequent exodus from Egypt, and the events at Sinai, are grounded in the fact that God is acting on the basis of his promises to the patriarchs.[83] Thus Dahlberg proposes that the Joseph story serves both to round off the book of Genesis and to provide a bridge between Genesis and Exodus.[84] Again, the patriarchal accounts and the book of Exodus are interconnected in their present form.

This connection between the Joseph narrative and the book of Exodus is significant for this study. If the theme of the Pentateuch is "the partial fulfilment - which implies also the partial non-fulfilment - of the promise to or blessing of the patriarchs",[85] then the links with Exodus, and therefore with the rest of the Pentateuch, highlight the significance of the promises in the final form of Genesis 37-50. The Abrahamic promise theology thus makes an important contribution to the meaning of the Joseph narrative as a whole.

There is also one other part of the Joseph narrative that, for many readers, would have suggested links with the later story of Israel. In its present form, chapter 38 ends with the birth of Perez and Zerah (38:27-30). For a reader of this text in monarchical or post-monarchical Israel, the mention of Perez raises connection with the later David covenant traditions. This is, of course, heightened by the genealogy of Perez in Ruth 4:18-22, leading to David, especially in the light of the specific reference to Tamar in Ruth 4:12.

Joseph and Moses

One further comparison also needs to be pursued. Moses is the archetypal covenant figure, being prophet, priestly intercessor and leader of the people.

---

83 Sarna, *JPS Torah Commentary*, 254.

84 Dahlberg, 'The Unity of Genesis', 128 notes that "the Joseph story seems to exceed the requirement for a mere bridge." He suggests that "the Joseph story does provide, *de facto*, a transition from the patriarchal narratives to the Exodus. But, more important, it functions as a completion to and consummation of everything in the book of Genesis that precedes it." The transitionary function of the Joseph story is also pointed out by F.R. McCurley, *Genesis, Exodus, Leviticus, Numbers*. Proclamation Commentaries. (Philadelphia: Fortress, 1979) 62-63; Adar, *The Book of Genesis*, 137; Humphreys, *Joseph and His Family*, 194; Clines, *The Theme of the Pentateuch* (1997), 91-92.

85 Clines, *The Theme of the Pentateuch* (1997), 30.

Many of the offices that developed later in the history of Israel traced their origins to Moses. It is, therefore, perhaps initially surprising to note a number of parallels between the Joseph and Moses stories.

Some of the parallels may be set out as follows

- both are substantially set in Egypt, which is a rare feature in the Old Testament.
- in both, a disaster occurs in the sphere of nature (famine and plagues).
- both men marry non-Israelite wives (Gen 41:45; Exod 2:21).
- both figures gain significant status at the Egyptian court (Gen 41:40-44; Exod 2:10).
- both Joseph and Moses spend time in a place apparently unrelated to their mission, where they seemingly achieve nothing. Moses spends 40 years in Midian; Joseph spends about 17 years (Gen 37:2; 41:46) in Potiphar's house and in prison.
- in both accounts there are lists of descendants (Gen 46:8-27; Exod 6:14-27), and mention of the patriarchal promises (for example, Gen 46:3; 50:24; Exod 2:24; 6:2-8).[86]

This is, of course, not to say that Joseph and Moses are portrayed identically, or that the two stories have emerged from the same intellectual setting. In fact, this is far from being the case, for the differences between the two are significant

- there is no revelation or appearance by God to Joseph, but Moses is portrayed as receiving God's words and guidance in the burning bush, at Sinai, at the tent of meeting and in many other places.
- Moses fights against Pharaoh; Joseph acts on Pharaoh's behalf.
- there is a contrast in their destinies. Moses starts off in a position of status in Egypt yet renounces it; Joseph becomes a leader in Egypt.
- Joseph takes 'Israel' from Canaan to Egypt; Moses takes Israel from Egypt to the verge of Canaan.[87]
- the early Moses story follows the traditional patterns of heroic tales, with an emphasis on extraordinary episodes and liminal situations.[88] By

---

86 See, for example, Ruppert, *Die Josephserzählung*, 119-121, 219-223. Irvin in Thompson and Irvin, 'The Joseph and Moses Narratives', 190 also argues that both of these stories are 'hero tales', and deal with the success of the unpromising. However, the differences between the two suggest that, while Moses is depicted in heroic terms, Joseph is not.

87 Thus, C.J.H. Wright, *Living as the People of God* (Leicester: Inter-Varsity Press, 1983) 128 has proposed that, in this respect, "*Moses* stands as the counterpart to Joseph."

88 R.S. Hendel, *The Epic of the Patriarch: The Jacob Cycle and the Narrative Traditions of Canaan and Israel*. HSM, 42. (Atlanta: Scholars, 1987) 138-140.

contrast, there is little focus on Joseph's birth, marriage or death;[89] only a little on his moving to Egypt; a lot on his life in Egypt in non-liminal settings.

Thus, while the many similarities lead to a linking of Joseph and Moses, their characters are drawn and stories are told in very different ways.[90] It is as if a link has been forged in order to accentuate the differences between the two. The implications of this contrast will be developed in the following chapter when the characterisation of Joseph is considered at length.

For this stage of the argument, however, the similarities between Joseph and Moses (and their stories) serve to establish a link between the Joseph narrative and the subsequent account of Moses in the remainder of the Pentateuch. Since the Moses story continues and develops the fulfilment of the covenant promises, this binds the final form of the Joseph story into God's overarching covenant purposes to establish the descendants of Abraham, living in Canaan in relationship with him, as his way ultimately to bless all of humanity.

It is thus proposed that the Joseph narrative is a work that has been enmeshed in its wider contexts, both in the book of Genesis and in the Pentateuch as a whole. Clearly, then, it cannot simply be read as a wisdom tale in narrative form, for its meaning is, in part, derived from its canonical context as the final part of Genesis and as a link between the patriarchal accounts and the Moses stories.

---

89 *Contra* Niditch, *Underdogs and Tricksters*, 70 who suggests that Joseph's birth is "a magically induced event belonging to the tale of rivalry between Rachel and Leah."
90 Culley, *Themes and Variations*, 160-161.

CHAPTER 10

Wisdom and Genesis 37-50

It has already been concluded that the Joseph story is not simply a 'wisdom narrative', although significant 'wisdom-like elements' have been identified in the exegesis of chapters 37-50. It is now proposed to consolidate these exegetical observations in order to discern the shape or nature of the 'wisdom-like elements' of the story. These will be studied under the headings of Joseph's public wisdom, Joseph's private wisdom, Joseph's tested character, and the nature of divine activity and human initiative.

Joseph's Public Wisdom

The Egyptian court is the primary arena in which Joseph's public wisdom is displayed. During the account of Joseph's rise to prominence (chapters 39-41), his family is completely absent. While Joseph's rise will be considered in detail in a later section, this part of the study will examine how Joseph seized opportunities and used power at the public level.

Joseph's Use of Power at Court

In the first two sections of chapters 39-41 (39:1-20; 39:21-40:23), there are several cameos of Joseph prospering as he exercises responsibility. Gen 39:2-6 outlines how Joseph succeeds in the service of Potiphar and becomes overseer of the house and the fields. At a later stage, despite being cast into prison, Joseph is again entrusted with the care of others and succeeds at the task (39:21-23).[1] Both of these descriptions serve as appetisers for the implied reader as the events of chapter 41 unfold.

Furthermore, the events of chapter 40 also disclose Joseph's fundamental values. When Joseph sees that the cupbearer and baker are troubled, he shows genuine care in seeking to find out the nature of their concerns (40:6-7). In addition, although he acknowledges that interpretations belong to

---

1   Seybold, 'Paradox and Symmetry', 63 observes that this is in spite of his "diminishing freedom from that of favorite son, to trusted servant, to favored prisoner."

God, Joseph urges the officials to tell *him* their dreams (40:8). His understanding of God's control leads naturally into his taking initiative to help, expecting God to work through him.

Indeed, there is one additional example of Joseph's initiative in his approach to the cupbearer. After he has revealed a favourable interpretation to this official, Joseph boldly but deferentially asks the cupbearer to 'remember' him to Pharaoh (40:14-15). Joseph thus shows decisiveness not only in offering to interpret the dream, but also in creating an opportunity to reverse his unjust circumstances by speaking up.

A similar pattern is found in chapter 41, where Joseph not only interprets Pharaoh's dream, but shows presence of mind in the midst of the crisis by proposing a rescue plan to deal with the forthcoming famine (41:33-36). Joseph manages his circumstances and opportunities in order to bring about his desired goal. In particular, he is eloquent and persuasive in his speech.[2] Our previous exegetical material has concluded that there are strong wisdom hints in this chapter. In interpreting Pharaoh's dream, Joseph is accomplishing what the wise in Egypt were expected to do, but could not (41:8). Joseph's solution calls for one who is נבון וחכם - strong wisdom terminology - to be set over the land. Pharaoh sees that such a description fits Joseph, and so appoints him to the life-preserving task of collecting and distributing food. Joseph's initiative in suggesting how to deal with the crisis has resulted in his gaining opportunity to use the power of the state to meet human need.[3] Such is the ideal picture of Joseph as an administrator that there is not even mention of any opposition or intrigue in the court, though it surely would have occurred in the promotion of a 'foreigner' at court.[4]

Joseph's plan is implemented in the rest of chapter 41, as well as in 47:13-26. This study has argued that both these descriptions view Joseph's innovations in a positive way, despite the reservations that many modern writers have about enslavement of the Egyptians. The reforms reveal

---

2   N. Shupak, 'Egyptian "prophetic" writings and biblical wisdom literature', *BN* 54 (1990): 93 notes the parallels with Egyptian wisdom literature at this point. Under the heading 'the value of eloquence', Shupak observes that "[t]his faculty plays an especially significant part in the Egyptian tale [of the Eloquent Peasant], as well as in the Biblical story of Joseph, which is also associated with the wisdom tradition. In both, command of language is presented as a means of salvation from catastrophe or even of rising to greatness."

3   Fretheim, 'The Book of Genesis', 594 notes that Joseph, in his use of power, actively works for the public good.

4   R. Rainy, 'Joseph's Forgetting', *The Expositor* 3rd Series 4 (1886): 401-402. *Contra* M. Samuel, 'Joseph - The Brilliant Failure', *Bible Review* 2 (1986): 41 who suggests that "[h]e was an actor who always had to 'upstage' his fellow actors, *and he expected them to like it*." The absence of any comment by other Egyptian officials makes Samuel's view unlikely.

insight and perseverance, while they result in the Egyptians having access to food during the years of famine (41:56). Indeed, Egypt's bounty was sufficient to spill over to surrounding nations who came to buy grain to keep themselves alive (41:57; 42:2). In chapter 41, there is no mention of enslavement but only of the provision of food and thus the preservation of life. Even in chapter 47, the narrator closes off the incident by recording the Egyptian's gratitude to Joseph for saving their lives (47:25). Certainly, Joseph has so managed this public crisis as to strengthen the hand of the Pharaoh, as well as to bring life to Egypt and the surrounding nations. As Wintermute has argued, "[t]he greatness of Joseph's administrative ability is judged in terms of his results in acquiring all the land in Egypt for the king."[5]

Joseph's use of power is, therefore, not ambiguous or suspect,[6] but rather reflects values that would be regarded as important in court wisdom circles (see Prov 22:29).[7] However, Weeks has suggested that more attention in these chapters is given to dream interpretation than to Joseph's administrative roles.[8] Yet, it appears from 41:37 that Pharaoh and his advisers were impressed by Joseph's plan rather than mesmerised by his ability to interpret dreams. Furthermore, Weeks' analysis cannot embrace 47:13-26 being part of a cohesive 'Joseph narrative'. He claims it is not clear that the intention of Gen 47:13-26 is to portray the advantage to the

---

5   Wintermute, 'Joseph', 985.

6   *Contra* D.R. Shevitz, 'Joseph: A Study in Assimilation and Power', *Tikkun* 8 (Jan/Feb 1993): 51-52, 76 who suggests that the Joseph story reveals a Jewish ambivalence about power and assimilation. On the one hand Joseph's accomplishments are admired, but counter-examples such as Moses and Mordecai reflect negatively on Joseph and his 'civil religion'. At 52, Shevitz expresses the view that "Joseph is more comfortable serving Pharaoh than serving God."

7   E. Robertson, *The Old Testament Problem* (Manchester: Manchester University Press, 1950) 218 regards Joseph as "the perfect example of Hebrew ability, business acumen and enterprise suitably rewarded. ... the only effect on Joseph of rank and station is to bring out more clearly his basic nobility of character." Coats, 'The Joseph Story and Wisdom', 290 views the story in chapters 39-41 as having "an obvious didactic function. It demonstrates to future administrators the proper procedure for using power." Joseph is also seen as a model administrator by Wintermute, 'Joseph', 983-984; Niditch, *Underdogs and Tricksters*, 121; Frost, *Patriarchs and Prophets*, 41-42. J.A. Loader, 'Jedidah or: Amadeus. Thoughts on the Succession Narrative and Wisdom', in *Studies in the Succession Narrative*. Ou Testamentiese Werkgemeenskap in Suid-Afrika, 27 & 28: Old Testament Essays, ed. W.C. van Wyk. (Pretoria: Ou Testamentiese Werkgemeenskap in Suid-Afrika, 1986), 175-176 also sees a number of parallels between the Joseph story and Egyptian wisdom texts, such as a royal court setting; the emphasis on a wise person being able to speak well; the need to control one's sexual passion; the virtue of self-control; and respect for authority.

8   Weeks, 'Joseph, Dreams and Wisdom', 9-10.

king of Joseph's actions as a great administrator.[9] Weeks regards the unit as secondary, and simply explaining the situation in Egypt (verse 26), suggesting that verse 22 setting out the exception of the priestly land is irrelevant to an intention to idealise Joseph. It is telling that even Samuel concedes that, in Joseph's manipulation of public affairs

> the exercise of his powers was directed not primarily at personal aggrandizement and self-inflation, but at the satisfaction of his craftsmanship. He was farsighted and responsible in public service.[10]

While the unique circumstances of Joseph's life preclude his rise to power being a pattern for others,[11] he clearly shows the right way to use power once in a position of authority.[12] As Rainy comments, Joseph showed great skill "in framing and executing his plans, in watching and guiding the progress of far-reaching designs, in helming a great people through years of intoxicating plenty and crushing want".[13]

It is important to realise that wisdom texts generally assess the use of power by whether it is able to achieve the desired result or not. As Curtis indicates, "[w]isdom can be defined as the ability to succeed; it is the ability to form a correct plan to get a desired result."[14] There is a particular concern for harnessing one's opportunities and resources to meet a required goal, rather than a moral evaluation of the goal itself (such as enslavement, the

---

9   Weeks, 'Joseph, Dreams and Wisdom', 15. At 14, he comments that: "[t]he proverbial literature does, in fact, given frequent advice for the correct use of power, emphasising above all else the importance of honesty (cf. Prov 17:8, 29:4) and justice (cf. Prov. 16:10, 12; 29:14). This emphasis also appears in the Egyptian material, and it is probably implicit in the idea of 'discernment and wisdom', yet nowhere are we shown Joseph exhibiting such just dealing. This is an essential difference between the JN [Joseph narrative] and the Solomon story, where Solomon's justice and forensic ability are stressed. If the JN, or at least ch. 39-41, is indeed intended to exemplify and teach wisdom ideals for administration, the omission of this key wisdom concept is astonishing." This book agrees with Weeks about his assessment of the teaching of Proverbs, but not in his view of the Joseph narrative. Joseph does not teach about the use of power, but instead Joseph exemplifies the proper use of power.

10   Samuel, 'Joseph - The Brilliant Failure', 42.

11   As Weeks, 'Joseph, Dreams and Wisdom', 7 rightly points out.

12   Thus, Coats, 'The Joseph Story and Wisdom', 290 comments that "the focus of the kernel falls on the proper use of power by a royal administrator already in office."

13   Rainy, 'Joseph's Forgetting', 403-404. Cohn, 'Narrative Structure', 13 makes an interesting comparison between Jacob and Joseph in this regard: "[w]hile Jacob is cunning, Joseph is wise. Jacob seizes the moment and acts to protect himself. Joseph is deeper, always planning for the future and biding his time."

14   E.M. Curtis, 'Old Testament Wisdom: A Model for Faith-Learning Integration', *Christian Scholar's Review* 15 (1986): 215.

positive view of Egypt or the non-acquisition of the priests' lands).[15] In other words, the major focus is on the pragmatic ability to succeed in a task or cope with reality. It is worth noting that wisdom terms in the Old Testament refer to a wide range of activities such as craftsmen skilfully shaping precious metals (1 Chr 22:15; 2 Chr 2:7), or sailors navigating and repairing ships (Ezek 27:8-9). Heaton thus observes that "wisdom at every level is the ability to cope, to design and execute, to plan and put into practice, to succeed by 'know-how', to steer by knowing the ropes (and often by pulling strings)."[16] This is precisely what is reflected in Joseph's public activities, since his plans do not fail in any respect when put to the test (41:47-57).

As a further indication that a court audience is at least partly in view, it has also been noted that, when the brothers appear before Joseph in a 'court-like' setting, Judah's speech in 44:18-34 "is a model of courtly petition".[17] The importance of speaking and arguing well appears to be significant and not incidental to the story.

The Goal of Preserving Life

Life is not only a common wisdom symbol, but an important wisdom goal. The contrasting results in Proverbs 9 are that those who follow Lady Wisdom will find 'life' (Prov 9:11), whereas those who succumb to Dame Folly find only death (Prov 9:18). This is the fundamental wisdom choice, and appropriately concludes the introductory nine chapters of Proverbs. Following the loose woman leads to death (Prov 2:18, 22), but wholeheartedly pursuing wisdom (Prov 2:1-10) is to take the path of life (Prov 2:19, 21). This contrast between the paths of life and death is also prominent in Proverbs 5-7 (5:5-6, 22-23; 6:20-23; 7:1-2, 22-23, 27). Those addressed in the book of Proverbs are constantly urged to be shaped by wisdom's teaching and live (for example, Prov 3:1-2; 4:3-4, 10-13). Chapter 8 is pivotal in Proverbs 1-9, and it ends with the solemn call of Lady Wisdom that those who find her find life, while those who hate her love death. The clear goal of wisdom is thus to find life.[18]

While it is likely that Joseph is partially motivated by a desire to reverse

---

15 Curtis, 'Old Testament Wisdom', 216 adds that "Isa. 40:20 and Jer. 10:6 describe people who are wise or skilled in making idols, and certain wise men of Egypt and Mesopotamia were wise or skilled in magic or divination (Gen. 41:8; Isa. 44:25 and Dan. 2:10-12). … the primary element in wisdom is its ability to accomplish a goal rather than its moral character."

16 E.W. Heaton, *The Hebrew Kingdoms*. New Clarendon Bible: Old Testament, 3 (Oxford: Oxford University Press, 1968) 166.

17 Humphreys, 'Joseph Story, The', 492.

18 Thus Murphy, *The Tree of Life*, 104 notes that "[l]ife is the kerygma of the Book of Proverbs … and it is the great promise of wisdom".

his unjust treatment, this issue is not made explicit in chapter 41. The focus is on life. There is no mention of vengeance (or otherwise) towards Potiphar or his wife for their less-than-fair treatment of Joseph. While his ongoing relationship with his brothers will be the focus of chapters 42-45, the narratives of 41:47-57 and 47:13-26 are concerned with how Joseph's plan led to the saving of lives, inside and outside Egypt. Jacob alerts the implied reader to this in 42:2 when he tells his sons to go to Egypt for grain so that they may live and not die. There is life in Egypt, for Joseph is in Egypt. It is further emphasised by Joseph in his conversations with the brothers, for in 42:18 he tells them what they need to do in order to live. In the recognition scene (45:5-8) Joseph reflects back on the reason for his being sent to Egypt and tells the ten (45:5)

כי למחיה שלחני אלהים לפניכם

Thus, chapters 42-45 clarify the purpose or goal of Joseph's rise to power. Although the book of Genesis ends with the death of Joseph, he is remembered as the one who preserved life, both for the descendants of Abraham, and for the wider world. Indeed, even in his death he is the architect of Israel's future life, for his bones are to be carried into the promised land, the land where they will find life. Brueggemann aptly observes that "the wise man not only finds life, but finds ways of bringing it to others. The Joseph narrative is a clear example of this conviction."[19]

Dream Interpretation and Wisdom

It has often been argued that Joseph's ability to interpret dreams are an expression of mantic wisdom. Müller, for example, has suggested that Joseph's mantic abilities reflect a "weisheitliche[n] Prägung", adding that the Daniel stories later amplify this type of wisdom.[20] More recently, Gammie has observed that, although mantic wisdom is infrequent in the Hebrew Bible, it is "unmistakably present ... in the novella (didactic tale) of Joseph (Genesis 37-50)".[21]

---

19 W. Brueggemann, 'Scripture and an Ecumenical Life-Style: A Study in Wisdom Theology', *Int* 24 (1970): 17.

20 H-P. Müller, 'Magisch-mantische Weisheit und die Gestalt Daniels', *Ugarit-Forschungen* 1 (1969): 85. He notes that "[s]chließlich hat das Alte Testament in den Daniellegenden den Typus des mantischen Weisen Israels gezeichnet. ... In gewissen Maße gehört schon de Gestalt des Joseph hierher." See also Robinson, *Mysterious God*, 10, who sees the ability to interpret dreams as "a charism given by God to Jewish sages".

21 J.G. Gammie, 'From Prudentialism to Apocalypticism. The Houses of the Sages Amid the Varying Forms of Wisdom', in *The Sage in Israel and the Ancient Near East*. eds. J.G. Gammie and L.G. Perdue. (Winona Lake: Eisenbrauns, 1990), 482-

Certainly, it is significant that the dreams of Genesis 37, 40-41 are atypical, being 'symbolic dreams' or 'visual symbolic message dreams' (seen elsewhere in the Old Testament only in Judg 7:13-15 and Daniel) rather than the more frequent 'auditory message dreams'.[22] Ehrlich, who includes Gen 37:5-10 in his category of 'symbolic dream', notes that "»[s]ymbolische Träume« sind solche, die einer Deutung bedürfen".[23] On this view, Joseph's dreams in chapter 37 are symbolic since they need interpretation. Their general sense is, however, made fairly transparent by the context. Indeed, one could argue that the remainder of the Joseph story unpacks the more specific meaning of the dream.

Oppenheim argues that "'[s]ymbolic dreams' are, in the Old Testament, reserved for the 'gentiles.'", although an exception may need to be made in the case of Joseph's dreams in 37:5-11.[24] It is likely that symbolic dreams are normally used for Gentiles since this is a way of avoiding Yahweh giving a message to one who does not yet acknowledge him. However, it is probable that the reason for the use of a symbolic dream in chapter 37 is that God is able to make the future known but in such a way as not to give Joseph any message or instructions.

Given the atypical nature of the dreams in the Joseph narrative, it is surprising that so little is made of the 'art of interpretation' of such dreams. Arguably, Joseph uses skill in understanding which might be the significant parts of the dreams in chapter 40,[25] and perhaps in his word-play about

---

483. His definition of mantic wisdom it that it is concerned "with the interpretation of dreams and hidden signs or omens, with the utterance of spells to inflict harm on an enemy, or with the formulation of sayings to exorcise an unwanted spirit."

22 R.K. Gnuse, *Dreams and Dream Reports in the Writings of Josephus: A Traditio-Historical Analysis*. AGJU, 36. (Leiden: E.J. Brill, 1996) 73-92. The standard exposition of this is that of Oppenheim, 'The Interpretation of Dreams', 206ff. Da Silva, *La symbolique des rêves*, 41-50 also classifies the Old Testament dreams into 'rêves-message' and 'rêves symbolique'. At 42, she writes: "[p]armi les récits de rêves on peut distinguer deux groupes principaux: ceux dont le rêve transmet un ordre de la divinité, et ceux dont le rêve transmet une information sur l'avenir." At 47 she adds that "[l]e rêve symbolique est un rêve prémonitoire en ce sens qu'il dévoile l'avenir du rêveur. Cet avenir est transmis en forme d'images allégoriques et muettes. Le sens n'étant pas toujours clair ils ont, par conséquent, besoin d'être interprétés par un spécialiste." Ehrlich, *Der Traum*, chapter 1, has also proposed the third category of 'the incubation dream', which he sees in 1 Samuel 3, Genesis 28 and 1 Kings 3.

23 Ehrlich, *Der Traum*, 58.

24 Oppenheim, 'The Interpretation of Dreams', 207. In this he is followed by A. Jeffers, 'Divination by Dreams in Ugaritic Literature and in the Old Testament', *IBS* 12 (1990): 169, 171. However, in order to do so he has to distinguish Joseph's 'symbolic' dreams in 37:5-11. Jeffers, at 168-171, describes these as 'simple message dreams' on the basis of their not needing an interpreter.

25 Thus, Caquot, 'Les songes', 113 notes that "[t]oute l'habilité de Joseph consiste à

'Pharaoh will lift up your head'. In addition, his interpretation in chapter 41 is insightful in his perception that the two dreams are one and that each ear of grain and cows represents a one-year time period. Yet, Weeks is probably correct in his view that

> the accounts of dreams in the JN [Joseph narrative] show no particular knowledge of, nor interest in, any system or branch of learning concerned with dreams, and Joseph is not depicted as 'learned' or as an 'expert' in his interpretation.[26]

It has already been observed that, when Joseph interprets Pharaoh's dreams, both the comments of Pharaoh and his courtiers (41:37), and the subsequent narrative description (41:47-57), focus on Joseph's rescue plan rather than on amazement at his gift of dream interpretation. The narrator simply does not mention any other incident in which Joseph interprets dreams.[27] Gnuse has also pointed out that the narrative shows a concern to attribute the interpretation to God's enabling (40:8; 41:16) rather than Joseph's special powers.[28] Ruppert has even suggested that Joseph's ability to interpret dreams, rather than exalting wisdom, acts as "ein indirektes, aber vernichtendes Urteil über die ägyptische Wahrsagekunst und Weisheit" - in other words, a polemic against Egyptian wisdom.[29]

Thus, if there is any implication that Joseph is wise because he can interpret dreams, it is much more likely to be simply a matter of his general skilfulness or insight, rather than an assertion of his mantic wisdom ability. Indeed, the dream that dominates the entire narrative is not that of chapter 41, but rather the dream of Joseph's rise to prominence in chapter 37, a dream that requires no specialist to interpret it.[30] Weeks argues that the

---

    trouver un sens aux *trois* sarments et aux *trois* corbeilles.

26   Weeks, 'Joseph, Dreams and Wisdom', 23. In particular, he notes at 22-23 that "there is no indication here of a scientific method for dream-interpretation." While Fox, 'Wisdom in the Joseph Story', 32-33 is probably right in seeing that Joseph is not a model for how to interpret dreams, he does not discuss his wisdom in dealing with the problems raised by the dreams.

27   The mention of Joseph's cup for divination (44:6) is part of the ruse, portraying Joseph as an Egyptian official, without any indication whether it was so used or not.

28   Gnuse, *Dreams and Dream Reports*, 71 notes that "the art of interpretation is connected only with Joseph and Daniel where special effort goes into attributing the power of interpretation to God, so that Joseph and Daniel appear as prophets not oneirocritics." See also R.K. Gnuse, *The Dream Theophany of Samuel* (Lanham: University Press of America, 1984) 61, and R.K. Gnuse, 'The Jewish Dream Interpreter in a Foreign Court: The Recurring Use of a Theme in Jewish Literature', *JSP* 7 (1990): 37.

29   Ruppert, *Die Josephserzählung*, 72. See also 76.

30   Irvin in Thompson and Irvin, 'The Joseph and Moses Narratives', 189 notes, in

prominence of the dreams yet lack of mantic wisdom precludes any significant wisdom influence in the Joseph story.[31] Yet, this is to argue his case too highly. As will be asserted in the remainder of this chapter, Joseph's wisdom is seen rather in his public activity and his actions within the family, while the narrative also shows wisdom-like concerns in its depiction of God's present but hidden activity.

Joseph's Private Wisdom

There has been much debate in recent years over the social setting of wisdom, but substantial connections have been made with both the court and family.[32] Thus, having examined Joseph's public activity in and around the court, we now turn to the realm of the family.

Joseph's Use of Power in the Family

The brothers are entirely absent from chapters 39-41, but are then foregrounded for the following section. In chapters 42-45, the power structure of chapter 37 is reversed. When Joseph travels to the brothers at Dothan, the ten see him coming and hatch plans to dispose of him. Joseph is powerless to stop them. In Egypt, Joseph recognises the brothers but does not disclose his identity. Just as the brothers previously had the power of life and death over Joseph, the tables are now turned as Joseph is a powerful official who controls the distribution of food during the famine. He can now treat them as he wills, apparently with little accountability to anyone. Such a scenario provides a clear opportunity for the reader to discern Joseph's attitudes towards the brothers who have wronged him.

This study has argued that chapters 42-45 provide a positive view of Joseph in the private setting of the family. Some commentators, however, have been troubled by Joseph's use of deception, his deliberate false accusations (42:9), his refusal to stop when the brothers admit their guilt (42:21-22) his long imprisonment of Simeon (42:24; 43:23), as well as his

---

relation to the dreams of chapter 37, that "these early dreams, for which interpretation was scarcely necessary, still serve the function of dreams in tales, which is *to come true*." *Contra* Green, *What Profit for Us?*, 152-153, who suggests that it is not only the dream of chapter 37 but also the other four dreams that hang over the narrative as a whole.

31 Weeks, 'Joseph, Dreams and Wisdom', 22-23, 45.
32 Substantial connections with the court are suggested by the number of sayings that are connected with the king, and have been proposed by von Rad, 'Ancient Wisdom', 292-300, Brueggemann, *In Man We Trust*, and many others. A family, village or clan setting has been proposed more recently by Westermann, *Roots of Wisdom*, especially 24-28.

previous failure to 'call home' and let Jacob know he was alive.[33] They have therefore suggested that Joseph was seeking vengeance[34] or, at the very least, trying to exercise power over them for selfish reasons.[35]

Such theories fail on several counts. Firstly, Joseph's actions were necessary for him to test whether his brothers had changed, and so bring about an enduring reconciliation within the family. The clearest parallel to this occurs in the narrative prologue to the book of Job (a clear wisdom narrative text), where God allows some otherwise questionable events (Job 1:13-19; 2:7) in order to test Job. Despite the reservations of some modern commentators, the wisdom writer of Job appears to assume that the testing process justified such actions.

Secondly, such readings do not account for all of the text. They cannot explain, for example, Joseph's acts of kindness towards them (42:25), nor his willingness to let nine brothers return to Jacob (42:19). Furthermore, Joseph is not portrayed as one who gloats over his plan, but rather one who weeps. Several times he has to withdraw himself from their presence in order to keep his ruse intact (42:24, 43:30). Nor would a motive of revenge explain why the innocent Benjamin has to be brought down (42:20), knowing the effect on Jacob. Benjamin's presence can only be justified on the basis that this is the only way to test how they will treat the favoured younger brother. Finally, when chapters 42-45 are read in the context of the whole story, they do not depict Joseph as a man of vengeance. Genesis 50:15-21 provides the perfect opportunity for Joseph to take revenge, but he refuses to do so on the basis that God used their evil actions to bring about good. While the reader may not initially be sure about Joseph's motives, by the end of the story it is clear that they are not revenge. As Fretheim concludes, [h]e rejects violence and revenge, and hence brings closure to the snowballing effects of dysfunctionality. ... The one who has ample reason to retaliate chooses reconciliation instead of retribution."[36]

Admittedly, Joseph's failure to contact his father at an earlier stage is difficult to explain, and some have suggested that his explanation for the naming of Manasseh (41:51) reflects a less-than-filial piety. Ages, for example, comments that "the Joseph saga becomes the paradigm of the Jew who lives in a non-Jewish culture so completely that he forgets to call home."[37] However, this needs to be balanced with Joseph's repeated

---

33 For example, Robinson, *Mysterious God*, 7.
34 For example, Redford, *Biblical Story of Joseph*, 103; Miscall, 'Analogies', 34; Wildavsky, *Assimilation versus Separation*, 103.
35 Turner, *Announcements of Plot*, 159-160 proposes that Joseph is attempting to fulfil the second dream, although he concedes that Joseph was not solely motivated by revenge.
36 Fretheim, 'The Book of Genesis', 594.
37 Ages, 'Why Didn't Joseph Call Home?', 46. However, at 42-44, he notes that,

concern for his father's well-being (43:7, 27),[38] and is therefore most likely to be accounted for by the need to test the brothers. This view is reinforced by the observation that, immediately after he has revealed himself to his brothers (45:5-8), he gives them a reassuring message to his father (45:9-13) even before he embraces his brother Benjamin (45:14). Subsequently, of course, he provides amply for his father (46:11-12), and carries out Jacob's burial instructions with proper dignity (50:1-11) Thus, whatever the reason for Joseph not 'calling home', his filial love does not appear to be in doubt.

One cannot, of course, rule out entirely that there was an element of punishment in Joseph's treatment of his brothers, but perhaps this was necessary to bring them to a change of heart.[39] Indeed, Niditch has suggested that inflicting a just amount of punishment is a common characteristic of Ancient Near Eastern wisdom figures.[40] However, texts like Prov 20:22 and 24:29 appear to preclude this being the main motive of a wise person's actions, and Joseph does not speak in these terms.[41]

These chapters, then, appear rather to outline a shrewd test of the brothers by Joseph. It has been argued earlier that a close parallel to this is the narrative about Solomon in 1 Kings 3, where Solomon demonstrates his wisdom by creating a test that reveals which of the two women had maternal feelings. Thus, Joseph's clever ruse does not preclude his being pictured as wise, and the success of the ruse, like that of 1 Kings 3, is strongly suggestive of wisdom. Indeed, Joseph uses his position of courtly power to bring about a lasting reconciliation within his family.

The Goal of Reconciliation

In Joseph's public activity, his goal appeared to be 'to bring life'. In his private activity, however, his goal is even more ambitious. Joseph is

---

while the Jewish rabbis have criticised Joseph (for example, for asking the butler to intercede for him once he was released; for almost giving in to Potiphar's wife; for the non-Jewish rite of embalming his father), "nowhere in the rabbinic tradition is there any criticism of Joseph for failing to communicate with his family back in Canaan during the years of plenty." Kugel, 'The Case Against Joseph', 276, also comments on Joseph's failure to contact his father.

38   Rainy, 'Joseph's Forgetting', 410.

39   Vawter, *On Genesis*, 418; Niditch, *Underdogs and Tricksters*, 102; Boice, *Genesis*, 123. Weeks, *Early Israelite Wisdom*, 94 comments that "it is hard to believe that there is no element of punishment present". D.A. Hubbard, 'The Wisdom Movement and Israel's Covenant Faith', *TynBul* 17 (1966): 14-15 sees Joseph's "craftiness in manoeuvring his brothers into a place where he had the upper hand, yet willingness to forgive upon evidence of their contrition."

40   Niditch, *Underdogs and Tricksters*, 121.

41   De Vaux, *Early History*, 296 cites Prov 14:29; 15:18 and 24:29.

seeking to bring about the family reconciliation that has been so elusive throughout the book of Genesis. It is this goal, more than anything, which establishes Joseph as wise in chapters 42-45.

Harris has recently argued that there are strong intertextual links between Prov 6:1-19 and the Joseph story.[42] It is significant that the climactic practice that God hates in verses 16-19 is that of sowing discord within a family (verse 19b). If this intertextual link can be established, then Joseph, seeking reconciliation within the family, is the antithesis of Jacob's other sons. At the very least, however, Joseph is the embodiment of the wisdom virtue of promoting family harmony that is implied by Prov 6:16-19.

Along similar lines, Joseph appears to exemplify Prov 17:9 which indicates that forgiving a wrong performed against you can foster a healthy relationship with the offender. Furthermore, Joseph acts consistently with the advice given in Prov 20:22; 24:29 of not paying others back for the evil they have done to you. Joseph seems intent on fostering the proverbial goal of reconciliation rather than revenge.

If Joseph's goal were merely revenge, then it could have been achieved much more ruthlessly, and without involving Benjamin. If his goal were simply to disclose his high status, or to demonstrate his power to make his brother bow down to him, then this was possible as soon as they arrived in chapter 42, and is achieved in Gen 43:26. Instead, Joseph is seeking to create a full-blooded reconciliation that will ensure the ongoing survival of the family. He wants more than a truce; he wants to break the cycle of deceit and mistrust, and to enable the fullness of שׁלוֹם. It has been well observed that while each part of the Joseph story involves conflict, "the narrative as a whole is a story of reconciliation."[43]

It is for this reason that Joseph wants to see the brothers changed. Schimmel comments that "Joseph's piety resides in this - he would rather see his enemies purified of their sinfulness than punish them for it."[44] Joseph would have been entitled to punish the guilty brothers, but he chooses the higher way of restoring harmony and trust in the family. Thus Ackerman can rightly claim that reconciliation among the brothers is an important sub-theme of the Joseph story.[45]

For reconciliation to occur, the brothers must be faced with the full horror of what they have done. This is why the brothers' expression of guilt in 42:21-22 was not enough, for they had not yet faced the enormity of their

---

42 Harris, *Proverbs 1-9*, 149-153. Harris' argument is outlined in footnote 58 below.
43 H.J. Flanders, R.W. Crapps and D.A. Smith, *People of the Covenant*. 3rd edn. (New York: Oxford University Press, 1988) 135. An interesting comparison might be made here with the Moses narrative, where there is conflict between Pharaoh and Moses but no reconciliation.
44 Schimmel, 'A Paradigm for Repentance', 63.
45 Ackerman, 'Joseph, Judah and Jacob', 95.

offence. The cleverness of Joseph's ruse is that it provides a possibility of the brothers leaving the favourite son behind while going free themselves (44:17). Joseph ironically invites them to go לשלום, and thus settle for much less than reconciliation. It is only Judah's powerful speech, including his reflection on the effect of such a loss to their father (44:30-31), which reveals that the brothers see both the ugliness of such an action and choose not to repeat it.

In this context, the meal of Gen 43:26-34 takes on an ironic dimension. The threefold use of שלום in verses 27-28 - "a veritable burst of *šālôms*"[46] - alerts the implied reader to the significance in the Ancient Near East of sharing a meal as a symbol of שלום. However, relationships have not yet been restored as the brothers have recognised neither their full guilt, not the real identity of their host. There is the appearance of שלום but Joseph and his brothers are still sitting separately (43:32). As Ackerman comments, "[t]he brothers are together, but they are not a family. Only after they have passed the test in chapter 44 does reconciliation begin."[47]

Once Joseph has demonstrated to all that the brothers have changed, he discloses himself to them as 'your brother' (45:4), and he embraces and weeps with them (45:15). He does not speak of restitution, but expresses warmth of relationship. Friedman describes it well

> what brings this chain of deception to an end: forgiveness. The sequence of deceptions that causes this family so much suffering finally comes to an end when Joseph chooses not to take revenge on his brothers. True, Joseph causes them discomfort, but only to the point of recognizing their past wrong. He does them no harm corresponding to what they have done to him, despite the fact that it is clearly in his power to do so. ... Wherever the deception begins, it ends when one family member puts family above revenge, when one who is manifestly entitled to retribution chooses not to take it.[48]

It is Joseph's response that enables reconciliation, and he has clearly been working towards this goal. The restoration of relationships is accomplished from Joseph's perspective as early as chapter 45, although he needs to reaffirm it to his still-anxious brothers in 50:15-21.[49]

It is interesting to note that, while the brothers are absent in chapters 39-41, the narrator recounts the story of Joseph's public wisdom in a court

---

46   Humphreys, *Joseph and His Family*, 95.
47   Ackerman, 'Joseph, Judah and Jacob', 95.
48   Friedman, 'Deception for Deception', 30.
49   Niditch, *Underdogs and Tricksters*, 118 suggests that "events necessary for reconciliation in the Joseph narrative begin in chapter 42, with a climax in chapter 45 and additional aspects of resolution covering a few more chapters."

setting. In Gen 42:1-45:15, when Pharaoh is absent, the narrator has provided the reader with a tale of Joseph's private wisdom in a family setting.[50] Both these major sections of the story - and major spheres of life - contribute to Joseph's characterisation as wise. Thus, the Joseph narrative appears to depict both Joseph's public and his private activity as in accordance with wisdom ideals.

Joseph's Tested Character

The first two sections of this chapter have been concerned with Joseph's actions whether in private or in public. However, the wisdom books look not only at individual actions but also at the character of the person who acts wisely. Indeed, Boström has argued that, in the book of Proverbs, it is preferable to talk of a connection between character and consequences rather than between acts and consequences. He writes that "[t]he consequences mentioned in the book of Proverbs do not relate primarily to particular acts performed but rather to the total life-style and disposition of the person."[51] Therefore, this section will examine Joseph's underlying character as a factor that is more than his isolated actions.

Joseph in Chapter 37

It is interesting that several writers who argue strongly for wisdom elements in the Joseph story have contended that Joseph acts immaturely and unwisely in chapter 37.[52] This, they allege, does not disqualify Joseph from becoming wise and acting wisely from chapter 39 onwards.

Earlier in this study, however, it was argued that chapter 37 does not contribute significantly to the characterisation of Joseph. Firstly, it was argued that, from a structural viewpoint, verses 2-11 belonged together and constituted the exposition of this chapter, while verses 12-35 provided the

---

50   Thus, J.R. King, 'The Joseph Story and Divine Politics: A Comparative Study of a Biographic Formula from the Ancient Near East', *JBL* 106 (1987): 593 sees two sequences going on in the Joseph story: the tale of Joseph's rise within Jacob's family (chapters 37, 42-50) and Joseph's rise in Pharaoh's court (chapters 39-41). Similarly, Humphreys, 'Joseph Story, The', 491 proposes that chapters 37, 42-48, and 50 concern the internal affairs of the family of Jacob, while chapters 40-41 relate Joseph's adventures in the Egyptian court.

51   L. Boström, *The God of the Sages: The Portrayal of God in the Book of Proverbs*. CBOTS, 29. (Stockholm: Almqvist & Wiksell, 1990) 138. See also 90-91. In fact, Boström acknowledges that actions and character are intertwined as he often speaks of act/character-consequence relationship (for example, on page 125).

52   Loader, 'Chokma - Joseph - Hybris', 28; Wessels, 'The Joseph story', 55; Humphreys, *Joseph and His Family*, 25.

initial complication. This means that both Joseph's report on the brothers and his telling of the dreams to his family are part of setting the scene rather than events in the story that create a picture of Joseph's character.

Secondly, there is a curious avoidance in the chapter of Joseph's reaction to what had happened to him, with the narrative focus seeming to be on the brothers and their thoughts and plans. Most noticeable was the omission here of any record of protest by Joseph. This is made all the more striking by the fact of Joseph's pleading cries being mentioned later by the brothers (42:21). This apparently deliberate attempt to avoid using Joseph as a model makes it likely that he is also not a negative model in verses 2-11. The chapter precludes the reader from getting inside the head of Joseph and viewing events from his perspective.

If so, there is very little in chapter 37 that supports either a positive or a negative view of Joseph's character. However, even if Joseph's character in chapter 37 were not to be regarded so neutrally, it would only serve to disqualify the early Joseph from being wise. He would still be a model of a young man who learns wisdom by turning away from his earlier folly. Thus, the conclusions of this study are not largely affected by taking a less-flattering view of Joseph in chapter 37.

Joseph and Potiphar's Wife

In the light of the avoidance in chapter 37 of Joseph's reactions, there is a striking focus on Joseph's words and thoughts in the attempted seduction by Potiphar's wife. It has been argued that the characterisation of Joseph begins here, and does so by focusing on his values and loyalties. The unnamed wife of Potiphar is depicted stereotypically, while Joseph's mentioning of his reasons for refusal reveals what is important to him. He speaks of the abuse of his master's trust, and of his refusal to sin against God in so doing. While this language of 'sin against God' is found in other traditions, it was noted that such language is reminiscent of Prov 5:21-22, which is part of a passage dealing with an adulteress.

Indeed, the inclusion of this persistent seduction, as well as Joseph's verbal response, does not further the plot in any significant way. As Kugel has indicated this incident provides much more detail than is needed to advance the story, and seemingly is recorded to give the implied reader a deeper insight into Joseph's character.[53] Consistent with this is the observation that the narrative focus is on Joseph throughout the seduction incident. Potiphar's wife is unnamed and her fate is not told. The narrator records that she constantly spoke to Joseph (39:10), since a characteristic of the loose woman of Proverbs is her seductive speech. Williams has observed about the loose woman of Proverbs 5-7 that

---

53   Kugel, *In Potiphar's House*, 126.

her weapons are not so much her beauty or sexually seductive wiles as her manner of using language. It is her "coaxing words" (Prov 2:16; 6:24; 7:5, 21), her lips that drop honeyed words (5:3), her "flattering speech" (7:21), her mouth like a deep pit (22:14), that hold the power of entrapment.[54]

This explains the focus on Potiphar's wife repeatedly speaking to Joseph. Brenner has also noted that, when Genesis 39 and Proverbs 7 are read as intertexts, there is a basically similar paradigm

A nameless married woman desires a young man. The husband is absent. The woman initiates action. She tries to seduce the young man. She does so by speech acts rather than by reliance on her looks - her physical appearance is not reported. ... Unlike his intertextual counterpart, Joseph does not succumb to the woman's advances. The reward for this restraint as well as for his other virtues is great indeed.[55]

Yet the narrator skips over the content of her words, and records only Joseph's responses, which are a stark contrast to his silence of 37:18-28. Instead, the narrative focus on Joseph draws attention to his words and thus to his underlying character.[56]

Indeed, Harris has recently argued that there are more examples of intertextuality between the Joseph story and Proverbs 1-9. He proposes strong intertextual links of a lexical, linguistic and thematic nature between Prov 1:8-19 and Gen 37:12-36, and between Prov 6:1-19 and Judah's words (Gen 37:26-27, 36; 44:32-34). Harris, dating Proverbs 1-9 in the late exilic and early post-exilic period, concludes that there are covert citations from the Joseph story in Proverbs 1 and 6.[57]

---

54   J.G. Williams, *Those Who Ponder Proverbs: Aphoristic Thinking and Biblical Literature*. Bible and Literature Series, 2. (Sheffield: Almond Press, 1981) 25.

55   A. Brenner, 'Some Observations on the Figurations of Woman in Wisdom Literature', in *Of Prophets' Visions and the Wisdom of Sages*. JSOTSup, 162, eds. H.A. McKay and D.J.A. Clines. (Sheffield: JSOT Press, 1993), 204-205. See also D.K. Berry, *An Introduction to Wisdom and Poetry of the Old Testament* (Nashville: Broadman & Holman, 1995) 98.

56   Alter, 'Joseph and his Brothers', 60 notes that "character is revealed primarily through speech, action, gesture, with all the ambiguities that entails". Robertson, *The Old Testament Problem*, 211 also observes that in Hebrew narrative, "[w]here a modern story writer would devote long paragraph to an appraisement of the characters of his story, the Hebrew narrators can produce the same result more artistically by a skilful use of dialogue."

57   Harris, *Proverbs 1-9*, 155. At 22-23, he argues that past attempts to base these passages on Egyptian parallels overlook the intertextual connection between them

Harris's work is stimulating in its observations, although the obscurity of some of the links render it not compelling in its entirety. However, it notices a number of new and quite specific parallels between Proverbs 1-9 and the Joseph story.[58] This reinforces the more transparent intertextual connection between Genesis 39 and Proverbs 5-7.

However, Weeks has objected to seeing any wisdom elements in the incident with Potiphar's wife, noting that "it is a strange didacticism indeed which promises a prison sentence as the reward for virtue!"[59] Yet, this is to have too short term a focus for Joseph ultimately becomes vizier of Egypt

---

and the Joseph story.

58 Harris, *Proverbs 1-9*. At 54-56, he outlines common elements in Prov 1:8-19 and Gen 37:12-36. Among his examples, he notes the occurrence of בצע (Gen 37:26; Prov 1:19) = 'ill-gotten gain, profit', which is used elsewhere in Proverbs but only twice in the Torah, here and Exod 18:21 (where other parallels are not present). He adds that there is also a common imagery of 'devouring/consuming' in Genesis 37 and Prov 1:10-19, as well as the profit motif in both cases. Furthermore, in both passages "[t]hose who engage in plotting to get gain by violent means actually lay the groundwork for their own demise." At 135, in relation to Prov 6:1-19, he notes in particular that "Judah stands out in the Hebrew Bible as the only one who provides surety from someone else." and argues that the parent's words in Prov 6:1-19 echo and reverse the pattern set by Judah in the Joseph story. At 144, he points out that Judah's first words are to suggest they sell Joseph to the Ishmaelites/Midianites (Gen 37:26-27), and in his last words he tells the Egyptian overlord that he has gone surety for his brother (Gen 44:32-34). In Prov 6:1-5, the parent urges his son to extricate himself from a surety, and the last part of 6:19 speaks of 'one who sows discord between brothers', with the word for 'discord' or 'strife' being מדנים, which is used in Gen 37:36 as a proper noun to refer to the Midianites. He observes (144-145) that "[t]he first and last didactic lessons in Prov 6:1-19 concern familial relationships, as does the Joseph story. Judah plays a role both by dividing the family when he sells Joseph to the Midianites (the last thing mentioned in Prov 6:19) and by bringing the family together again when he goes surety for Benjamin (the first lesson in Prov 6:1-5). by reversing the order of acts associated with Judah, the parent in Prov 6:1-19 effects a reading of the text which ends with Judah's abominable act of selling his brother Joseph." At 147-148, he also notes then that the setting of going surety for Benjamin was a time of famine, in which Joseph showed his industriousness and wisdom in storing up food. This, he indicates, is the lesson of Prov 6:6-11.

59 Weeks, 'Joseph, Dreams and Wisdom', 12. He refers to other ancient examples of this motif and at 13 he concludes that "[n]one of these stories has any apparent origin in the wisdom tradition, while the very prevalence of the motif tells against any supposition that Gen. 39 was composed to illustrate wisdom teachings about adultery." However, many of his references are to texts that are probably written at a later time, and have crucial differences. Thus, in the cases of Hippolytus and Tenes, the woman is the stepmother, while in the story of Susannah, the sexes of the characters are reversed. Such differences significantly undermine the force of his argument. Similarly, Fox, 'Wisdom in the Joseph Story', 30-31.

and his imprisonment is, in the broader tale, one step along that path. Indeed, Weeks' view would also disqualify Job as a wisdom figure for, though he ultimately prospered, he too suffered setbacks. Even the book of Proverbs has the realism to observe that a righteous person may fall, yet will ultimately prevail (Prov 24:16)

כי שבע יפול צדיק וקם ורשעים יכשלו ברעה

In terms of the role of this incident in the Joseph story as a whole, it appears to operate as a way of testing Joseph's character in order to see if he will remain true to the way of life. He has not yet been entrusted with power either in the court or in his family. His character must first be tested to demonstrate his ability not to be seduced by the opportunities that power can bring.

The parallels with Proverbs 1-9 are again interesting here, since their focus is also on the development of character (Prov 1:2-7; 2:1-3:18), largely through the fundamental embrace of the call of Lady Wisdom (Prov 1:20-21; 4:4-27; 8:1-21; 9:1-6). There is comparatively little instruction in Proverbs 1-9 on what kind of actions to perform or refrain from, since the focus is rather on whether a person takes their basic stance in the way of wisdom or the way of folly. It is in the sentence literature of Proverbs 10-29 that much more specific guidance is given about wise and unwise actions. Indeed, the final form of the book of Proverbs requires a reader to consider first the issues of one's character and basic orientation, prior to being given detailed advice on how to live and act. Character formation, according to the book of Proverbs, precedes wise actions that will bring life.

Of course, this pattern is clearly evident in the Joseph narrative. Joseph's character is tested in chapter 39 and will be again in chapter 40, before he is entrusted with power in the Egyptian court and subsequently in his family. Once his character has been tested, he is then both permitted and able to act wisely in a wider sphere.

Joseph's Patient Enduring of Ingratitude

A second and less obvious form of testing occurs in chapter 40, where Joseph has to wait patiently after the cupbearer fails to make mention of him to Pharaoh (40:23). Despite Joseph's concern for the officials in prison (40:6-7), and his willingness to interpret their dreams (40:8), he appears to be no closer to his goal of release from prison. Joseph's only option is to persist in doing what he has done before - waiting patiently for a further two years (41:1).

On this occasion, the narrator records no speech by the characters (since there is presumably no contact), but makes the point by means of an editorial comment (40:23) followed by a time reference (41:1). Although

Joseph has been waiting since he has been seventeen, he has no alternative but to keep on waiting.[60] Kugel has argued that *"patience* is the cardinal virtue of the sage: since he knows that all happens according to the divine plan, the apparent triumph of the wicked must be only temporary."[61]

While the details are scarce, Joseph appears to combine a patient waiting for wrongs to be righted together with an ability to act decisively when necessary. Indeed, the story of Joseph and the cupbearer begins with Joseph taking initiative to enquire after the two officials (40:6-7), and continues with Joseph boldly urging them to tell him their dreams (40:8). Even more clearly, when Joseph interprets his dream, he adds a request that the cupbearer remember Joseph (40:14-15). This bold request leads to his release some two years later (41:9-13). Thus, Joseph displays an astute combination of necessary patience and a shrewd taking of initiative. This combination fits nicely with the fact that the book of Proverbs does not contrast patience and initiative, but rather patience and a quick temper (Prov 14:29; 15:18).[62] The patience of the wise was based on the belief that God will ultimately right wrongs if one continues to act wisely. Kugel concludes that "the cardinal virtue of patience characterizes this wise hero's action at every turn."[63]

Joseph's Refusal to Take Revenge

Joseph's treatment of his brothers has already been discussed under the heading of his private wisdom and it is not necessary to cover that ground again. However, it is worth pointing out in the present context that Joseph eschews the quick-tempered response of taking revenge, and opts instead for a shrewd plan that will lead to reconciliation. This, too, requires patience for it delays his opportunity to see his father and younger brother, but it ultimately restores wholeness to the family.

It is noteworthy that Joseph stands in strong contrast to the earlier impetuosity of Jacob and indeed the other patriarchs. Jacob's impatience led him to resort to trickery in order to gain what he wanted for himself (Genesis 27), requiring him to flee from his brother. Joseph, however, does not act impatiently out of a desire for selfish gain, but wisely combines

---

60   J.L. Kugel, 'Introduction to the Psalms and Wisdom', in *Harper's Bible Commentary*. ed. J.L. Mays. (San Francisco: Harper & Row, 1988), 400 suggests that here "Joseph, sage that he is, patiently greets each new turn, and ultimately assumes his place as ruler over Egypt."

61   J.L. Kugel, 'Wisdom and the Anthological Temper', *Prooftexts* 17 (1997): 22.

62   De Vaux, *Early History*, 296.

63   Kugel, 'Anthological Temper', 23. See also R.B.Y. Scott, 'The Study of Wisdom Literature', *Int* 24 (1970): 34. *Contra* Weeks, 'Joseph, Dreams and Wisdom', 16 who argues that "if the narrator intended Joseph to be primarily a didactic model of the ideals embodied in the wisdom literature, then he has made a poor job of it."

patience and action for justice. Indeed, Joseph's character is tested as he refuses the temptation to take revenge, both during and after Jacob's life (45:5-8; 50:15-21).

Joseph thus acts wisely not only in resisting Potiphar's wife, but also in his patient enduring of wrongs both in chapter 40 and in effecting reconciliation with his brothers.[64] Frost concludes that "the things for which the Wise Men so earnestly contended and the virtues which they so persistently inculcated are beautifully and tellingly set forth in the story of Joseph."[65]

Wisdom Vocabulary and Joseph

In chapter two of this study it was argued that the question of wisdom terminology was too narrow a basis on which to refute the identification of a wisdom text or wisdom influence. It was argued in particular that the formal transformation from the poetic language of the wisdom books to a prose narrative like the Joseph story may well affect the vocabulary used to outline the same concepts.[66]

An interesting parallel case here is Genesis 3. It is striking that nowhere in Genesis 3 do any of the usual Hebrew words for 'sin' appear as descriptions of the actions of Adam and Eve. Yet the concept is not only present but pervasive, and the chapter constitutes one of the foundational passages in the whole of the Bible on the subject of sin. The mere absence of characteristic vocabulary does not preclude the presence of an idea.

However, several studies of specific wisdom vocabulary have seen in the Joseph story enough of these terms to indicate the presence of wisdom-like ideas or elements. Whybray, for example, notes that the description of Joseph in Gen 41:33, 36 as וחכם נבון are "key-words in a key-passage"; thus supporting von Rad's view that Joseph is being characterised as an

---

64 Schimmel, 'A Paradigm for Repentance', 63 comments that Joseph was known as 'Joseph the Zaddik' not only because of his successful resistance of Potiphar's wife, but also for his piety evident in the testing of the brothers.

65 Frost, *Patriarchs and Prophets*, 41. Niditch, *Underdogs and Tricksters*, 120 also concludes that "the image of Joseph as wise man remains fully intact by the end of the tale; in fact, it is strengthened." Von Rad, 'The Story of Joseph', 20-21 notes the different emphasis on characterisation between the Joseph narrative and the patriarchal stories. He concludes that the Joseph narrative "must have its origin in a quite different intellectual and theological place." *Contra* Weeks, 'Joseph, Dreams and Wisdom', 6 who claims that "we should anticipate in such a didactic text a far more consistent idealisation of character, and a less ambiguous correlation between the behaviour of Joseph and the 'ideal' behaviour which, Von Rad claims, the proverbial literature upholds."

66 Whybray, *Intellectual Tradition*, 3 also suggests that characteristics of form and style are not likely to survive the translation from poetic wisdom to narrative texts.

ideal 'wise man'."[67]

Shupak has more recently made a study of wisdom terminology in both Hebrew and Egyptian wisdom, arguing that clusters of words that appear more frequently in wisdom texts are a helpful criterion for discerning wisdom influence.[68] She notes that wisdom vocabulary is used in non-wisdom texts in both Hebrew and Egyptian writings,[69] and concludes

> In both Israel and Egypt wisdom phrases and terms - when appearing outside wisdom literature and found together with other elements peculiar to wisdom, i.e., literary form and subject-matter - may be used as criteria to indicate a "wisdom influence" in other literary genres.[70]

It is on such a basis that she implies that there is evidence of wisdom influence in the Joseph story.[71]

These linguistic studies provide useful corroborative evidence that the description of Joseph as נבון וחכם (41:33) is an attempt to describe his character in wisdom terms. While such studies are not conclusive, they provide useful supporting evidence for the presence of wisdom-like elements in the Joseph story.

---

67   Whybray, *Intellectual Tradition*, 87. For a more recent view to the contrary, see R.P. Gordon, 'A house divided: wisdom in Old Testament narrative traditions', in *Wisdom in ancient Israel: Essays in honour of J.A. Emerton*. eds. J. Day, R.P. Gordon and H.G.M. Williamson. (Cambridge: Cambridge University Press, 1995), 96. Gordon uses a fairly narrow test of terminological parallels, largely those of the חכם root, but his work is much less detailed than that of Whybray on this point. On the question of the 'fear of God' in Gen 42:18, see the detailed argument by Weeks, 'Joseph, Dreams and Wisdom', 63-65, urging that the context here precludes a wisdom understanding of the term.

68   N. Shupak, *Where can Wisdom be found? The Sage's Language in the Bible and in Ancient Egyptian Literature*. OBO, 130. (Fribourg: University Press, 1993) 339-340. She proposes that "[i]t is the accumulation of several words, or the appearance of a single term together with other characteristic features in a passage outside the wisdom books, which may indicate a relationship of the passage to the wisdom literature."

69   Shupak, *Where can Wisdom be found?*, 352. She adds: "[t]hat the wisdom tradition influenced literary works otherwise unrelated to the Biblical wisdom literature appears therefore as quite a legitimate assumption, and there seems to be no reason for rejecting it, as a number of scholars in the field [she cites Murphy and Crenshaw] have attempted to do."

70   Shupak, *Where can Wisdom be found?*, 337.

71   Shupak, *Where can Wisdom be found?*, 352 and endnote 46 on page 421.

Divine Activity and Human Initiative

Up to this point it has been argued that the public and private actions of Joseph, as well as his underlying character, show significant wisdom-like elements that distinguish these chapters from the preceding patriarchal stories, in spite of their obvious connections. However, the distinctiveness of the Joseph story is taken one step further when the activity of God, and place of human actions, are examined. It will be argued that this particular blend of divine activity and human initiative reveals strong 'wisdom-like elements'.

Dreams as a Tool to Background God's Activity

The structural analysis of chapter 37 revealed that Joseph's dreams were part of the exposition, giving the necessary background information before the action itself started. This is an important observation, for it places the dreams outside the narrative events and thus giving perspective to them. The dream (for in reality the two dreams are one) of Joseph's rise to prominence looms over the entire Joseph story. It is very important for the implied reader to know from the outset that this is where the story is heading so that, when it happens, it will not be seen as accidental but rather as predetermined (by God). The dream is, however, not the event that provokes a reaction from the brothers, for they hated him before the dream (37:4). The dream is rather an unveiling of the course of the subsequent story.

The literary effect of having the dream at the beginning of the Joseph story is that it sends signals to the reader. In Genesis 37-41 dreams have the function of showing what God is going to bring about. This is made explicit in Gen 41:25, 28. In other words, when the Joseph story is read as a whole, there is an implied assertion that God is bringing about his purposes as Joseph's dream is fulfilled.

The delicate operation of the dream reveals the literary artistry of the text. At one level, it asserts that what will happen is the outworking of God's controlling will. At another level, the events of the story do not mention God's overt activity in bringing anything about.[72] The dream thus foregrounds the truth that the rise of Joseph is in conformity with the will and purposes of God, yet backgrounds the activity of God. Since the story starts with the dream, the implied reader is discouraged from thinking that the subsequent events are accidents that are out of God's hands. The dream reveals God's plans and purposes, showing that what happens is what God ultimately determines. In other words, God is exercising his powerful,

---

72   For a study of how deeds lead to consequences in the Joseph narrative, see E. Otto, 'Die 'synthetische Lebensauffassung' in der frühköniglichen Novellistik Israels', *ZTK* 74 (1977): 387-400.

sovereign, kingly rule of events in the world, even though God does not come into the foreground by intervening or acting to bring this about. After the dream has shaped the reader's perspective, the focus is then on the human actions which bring these events to pass.

It is at this point that wisdom-like ideas are manifest. Weeks has objected that the depiction of Joseph as a dream interpreter does not qualify him as a wisdom figure.[73] What this observation is partially true, Weeks appears to miss the broader connection between Joseph's dream and wisdom. It is not claimed that Joseph is wise because he is the recipient of a dream, for that would only make him as wise as the chief baker who was beheaded. Instead, Joseph's dream is a clever way of asserting a wisdom understanding of God, in which the deity works behind the scenes to bring about his purposes, through natural processes and human actions. This connection between Joseph's dream and wisdom has not often been noticed.

The Absence of Divine Intervention

The backgrounding of God is of major importance in distinguishing the Joseph narrative from the preceding patriarchal accounts as well as the subsequent Moses stories.[74] Thus, God is portrayed as appearing to Abraham, Isaac and Jacob, and confirming his covenant with each of them (Gen 12:1-3; 15:1-21; 17:1-22; 22:15-18; 26:2-5, 24; 28:10-17; 35:9-12). Similarly, God meets Moses in the burning bush (Exodus 3) and on Mount Sinai (Exodus 19). The summary at the end of the Pentateuch is that Moses was one whom the Lord knew face to face (Deut 34:10).

By way of contrast, God rarely appears in the Joseph story, and never to Joseph.[75] The narrator's use of יהוה in Gen 39:3-5, 21-23 makes the claim that Joseph is serving Israel's covenant God, but Joseph neither sees God nor hears him speak, let alone receives any instructions from him. God is more a hidden influence rather than a character on stage.[76] Furthermore,

---

73   Weeks, 'Joseph, Dreams and Wisdom', 48, 53-54.

74   Thus, Weeks, 'Joseph, Dreams and Wisdom', 55, 67 concedes that, in the Joseph story, "divine action is portrayed as subtle and enigmatic" when compared to both the Moses/Exodus and the patriarchal stories. Similarly, Culley, *Themes and Variations*, 146; J.S. Kselman, 'The Book of Genesis: A Decade of Scholarly Research', *Int* 45 (1991): 389; E.W. Hengstenberg, *History of the Kingdom of God Under the Old Testament*. 2 vols. (Cherry Hill: Mack, 1972) 1:199-200; Sarna, *Understanding Genesis*, 211; Keil and Delitzsch, *The Pentateuch*, 330

75   Niditch, *Underdogs and Tricksters*, 105. Nicol, 'Story-Patterning in Genesis', 215 notes that in Genesis 37-50, God "is more a hidden influence, a providence detected and spoken of by Joseph, rather than a character who intrudes regularly to interact with the other characters."

76   D. Patrick, *The Rendering of God in the Old Testament*. Overtures to Biblical

Joseph is not portrayed as praying to this God. As Sarna notes "[t]here are no direct divine revelations or communications to Joseph. He builds no altars. He has no associations with cultic centers. God never openly and directly intervenes in his life."[77] Westermann's analysis of the Yahweh sayings in Proverbs 10-31 reveals similar emphases and omissions.[78]

While theoretically these omissions could be a result of the narrator's oversight, this seems unlikely in the light of Gen 46:1-4. Once Joseph has been reconciled to his brothers in chapters 42-45, the patriarch Jacob begins to set out for Egypt. However, in a manner that reflects the usual pattern in the preceding patriarchal narratives, Jacob travels to a traditional holy place (Beersheba) and offers up sacrifices to the God of the patriarchs. God appears to him in an auditory or perhaps even visual experience,[79] speaks to Jacob and Jacob answers. Indeed, God gives Jacob instructions about what to do (אל־תירא מרדה מצרימה, verse 3) and leaves him with a promise (ואנכי אעלך גם־עלה, verse 4).

Jacob's encounter in Gen 46:1-4 is thus almost the complete opposite to Joseph's experience of God in chapters 37-45. Consequently, this very contrast draws attention to the sudden change in divine activity at this point of the Joseph story. God simply has not intervened to bring about his purposes. The closest that God came to intervening in the story was firstly in Joseph's dream, and secondly in the seven years of plenty and famine. However, the dream merely outlined what will be, and no command or instruction being recorded as given to Joseph to help his rise to prominence. It has also been argued that the description that the LORD was with Joseph (39:2, 21, 23) does not, in this context, connote God giving guidance to Joseph, while expressions like 'the LORD gave him success' or 'the LORD blessed the household' (39:3, 5, 23) do not imply that God does so by intervening in history. Indeed, no such intervention on Joseph's behalf is recorded in the narrative. In relation to the years of plenty and of famine, there is no suggestion in the narrative that these are anything other than normal earthly processes. God is not depicted as interfering with the cycles of nature to bring about either famine or plenty. He was simply revealing

Theology. (Philadelphia: Fortress, 1981) 22; McGuire, 'The Joseph Story', 12; Fretheim, 'The Book of Genesis', 594; U. Simon, *Story and Faith in the Biblical Narrative* (London: SPCK, 1975) 21.

77   Sarna, *JPS Torah Commentary*, 254.
78   Westermann, *Roots of Wisdom*, 130.
79   It is not clear whether this is a visual or an auditory encounter with God. Wenham, *Genesis 16-50*, 441 points out that in 1 Sam 3:15, this phrase refers to a purely auditory experience at night. Westermann, *Genesis 37-50*, 155 understands 'vision' here in the sense of 'revelation' not 'vision'. Sarna, *JPS Torah Commentary*, 312 suggests the use of 'speaking' not 'appearing' was "because the revelation is wholly verbal and without any visual aspect". Fretheim, 'The Book of Genesis', 652 argues that it "could be either oral or oral with a visual component."

what will be.

The picture of divine activity that is given here thus produces what is in the truest sense a distinctive theo-logy. A recurring element in the preceding patriarchal accounts is the intervention by God to rescue Abraham and his descendants, thus removing any threat to the continuation of the covenant promise. The Joseph narrative, by way of contrast, is characterised by the absence of divine intervention until chapter 46. This presentation of God's actions marks the Joseph story off from the texts which surround it, and raises the issue of the source of such a distinctive understanding of divine activity.

Of course, this is not to assert that the God of the Joseph story is different *in nature* from the God of the earlier patriarchal accounts. God is simply active in the story in a different *manner* than in the previous chapters.[80] Jacob's God is clearly Joseph's God, but the same God is active in different ways in the lives of these two men. God is undoubtedly present in Genesis 37-50, but he does not appear to Joseph nor does he intervene on Joseph's behalf.

In addition, in the Joseph story there is no polemic against (or even reference to) the gods of the Egyptians, in stark contrast to Exodus 1-15 which follows the Joseph story in the canon. There is also a fairly positive evaluation of Pharaoh, although in Egyptian thought he is the one in whom the human and divine merge. Thus there is no strong push of the distinctiveness of the God of Israel in this narrative, consistent with the more universal and less exclusivist attitude found in the wisdom corpus.

Weeks has objected, however, that "[t]he distinctiveness of the JN [Joseph narrative] in respect of its portrayal of God is essentially one of presentation rather than of presupposition."[81] While he argues that this need not be explained by wisdom influence, he fails to see that a wisdom understanding of God and his activity is different only at this level of presentation or emphasis. There is not a different doctrine of God in the wisdom books,[82] but there is a characteristic pattern of divine activity not as intervention but behind the scenes (Job 1-2) or in the normal everyday processes. Even the theophany of Job 38-41 is not a real exception, for there God does not do anything to ameliorate Job's situation, not does he give Job any instructions or commands. God simply invites Job to look

---

80 Fretheim, *The Pentateuch*, 91.

81 Weeks, 'Joseph, Dreams and Wisdom', 68.

82 R.E. Murphy, 'Religious Dimensions of Israelite Wisdom', in *Ancient Israelite Religion: Essays in Honor of Frank Moore Cross*. Ed. P.D. Miller, P.D. Hanson and S.D. McBride. (Philadelphia: Fortress, 1987) 450 rightly observes that "[w]isdom and salvation are not incompatible in human experience ... The teaching of Deuteronomy and Proverbs suggests that the Yahweh of both books is the same Yahweh who is at work on every level of experience."

around at the world and learn from it.

This pattern of God's behind-the-scenes activity has traditionally been described as God's providence.[83] Gibson observes that

> The theme of the Joseph epic, however, is the overriding providence of God in the affairs of men. He disposes things gradually and gently, overruling rather than interfering, working behind the scenes to bring good out of evil.[84]

The dream, in outlining what will come to pass, is a crucial symbol of God's behind-the-scenes control of events. The crises of the story present many obstacles to Joseph's rise to prominence but cannot thwart his eventual triumph. Goldingay has thus argued that the Joseph story centres on

> how Joseph's dream comes true despite and even through the affliction and humiliation brought about by the brothers who resented him, by the woman who loved him, by the master who misjudged him, and by the steward who forgot him.[85]

Therefore, although God does not himself appear as a character on stage, he is actively at work ordering situations and events so as to make all things come right for his chosen people and purposes. As Humphreys comments, "at least a glimpse of a divine providential guiding hand is caught behind the toss and tug of human interactions."[86]

Thus, the family is preserved in spite of natural disaster (famine) and human wickedness (betrayal of a brother). God's activity is clearly signalled to the readers in the narrator's comments that the Lord was with Joseph (Gen 39:2-5, 21-23),[87] implying that even these serious setbacks will not ultimately frustrate God's purposes. Indeed, Wintermute has observed

---

83 Indeed, Hengstenberg, *History of the Kingdom*, 1:191 has urged that "[p]rovidence appears so prominently in the history of Joseph, that it would be superfluous to draw attention to it in detail."

84 Gibson, *Genesis*, 249. Similarly, Licht, *Storytelling in the Bible*, 139.

85 Goldingay, 'The Patriarchs', 21.

86 Humphreys, *Joseph and His Family*, xi. Similarly, Good, *Irony*, 111; Blenkinsopp, *Wisdom and Law*, 43; Savran, *Telling and Retelling*, 86.

87 In relation to the motif of God being 'with Joseph', T.W. Mann, *Divine Presence and Guidance in Israelite Traditions: The Typology of Exaltation*. John Hopkins Near Eastern Studies. (Baltimore: John Hopkins, 1977) 112 observes a strong connection between divine presence and human success, as seen most clearly in Gen 39:2. He notes that "the *form* of divine presence expressed by Yahweh's being "with" someone clearly is not analogous to phenomena such as the pillar of cloud and fire, and the *function* is not really that of guidance."

that "[e]ach time that Joseph's social status is improved, we are reminded that it is under the auspices of God." (39:4-5, 21, 23; 41:38-40).[88] Furthermore, both Joseph and Pharaoh specifically allude to God's role in Joseph's public wisdom (41:16, 38-39). Though his work is behind the scenes, God is nonetheless very active in effecting his purposes throughout the Joseph story.[89]

Indeed, Joseph's own analysis of what has happened (45:5-8; 50:19-21) reinforces this theological interpretation. Last century Lange suggested that "[t]he key of Joseph's history, as a history of providence, is clearly found in the declaration made by him in ch. xlv. 5-8, and ch. l. 20."[90] However, Weeks has recently argued that these passages are not "expressions of great theological profundity",[91] and ought to be read in a much more limited way. He views such sayings having only a literary purpose of summarising the divine role in the plot and that they are therefore limited to their context rather than being "great theological pronouncements with general applicability".[92]

This, however, does not seem to do justice to the texts themselves. While care needs to be taken not to read back the later doctrine of 'predestination' into these verses,[93] they do appear to be drawing some general principles out of the events that have happened. In the absence of any speech by God, Joseph's role in the story once the ruse is ended is that of a reliable character. In the light of Joseph's tested character and manifest discernment, his interpretive words are of great import for the reader.

The paucity of Joseph's words in the story make any of his utterances potentially very significant. In chapters 45 and 50, his words come at climactic points. Immediately after Joseph reveals himself to his brothers

---

88 Wintermute, 'Joseph', 984.
89 De Vaux, *Early History*, 296 comments that "although God neither appears nor speaks in the story of Joseph ... he guides everything that happens." E. Segal, 'Human Anger and Divine Intervention in Esther', *Prooftexts* 9 (1989): 251 also notes that "in the Joseph story ... God's behind-the-scenes operations constitute an unquestioned assumption of the story."
90 Lange, *Genesis*, 581.
91 Weeks, 'Joseph, Dreams and Wisdom', 66. At 56-59, Weeks proposes that these verses in chapters 45 and 50 are not climaxes to the story and are not true parallels to such wisdom texts as Prov 19:21; 16:9; 20:24; 21:30ff and Amenemope 19:16. He suggests that the Joseph narrative integrates human and divine efforts, while the wisdom sayings contrast them.
92 Weeks, 'Joseph, Dreams and Wisdom', 66. At 66-67 he suggests that a theologically didactic motive is absent from the narrative.
93 Turner, *Announcements of Plot*, 169 rightly warns, in relation to Gen 45:5 and 50:20, that "[t]hese sentences are not to be taken, as they are so often, as predestinarian theologoumena" but are simply confirming that "attempts to thwart God's purpose merely speed its triumph."

(45:1, 4), he does not explain why he concocted the ruse of chapters 42-44. Instead, Joseph returns to the events of chapter 37 and gives a theological interpretation of what has happened since that time. In his analysis of those incidents he pronounces that God has been furthering his purposes to keep alive many 'survivors', including the promised line. Furthermore, God's hidden but guiding control over events is the theological principle which precludes Joseph taking revenge on his brothers.

Chapter 50 also comes at a crucial stage. Immediately after the death and burial of Jacob there is potential for the reconciliation within the family to unravel. As far as the plot is concerned, Joseph needed only to reassure the brothers that he would not harm them even though the restraining hand of his father was gone. However, Joseph does much more than this. He clearly states that he will not usurp the role of God in taking revenge, but he adds the more general principle that God has worked through the series of events to bring about his purposes of keeping many people alive (לְהַחֲיֹת עַם־רָב, verse 20). This latter statement is unnecessary for the plot, but aids the implied reader in their understanding by identifying a key theme or principle underlying the story. Thus, Humphreys concludes that "[i]n observing that 'you meant evil against me, but God meant it for good,' Joseph seems to cite a wise saying to underscore the narrative's theological message."[94]

Boström has argued for a mediating position, noting that "although these texts provide a number of pertinent illustrations of the teachings of the sages, it is difficult to find specific passages that assert the Lord's sovereignty in the outworking of his purposes independently of or contrary to man's actions."[95] In so doing he is suggesting that texts such as Prov 16:1, 9, 33; 14:12; 20:9; 21:1, 30-31, 25:2 have a different emphasis from the Joseph story. Boström argues that Genesis 37-50 has "few explicit statements concerning the relationship between God's activity and man's that can serve as parallels" to these texts, although he does concede in a footnote "See, however, Gen 45:5-8".[96] This is arguably too subtle a distinction, particularly in light of Boström's admission that the Joseph narrative shows "signs of a wisdom perspective" and "certainly can be used

---

94   Humphreys, *Crisis and Story*, 87-88. De Vaux, *Early History*, 296 also describes
       Gen 45:8 and 50:20 as "sapiential teaching". *Contra* A. de Pury, *Promesse Divine
       et Légende Cultuelle dans le Cycle de Jacob: Genèse 28 et les traditions
       patriarcales*. Études Bibliques, 2 vols. (Paris: J. Gabalda, 1975) 1: 153: "Lorsque
       Dieu se sert du *mal* des hommes pour le tourner en bien (Gen 50:20), nous sommes
       aux antipodes de la sagesse. ... Sous la plume du Yahviste, l'histoire de Joseph
       quitte la domaine de la sagesse pour s'insérer dans la perspective de la « théologie
       de la grâce» qui est propre à ce narrateur." For a similar view see Ruppert, *Die
       Josephserzählung*, 208-217.
95   Boström, *The God of the Sages*, 188. Similarly, Scullion, *Genesis*, 289.
96   Boström, *The God of the Sages*, 180.

as illustrations of wisdom teachings and the way the Lord leads everything to serve his purposes in spite of man's interference".[97]

Indeed, the idea of God working behind the scenes to bring about his purposes despite and sometimes through human actions is central to the whole story.[98] It is foregrounded in Gen 45:5-8 and 50:19-21, where the contrast is explicitly between the human actions of the brothers and God's determination to preserve life through raising Joseph to prominence. In addition, it has been argued above that the dream motif addresses this very issue. The brothers try to dispose of the dream by eliminating the dreamer (Gen 37:19-20), but God causes Joseph to rise to power nonetheless (Gen 39:2-5, 21-23; 41:37-45).[99] When the brothers bow down to him in Egypt, the dreams are then recalled (Gen 42:6-9) in order to invite the reader to see Joseph's rise to power as the fulfilment of the dream of chapter 37. It is again a narrative rather than a poetic way of paralleling the sentence sayings of Proverbs. Thus, Jagersma appears justified in arguing that Gen 45:8 and 50:20 present the theme of the story, and adds that "[t]hese words above all make us think of the wisdom teachers."[100]

The notion of God working behind the scenes is, of course, a concept central to the wisdom books. Most recently Barr has pointed out that "the Wisdom literature constituted something of an exception to the general Old Testament emphasis on God's actions in the world."[101] He notes that

> In this literature, while it is known that God may and does act in human affairs, there is no impression that any particular series of historical acts are the sole or even the central foundation for all knowledge of him.[102]

This is not to assert that the wisdom view of God is that he is inactive (for example, Prov 15:25; 16:2, 9; 17:3; 19:17; 20:22), but rather to claim that he is described as acting in a distinctive way in books like Proverbs. His actions

---

97 Boström, *The God of the Sages*, 180.
98 Savage, 'Literary Criticism', 91.
99 Thus McCurley, *Genesis, Exodus*, 62, cites Prov 19:21; 16:9; 20:24 and observes the parallels: "the Joseph story begins with the evil plans of the brothers … (37:18) and ends with a double statement that God made it work out for good: to preserve life. … as in the teaching of Proverbs, God has had the last word!"
100 H. Jagersma, *A History of Israel in the Old Testament Period* trans. J. Bowden. (Philadelphia, Fortress, 1982) 34. See also E.W. Heaton, 'The Joseph Saga', *ExpTim* (1947-8): 135, although he dates the Joseph narrative in a much later time.
101 J. Barr, 'Divine Action and Hebrew Wisdom', in *The Making and Remaking of Christian Doctrine*, eds. S. Coakley and D.A. Pailin. (Oxford: Clarendon, 1993), 1.
102 J. Barr, *Old and New in Interpretation. A Study of the Two Testaments*. 2nd edn. (London: SCM, 1982) 72.

are not 'mighty acts' of a type comparable to the dividing of the Red Sea or the toppling of the walls of Jericho. They are more like an active presence of God in the order of the world, actions that are going on all the time but which may not be obvious or perceptible.[103]

Of course, this is not to deny that God can act in more direct or overt ways, but such actions are not focused on in the wisdom books.[104] God is pictured as working in and through his creation, and his ordering of the 'natural' processes of life. While some speak of this type of activity as another form of intervention,[105] it seems preferable to highlight the distinctive focus of wisdom in ways other than God's incursions into history.

Of course, the notion of God's behind-the-scenes activity is not confined to the wisdom corpus, since God is seen in charge of events in broad range of Old Testament traditions. Crenshaw has thus observed that "[t]he hidden control of God over human affairs despite man's intentions is a basic assumption of the Yahwist, Elohist, deuteronomist, and prophecy".[106] Yet, Humphreys has appropriately responded that

Crenshaw is certainly correct when he observes that within Israelite religious traditions and circles the theme of the hidden providence of God is too common to be designated as a sure sign of wisdom material. Yet it is a theme that is developed in material that on other grounds can be designated 'wisdom.'[107]

This study has argued that there are many other links with wisdom thinking in the Joseph narrative, which makes it probable that some connection can also be drawn with the notion of God's background ordering of events.

Further evidence of this may be gained by a brief study of the way in which the non-wisdom literature uses the motif of 'providence'. Given the constraints of this study, two examples will suffice. Firstly, Eichrodt suggests that the theme of providence is found right through the patriarchal stories, though he concedes that "the Joseph story in particular is the classic expression of a morally profound belief in Providence".[108] One place where

---

103 Barr, 'Divine Action', 7.
104 Barr, 'Divine Action', 6 points out that "[i]n the Wisdom literature God seems not to act, or to act only little and in a muted or distant way." At 8 he notes that the book of Proverbs "shows a different mode of perceiving the world, in which interventive action by Yahweh is muted or absent".
105 Thus Patrick, *The Rendering of God*, 83 suggests that the term 'divine intervention' "can also be applied to the hidden work of divine providence", citing the Joseph story as an example.
106 Crenshaw, 'Method', 138-139.
107 Humphreys, *Joseph and His Family*, 188-189.
108 W. Eichrodt, *Theology of the Old Testament.* Vol. 2, trans. J.A. Baker. (London:

it is prominent is in the wife-sister stories of Abraham and Sarah in chapter 12 and 20. In each case God works to bring about his purposes to preserve the covenant line by keeping Sarah safe. However, the means God uses differ markedly from those employed in the Joseph narrative. In Gen 12:17, God directly intervenes and afflicts Pharaoh with plagues, while in Gen 20:3-7, God appears to Abimelech in a dream revealing the truth about Sarah *and instructing him about the necessary response.* While there are elements of God's hidden working in these stories, they provide a stark contrast with the absence of divine intervention in the Genesis 37-50.

A second example can be found in 1 Samuel 9, when Saul 'coincidentally' is led to Samuel while looking for his father's donkeys. While this apparently accidental meeting leads ultimately to the anointing of Saul as king, God intervenes at several points. Thus, for example, God reveals his plans to Samuel the prophet (1 Sam 9:15-17) and gives him explicit instructions for Saul. Furthermore, words of reassurance are given to Saul (1 Sam 10:1-6, 9-10) to confirm what Samuel had spoken to him. By contrast, in Genesis 39-45, God is apparently silent, and no mention is made of any command or instruction given to Joseph. Even in chapter 37, when Joseph meets a man in Shechem who tells him the location of his brothers (Gen 37:15-17), there is no word from God, nor any instruction for him to follow his brothers. The character God is much more behind the scenes in the Joseph story. Thus, Robinson concludes that

> the conception of divine providence found in Gen 39-41 is very much in keeping with the doctrine of the Book of Proverbs. Joseph's success is due to his skill, competence, reliability and self-discipline, not to direct divine interventions.[109]

The Role of Human Actions

A further indicator of the presence of 'wisdom-like elements' is the narrative's understanding of the place of human actions. This has two component elements. Firstly, despite the strong emphasis on God's overruling of events, there is significant room for human initiatives and responsibility. Secondly, on several occasions the narrator asserts that actions are undertaken, or situations brought about by God, yet the narrative

---

SCM, 1967) 169. In terms of the patriarchal accounts he sees tales of 'providence' in the 'abduction' of Sarah, the whole Jacob saga with themes of testing, purifying and blessing, and the story of Joseph.

109 Robinson, *Mysterious God*, 10. So also Frost, *Patriarchs and Prophets*, 43 who comments that the Joseph story "is the great illustration of that truth which was perhaps more dear to the hearts of the Wise Men than any other".

clearly indicates that these are accomplished through human agents. In other words, the same action is ascribed to both God and human beings.

Firstly, then, human initiative is strongly emphasised in the Joseph story. For example, God preserved many people through seven years of famine not by sending flocks of quail, but rather by Joseph's wise agricultural policies. Similarly, Joseph is not commanded by God either to gather grain or to forgive his brothers. Instead, he has to discern what will bring about life or peace, and act accordingly.

A particular feature of Joseph's characterisation is that he seizes opportunities to change situations that are not right. Thus, with both the cupbearer and with Pharaoh, Joseph not only interprets the dream but continues to make a request (Gen 40:14-15) or to offer wise advice (Gen 41:33-36). While Joseph elsewhere emphasises God's purposeful control of events (Gen 45:5-8; 50:19-21), this does not preclude Joseph taking genuine initiatives. Savran summarises this aspect with great clarity

> providence is not presented as a wholly passive ideal, according to which humans lack all initiative and respond blindly to the gestures of a puppet master. Joseph's seizing the opportunity in 41:33-36 is an expression of the necessary human response to providence: success comes out of a combination of patience, proper understanding of the auspicious moment, and appropriate action such as dovetails with the larger divine plan.[110]

Furthermore, the initiatives that Joseph takes are, in human terms, precisely what cause him to rise to a position of power. When the cupbearer, as requested, finally remembers Joseph (Gen 41:9-13), Joseph is summoned to appear before Pharaoh and is given further opportunity. After Joseph interprets Pharaoh's dream and outlines what action needs to be taken, it is Joseph's proposal (הדבר) that seemed good to Pharaoh and the court (Gen 41:37). Thus, Joseph's forthright initiatives led to his appearance before Pharaoh and his elevation to a position of great authority in Egypt.[111]

It has been suggested by some writers that the strong emphasis on divine control evacuates human action of any significance, making the human characters little more than puppets.[112] However, Humphreys has rightly responded that "[w]e do not suddenly discover at the end that we have been

---

110 Savran, *Telling and Retelling*, 86.

111 Ackerman, 'Joseph, Judah and Jacob', 86 comments that "Joseph's rise to power in Egypt results from a combination of pious behavior, divine help, and his wise advice at court."

112 For example, Redford, *Biblical Story of Joseph*, 74 suggests that "God had manipulated the principals of the drama like so many marionettes."

an audience in some grand puppet show staged by a divine puppeteer",[113] because the characters are presented as having made real choices and are held accountable for their actions.

Indeed, the Joseph narrative not only highlights the proper place of human initiatives but also holds characters responsible for their wrong choices.[114] For example, the brothers who have betrayed Joseph are tested by him to see if they have changed. They admit their responsibility (Gen 42:21-22) and through their spokesman Judah refuse to repeat their offence (Gen 44:18-34). This test needs to be completed before Joseph can effect reconciliation in the family. Thus, when Joseph reveals himself to his brothers, he identifies himself as the one whom they sold into slavery (Gen 45:4). This emphasis on human accountability leads Wenham to propose that "[i]f divine overruling is one theme of the Joseph story, human responsibility is its counterpoint".[115]

Loader also notes that the tension between the 'divine' plane and the 'human' plane is a common theme in both the Joseph story and proverbial wisdom. He understands this to be a sapiential theology of history in which "God controls events unobtrusively **and** men are actors in their own right."[116] Elsewhere he describes this dual theme as "[o]n the one hand, **God is quietly and unobtrusively in control of events** in the human world ... On the other hand, **human history is acted by human actors** with their own decisions, schemes and mistakes."[117]

This distinctive emphasis is different from the predominant pattern in the historical books, where God is the decisive actor and the human leaders are evaluated on the basis of whether or not they were obedient and trusting. Thus Moses was disqualified from entering the land because he did not *trust* in God at the waters of Meribah (Num 20:12), while Saul is condemned for his lack of obedience (1 Sam 15:10-23, especially verse 22). Indeed, earlier in the patriarchal accounts, Abraham is held out as a model of faith because of his utter obedience (Gen 22:1-18, especially verse 12). What is common in these three cases is that their obedience to, or trust in, God's specific command was being assessed. Joseph, by way of contrast, receives no specific command from God, but prospers because he acts wisely and responsibly as an outworking of his values and character.

---

113 Humphreys, *Joseph and His Family*, 128.
114 Thus, Humphreys, *Crisis and Story*, 88 observes that "[t]he divine action occurs behind the scenes, hidden from the human actors, and it neither annuls nor excuses their actions and intentions. Human beings remain accountable, and destructive forces loosed at the outset roll back over the seemingly accursed family."
115 Wenham, *Genesis 16-50*, 359.
116 Loader, 'Jedidah or: Amadeus', 197. He also notes that it occurs in the Succession Narrative and the book of Esther.
117 Loader, 'Jedidah or: Amadeus', 191. The emphasis is his.

Boström, in noting that a "firm belief in the close relationship between act/character and consequence" is characteristic of wisdom, suggests that "[t]he important matter for the sages was to affirm the view that men are responsible for their way of life and must face the consequences."[118]

This leads to a robust view of human possibility in the Joseph narrative. Thus Brueggemann writes that "[i]n the Joseph story, for example, perhaps wisdom par excellence, … [Joseph] has the wits and courage to feed the world and bring life to the empire, and his humanity consists in seizing the opportunity to do so."[119] Joseph is a clear example of a person who believes that leaving everything to God is not an act of faith, but rather an abdication of the responsibility entrusted to humanity.[120] This pattern, seen in the wisdom books, is not that people act independently of God but simply that they assume the responsibility that human beings are given in God's purposes. They act, as it were, like "adult sons who have been trusted and are still trusted by an amazing father."[121] While the question of setting has not been a major focus of this study, it does seem likely that such a positive view of human achievement has emerged from a stable, prospering period of Israel's history, such as existed in the time of Solomon or Hezekiah.[122]

Secondly, God's purposes are largely brought about by human agents, and most commonly it is through Joseph's actions and initiatives. At several places in the Joseph narrative, Joseph achieves results which are then ascribed to God. In Gen 40:8 states that interpretations belong to God, yet Joseph urges the cupbearer to tell him the dream and he interprets it (Gen 40:12-13). Similarly, in Gen 41:16, Joseph informs the Egyptian ruler that God will answer Pharaoh, but it is Joseph who explains the dream (Gen 41:25-32). In Gen 41:28, Joseph asserts that God has caused Pharaoh to see what he is about to do, but he does so through Joseph's explanation of the dream. In other words, God's purposes at this stage are brought about largely by Joseph's actions and initiatives. God acts through the agency of Joseph, although the narrator does not record God telling Joseph what to do or say. Thus, God works through human initiatives in the Joseph story.[123]

---

118 Boström, *The God of the Sages*, 116.
119 Brueggemann, 'Scripture and an Ecumenical Life-Style', 16.
120 Brueggemann, 'Scripture and an Ecumenical Life-Style', 13.
121 Brueggemann, 'Scripture and an Ecumenical Life-Style', 18.
122 Brueggemann, 'Scripture and an Ecumenical Life-Style', 8 writes about Proverbs as follows: "It is not the postexilic reaction to the disillusionment of the exile. Rather, *it is a mood of strong men in times of success*." The same sentiments could easily be applied to the Joseph narrative.
123 Gibson, *Genesis*, 291-292 points out that "[t]he two former Patriarchal epics think on the whole in terms of God interfering in and with the normal … The Joseph epic, on the other hand, … invites us to think of God as working always behind the scenes, controlling but not forcing the pace of events, permitting things to happen rather than directly causing them to happen, achieving his purpose through men's

However, God also works to overrule some human actions in the story. The classic examples of this can be seen in Gen 45:5, 8 and 50:20, where the brothers' plot to harm Joseph was turned on its head by God who caused Joseph to rise to power anyway. Thus, God determines the eventual outcome in both these strands, sometimes working through human initiatives and sometimes overruling them.

It is significant that a similar place for human action, under the broad umbrella of God's ordering of his world, emerges from the book of Proverbs. A fundamental tenet of Proverbs is that God determines what happens. Whybray has made a useful study of the 'Yahweh sayings' in the book, and argues that Prov 15:33-16:9 are a kind of theological kernel of the sentence sayings. In these ten verses, of which nine are Yahweh sayings, there emerges a common thematic element "they all specifically recognise Yahweh as constituting the ultimate authority and as the undisputed arbiter of human destiny."[124] As in the Joseph story, God finally determines what happens. Yet the book of Proverbs also explores the place of human action and responsibility, and both the strands discerned in the Joseph story are evident. Thus, in sayings like Prov 16:1, 9; 21:30-31, God is pictured as overriding human plans that are contrary to his purposes. It has previously been argued that these substantially parallel the concepts in Gen 45:5, 8; 50:20.

However, there are also many proverbs that urge humans to take action in order to bring about God's purposes. Thus, for example, the unit in Prov 3:1-12 generally outlines in the alternate verses the wisdom picture of a full life. This includes long life and שלום (verse 2), favour (חן) and a good reputation (verse 4), straight paths (verse 6), physical health (verse 8), abundant food and drink (verse 10) and God's delight and love (verse 12). Yet all of these are seen in the chapter as the result of the human actions in the odd-numbered verses. This includes remembering the teaching (verse 1), holding on to חסד ואמת (verse 3), trusting in God (verse 5), fearing the Lord and turning from evil (verse 7), honouring God with your wealth (verse 9) and not despising God's discipline (verse 11).

God often works through wise human actions. In the sentence sayings, Prov 10:3 claims that the Lord will not let the righteous go hungry, but Prov 10:4-5 suggest that this happens through diligent human actions in gathering the crops.[125] God, it seems, also works through giving wisdom to human beings. In Prov 2:8, it is claimed that God guards (נצר) and watches over (שמר) the way of his faithful ones, while in Prov 2:11 it is prudence and understanding which guard (נצר) and watch over (שמר) the wise. Again, God works through human agency.

---

actions rather than upon or in spite of them."
124 Whybray, 'Yahweh-sayings', 158.
125 Schultz, 'Unity or Diversity', 284.

Thus, in the book of Proverbs as in the Joseph story God works in two ways to order his world according to his purposes. At times he works through granting wisdom to men and women and their actions further God's plans. At other times, he overrules those human plans which would work against his goals and intentions.

Indeed, one interesting feature of the book of Proverbs is that, while it asserts a connection between one's acts/character and the consequences that will follow,[126] it often does not explore how these consequences will come about (for example, Prov 1:19).[127] Boström finds an interesting illustration of this in Prov 5:21-23, where God weighs a person's iniquities, but also that a person's iniquities will catch that person out. There is no explanation of how God weighs these wicked actions. It may be by direct divine intervention or may simply happen through bringing upon a person the consequences of their folly.[128]

It is thus argued that the pattern in the Joseph story of hidden divine activity and evident human responsibility is one that has great affinity with mainstream wisdom ideas.

What is clear is that the place of human initiative is not promoted at the expense of God's strong control of events. It is significant, perhaps that both the wisdom and covenant strands have a common view that God is in absolute control over his world. This is a promising theme for revealing the interaction between the two strands in the Joseph story. In many covenant texts, God's rule or control is achieved either by divine intervention ('the mighty acts of God', as in the exodus or conquest) or by human beings obediently carrying out God's instructions (for example, Abraham, Moses, Joshua). In some wisdom texts, however, God's sovereign ruling over his people and his world is often furthered by human initiatives. It thus appears that the broader, all-encompassing category of God's active rule can be accomplished either by humans taking wise initiatives, or by the way God builds order into everyday life, as well as God's rule being promoted by the obedience of God's people to his instructions, and by God's own direct intervention.

---

126 Boström, *The God of the Sages*, 90-91.
127 Boström, *The God of the Sages*, 112. At 126, he comments that "passive and impersonal constructions are employed intentionally for the sake of leaving all alternatives open concerning the way the consequences of a person's character and activities will be realized."
128 Boström, *The God of the Sages*, 91.

CHAPTER 11

Covenant and Wisdom in Genesis 37-50

Unity and Diversity in the Joseph Story

The previous two chapters have established that there are (at least) two clear threads or strands in Genesis 37-50. Irrespective of the question of origins or putative sources, the final form of the text testifies to the presence both of 'wisdom-like elements' and themes, as well as motifs and concerns that revolve around the Abrahamic covenant promise.

Furthermore, neither of these two aspects can be viewed as a subset of the other. On the one hand, too much detail is given of the wider family and the future blessings for the whole to be simply a wisdom tale, and the chapters are too strongly tied in to the preceding patriarchal stories and the subsequent book of Exodus.[1] Yet, on the other hand, there is too intense a focus on the rise and testing of Joseph, and on his inner struggles as he exercises power over his brothers. This is neither a mere wisdom novella, nor solely part four of the patriarchal sagas.

Instead, Genesis 37-50 appears to be a unified narrative, an artistic whole, in which both these strands are prominent. As Licht observes, while the story of Joseph is not uniform in its various parts, "it certainly is a narrative unit composed as a whole, rather than a sequence of stories haphazardly tied together."[2] This study has proposed that all the material of Genesis 37-50 is related to the person of Joseph, even the initially problematic chapter 38. The story moves from the introduction of Joseph as a young man to the closure of his death at the age of 110, from tension through to resolution.

An interesting characteristic of the final form of the text is the way in which the Joseph story is interwoven with the broader and preceding Jacob narrative. The Joseph story is described as the *toledot* of Jacob (Gen 37:2), and Jacob is not buried until the last chapter of the story (Gen 50:7-14).

---

1 *Contra* Redford, *Biblical Story of Joseph*, 247 who suggests that "the events of the Joseph Story do not dovetail either with the immediate context of the Patriarchal and Exodus narratives".

2 Licht, *Storytelling in the Bible*, 141-142.

While Jacob is absent from chapters 38-41, his presence is ominous in chapters 42-45. During this time of testing of the brothers, the two key figures of Joseph and Jacob are both influential, but are kept apart from each other. However, the merging of the two accounts is heightened when Jacob moves to Egypt and interacts with Joseph. As Scullion observes, "from chapter 46 onwards, the end of the Joseph story and the end of the Jacob story have been woven together".[3] This is not to imply that they become reduced to a single story. The Jacob story remains one in which the patriarch is 'clever' or 'crafty', while Joseph emerges as one who is 'wise' or 'righteous'.[4] Yet, the same incidents at the end of Genesis, such as the 'blessings' or testamentary words of chapters 48-49, serve to effect a sense of closure to both narrative streams. This closure, however, often takes the form of including in chapters 46-50 concerns which do not relate solely to Joseph but which are significant in rounding off the account of Jacob.[5]

Humphreys notes that there are some elements which mitigate against isolating the Joseph narrative as a distinct unit, such as the fact that the main characters have been introduced earlier in Genesis, and that Exod 1:8 links that book with Joseph by referring to a new king 'who did not know Joseph'.[6] At an even later stage, Josh 24:32 speaks of Joseph's burial by a subsequent generation. However, Genesis 37-50 opens with special attention to Joseph in Jacob's family (37:1-4) and concludes with a notice about his death (50:26). The younger son motif, which the Joseph story borrows from the earlier patriarchal accounts, also fuses the final chapters of Genesis with what precedes.[7] Thus, it seems preferable to view the Joseph narrative as a unified text in its own right, but as one whose concerns have been intertwined with the other material in its canonical context.

What is remarkable in Genesis 37-50 is how the twin emphases of

---

3 Scullion, *Genesis*, 287. See also von Rad, *Genesis*, 439.
4 Wills, *The Jew in the Court*, 36 argues it is important to distinguish 'cleverness' from 'wisdom'. A story of cleverness depicts a protagonist who is clever enough to get what he wants (such as Jacob); a story of wisdom depicts a protagonist who is wise and righteous enough to get what he or she deserves (such as Joseph). W. van Heerden, 'A bright spark is not necessarily a wise person. Old Testament and contemporary perspectives on wisdom and intelligence', *Old Testament Essays* 9 (1996): 522 comments that "[c]leverness is like a sharp-focus lens. Wisdom is like a wide-angle lens."
5 This would include the repetition in 48:4-5 of the divine promise of progeny, the blessing of Pharaoh by Jacob in 47:7, 10, and Jacob's last words in 49:29-32, recalling solemnly the burial of his ancestors and their wives.
6 Humphreys, *Joseph and His Family*, 12.
7 Niditch, *Underdogs and Tricksters*, 78 describes Joseph as "the next generation's Jacob, the successful younger son whose youngest son in turn will carry on his leadership."

'covenant' and 'wisdom' are rendered in such a prominent way, yet without either emphasis undermining the other. Humphreys describes it as in part a courtier's story, but in essence a family's story.[8] This captures the duality well, although it tends to overlook the fact that in securing reconciliation within the family, wisdom-like themes and characteristics emerge. The Joseph story brings into view an emphasis on God's behind-the-scenes activity to preserve his chosen line together with a clear portrayal of Joseph's initiative that brings benefit to himself, his family and the whole world.[9]

This twin focus has been recently explored by Culley in a careful study of action sequences in narrative.[10] He discerns two 'action sequences' in the Joseph story - "Joseph's rise to power in Egypt and the rescue of the family of Jacob from famine."[11] The first sequence features the victim taking initiative to correct his own situation, although God appears to be behind it all. The second sequence - the rescue from famine - does not emerge until well into the story and is made explicit in Gen 45:4-9. This invites the reader to reread the story of Joseph's misfortune in a new light.[12] His conclusion is that the final narrative "is a merging of an attractive story about Joseph's rise to power with an important rescue story that is critical for the future of the people of Israel."[13]

However, Culley rightly insists that each action sequence retains its own distinctive contribution and thrust

> Nevertheless, the narrative concerning Joseph's dreams, the misfortune and the brothers seems to resist simply being absorbed into and dominated by the larger story of the rescue of the people. For one thing, it makes such a good story that it stands out from the major rescue story and calls for attention on its own. Then too, as we have noted, the subordinate role of this segment about the rise of Joseph is not signalled until the comment of Joseph in Genesis 45 ... In the present Joseph story, the tension between the two parts sets two perspectives in balance so that the story about the misfortune and rise of Joseph and the story about the rescue of the people can be played off against each other with neither losing its force.[14]

---

8 Humphreys, *Joseph and His Family*, 11.
9 W.J. Dumbrell, *Covenant and Creation: An Old Testament Covenantal Theology* (Exeter: Paternoster, 1984) 77; Goldingay, 'The Patriarchs', 22.
10 Culley, *Themes and Variations*, especially 156-168.
11 Culley, *Themes and Variations*, 159.
12 Culley, *Themes and Variations*, 161.
13 Culley, *Themes and Variations*, 162.
14 Culley, *Themes and Variations*, 161.

In other words, the presence of the 'rescue from famine' sequence, which is roughly co-extensive with the Abrahamic promise elements, does not extinguish the earlier emphasis on Joseph's human initiative and God's backgrounded activity. Both action sequences retain their narrative and thematic power.

Furthermore, the first action sequence (Joseph's rise to power) does not stand alone, since it does not come to a clear end prior to the beginning of the second sequence.[15] This is accentuated if Joseph's rise to power is broadened - as this study has proposed - to include his securing of reconciliation within his family. In the very last chapter, Joseph is portrayed as prominent in the burial rites of Jacob (Genesis 50:1-14), and effective in his reassurance to his anxious brothers (Genesis 50:15-21). Thus, the first action sequence is still prominent at the end of the story, and not overshadowed by the rescue of the covenant line from famine.

The final form of the Joseph story thus reveals a unified text which has a twin thrust. This study has proposed that this thrust is the creative tension between the Abrahamic covenant promise elements and the 'wisdom-like elements', which combine to form the text preserved in Genesis 37-50. Both the unity of the whole and the diversity of the component parts are reflected in, and foundational to, the Joseph narrative.

The Search for an Integrative Model

A number of writers have sought to explain the interaction of wisdom and other perspectives in scripture by a variety of analogies or models. It is appropriate at this stage of the study to examine some of these suggested analogies in order to see if they can elucidate the relationship between the 'wisdom-like' and Abrahamic promise elements in the Joseph narrative.

Martens notes that both wisdom and covenant have similar goals of a better life or life in all its richness. He then develops a road or travel analogy in commenting that[16]

> Wisdom is no cul-de-sac. Rather it represents a parallel traffic lane, according to the modern divided highway or dual carriageway, in which for an interval the wisdom route and the history-of-salvation route are shown parallel, leading toward the same goal.

---

15 Culley, *Themes and Variations*, 162 comments that "[t]he story of Joseph's rise to power can almost stand alone except that, as I have said, the sequences we identified do not come to clear endings all at once but seem to disperse throughout the larger narrative."

16 Martens, *God's Design*, 225.

One helpful aspect of this analogy is that Martens seeks to preserve the integrity of both wisdom and salvation history, suggesting that they are both part of a larger whole, which he identifies as God's design. He seeks to relate how both wisdom and salvation history deal differently with this overarching motif[17]

> In wisdom the issue is not so much what the design is but that design and order govern the universe. It is in the Israelite story of salvation that the precise nature of the design is explicated.

It will be argued later in this chapter, however, that the focus of the Joseph story is not on God's 'design', but rather on the various forms of his control of events or active rule.

Furthermore, it is by no means self evident that wisdom and salvation history are parallel roads. Indeed, wisdom tends to meander into everyday life more than other parts of the Old Testament. Kidner notes that the wisdom strand particularly focuses on those "details of character small enough to escape the mesh of the law and the broadsides of the prophets".[18] Perhaps a better road analogy is not a divided highway, but a variety of routes to travel, for example, from Paris to Rome. The person who is interested in rural areas and small villages might travel via the Loire Valley, and linger in Provence and Tuscany before travelling on to Rome. Those interested in rugged mountain scenery might insist on travelling via the majestic French and Swiss Alps, and the Italian Dolomites. Those interested only in a quick trip might travel by direct autoroutes all the way, or even think of flying. Those interested in a more Germanic flavour might travel via Alsace-Lorraine into southern Germany and Austria before heading south into Italy. All these routes would have the same goal, but the travellers would spend their time differently, and take notice of different features along the way.

However, even this modification of Martens' analogy is inadequate in one further respect. While it shows that it is possible to have a common starting and finishing point (but with different observations and experiences on the way), it says nothing about the interrelationship between the various routes or roads. In terms of wisdom and covenant, it might explain how they can co-exist, but it does not explain how they intersect or relate to each other.

Goldingay has helpfully focused on the interrelationship between salvation history and wisdom, and tries to relate them together around the twin foci of creation and redemption.[19] The complex relationship between

17 Martens, *God's Design*, 226.
18 D. Kidner, *Proverbs*. TOTC. (London: Inter-Varsity Press, 1964) 13.
19 J. Goldingay, *Theological Diversity and the Authority of the Old Testament* (Grand

creation and redemption, he asserts, can be summarised in the following four statements

1. The world God redeems is the world of God's creation.
2. The world that God created is a world that needs to be redeemed.
3. Human beings are redeemed to live again their created life before God.
4. The redeemed humanity still looks for a final act of redemption or new creation.

A closer look at these four summary statements is in order. The first two establish the connection between creation and salvation history (or covenant), and ensure that both voices are heard. God's purposes are wider than the covenant people, yet they are also focused on Israel, and effected through them. The last statement indicates the incompleteness and forward-looking nature of the Old Testament. When these three assertions are read together, they outline the flow of Old Testament theology. They highlight the movement from creation, through God's redeeming acts in different generations, to the future hopes variously described as redemption or new creation. This is the big picture or the broad canvas of the Old Testament. Yet Goldingay also sees the smaller picture where the focus is on everyday life and its continuities and order. Here again he recognises that both creation and redemption have a part to play - people are redeemed to live their created life before God.

This synthesis seems, therefore, to be a very promising framework upon which to develop an Old Testament theology. It picks out the key concerns of creation and redemption, and takes in the movement throughout and beyond the entire testament. Furthermore, it gives the smaller picture of everyday life, so that it includes more than simply the mighty acts of God. Both the continuities and discontinuities in life are catered for.

There are, however, two matters of concern that should be raised in reference to Goldingay's synthesis. Firstly, the nature of the human response ('redeemed to live again their created life before God') needs to be clarified. The danger here is the implication that the wisdom materials are a human response to God's redemptive acts in salvation history. Scobie, however, rightly points out that wisdom "is not a response to divine activity at all, but is a type of response to the world and to human experience".[20] Perhaps what is needed here is a broader understanding of the human

---

Rapids: Eerdmans, 1987). For an outline and evaluation of Goldingay's view, see Wilson, 'Place of Wisdom', 67-68, which is the basis of the material here.

20 C.H.H. Scobie, 'The Place of Wisdom in Biblical Theology', *Biblical Theology Bulletin* 14 (1984): 44. He notes that wisdom is not responding to God's mighty acts, but instead to order evident in creation.

response so that it includes responding to God's redemptive acts (so mainly the Torah and the prophets) and to God's order in creation (especially in the wisdom materials).

The second issue requiring clarification is the precise connection between creation and redemption. While Goldingay's principles seem to contain the main ingredients for holding creation and redemption in tension, the precise nature of the final product is not satisfactorily explained. Goldingay neither proposes nor denies the existence of any category or motif that includes both creation and redemption, and only explains their connection in fairly general terms.[21] This, then, is a promising analogy but one which does not sufficiently explain the intersection of wisdom and covenant promise.

Marshall uses the analogy of a rope as a way of understanding the various emphases of biblical theology. He sets it out as follows

> The first picture is that of a climbing rope which is made up of various strands that are twisted together and run along the length of the rope. Some strands go through the whole length, while others run for limited stretches, but the effect is that it is the same rope throughout because there is continuity from one part to the next (even if the actual connecting links are not identical throughout its length), there are no breaks, and the rope can do much the same things at any points in its length. The strands running the whole length are the major locus of the rope's identity and unity, but shorter ones also do duty over limited periods.[22]

He adds that "the task of biblical theology is to tease out, identify and describe the different strands and show how they are interwoven at any given point."[23] This is a crucial part of what is being attempted in this study.

The value of this analogy is twofold. Firstly, it proposes that the various strands are part of a larger whole which encompasses the two or more threads and binds them together. Secondly, it does not assume that both

---

21 Later in this chapter, the views of S. Lee, *Creation and Redemption in Isaiah 40-55*. Jian Dao Dissertation Series, 2. (Hong Kong: Alliance Biblical Seminary, 1995) will be discussed. Lee argues that, in Isaiah 40-55, the ideas of God as creator and redeemer are subsumed under the broader theme of Yahweh's sovereignty, explicitly modifying Goldingay's analysis on page 197.

22 I.H. Marshall, 'Climbing Ropes, Ellipses and Symphonies: the Relation between Biblical and Systematic Theology', in *A Pathway into the Holy Scripture*. eds. P.E. Satterthwaite and D.F. Wright. (Grand Rapids: Eerdmans, 1994), 208. An earlier form of this analogy, given in a lecture in 1986, is referred to in Wilson, 'Place of Wisdom', 68.

23 Marshall, 'Climbing Ropes, Ellipses and Symphonies', 209.

strands are equally prominent in all parts of the rope. Rather, it suggests that this issue should be resolved by a closer examination of the rope itself, which is the reason for the detailed exegetical study of Genesis 37-50.

A similar analogy is that of a symphony, briefly alluded to by Marshall and explored in much greater depth by Poythress.[24] Marshall notes that, just as the different kinds of musical instruments (string, wind, percussion) produce, in a variety of ways, sounds that can be combined in symphony, so the different kinds of biblical literature and emphases can be combined in a theological synthesis.[25]

Poythress has developed this analogy in his book *Symphonic Theology*, which is subtitled 'The Validity of Multiple Perspectives in Theology'.[26] He suggests that the different perspectives in a text "are like facets of a jewel. The whole jewel ... can be see through any *one* of the facets, if we look carefully enough. But not everything can be seen equally through only one facet."[27] The aim of such a study is not 'harmonization', by which he means making the texts say the same thing, for this needs to be "balanced by an appreciation of divinely ordained diversity."[28] He explains that he calls this procedure "*symphonic theology* because it is analogous to the blending of various musical instruments to express the variations of a symphonic theme."[29]

Often Old Testament theologies are written as if there is one centre - the solo to which all the other music connects, and by which it finds its meaning. On this view, the parts of the Old Testament that do not fit easily are usually relegated to being an interlude, or a chorus - in other words, something which is valid because and only because it relates to the solo, or main thread. However, many contributions are involved in a symphony. Some instruments are there to give the foundation or beat; others to offer a harmony that nuances the tune; some will accentuate highlights or anticipate a forthcoming climax. Some of these instruments will fade in and out, while others may begin late or end early. Different instruments will dominate, or at least add their distinctive touches at different points of the symphony. It is, in the end, not just a collection of contributions, but a symphony - a musical piece whose richness has come about from the

---

24 Marshall, 'Climbing Ropes, Ellipses and Symphonies', 215-217; V.S. Poythress, *Symphonic Theology: The Validity of Multiple Perspectives in Theology* (Grand Rapids: Academie, 1987).

25 Marshall, 'Climbing Ropes, Ellipses and Symphonies', 216.

26 Poythress, *Symphonic Theology*, 16 defines a 'perspective' as a consistent, pervasive, developed way of looking at an object of study, in which a thematic or other interest controls selection of material and emphasis.

27 Poythress, *Symphonic Theology*, 37.

28 Poythress, *Symphonic Theology*, 86.

29 Poythress, *Symphonic Theology*, 43.

presence of, and interaction between, the various instruments. The individual distinctives of all parts of the orchestra combine together to present the richness of a symphony.

This analogy, like that of the rope, suggests that a closer study of the text will reveal what instrument is played at each point, and where the instruments overlap. Furthermore, it is a useful reminder to look beyond the distinctive parts to the larger whole. While the wisdom and covenant elements are not equally prominent in all sections of the Joseph narrative, both are important in giving the fullness of the final product.

It is therefore proposed that the wisdom and covenant emphases of the Joseph story are interwoven like the strands of a rope, or blended like distinctive instruments in a symphony. The usefulness of these analogies will depend on the extent to which they illuminate the intersection of the two ideas, and it is therefore proposed to review Genesis 37-50 in the light of these analogies.

The Integration of Wisdom and Covenant

Many scholars who explore the interrelationship of the various component parts with the story are interested primarily in the question of the redactional history of Genesis 37-50. This study, however, has focused on the interrelationship between the wisdom and covenant strands at the level of the final form of the text.

A number of other writers have also drawn attention to this twin focus. Wessels, for example, has proposed that these chapters can be read at two levels

> First, it is a wisdom novelette ... we can take it out of its present context and still read and understand it as a story without having to know that precedes it or what follows in Exodus. ... On the other hand, the story also fits well into its present context, for the very reason that it draws on material from this context, that is its origin lies there. This context represents the second level at which the story can be read. At this level it is seen as part of the "salvation history" line that explains Israel's entrance into Egypt and provides the substructure for the exodus.[30]

---

30 Wessels, 'The Joseph story', 56-57. In terms of how the Joseph narrative was a wisdom novel yet integrated into the *Heilsgeschichte* story, Loader, 'Chokma - Joseph - Hybris', 26 proposes the existence of old tribal traditions that a wisdom writer could see were useful for building a wisdom novel around, and the final product was seen to be able to fit nicely into the *Heilsgeschichte* ancestral narratives.

Longacre has explored, in diagrammatic form, his understanding of the interrelationship between what he calls 'the Joseph story' and the broader concerns of Jacob and his family - when Joseph is not mentioned or offstage - within the *tōlĕdôt yaʿĕqōb*. Joseph, he rightly points out, "is not the *whole* concern of [chapters] 37-50."[31] He regards these two foci as 'interwoven strands', that are present in the fourteen sections of Genesis 37-50. Both streams, he says, are jointly present in chapter 37, in the trips to Egypt in Gen 42:1-47:12, and in chapters 49-50. However, in the Tamar story of chapter 38, there is only a focus on Jacob and his family, while chapters 39-41 and 47:13-48:22 are concerned solely with Joseph.[32] Thus, at times the twin streams are joined together in their concerns, whilst at other times, one or the other stream will be dominant.

This study has argued that the two streams can perhaps better be identified as a 'wisdom-like' stream and one concerned with the Abrahamic covenant. In other words, Genesis 37-50 deals with both the survival of the line of promise and the wise initiatives of Joseph. Furthermore, it has been argued that, on occasions, both are in view at the same time, such as in chapters 42-45.

It is therefore proposed to review chapters 37-50 in order to discern where the two strands are joined together, and to indicate where one dominates the other. Much of this is drawing together and shaping the material outlined in Part 2 of this study.

Chapter 37 begins with the explicit mention of the *toledot* of Jacob, followed immediately by the mention of Joseph (37:2). At the outset, both Joseph and the broader family of Jacob are in view. This study has argued, against the views of many scholars, that a negative portrayal of Joseph is not given in chapter 37, but has equally insisted that the focus of the chapter is not to depict him in positive light either. Instead, there is a curious avoidance of information that enable a clear characterisation, such as Joseph's thoughts or words as he is attacked by his brothers and sold into slavery. The chapter, it is suggested, serves to outline the extent of the disharmony and fractured relationships within the line of promise, as well as giving prominence to the dream of Joseph about his rise to power. It has been argued that this dream, which hangs over the larger narrative, is a 'wisdom-like' device which reveals God's plan but backgrounds his activity.

Thus, both streams co-exist in the opening chapter, but in different verses. The dream is presented as part of the exposition (verses 5-7, 9), while the tensions within the family permeate the whole chapter, including the exposition (verses 2-4, 8, 10-11, 18-33). It appears that the rise of

31 Longacre, *Joseph: A Story of Divine Providence*, 23.
32 Longacre, *Joseph: A Story of Divine Providence*. 22-23.

Joseph will take place in such a setting of family rivalry and disharmony. Joseph's rise to prominence, which reflects a 'wisdom-like' focus on backgrounded divine activity, is thus juxtaposed with the motif of the promised line threatening to self-destruct.

Chapter 37 therefore serves a twofold purpose, addressing the concerns of both strands. Firstly, in relation to the covenant stream, it raises the crucial threat to the Abrahamic promises that will be resolved in the rest of the book of Genesis. Significantly, no indication is given in the chapter of how this threat will be overcome. However, the subsequent course of events discloses that this will not be effected by overt divine intervention.

Secondly, in relation to the wisdom stream, it outlines the overarching purpose of God (to raise Joseph to power), while introducing the initial complication (Joseph sold as a slave and sent to Egypt). Chapter 37 thus outlines the goal of the focus on Joseph, explains why this will be difficult, yet does not demonstrate how this goal will be achieved.

In other words, the chapter introduces obstacles to both streams, but gives no explanation about how these will be overcome, or how the two streams will interact in the remainder of the narrative.

Chapter 38 is often by-passed in the study of the interrelationship of the two strands, since Joseph is entirely absent from the chapter. Since the story of Tamar will be examined at length in the next section of this chapter, it is not proposed to deal with it at this point. However, it will be argued that the significance of chapter 38 is that it operates as a microcosm of the whole story, showing how the threat to the line of Judah is overcome by human shrewdness. This has important implications for the interrelationship of the two streams.

Chapters 39-41 do not really focus on the broader family of Jacob, but instead reveal how Joseph's rise to power comes by virtue of his fear of the Lord (seen in the incident with Potiphar's wife) and his patient trust in God, leading to some wise human initiatives. There is no mention at this stage of how these events will impact on the broader family.

However, when we come to chapter 42, we see very quickly that one threat to the promised line (death because of the famine, 42:2, 5) is able to be overcome because Joseph has prudently gathered grain in Egypt during the years of plenty (42:1). In other words, Joseph's wisdom not only leads to success for him (41:39-45), or to blessing for the nations (41:57), but also becomes the means used to overcome the threat to the patriarchal promises. Wisdom serves its own goals, but also contributes to a key goal of the covenant strand - the survival of the chosen descendants of Abraham.

Furthermore, in chapters 42-45 as a whole, Joseph's clever ruse is the process by which reconciliation is achieved in Jacob's family. While family harmony is a broader wisdom goal, it is also the state of affairs that can best ensure that the descendants of Jacob will survive and establish a nation.

At this point the symphonic analogy is useful. If the music of Joseph's rise to power in chapters 39-41 seemed self-contained, a careful ear will discern that the melody has continued right up to the end of chapter 45. Of course, a new musical thread has also become present, but the two harmonise well and there is symphony not cacophony.

46:1-4 then makes it clear that the family's movement from Canaan to Egypt is endorsed by God. However, while God gives permission or instruction to Jacob to go to Egypt, it is also Joseph's actions and words that have made it possible. Furthermore, there is a focus on the broader family from 46:5-47:12, but even here Joseph is the one who gives advice and takes charge (46:31-47:12). The explicit mention that he provides for his family (that is, ensuring the continuation of the promises) in 47:12, is filled out by 47:13-26. In 47:27-28, this state of affairs (which has come about through Joseph's initiatives) has led to both survival and multiplication of the promised line. In the short unit in 47:29-31, Jacob ensures that the ancestral promises will not be forgotten, but this, too, will happen because of the actions of Joseph in swearing not to bury Jacob in Egypt.

Longacre has allocated both 47:13-31 and chapter 48 to the Joseph side of the story alone.[33] However, the analysis above strongly suggests that all of chapter 47 deals at least implicitly with the broader family as well.

In relation to chapter 48, Longacre severs it from 49:1-28, arguing that the broader family is in view only in chapter 49.[34] However, this study has concluded that chapters 48 and 49 belong together. More specifically, the fact that chapter 48 comes first implies that Jacob acknowledges the priority of Joseph in his family, while chapter 49 details how various testamentary words are given to all of the sons/future tribes. Of particular significance is the way in which both Joseph and Judah can be exalted, but in different ways. This makes it clear that the line of promise will not ultimately pass through the descendants of the wise Joseph, but rather through the line of Judah, as foreshadowed by 38:27-30. Joseph is thus prominent, but his rise to prominence also has implications for the broader family of Jacob, and for the future covenant promise.

The leading role of Joseph in 49:29-50:21 again reminds us of the message of the dream about Joseph's rise to prominence. It also highlights how the ongoing survival of the promised line is contingent on Joseph's character of fearing the Lord and genuinely pursuing reconciliation. The notion of God's behind-the-scenes plans, introduced by the dream in chapter 37 and made explicit in chapter 45, is now repeated as the story draws to a close.

The final section (50:22-26) ties Joseph's life more closely in the

---

33 Longacre, *Joseph: A Story of Divine Providence*, 23.
34 Longacre, *Joseph: A Story of Divine Providence*, 23.

promises to the patriarchs, for the next book (Exodus) is going to pick up this thread and develop it further.

Thus, throughout chapters 37-50, there is a forceful, independent emphasis on the rise of Joseph to success and power, as the outworking of his wise actions and character. This stream stands in its own right. Yet it is only partially true to say that this is an independent strand, since it is also interdependent with the other major stream of the survival and partial fulfilment of the patriarchal promises. The narrative does not present these promises as the sole reason for Joseph's success or his rise to power. Indeed, he is pictured as being entrusted with power because of his tested character and wise human initiatives under the overarching rule of God. On the other hand, it is clear that Joseph's rise to prominence, and his initiatives are the means that are used to ensure the survival of the covenant line. Were it not for Joseph providing food, a safe place to live, as well as forgiveness leading to family reconciliation, then it is difficult to see how the broader promised line, and thus the covenant promises, could have been preserved. Thus, the wisdom stream achieves its own goals, but also is the means in the Joseph story of overcoming the threats to the covenant promises.

The wisdom and the covenant strands are therefore integrated into a harmonious, but variegated symphony yet without the direct intervention of God. The rise of Joseph pervades the entire story, just as the dream of chapter 37 intimates. While Joseph's success could have led to the covenant promises being continued only in and through him, his initiatives extended to actions which secured reconciliation within the wider chosen family.

It is at least clear that neither the wisdom nor the covenant strands in Genesis 37-50 collapse into the other without remainder. The concerns of the wisdom strand are not exhausted by preserving the covenant promises, although the hidden rule of God and the wise initiatives of Joseph certainly do secure the fulfilment of those promises. Similarly, the covenant promises are not simply fulfilled in order for Joseph to rise to power, but will have further independent significance in the book of Exodus which follows. The two strands do intersect and are integrated, but the distinctives of each are retained.

Chapter 38 as a Microcosm

This study has previously argued that chapter 38 is in many ways a microcosm of the Joseph story as a whole. While it is not proposed to repeat that material, this section will propose that the many parallel themes between chapter 38 and the wider Joseph story are fruitful for exploring the interaction between wisdom and the Abrahamic promise.

Some recent studies have usefully explored the motif of the wise woman.

This figure of the wise woman is seen most clearly in 2 Samuel 14 and 20.[35] Schroer refers to the type of 'wise counselling women' and defines the category as follows: "women who, in decisive situations, diplomatically interfere in politics and authoritatively influence the way of the world by their counsel."[36] In 2 Samuel 14, the wise woman of Tekoa disguises herself by dressing as a widow and through the words of a parable persuades David to bring back Absalom.[37] In 2 Samuel 20, the wise woman of Abel preserves the life of her town by exercising initiative in negotiating with Joab.[38] Camp suggests that these stories "provide two of the clearest representatives of what has been called clan or family wisdom."[39]

---

35 Camp, *Wisdom and the Feminine*, 120 argues that "the wise women of Tekoa (2 Sam 14) and of Abel (2 Sam 20) were representatives of a non-regular but recurrent leadership role for women in pre-monarchic Israel."

36 S. Schroer, 'Wise and Counselling Women in Ancient Israel: Literary and Historic Ideals of the Personified Ḥokmâ, in *A Feminist Companion to Wisdom Literature*. Feminist Companion to the Bible, 9, ed. A. Brenner. (Sheffield: Sheffield Academic Press, 1995), 71. Schroer notes that both the אשה חכמה of Tekoa who cleverly persuades David to stop banishing Absalom (2 Samuel 14) and the אשה חכמה of Abel-Beth-Maacah (2 Sam 20:15-22), "employ diplomatic tricks skilfully" and "refer to wisdom traditions".

37 A. Brenner, *The Israelite Woman: Social Role and Literary Type in Biblical Narrative*. Biblical Seminar Series. (Sheffield: JSOT Press, 1985) 35 comments that "the skill with which the woman commences to introduce David's problem, her talent for pursuing the analogy between her troubles and the king's through recurrent references to her own case, and, finally, the way she deals with the king when he calls her bluff all point to the fact that she is much more than an accomplished actress who repeats, parrot-like, what Joab has ordered her to say. She has the presence of mind to seize upon a situation, judge it for herself, and manipulate it to her own advantage. ... This 'wise' woman ... can be counted on for sensing undercurrents of emotions and opinions, and for utilizing them. She can adapt easily to changes in the atmosphere, and redirects these changes according to her purpose through improvization." Similarly, W.A.M. Beuken, 'No Wise King Without a Wise Woman (I Kings III 16-28)', in *New Avenues in the Study of the Old Testament: A Collection of Old Testament Studies Published on the Occasion of the Fiftieth Anniversary of the Oudtestamentisch Werkgezelschnap and the Retirement of Prof. M.J. Mulder*. OTS, 25, ed. A.S. van der Woude. (Leiden: E.J. Brill, 1989), 9; Camp, *Wisdom and the Feminine*, 121.

38 Brenner, *The Israelite Woman*, 36-37 notes that the wise woman of Abel-beth-Maacah (2 Sam 20:14-22) "uses rational consideration, persuasion and rhetoric rather than spontaneous action, and she succeeds in achieving what she has set out to do."

39 C.V. Camp, 'The Female Sage in Ancient Israel and in the Biblical Wisdom Literature', in *The Sage in Israel and the Ancient Near East*. eds. J.G. Gammie and L.G. Perdue. (Winona Lake: Eisenbrauns, 1990), 188. She discusses the passages on pages 185-190. See also C.V. Camp, 'The Wise Women of 2 Samuel: A Role Model for Women in Early Israel', *CBQ* 43 (1981): 14-29.

A third figure who can be regarded as a wise woman is Abigail in 1 Samuel 25. Although she is not explicitly described as wise - she is called טובת־שכל or 'of good understanding' (1 Sam 25:3)[40] - she is contrasted strongly with her husband, Nabal, whose name means 'fool' (1 Sam 25:25). She is, at the very least, the opposite of a 'fool' and the foundational wisdom contrast is between wisdom and folly (Prov 9:1-6, 13-18). Furthermore, she acts decisively to avert an imminent disaster (1 Sam 25:18-19) and displays both diplomacy and rhetorical skill in her words to David (1 Sam 25:24-31).[41] Brenner has argued that, although she shows insight, she is not called 'wise' because she is only seeking to further her own ends.[42] However, while Abigail does preserve her own life and ultimately becomes David's wife (1 Sam 25:42), she appears to have responded to an issue of justice (1 Sam 25:14-17), preserved the life of the male servants (1 Sam 25:22, 34), and prevented David from incurring bloodguilt (1 Sam 25:33). Her actions thus had a wider effect than simply her own interests, and she can therefore appropriately be called 'wise'. It is thus possible to identify a woman as a wisdom figure even when she is not explicitly described as 'wise' in the text.[43]

Several features of these narratives are striking. Firstly, all these stories have a setting in the ongoing account of God's covenant people, yet each woman is faced with a dilemma which is resolved without any mighty act by God. In 2 Samuel 14 the broken relationship between David and Absalom is restored simply by human discussions in a court setting, while in 2 Samuel 20 God does not need to intervene in battle because the fighting is averted through the persuasive negotiations of the wise woman

---

40 T.E. Fretheim, 'שכל', in *New International Dictionary of Old Testament Theology and Exegesis*. 5 vols., ed. W.A. VanGemeren. (Grand Rapids: Zondervan, 1997), 3:1243 notes that שכל "is commonly used in literature associated with wisdom." Schroer, 'Wise and Counselling Women, 72 notes that Abigail prevents bloodshed by her decisive action, diplomacy and rhetoric, and thus through her wisdom preventing David from acting precipitously.

41 Brenner, *The Israelite Woman*, 40 comments that "[a]s in the cases of the two 'wise' women associated with Joab, an important component of Abigail's intelligence is her eloquence. The speech she delivers to David - which, together with her tribute, brings about his reconciliation and their eventual marriage - is a beautifully constructed piece of manipulation, carefully designed to further her own ends".

42 Brenner, *The Israelite Woman*, 40-41, 45.

43 It is also worth observing that Beuken, 'No Wise King', 1-10 has argued that the mother in 1 Kings 3 should also be regarded as wise. He proposes that the two whores of this chapter personify wisdom and folly, and, adds (10) that "[b]y listening to the inclinations of her motherly heart she [the 'good whore'] can speak wise words to king Solomon." Since this case is not as obvious as the other wise women, it is proposed not to deal with this incident. If, however, she were to be classified as 'wise', then it would further strengthen the argument of this study.

of Abel. In 1 Samuel 25, Abigail quickly gathers food and drink for David and his men (1 Sam 25:18) but keeps her foolish husband unaware of her initiative (1 Sam 25:19). When Abigail meets David, she pleads her case with a deferential attitude (1 Sam 25:23-24) and reasoned arguments (1 Sam 25:24-31).

This twin emphasis on human initiative and aptly chosen words is exactly what occurs in the Joseph narrative and, it has been argued, is a focus of the theology of the sages. God's kingly and often covenant purposes are furthered by wise human actions rather any overt divine intervention. God is working behind the scenes, accomplishing his outcomes through human initiatives. In the case of Tamar, she acts to avoid the extinction of her husband's line and, with that, the entire family of Judah. She, like Joseph, does not wait for a command from God but rather assesses the seriousness of the situation and acts decisively. She chooses an opportune time (Gen 38:12-13) and when propositioned by Judah she skilfully uses words to negotiate with him. She is able to secure possession of his signet ring, cord and staff (Gen 38:16-18), so that she will have the evidence that she needs when she is discovered to be pregnant (Gen 38:25). She, like the other wise women, shows initiative in her actions, shrewdness in her speech, and success in her plans.

In addition, there is an overlap between what each of the wise women are seeking to accomplish. The wise woman of Tekoa sought to bring about family reconciliation between David and Absalom (2 Sam 14:13). The woman of Abel aimed at preserving the innocent lives of those caught in the city with Sheba (2 Sam 20:21), while Abigail attempted to save the lives of the male servants (1 Sam 25:31, 34). In each case, David or someone acting on David's behalf, is turned towards a new course of action that both has a better outcome and is generally more just (1 Sam 25:39; 2 Sam 14:21; 20:19-21). Jackson describes this as "an alternative dispute-resolution technique."[44]. In Tamar's case, her actions were designed to preserve the life of her husband through his descendants (Gen 38:8, 14; see 2 Sam 14:7), and led to the preservation of the line of Judah from which David would come (Gen 38:27-30). This led ultimately to reconciliation within the family (Gen 38:26), and the righting of the injustice committed against Tamar and Er.

Furthermore, the incident in 2 Samuel 14 is characterised by two other features. Firstly, there was a clever ruse involved (2 Sam 14:2-3) which was

---

44 B.S. Jackson, 'Practical Wisdom and Literary Artifice in the Covenant Code', in *The Jerusalem 1990 Conference Volume*. Jewish Law Association Studies, 6, eds. B.S. Jackson and S.M. Passamaneck. (Atlanta: Scholars, 1992), 66. In relation to the 'wise woman' of Abel in 2 Sam 20:16-22 he notes that "[t]he dispute here is resolved not by war, but by practical wisdom: a common sense solution supported by a popular saying."

undertaken to bring about reconciliation within a family. Abigail also used deceit in her plan by not informing her husband (1 Sam 25:19). In a similar vein, Tamar disguised her appearance so that Judah would not recognise her, and was successful in outwitting her male counterpart (Gen 38:14-16). In securing a pledge from Judah, and later disclosing it, she was able to gain a public vindication of her actions.

Secondly, the clothing motif surfaces (2 Sam 14:2) as the wise woman of Tekoa dresses in disguise in order to be successful in her plan. In Genesis 38 the clothing motif is also present as Tamar takes off her widow's garments and puts on those of a prostitute so as to deceive Judah (Gen 38:14).

There are, therefore, compelling reasons for viewing Tamar as a wise woman. What, however, is the significance of this conclusion for an understanding of the relationship between wisdom and covenant in the Joseph narrative?

Firstly, if both Tamar and Joseph are characterised as wisdom figures, it is worth asking whether their stories share any other elements in common. In fact, parallels may be observed with most sections of the Joseph narrative. Throughout the entire Tamar story, God appears to be at work behind the scenes, while the human actions of the characters are foregrounded. While Yahweh puts both Er and Onan to death (Gen 38:7, 10), no details are given that enable a reader to discern whether their deaths are due to specific divine intervention or whether they simply happen as a result of 'natural causes', but they are depicted theologically as the work of Yahweh. Other than this God has no overt role in chapter 38. This theme of God's hidden rule has also been highlighted in the Joseph story, where God is active, but active behind the scenes.

Chapters 39-41 outline the reversal of the injustice meted out to Joseph. Though sold as a slave (by his brothers), falsely accused (by Potiphar's wife), and ungratefully forgotten (by Pharaoh's cupbearer), Joseph exercises initiative and finally rises to a position of great authority in the land. Tamar is treated unjustly by Judah when he withholds Shelah from her, leaving her in the "liminal state where she was neither a virgin daughter nor a child-bearing wife".[45] Tamar, by her initiative, has this injustice reversed by being taken back into the family and bearing children to carry on the name of Er. In both stories, the two wronged characters not only take initiative, but also secure their goal by means of assertive and effective speech. Furthermore, in the reversal of the injustice, both Tamar and Joseph manage to promote life in the face of the threat of death. Tamar brings life into the world through the birth of her sons, overcoming the deaths of Er and Onan, as well as the self-defeating actions of Judah.

---

45 Camp, *Wisdom and the Feminine*, 127.

Joseph brings life to a world facing death because of famine.

In chapters 42-45, the parallels are not quite as overt, but are nonetheless real. The theme of life noted above in the Tamar story is also found in Joseph's theological explanation in 45:5-8. Even more significant here is that both Tamar and Joseph are able to effect a family reconciliation. Tamar was sent back to her father's house by Judah, with the result that Shelah could produce no descendants until her return. Judah appears to regard her as 'tainted by death', and refuses to allow her to bear children in the name of Er. This study has already argued that chapters 42-47 outline how Joseph effects a lasting reconciliation in his wider family. It is also noteworthy that both these reconciliations are brought about through clever ruses, deceiving those who had sought to deceive Tamar and Joseph. Tamar disguises herself and deceives Judah, while Joseph does not reveal himself to his brothers but instead accuses them of being spies. Both these ruses also involved the use of garments, with Tamar putting on the clothes of a prostitute and Joseph hiding behind the robes of the powerful vizier.

The structural parallels between chapter 38 and the Joseph story have already been demonstrated, moving from an outline of the family situation, through the use of human initiative and planning, to the birth of descendants against the odds.[46] Both chapters 48-50 and 38:27-30 outline the future members of the family - and in both cases, the covenant line - that have been preserved.[47] Robinson points out that "[t]he story of Tamar shares with the Joseph story ... the theme of how a risk to the divine promise was averted".[48] The descendants of Judah, from which David will come, are a particular focus of both accounts. Furthermore, the families only survive because of the transformation of Judah in chapter 38 and the transformation of the brothers made evident in Judah's speech in chapter 44. In both cases, it is the clever ruse of Tamar and Joseph that transforms Judah and keeps the covenant line alive.

The frequency and spread of these common elements suggest strongly that the Tamar story is a kind of microcosm of the larger Joseph story, and that its function in the final form of Genesis 37-50 is to anticipate themes in the subsequent chapters. Thus Goldman is right in observing that, "[t]hough Tamar never *directly* enters into the Joseph tale, her tale is very much of a

---

46 G.D. Vreeland, 'The Joseph Narrative - Genesis 37-39: An analysis of three modern textual approaches', (Dissertation, PhD, Trinity Evangelical Divinity School, 1994) 429 also observes that "[a]nother factor that links chapter 38 to the rest of the patriarchal narratives as well as the Joseph narrative is the etymologies on the names of his sons. Like Joseph he [Judah] has two sons, and like chapter 41:51, 52 there are two etymologies for the names of his two sons."

47 Rendsburg, *The Redaction of Genesis*, 83-86 also demonstrates many verbal and other parallels between chapters 38 and 49.

48 Robinson, *Mysterious God*, 15.

piece with both the spirit and circumstances of the Joseph narratives."[49]

Secondly, since chapter 38 functions as a microcosm of the broader Joseph narrative, it is a fruitful source for exploring the intersection of covenant and wisdom elements. Camp, commenting on the wise women in 2 Samuel 14 and 20, notes that "[t]hese stories in 2 Samuel present two women whose values - justice, well-being, life, the heritage of Yahweh - are covenant values. But they are also wisdom's values (cf. Prov 8.18-21, 32-36; 22.22-23; 23.10-11; 2.20-22)."[50] In other words, their wise actions and words not only achieve the wisdom goal of life and justice but also God's covenant purposes of the survival and prospering of Israel under David. In both situations, and also in the case of Abigail, God's covenant community is maintained, but it is enriched because of these wise women. Their aim is not solely to exalt the chosen line of David, but that happens as a consequence of their pursuit of wisdom values like life, reconciliation and justice. The covenant could have been maintained without the actions of these wise women, but their efforts enrich and promote the covenant community. These observations suggest that wisdom does not simply feed into covenant without remainder, but rather that both wisdom and covenant promote an even broader, more all-encompassing concept.

In a similar vein, Tamar is not solely concerned to promote the covenant line of promise. She seeks to fulfil her obligation to Er, and to correct an injustice committed by Judah. Camp points out that Tamar's actions lead to "the strengthening of family unity and hence, both actually and symbolically, of the whole community social structure."[51] In pursuing these goals successfully she additionally, but incidentally, preserves the chosen line of Judah. Her shrewd wisdom was the means God used to further his broader purposes, which include the later establishment of Israel, but also the promotion of justice, family reconciliation and the loyal fulfilment of responsibilities. The two are "contiguous" in chapter 38,[52] and this again makes clear how human wisdom serves God's wider purposes. However, it

---

49 S. Goldman, *The Wiles of Women/The Wiles of Men: Joseph and Potiphar's Wife in Ancient Near Eastern, Jewish, and Islamic Folklore* (Albany: State University of New York Press, 1995) 101.

50 Camp, *Wisdom and the Feminine*, 123.

51 Camp, *Wisdom and the Feminine*, 127.

52 Camp, *Wisdom and the Feminine*, 132 makes comparisons with the stories of Tamar and Ruth in this regard: "the goals of Tamar and Ruth are not only those of personal gain but are, like those of female Wisdom, concerned with the larger issues of social justice and social order. Further, both Tamar and Ruth act implicitly, but only implicitly, to further *God's* work, the establishment of the people of Israel and, in particular, of the house of David. The narratives thus reveal how pragmatic wisdom can be understood to work in God's interest ... Human pragmatism, social justice and theological purpose are contiguous in the narratives".

is also clear that Tamar achieves, and God desires, something more that the mere preservation of the covenant line. It is not simply that wisdom facilitates God's covenant purposes, but rather that human wisdom and the promotion of the covenant are both part a larger, more inclusive category.

God's Active Rule

In both the microcosm of chapter 38 and the wider Joseph narrative, then, wisdom and covenant appear complementary, yet without either being a subset of the other. This section of the study will examine how these two strands are embraced by a more foundational concept. The identification of this broader category is, in some ways, an offshoot of the study of the integration of wisdom and covenant in the Joseph story, but it also sheds much light on God's overarching purposes.

A number of recent studies, in both wisdom and non-wisdom books, have suggested some fruitful directions in this regard. The proposal by Goldingay - that the Old Testament can be integrated around the twin foci of creation and redemption - has already been mentioned.[53] While this was a significant step forward, it has previously been noted that the precise connection between creation (grounding wisdom) and redemption (grounding covenant) has not been sufficiently developed.

Goldingay's proposal has been usefully explored by Lee in relation to Isaiah 40-55. Lee notes that, while Goldingay views "creation and redemption in the Hebrew Bible as two divergent ideas that need to be unified theologically", his study of Isaiah 40-55 "shows that they are already unified under the theological theme of YHWH's unique sovereignty."[54] On Lee's view, then, the broader category can be identified as God's sovereignty. He also makes the significant observation that, in relation to Isaiah, "it does not imply either that the one motif is subordinated under the other, or that the two motifs are in fact denoting one and the same reality."[55] In Isaiah 40-55, as in Genesis 37-50, both strands retain their own integrity, and both ideas remain distinct as well as

---

53 Goldingay, *Theological Diversity*, 200-239.
54 Lee, *Creation and Redemption*, 197. On pages 129-142, he grounds this in a persuasive philological argument that ברא in the Hebrew Bible has connotations of 'sovereign power and control' rather than 'creation out of nothing' or 'novelty'. The connection between creation and wisdom is not a forced one, since, at page 197, Lee notes that "[t]he biblical doctrine of creation has more to do with a sovereign creator here and now than the origin of species there and then". In other words it concerns his activity in presently ordering his creation, which is very close to what has been shown of God's activity in the Joseph narrative.
55 Lee, *Creation and Redemption*, 196.

interrelated. Lee's conclusion is that "YHWH's sovereignty is illustrated by both his powerful acts in creation and history"[56] In other words, God is sovereignly active in the everyday world of the creation as well as in his divine incursions into history.

Smith, in writing on the book of Job, has also argued that the concept of God's sovereignty is useful for integrating wisdom into Old Testament theology. He proposes that Job has a unifying theme - that God sovereignly rules over individuals, nations and nature.[57] This theme, he claims, is similar to the basic thrust of the Pentateuch, historical and prophetic books that God sovereignly rules over Israel, the nations and nature.[58] With respect to the co-existence of the wisdom and salvation history strands, he concludes that

> Both wisdom and non-wisdom traditions have a distinctive place in OT theology. They are different, but they do not contradict each other. Both point to the same fundamental relationship between God and the world. God rules over everyone and everything.[59]

Like Lee, Smith specifically considers Goldingay's proposal and suggests that "[t]his central theme - God rules over Israel, the nations and nature - is superior to Goldingay's dual emphases on creation and redemption because it encompasses and stands behind both."[60] Smith gives four reasons for preferring this theme of God's sovereign rule

> 1) It does not focus just on the two powerful events of creation and redemption, but on all God's powerful deeds and words. 2) It encompasses not only God's great positive deeds (creation and redemption) but his just judgment of nature and nations and his daily

---

56 Lee, *Creation and Redemption*, 194. This is to argue against G. von Rad, 'The Theological Problem of the Old Testament Doctrine of Creation', in *The Problem of the Hexateuch and other essays*. trans. E.W.T. Dicken. (London: SCM, 1984), 142 who sets out a thesis "that in genuinely Yahwistic belief the doctrine of creation never attained to the stature of a relevant, independent doctrine. We found it invariably related, and indeed subordinated, to soteriological considerations".

57 G.V. Smith, 'Is There a Place for Job's Wisdom in Old Testament Theology?', *Trinity Journal* 13NS (1992): 16 rightly observes that "[t]he various theologies represented in Job agree on the fundamental theological principle that *God sovereignly rules over individuals, nations, and nature.* ... He rules over his creation through his power and his wisdom, over the nations through wars and famines, and over the final events of human history, including death itself. All animals, all people, and all nations are controlled by his almighty rule."

58 Smith, 'Is There a Place', 17.

59 Smith, 'Is There a Place', 18.

60 Smith, 'Is There a Place', 19.

providential care of history and nature as well. 3) It is not focused on a few historical points, but on the many ways his wisdom, instructions, laws, and prophetic warning bring about his rule over individuals, nations, and parts of nature. 4) It does not depend on the chronological relationship of creation and redemption, which makes one more prominent at one time and the other at another time, but applies to all times and in many ways.[61]

Schultz's recent study of the interrelationship of wisdom and covenant strongly affirms the usefulness of this theme of God's sovereign rule for understanding the wisdom corpus.[62]

The centrality of God's sovereignty to the wisdom corpus has also been separately proposed by Spina and Boström. Spina suggests a category of 'reformed wisdom', by which he means a reaction to a royal wisdom which failed to uphold the Israelite state. He notes that a feature of this perspective is that "all human activity must be chastened by the belief that Yahweh is in control, not man, and that no matter how skilfully wisdom is used the future of Israel and its institutions are in the hands of a sovereign God."[63]

Boström's careful study of the doctrine of God in the book of Proverbs argues that the sovereignty of God is foundational to the book.[64] He points out that

The sovereignty of the Lord in the book of Proverbs primarily appears when it is stated that he directs and rules all things, when his ways are declared to be incomprehensible to man, and in the assertion that God directs all things to suit his will and his purpose irrespective of or even contrary to man's actions.[65]

It is this understanding of God's 'overlordship' that calls for a human

---

61 Smith, 'Is There a Place', 19.
62 Schultz, 'Unity or Diversity', 290. He specifically comments that "Smith's recent proposal to construct an Old Testament theology on the basis of the Old Testament portrayal of God's sovereign rule over individuals, nations, and nature certainly would accommodate wisdom literature quite comfortably." See also Loader, 'Chokma - Joseph - Hybris', 27 who suggests that "[h]uman chokma means to integrate with God's order. Therefore chokma means to take the overlordship of God seriously."
63 F.A. Spina, 'Qoheleth and the Reformation of Wisdom', in *The Quest For the Kingdom of God: Studies in Honor of George E. Mendenhall*. eds. H.B. Huffmon, F.A. Spina and A.R.W. Green. (Winona Lake, Eisenbrauns, 1983), 276. At 277, he makes it clear that he understands fearing God to be equated with the recognition of Yahweh's sovereignty.
64 Boström, *The God of the Sages*, 112, 169.
65 Boström, *The God of the Sages*, 169. This is amplified at page 191.

response of fearing the Lord.[66]

Boström also makes the broader observation that the notion of God's sovereignty is not restricted to the book of Proverbs. It is, he observes a common view in the wisdom corpus, shared in particular by the books of Job and Ecclesiastes.[67] Indeed, he observes that "it is probably correct to say that a belief in God's sovereignty more or less characterizes the OT as a whole and that the belief in the Lord as supreme ruler constitutes a basic shared assumption of the biblical authors."[68]

This series of studies suggests that God's sovereignty may be a useful way of describing this broader category. However, the drawback of this term is that it can easily carry too much baggage from systematic or historical theology. While the notion of God's sovereignty is theologically legitimate to use - in that it explains the authoritative nature of God's rule - it might be preferable to look for a more precise and descriptive term.

It is proposed, therefore, to use the phrase 'God's active rule'. However, this cluster term requires some explanation and justification. What is envisaged by the term is the notion that God is purposefully bringing about his goals. In this sense, God is active rather than passive. Yet, it does not necessarily imply that God is *seen* to be active, for he may well be active behind-the-scenes. What is implied in using the expression is that God is rul*ing* rather than merely being the one with the title of 'ruler'. It focuses on activity not simply entitlement, and would preclude a scenario in which God simply wound up the world and then just watched it run.

Brueggemann has recently focused on the hiddenness or hidden rule of Yahweh as a motif that is prominent in the wisdom corpus.[69] He comments that

> The countertestimony of wisdom is that in much of life, if Yahweh is to be spoken of meaningfully, it must be a Yahweh who is not direct and not visible, but who in fact is hidden in the ongoing daily processes of life ... it [wisdom] dares to make a claim about Yahweh's faithful sovereignty and sovereign fidelity in all of those dimensions of life where the Yahweh of the great verbs is not evident.[70]

---

66 Boström, *The God of the Sages*, 187.
67 Boström, *The God of the Sages*, 169, 177, 187-188.
68 Boström, *The God of the Sages*, 179.
69 W. Brueggemann, *Theology of the Old Testament: Testimony, Dispute, Advocacy* (Minneapolis: Fortress, 1997) 333-342 studies this under the heading of 'The Hidden Rule of Yahweh', under which are two subheadings: 'Wisdom Theology' and 'Yahweh as Hidden Guarantor of Order'.
70 Brueggemann, *Theology of the Old Testament*, 335. At 338 he adds, in relation to the connection between deeds and consequences: "Yahweh is *not at all visible* in this

Thus, he is speaking about the reality of God's sovereignty, but under the
rubric of 'the hidden rule of Yahweh'.[71] This is a genuine exercise of rule or
authority by God, and it does demand that human beings discern it and
embrace it.[72] God's hidden rule is clearly evident in his 'providential'
ordering of events

> The hiddenness that runs through and beneath and beyond what is
> visible in Israel's life is marked by Yahweh's sovereignty (Yahweh's
> resolve to have Yahweh's own way) and by Yahweh's fidelity
> (Yahweh's good, positive, and benign intention for Israel and for the
> world). This substantive content to Yahweh's hiddenness is
> commonly understood as an affirmation of Yahweh's providence.[73]

God thus accomplishes his purposes, but in such a way as they appear to
be brought about by circumstances or human initiatives.[74] This is often
referred to as 'providence' but the concept of providence is a problematic
one. Even Brueggemann himself concedes that "*[p]rovidence* is not a
biblical word, and we cannot easily point to a semantic field to express this
conviction about Yahweh".[75]

Just as Brueggemann discerns the concept of 'providence' but uses the
descriptive term 'the hidden rule of Yahweh', so this study suggests that the
reality of God's sovereignty can be more neutrally described as 'God's
active rule'.

Of course, God's active rule, or ruling, can take many forms. God can
raise up nations, defeat armies and kill individuals. However, he can also
raise up women and men to win battles, persuade a nation, or model an
alternative way of behaving. In both cases, God is actively accomplishing
his purposes, but through different means. In other words, God's active rule

---

process. But, according to Israel, Yahweh is *nonetheless indispensable* for the
process. This is not, in Israel's horizon, a self-propelled system of sanctions, but it is
an enactment of Yahweh's sovereign, faithful intentionality."

71 Brueggemann, *Theology of the Old Testament*, 355 also notes that a "second way in
   which Israel presents its countertestimony that Yahweh is sovereign but hidden is to
   speak about the "plan of Yahweh.""

72 Brueggemann, *Theology of the Old Testament*, 342.

73 Brueggemann, *Theology of the Old Testament*, 352.

74 G.L. Goldsworthy, *Gospel and Wisdom: Israel's Wisdom Literature in the Christian
   Life* (Exeter: Paternoster, 1987) 145 thus comments that "[w]isdom is a theology of
   covenant adulthood, both corporate and individual. It recognizes that an important
   aspect of man's relationship to God is his responsibility to think and act in a world
   that is not, and was never meant to be, an open book nor a static, passive blob of
   matter."

75 Brueggemann, *Theology of the Old Testament*, 352.

is a category that can embrace not only the mighty acts of the exodus, but also the notion of God's hidden yet effective rule. In the Joseph story the specific motif associated with God's active rule is his purposeful, behind-the-scenes, ordering of events, raising up Joseph to bring life to the world and to preserve the covenant people and promises. A term such as 'God's active rule' is thus able to describe both God's covert as well as his overt activities. The overarching unity is God's purposeful and powerful controlling of events. God's controlling or ruling or superintending what happens is common to both the Joseph story and the records of the mighty acts of God, even though God can use differing means. Within the Joseph story, God's active rule is largely hidden but is nonetheless both active and effective.

It is therefore proposed that the wisdom and covenant strands of the Joseph story can be encompassed in this broader category of God's active rule. It is not that wisdom is made acceptable by being connected to covenant, but that both serve a broader goal - God's control or active rule, and what it means to live in light of that control. Wisdom thus acts as a 'contrepoint thé ologique' to other emphases in the Old Testament.[76] As Scobie points out, "[w]isdom challenges the often-held assumption that revelation in *history* is all that counts in biblical theology."[77]

The notion of God's active rule, then, is the nature of the rope as the various strands are woven together, and is the thrust of the symphony that is found in Genesis 37-50. Indeed, the Joseph story could be understood as an 'unfinished symphony', since the message of God's active rule continues on through the rest of the Old Testament.

Within Genesis 37-50, the dream of chapter 37 stands at the very beginning of story as the icon of God's active rule. While God's rule is generally hidden in these chapters, the dream announces God's overarching purposes that the narrative subsequently describes being accomplished. It has earlier been argued that Joseph's dream sends signals to the implied

---

76 J. Lévêque, 'Le contrepoint théologique apporté par la réflexion sapientielle', in *Questions disputées d'Ancien Testament*. BETL, 33, ed. C. Brekelmans. (Leuven: Leuven University Press, 1974), 185 uses the image of a 'theological counterpoint' to explain wisdom's place in Old Testament theology. He is borrowing from the language of music. R.E. Murphy, 'Wisdom and Yahwism', in *No Famine in the Land: Studies in Honor of John L. McKenzie*. eds. J.W. Flanagan and A.W. Robinson. (Claremont: Scholars, 1975), 120 also makes a pointed observation in proposing that "[i]nstead of inserting wisdom into Yahwism, with Yahwism as a kind of implicit determinant of orthodoxy, one might rather turn the question around: How is Yahwism to be inserted into wisdom, into what was the daily experience of the Israelite?" See also Scobie, 'The Place of Wisdom', 44; Goldsworthy, *Gospel and Wisdom*, 132.

77 Scobie, 'The Place of Wisdom', 47.

reader that what will happen is in conformity with the plans of God, yet without foregrounding any divine activity. It lifts the veil in order to reveal God's purposes for Joseph, his father and brothers, and thus discloses the very heart of the story.

This can be seen very clearly in several crucial sections of the text. In Gen 42:6-9, when the brothers bow down to Joseph, the narrator includes the comment in verse 9 that

ויזכר יוסף את החלמות אשר חלם להם

Thus, as the events of the dream begin to fulfilled, the dream itself is explicitly recalled.

The nature of dreams in the Joseph story is most clearly explained in chapter 41. In the court of the one who is supposedly sovereign over Egypt, Joseph explains that the dreams disclose what God - the ultimate sovereign who actively rules all his world - is about to do (Gen 41:25, 28)

ויאמר יוסף אל־פרעה חלום פרעה אחד הוא את אשר האלהים
עשה הגיד לפרעה:
הוא הדבר אשר דברתי אל־פרעה אשר האלהים עשה
הראה את־פרעה:

Furthermore, the doubling of Pharaoh's dream and, by implication, Joseph's dream in chapter 37, has the significance that it is firmly established by God, and that he will soon bring it about (Gen 41:32)

ועל השנות החלום אל־פרעה פעמים כי־נכון הדבר מעם
האלהים וממהר האלהים לעשתו:

It has also been argued in the previous chapter that the descriptions of divine and human activity are telling. Thus, in Gen 40:8, Joseph informs the cupbearer that interpretations belong to God, but he both urges the official to tell *him* the dream and then proceeds to interpret it (Gen 40:12-13). In addition, Joseph advises Pharaoh that God will answer Pharaoh (Gen 41:16), yet God apparently does so through the words of Joseph (Gen 41:25-32). The character Joseph - a reliable character at this point - thus makes it plain that God is actively bringing about his purposes through human agents.

In this extended narrative, where God rarely acts visibly or openly, God nonetheless acts to achieve his goals through the very ordinary means of human activity and initiative. God is actively ruling, but the nature of this rule in Genesis 37-50 is largely hidden.

CHAPTER 12

Conclusions

This book has studied the interaction between wisdom and covenant in a particular Hebrew narrative, the story of Joseph. As a result, a number of conclusions have already been advanced. A summary of these, together with some suggestions for further study, will be presented in this closing chapter. These conclusions can be grouped into three main areas: methodological issues; the interpretation of the Joseph story and its connection with wisdom; and the intersection of wisdom and covenant ideas.

Methodology

The first part of this study has argued that there has been a lack of methodological rigour in the study of wisdom influence in non-wisdom texts. There has often been an imprecise use of terminology, such as a failure to distinguish between identifying 'wisdom influence' and classifying a piece of writing as a 'wisdom text'. It has been proposed that 'wisdom literary influence' can be ascertained by identifying 'wisdom-like elements' in a text, and then asking how significant these elements are to the text as a whole. This is preferred to the 'proverbial correlative view' of von Rad and his followers (which involves a flat reading of the text),[1] and to 'social setting approach' which denies any wisdom influence unless the text can be shown to have emerged from a wisdom *Sitz im Leben* (so Crenshaw). While the question of social setting is an important one, the 'literary influence method' is less speculative in that it is dealing with the final form of the text, and is particularly valuable for identifying the interconnection of wisdom ideas and those in other streams of the Old Testament. For this reason one can be content to identify 'wisdom-like elements', by which is meant an element (idea, theme etc.) which is

---

1 The 'proverbial correlative' view is an apt phrase coined by Wills (in *The Jew in the Court*, 32). By it he means that the question of wisdom influence is determined largely by finding or dismissing proverbial sayings 'equivalent' to components of a narrative.

prominent in the canonical wisdom books without necessarily asserting that it has come from a wisdom setting.

Related to these terminological questions is the need to take seriously the narrative form of a text in determining 'wisdom literary influence'. In identifying wisdom elements in a psalm, one can expect distinctive wisdom words and forms to be discovered, since both are poetic texts. However, if one is moving from the (largely) poetic wisdom literature to a *narrative* like the Joseph story, then the nature of the text as narrative prose must be taken seriously. A narrative can promote a wisdom understanding of life by means of a story, or characterisation, or even a recurring motif. It can do so in the absence of distinctive vocabulary or wisdom genres, since these features may legitimately disappear in the process of moving from poetry to prose. This provides a further reason to undertake a literary reading of a narrative as a whole, trying not only to identify any 'wisdom-like elements', but also the key themes and thrust of each part of the story in the light of the whole. Such an approach deals most appropriately with the fact that a text is narrative.

These methodological issues could be tested further by applying them to other narrative texts in order to see if they avoid the impasse that has often confused this area of Old Testament study. Indeed, the question of 'wisdom literary influence' on apocalyptic, prophetic or even hymnic texts may also be aided by clarifying what wisdom characteristics can properly be expected to survive the change in literary genre.

Wisdom and the Interpretation of the Joseph Story

Since the Joseph narrative is one in which 'wisdom-like elements' have been both discerned and denied, a detailed exegetical and literary study of Genesis 37-50 has been undertaken. This study has concluded that the text as a whole is not a 'wisdom narrative', but that many 'wisdom-like elements' have been woven into it. A number of other exegetical conclusions have been reached, some of which have an important bearing on the place that wisdom has in the narrative.

In chapter 37, the dream motif is introduced as a way of outlining the nature of God's overarching purposes, with the dream serving to highlight God's ongoing activity without foregrounding God as a character. It has been argued that the pattern of God's hidden rule - accomplishing his purposes through the rise of Joseph to power - is symbolised by the dream, and looms over the story as a whole. However, Joseph's character is left largely undeveloped in the opening chapter, so that he is portrayed as neither wise nor unwise.

It is then argued that chapter 38 is an integral part of the final form, since it operates as a microcosm of the story as a whole. Tamar, characterised as a 'wise woman', shows discernment and initiative in preserving life and regaining justice in the family. Her shrewd actions thus mirror and anticipate Joseph's in chapters 39-45, and lead to the survival of the covenant line (as do Joseph's in chapters 46-50). The wisdom depiction of Tamar thus offers further confirmatory evidence that this chapter performs important functions in the final form of the narrative.

Chapters 39-41 reveal the first stage of the fulfilment of the dream - the rise to power of Joseph. In these chapters the purposeful but hidden divine activity is matched by Joseph's wise actions. Joseph successfully resists the sexual temptation of the adulteress, and patiently endures the setback caused by the ingratitude of the cupbearer. Significant parallels have been demonstrated between this section and the structure of the book of Proverbs, implying that Joseph's character is being tested, before he is given opportunity to exercise power. In chapter 41, Joseph takes bold initiatives to preserve life when given the opportunity. Joseph is portrayed as one who wisely uses power for the sake of others, which will ultimately include keeping the chosen family of Jacob alive. These are vital aspects of the Joseph narrative which reflect the theological milieu of wisdom.

A further contribution of this study is the argument that chapters 42-45 also portray Joseph's wisdom, but in the area of the family (rather than the court, as in chapters 39-41). Joseph's wisdom is seen in his elaborate ruse which enables past wrongs to be faced and reconciliation achieved. He brings life and restores wholeness to his family, as well as refusing to seek revenge. Chapter 45 makes explicit that this is all part of *God* bringing his purposes about, but the actual means used are the plans and actions of Joseph. In its canonical context, reconciliation in the family will also secure the future of the chosen covenant line. This section is thus not to be viewed as a cruel test, but rather a ruse which brings life and reconciliation and which secures God's covenant purposes. It is Joseph's human wisdom rather than any overt divine activity that leads to the accomplishment of God's overarching plan.

While chapters 46-50 display a few 'wisdom-like elements' (such as 47:13-26; 50:15-21) their major effect is to bring the focus of the reader back to the wider concerns of the book of Genesis, in particular the motif of the covenant promise of descendants. These chapters reveal that the Joseph story is not only a literary unit with its own integrity, but it is also embedded in a broader narrative context.

In the story as a whole, it is argued that Joseph shows public wisdom in the court and private wisdom in his family. Furthermore, it is proposed that the doctrine of divine activity or God's hidden rule in the Joseph story has wisdom features. In particular, the backgrounded nature of divine activity (symbolised by the dream) and the foregrounding of human actions, means that God acts through the agency of Joseph, yet without telling Joseph what to do.

Thus, it is concluded that 'wisdom-like elements' are not only prominent in chapters 39-41, but also in the story as a whole through the actions of Tamar, the themes of reconciliation in the family, and the backgrounded divine activity.

The Intersection of Wisdom and Covenant

The final, synthetic part of this study draws together the earlier observations about the place and importance in the Joseph narrative of both the covenant promise elements and the 'wisdom-like elements' and explores the interaction between them in the final form of the text.

It is noted that the Joseph narrative serves to further the patriarchal promises in several ways. Firstly, it highlights the promise of descendants, so that the events of these chapters enable the chosen line both to survive the threat of famine and to gain stability through reconciliation. Secondly, the promise to be a blessing to the nations is also partially fulfilled through Joseph's collection and distribution of grain, bringing life to Egypt and the surrounding countries. These appear to be God's overarching purposes, and are effected in chapters 37-50. However, the Joseph narrative clearly portrays that God's purposes are brought about not by divine intervention, but rather through the wise human activity of Joseph.

A number of specific conclusions have been made concerning the interaction of wisdom and covenant in the Joseph narrative.

Firstly, it is clear wisdom and covenant concerns can co-exist in the same narrative, even though they are different. The combination of these ideas in the Joseph narrative does not lead to dissonance, for their perspectives are integrated. They are not ideologically incompatible views.

Secondly, it has been argued that both the wisdom and covenant emphases have been synthesised into a broader category encompassing both of these strands. This category can be described as God's 'active rule' or more theologically as God's sovereignty over his world and his people. In many covenant texts, God's rule is achieved either by divine intervention ('the mighty acts of God') or by human beings obediently carrying out God's instructions (for example, Moses, Joshua). God's sovereign ruling over his people and his world, is often promoted by hidden divine activity and evident human responsibility in wisdom literature and in the Joseph narrative. In the Old Testament it appears that the broader, all-encompassing category of God's kingly rule can be accomplished either by humans taking wise initiatives, by human obedience to God's instruction, or by God's direct activity.

Thirdly, some scholars believe that the covenant model of divine and human activity is the only one, and that wisdom has to be assimilated to covenant in order to become part of Old Testament faith. However, once

God's active rule is seen to be the broader category, then both these intertwined strands (and perhaps others) assume their own validity as part of the variegated whole of the Old Testament. There is no inconsistency or contradiction between the two strands, for neither exhaustively explains how God rules his world. Instead, they both contribute to the fuller picture. Hence, the presence of non-wisdom elements in a text does not preclude wisdom influence in a narrative. These are simply to be viewed as different although compatible ways of God exercising his overarching rule.

Fourthly, what the Joseph narrative adds to the Old Testament is its observation that the preservation of God's chosen covenant line of people can be accomplished by ways other than divine intervention or obedience to covenant stipulations or God's revealed words. Joseph's human initiatives, his ability to see what works in life and what will bring success are wisdom-like ideas which become the means God uses to preserve his covenant, and ultimately his kingly rule. Indeed, his actions extend far beyond the covenant people, as he preserves life and thus brings blessing to the 'whole world'.

The theological or ideological compatibility of covenant and wisdom thus becomes patently clear. The way of wisdom is not in conflict with the path of obedience (for the fear of the Lord is the beginning or first principle of wisdom), but is an appropriate option at a time or place when God has not specifically revealed his will. It has value in bringing life to others, and establishing God's kingly rule in everyday life. Wisdom thus has its own goals which are not exhausted by the goals of the covenant stream. Wisdom takes seriously the responsible and ongoing task that God has entrusted to humanity.

Such a view of the place of wisdom in Old Testament theology has enormous ramifications for the way that God's present people live out their daily lives (leaving aside, for the moment, the important but complex question of reading the Old Testament as part of the whole Bible, in the light of Christ). While there are many matters on which God has spoken in scripture, there is ample room as well for wise actions and shrewd discernment about what works and will promote the good. The wisdom books, and wisdom-like themes in non-wisdom books, have much to contribute at this point. Further study is needed to determine whether the concept of God's overarching rule is useful in integrating the perspectives of the other strands of the Old Testament.

How, then, do wisdom and covenant intersect in the Joseph narrative? Joseph's wise actions and initiatives enable and achieve the preservation of God's covenant line, as well as having a wider utility. Rather than the two being in conflict, in the Joseph story a wisdom-like figure, acting wisely, promotes the accomplishment of God's covenant promises, as well as bringing life and success to those who seek wisdom (Prov 2:1-4; 3:1-12). God's kingly rule is seen in both the preservation of his covenant people and in the success that flows from Joseph's tested wisdom.

The narrative artistry of the Joseph story is an appropriate note on which to finish. The very difficulty that source critics have perceived in unsrambling the putative sources in Genesis 37-50 is a powerful testimony to the way in which the author or redactor has understood the unity which lies behind the diverse components. The final form of the Joseph narrative has genuine narrative integrity, regardless of its prehistory. This is far from being a monochrome text, yet the elements of each strand are juxtaposed and interwoven in such a way as to highlight both the unity of the whole, and the distinctive contributions of each part.

The theological synthesis of Joseph story thus celebrates the place of wise personal initiatives that promote the wellbeing of both family and community. Such discerning actions have a genuine place in furthering God's purposes and ultimately can be the means that God uses to extend his active rule as king. In this well-integrated story, there is room both for God to be active behind the scenes and for humans to exercise responsibility in the foreground. Wise and godly human initiatives do not undermine God's sovereign, active rule over his world and his people, but can be the very means that God uses to promote his wisdom and covenant purposes.

Bibliography

Aalders, G.C. *Genesis Volume II*. Bible Student's Commentary. Translated by W. Heynen. Grand Rapids: Zondervan, 1981.

Abrams, M.H. *A Glossary of Literary Terms*. 4th edn. New York: Holt, Rinehart & Winston, 1981.

Ackerman, J.S. 'Joseph, Judah and Jacob'. In *Literary Interpretations of Biblical Narratives II*, Edited by K.R.R. Gros Louis. Nashville: Abingdon, 1982, 85-113.

Adar, Z. *The Book of Genesis: An Introduction to the Biblical World*. Translated by P. Cohen. Jerusalem: Magnes Press, 1990.

Adcock, N. 'Genesis 41:40b'. *ExpTim* 67 (1956): 383.

Ages, A. 'Why Didn't Joseph Call Home?'. *Bible Review* 9 (1993): 42-46.

Alexander, T.D. 'From Adam to Judah: The Significance of the Family Tree in Genesis'. *EvQ* 61 (1989): 5-19.

Aling, C.F. *Egypt and Bible History*. Grand Rapids: Baker, 1981.

Alonso-Schökel, L. 'Sapiential and Covenant Themes in Genesis 2-3'. In *Studies in Ancient Israelite Wisdom*. Library of Biblical Studies. Edited by J.L. Crenshaw. New York: KTAV, 1976, 468-480.

Alter, R. 'Joseph and his Brothers'. *Commentary* 70 (1980): 59-69.

— *The Art of Biblical Narrative*. New York: Basic, 1981.

— *The World of Biblical Literature*. New York: Basic, 1992.

— *Genesis: Translation and Commentary*. New York: W.W. Norton, 1996.

Andersen, T.D. 'Genealogical Prominence and the Structure of Genesis'. In *Biblical Hebrew and Discourse Linguistics*. Edited by R.D. Bergen. Dallas: Summer Institute of Linguistics, 1994, 242-266.

André, G. *Determining the Destiny: PQD in the Old Testament*. CBOTS, 16. Uppsala: CWK Gleerup, 1980.

Andrew, M.E. 'Moving from Death to Life. Verbs of Motion in the Story of Judah and Tamar in Gen 38'. *ZAW* 105 (1993): 262-269.

Argyle, A.W. 'Joseph the Patriarch in Patristic Teaching'. *ExpTim* 67 (1955/56): 199-201.

Ashley, T.R. *The Book of Numbers*. NICOT. Grand Rapids: Eerdmans, 1993.

Astour, M.C. 'Tamar the Hierodule. An Essay in the Method of Vestigial Motifs'. *JBL* 85 (1966): 185-196.

Ausloos, H. 'The Deuteronomist and the Account of Joseph's Death (Gen 50,22-26)'. In *Studies in the Book of Genesis: Literature, Redaction and History*. Edited by A. Wénin. BETL 155. Leuven: Leuven University Press, 2001, 381-395.

Bach, A. 'Breaking Free of the Biblical Frame-Up: Uncovering the Woman in Genesis 39'. In *A Feminist Companion to Genesis*. Feminist Companion to the Bible, 2. Edited by A. Brenner. Sheffield: Sheffield Academic Press, 1993, 318-342.

— *Women, Seduction and Betrayal in Biblical Narrative*. Cambridge: Cambridge University Press, 1997.

Bailey, N.A. 'Some Literary and Grammatical Aspects of Genealogies in Genesis'. In *Biblical Hebrew and Discourse Linguistics*. Edited by R.D. Bergen. Dallas: Summer Institute of Linguistics, 1994, 267-282.

Bal, M. *Lethal Love: Feminist Literary Readings of Biblical Love Stories*. Indiana

Studies in Biblical Literature. Bloomington: Indiana University Press, 1987.

Baldwin, J.G. *The Message of Genesis 12-50: From Abraham to Joseph*. Bible Speaks Today. Leicester: Inter-Varsity Press, 1986.

Bar, S. *A Letter That Has Not Been Read: Dreams in the Hebrew Bible*. Cincinnati: Hebrew Union College Press, 2001.

Barr, J. *Old and New in Interpretation. A Study of the Two Testaments*. 2nd edn. London: SCM, 1982.

— 'Divine Action and Hebrew Wisdom'. In *The Making and Remaking of Christian Doctrine*. Edited by S. Coakley and D.A. Pailin. Oxford: Clarendon, 1993, 1-12.

Becking, B. '"They Hated Him Even More": Literary Technique in Genesis 37.1-11'. *BN* 60 (1991): 40-47.

Beek, M.A. *A Journey Through The Old Testament*. Translated by A.J. Pomerans. London: Hodder & Stoughton, 1959.

Berlin, A. *Poetics and Interpretation of Biblical Narrative*. Bible and Literature Series, 9. Sheffield: Almond Press, 1983.

Berry, D.K. *An Introduction to Wisdom and Poetry of the Old Testament*. Nashville: Broadman & Holman, 1995.

Beuken, W.A.M. 'No Wise King Without a Wise Woman (I Kings III 16-28)'. In *New Avenues in the Study of the Old Testament: A Collection of Old Testament Studies Published on the Occasion of the Fiftieth Anniversary of the Oudtestamentisch Werkgezelschnap and the Retirement of Prof. M.J. Mulder*. OTS, 25. Edited by A.S. van der Woude. Leiden: E.J. Brill, 1989, 1-10.

Birch, B.C. *Let Justice Roll Down: The Old Testament, Ethics and Christian Life*. Louisville: Westminster/John Knox, 1991.

Bird, P. 'The Harlot as Heroine: Narrative Art and Social Presupposition in Three Old Testament Texts'. *Semeia* 46 (1989): 119-139.

Black, A. 'Joseph: an Ethical and Biblical Study'. *The Expositor* 6th Series 1 (1900): 63-78, 111-121, 217-230, 289-308, 444-459.

Blenkinsopp, J. *Wisdom and Law in the Old Testament: The Ordering of Life in Israel and Early Judaism*. Oxford Bible Series. Revised edn. Oxford: Oxford University Press, 1995.

— *The Pentateuch*. ABRL. New York: Doubleday, 1992.

Blum, E. *Die Komposition der Vätergeschichte*. WMANT, 57. Neukirchen-Vluyn: Neukirchener Verlag, 1984.

Blythin, I. 'The Patriarchs and the Promise'. *SJT* 21 (1968): 56-73.

Boecker, H.J. 'Überlegungen zur Josephsgeschichte'. In *Alttestamentlicher Glaube und Biblische Theologie: Festschrift für Horst Dietrich Preuss zum 65. Geburtstag*. Edited by J. Hausmann and H.-J. Zobel. Stuttgart: Kohlhammer, 1992, 35-45.

— 'Überlegungen zur Erzählung von der Versuchung Josephs (Genesis 39)'. In *Altes Testament - Forschung und Wirkung. Festschrift für Henning Graf Reventlow*. Edited by P. Mommer and W. Thiel. Frankfurt am Main: Peter Lang, 1994, 3-13.

de Boer, P.A.H. 'The Counsellor'. In *Wisdom in Israel and in the Ancient Near East*. VTSup, 3. Edited by M. Noth and D.W. Thomas. Leiden: E.J. Brill, 1955, 42-71.

Boice, J.M. *Genesis: An Expositional Commentary Volume 3: Genesis 37:1-50:26*. Grand Rapids: Zondervan, 1987.

Bos, J.W.H. 'Out of the Shadows: Genesis 38; Judges 4:17-22; Ruth 3'. *Semeia* 42 (1988): 37-67.

Boström, L. *The God of the Sages: The Portrayal of God in the Book of Proverbs*.

CBOTS, 29. Stockholm: Almqvist & Wiksell, 1990.

Boyd, W.J.P. 'Notes on the Secondary Meanings of אחר'. *JTS* New Series 12 (1961): 54-56.

Brenner, A. *The Israelite Woman: Social Role and Literary Type in Biblical Narrative.* Biblical Seminar Series. Sheffield: JSOT Press, 1985.

— 'Some Observations on the Figurations of Woman in Wisdom Literature'. In *Of Prophets' Visions and the Wisdom of Sages.* JSOTSup, 162. Edited by H.A. McKay and D.J.A. Clines. Sheffield: JSOT Press, 1993, 192-208.

Brisman, L. *The Voice of Jacob.* Bloomington: Indiana University Press, 1990.

Brongers, H.A. 'La Crainte du Seigneur (*Jirʾat Jhwh, Jirʾat ʾElohim*)'. *OTS* 5 (1948): 151-173.

— 'The Literature of the Old Testament'. In *The World of the Old Testament.* Translated by S. Woudstra. Edited by A.S. van der Woude. Grand Rapids: Eerdmans, 1989, 98-164.

Brown, F., S.R. Driver and C.A. Briggs. *A Hebrew and English Lexicon of the Old Testament.* Oxford: Clarendon, 1906.

Brueggemann, W. 'David and his Theologian'. *CBQ* 30 (1968): 156-181.

— 'Scripture and an Ecumenical Life-Style: A Study in Wisdom Theology'. *Int* 24 (1970): 3-19.

— *In Man We Trust: The Neglected Side of Biblical Faith.* Atlanta: John Knox, 1972.

— *Genesis.* Interpretation. Atlanta: John Knox, 1982.

— 'Genesis L 15-21: A Theological Exploration'. In *Congress Volume Salamanca.* VTSup, 36. Edited by J.A. Emerton. Leiden: E.J. Brill, 1985, 40-53.

— 'The Social Significance of Solomon as a Patron of Wisdom'. In *The Sage in Israel and the Ancient Near East.* Edited by J.G. Gammie and L.G. Perdue. Winona Lake: Eisenbrauns, 1990, 117-132.

— *Theology of the Old Testament: Testimony, Dispute, Advocacy.* Minneapolis: Fortress, 1997.

Bush, G. *Notes on Genesis.* 2 vols. New York: Ivison, Phinney & Co, 1860.

Caine, I. 'Numbers in the Joseph Narrative'. *Jewish Civilization: Essays and Studies* 1 (1979): 3-17.

Calvin, J. *A Commentary on Genesis.* Translated and edited by J. King. London: Banner of Truth, 1965, reprint of 1847 translation, originally in Latin 1554.

Camp, C.V. 'The Wise Women of 2 Samuel: A Role Model for Women in Early Israel'. *CBQ* 43 (1981): 14-29.

— *Wisdom and the Feminine in the Book of Proverbs.* Bible and Literature Series, 11. Sheffield: Almond Press, 1985.

— 'The Female Sage in Ancient Israel and in the Biblical Wisdom Literature'. In *The Sage in Israel and the Ancient Near East.* Edited by J.G. Gammie and L.G. Perdue. Winona Lake: Eisenbrauns, 1990, 185-203.

Campbell A.F. and M.A. O'Brien. *Sources of the Pentateuch.* Minneapolis: Fortress, 1993.

Candlish, R.S. *The Book of Genesis Expounded in a Series of Discourses.* 2 vols. Edinburgh: Adam and Charles Black, 1868.

Caquot, A. 'Les songes et leur interprétation selon Canaan et Israel'. In *Les songes et leur interprétation.* Sources Orientales, 2. Edited by A.-M. Esnoul, P. Garelli, Y. Hervouet, M. Leibovici, S. Sauneron and J. Yoyotte. Paris: Éditions du Seuil, 1959, 99-124.

— "Siméon et Lévi sont frères' (Gn 49,5)'. In *De la Tôrah au Messie*. Edited by M. Carrez, J. Doré and P. Grelot. Paris: Desclée, 1981, 113-119.

Carmichael, C.M. 'Some Sayings in Genesis 49'. *JBL* 88 (1969): 435-444.

— *Women, Law and the Genesis Traditions*. Edinburgh: Edinburgh University Press, 1979.

Carr, D.M. *Reading the Fractures of Genesis: Historical and Literary Approaches*. Louisville: Westminster John Knox Press, 1996.

— 'Βίβλος γενέσεως Revisited: A Synchronic Analysis of Patterns in Genesis as Part of the Torah (Part Two)'. *ZAW* 110 (1998): 327-347.

Cassuto, U. 'The Story of Judah and Tamar'. In *Biblical and Oriental Studies*. Translated by I. Abrahams. Jerusalem: Magnes, 1973, 29-40.

Childs, B.S. *Introduction to the Old Testament as Scripture*. London: SCM, 1979.

Christensen, D.L. 'Biblical Genealogies and Eschatological Speculation'. *Perspectives in Religious Studies* 14 (1987): 59-65.

Clements, R.E. 'Wisdom and Old Testament Theology'. In *Wisdom in ancient Israel: Essays in honour of J.A. Emerton*. Edited by J. Day, R.P. Gordon and H.G.M. Williamson. Cambridge: Cambridge University Press, 1995, 269-286.

Clines, D.J.A. *The Theme of the Pentateuch*. JSOTSup, 10. Sheffield: JSOT Press, 1978. 2nd edn. Sheffield Academic Press, 1997.

—'Images of Yahweh: God in the Pentateuch'. In *Studies in Old Testament Theology*. Edited by R.L. Hubbard, R.K. Johnston and R.P. Meye. Dallas: Word, 1992, 78-98.

—(ed.) *The Dictionary of Classical Hebrew Volume I*. Sheffield: Sheffield Academic Press, 1993.

—(ed.) *The Dictionary of Classical Hebrew Volume II*. Sheffield: Sheffield Academic Press, 1995.

— 'God in the Pentateuch: Reading against the Grain'. In *Interested Parties: The Ideology of Writers and Readers of the Hebrew Bible*. JSOTSup, 205. Gender, Culture, Theory, 1. Sheffield: Sheffield Academic Press, 1995, 187-211.

Clines D.J.A. and J.C. Exum. 'The New Literary Criticism'. In *The New Literary Criticism and the Hebrew Bible*. JSOTSup, 143. Sheffield: Sheffield Academic Press, 1993, 11-25.

Coats, G.W. 'Widow's Rights: A Crux in the Plot of Genesis 38'. *CBQ* 34 (1972): 461-466.

— 'The Joseph Story and Wisdom: a Reappraisal'. *CBQ* 35 (1973): 285-297.

— 'Redactional Unity in Genesis 37-50'. *JBL* 93 (1974): 15-21.

— *From Canaan to Egypt: Structural and Theological Context for the Joseph Story*. CBQMS, 4. Washington: Catholic Biblical Association, 1976.

— *Genesis, With an Introduction to Narrative Literature*. FOTL, 1. Grand Rapids: Eerdmans, 1983.

— 'Joseph, Son of Jacob'. In *The Anchor Bible Dictionary*. 6 vols. Edited by D.N. Freedman. New York: Doubleday, 1992, 3: 976-981.

Cohen, J.M. 'An Unrecognized Connotation of NŚQ PEH with Special Reference to Three Biblical Occurrences'. *VT* 32 (1982): 416-424.

Cohn, R.L. 'Narrative Structure and Canonical Perspective in Genesis'. *JSOT* 25 (1983): 3-16.

Coote, R.B. and D.R. Ord, *The Bible's First History*. Philadelphia: Fortress, 1989.

Coppens, J. 'La Bénédiction de Jacob: Son cadre historique à la lumière des parallèles ougaritiques'. In *Volume du Congrès: Strasbourg 1956*. VTSup, 4. Edited by G.W.

Anderson. Leiden: E.J. Brill, 1957, 97-115.

Crenshaw, J.L. 'Method in Determining Wisdom Influence Upon 'Historical' Literature'. *JBL* 88 (1969): 129-142.

— 'Prolegomenon'. In *Studies in Ancient Israelite Wisdom*. Library of Biblical Studies. Edited by J.L. Crenshaw. New York: KTAV, 1976, 1-60.

— 'Wisdom and Authority: Sapiential Rhetoric and its Warrants'. In *Congress Volume, Vienna 1980*. VTSup, 32. Edited by J.A. Emerton. Leiden: E.J. Brill, 1981, 10-29.

— 'Education in Ancient Israel'. *JBL* 104 (1985): 601-615.

— 'Wisdom Literature: Retrospect and Prospect'. In *Of Prophets' Visions and the Wisdom of Sages*. JSOTSup, 162. Edited by H.A. McKay and D.J.A. Clines. Sheffield: Sheffield Academic Press, 1993, 161-178.

Croatto, J.S. ''Abrek ,, Intendant" dans Gén.XLI, 41, 43'. *VT* 16 (1966): 113-115.

Culbertson, P. 'Blessing Jacob's Sons, Inheriting Family Myths'. *Sewanee Theological Review* 37 (1993): 52-76.

Culley, R.C. 'Stories of the Conquest: Joshua 2, 6, 7 and 8'. *HAR* 8 (1984): 25-44.

— *Themes and Variations: A Study of Action in Biblical Narrative*. SBLSS. Atlanta: Scholars, 1992.

Curtis, E.M. 'Old Testament Wisdom: A Model for Faith-Learning Integration'. *Christian Scholar's Review* 15 (1986): 213-227.

Dahlberg, B.T. 'On Recognizing the Unity of Genesis'. *Theology Digest* 24 (1976): 360-367.

— 'The Unity of Genesis'. In *Literary Interpretations of Biblical Narratives II*. Edited by K.R.R. Gros Louis. Nashville: Abingdon, 1982, 126-133.

Davidson, R. *Genesis 12-50*. Cambridge Bible Commentary. Cambridge: Cambridge University Press, 1979.

Demsky, A. 'The route of Jacob's funeral cortege and the problem of '*Eber Hayyarden* (Genesis 50.10-11)'. In *Minḥah le-Naḥum: Biblical and Other Studies Presented to Nahum M. Sarna in Honour of his 70th Birthday*. JSOTSup, 154. Edited by M. Brettler and M. Fishbane. Sheffield: Sheffield Academic Press, 1993, 54-64.

Dietrich, W. *Die Josephserzählung als Novelle und Geschichtsschreibung: Zugleich ein Beitrag zur Pentateuchfrage*. Biblisch-Theologische Studien, 14. Neukirchen-Vluyn: Neukirchener Verlag, 1989.

van Dijk-Hemmes, F. 'Tamar and the limits of patriarchy: Between Rape and Seduction'. In *Anti-Covenant: Counter-Reading Women's Lives in the Hebrew Bible*. JSOTSup, 81. Edited by M. Bal. Sheffield: Almond Press, 1989, 135-156.

Dillmann, A. *Genesis Critically and Exegetically Expounded*. Translated by W.B. Stevenson. Vol. 2. Edinburgh: T & T Clark, 1897.

Dods, M. *The Book of Genesis*. The Expositor's Bible. London: Hodder & Stoughton, 1896.

Donaldson, L.E. 'Cyborgs, Ciphers, and Sexuality: Re-Theorizing Literary and Biblical Character'. *Semeia* 63 (1993): 81-96.

Donner, H. *Die literarische Gestalt der alttestamentlichen Josephsgeschichte*. Heidelberg: Carl Winter, 1976.

Driver, S.R. *The Book of Genesis*. Westminster Commentaries. 12th edn. London: Metheun, 1926.

Dumbrell, W.J. *Covenant and Creation: An Old Testament Covenantal Theology*. Exeter: Paternoster, 1984.

Ehrlich, E.L. *Der Traum im Alten Testament*. BZAW, 73. Berlin: Töpelmann, 1953.

Eichrodt, W. *Theology of the Old Testament*. Vol. 2. Translated by J.A. Baker. London: SCM, 1967.

Emerton, J.A. 'Some Problems in Genesis XXXVIII'. *VT* 25 (1975): 338-361.

— 'An Examination of a Recent Structuralist Interpretation of Genesis XXXVIII'. *VT* 26 (1976): 79-98.

— 'Judah and Tamar'. *VT* 29 (1979): 403-415.

Endo, Y. *The Verbal System of Classical Hebrew in the Joseph Story: An Approach from Discourse Analysis*. Studia Semitica Neerlandica, 32. Assen: van Gorcum, 1996.

Fabry, H.-J. דִּבָּה *dibbāh;* זְבוּב *zᵉbhūbh'*. In *Theological Dictionary of the Old Testament*. Translated by J.T. Willis, G.W. Bromiley and D.E. Green. Edited by G.J. Botterweck and H. Ringgren. Grand Rapids: Eerdmans, 1978, 3:72-79.

Fischer, G. 'Die Josefsgeschichte als Modell für Versöhnung'. In *Studies in the Book of Genesis: Literature, Redaction and History*. Edited by A. Wénin. BETL 155. Leuven: Leuven University Press, 2001, 243-271.

Flanders, H.J., R.W. Crapps and D.A. Smith. *People of the Covenant*. 3rd edn. New York: Oxford University Press, 1988.

Fontaine, C.R. 'A Response to 'The Bearing of Wisdom''. In *A Feminist Companion to Samuel and Kings*. Feminist Companion to the Bible, 5. Edited by A. Brenner. Sheffield: Sheffield Academic Press, 1994, 161-167.

Fox, E. 'Can Genesis be Read as a Book?'. *Semeia* 46 (1989): 31-40.

Fox, M.V. 'Wisdom in the Joseph Story'. *VT* 51 (2001): 26-41.

Freedman, D.N. 'Who is like thee among the gods: the religion of early Israel'. In *Ancient Israelite Religion: Essays in Honor of Frank Moore Cross*. Edited by P.D. Miller, P.D. Hanson and S.D. McBride. Philadelphia: Fortress, 1987, 315-335.

Fretheim, T.E. 'The Book of Genesis'. In *The New Interpreter's Bible*. Vol. 1. Nashville: Abingdon, 1994, 319-677.

— *The Pentateuch*. Interpreting Biblical Texts. Nashville: Abingdon, 1996.

— 'שׂכל'. In *New International Dictionary of Old Testament Theology and Exegesis*. 5 vols. Edited by W.A. VanGemeren. Grand Rapids: Zondervan, 1997, 3:1243.

Friedman, R.E. 'Deception for Deception'. *Bible Review* 2 (1986): 22-31, 68.

Fritsch, C.T. '"God Was With Him": A Theological Study of the Joseph Narrative'. *Int* 9 (1955): 21-34.

Frost, S.B. *Patriarchs and Prophets*. London: John Murray, 1963.

Frymer-Kensky, T. 'The Sage in the Pentateuch: Soundings'. In *The Sage in Israel and the Ancient Near East*. Edited by J.G. Gammie and L.G. Perdue. Winona Lake: Eisenbrauns, 1990, 275-287.

Fung, Y.-W. *Victim and Victimizer: Joseph's Interpretation of his Destiny*. JSOTSup, 308. Sheffield: Sheffield Academic Press, 2000.

Furman, N. 'His Story Versus Her Story: Male Genealogy and Female Strategy in the Jacob Cycle'. *Semeia* 46 (1989): 141-149.

Gammie, J.G. 'Theological Interpretation By Way of Literary and Tradition Analysis: Genesis 25-36'. In *Encounter with the Text: Form and History in the Hebrew Bible*. Edited by M.J. Buss. Philadelphia: Fortress, 1979, 117-134.

— 'From Prudentialism to Apocalypticism. The Houses of the Sages Amid the Varying Forms of Wisdom'. In *The Sage in Israel and the Ancient Near East*. Edited by J.G. Gammie and L.G. Perdue. Winona Lake: Eisenbrauns, 1990, 479-497.

Gan, M. 'The Book of Esther in the Light of the Story of Joseph in Egypt'. *Tarbiz* 31

(1961): 144-149; English summary I-II.

Garrett, D. *Rethinking Genesis*. Grand Rapids: Baker, 1991.

Gemser, B. 'Be῾ēber haǰǰardēn: in Jordan's Borderland'. *VT* 2 (1952): 349-355.

Gevirtz, S. 'Simeon and Levi in 'The Blessing of Jacob' (Gen 49:5-7)'. *HUCA* 52 (1981): 93-128.

Gibson, J.C.L. *Genesis*. Daily Study Bible. Vol. 2. Edinburgh: Saint Andrew Press, 1982.

— *Davidson's Introductory Hebrew Grammar - Syntax*. 4th edn. Edinburgh: T&T Clark, 1994.

Gispen, W.H. 'What is Wisdom in the Old Testament?'. In *Travels in the World of the Old Testament*. Edited by M.S.H.G.H. van Vos, P.H.J.H. ten Gate and N.A. van Vehelen. Assen: van Gorcum, 1974, 75-79.

Gnuse, R.K. *The Dream Theophany of Samuel*. Lanham: University Press of America, 1984.

— 'The Jewish Dream Interpreter in a Foreign Court: The Recurring Use of a Theme in Jewish Literature'. *JSP* 7 (1990): 29-53.

— *Dreams and Dream Reports in the Writings of Josephus: A Traditio-Historical Analysis*. Arbeiten zur Geschichte des antiken Judentums und des Urchristentums, 36. Leiden: E.J. Brill, 1996.

Goldin, J. 'The Youngest Son or Where Does Genesis 38 Belong?'. *JBL* 96 (1977): 27-44.

Goldingay, J. 'The Patriarchs in Scripture and History'. In *Essays on the Patriarchal Narratives*. Edited by A.R. Millard and D.J. Wiseman. Leicester: Inter-Varsity Press, 1980, 11-42.

— *Theological Diversity and the Authority of the Old Testament*. Grand Rapids: Eerdmans, 1987.

Goldman, S. *The Wiles of Women/The Wiles of Men: Joseph and Potiphar's Wife in Ancient Near Eastern, Jewish, and Islamic Folklore*. Albany: State University of New York Press, 1995.

Goldsworthy, G.L. 'Empirical Wisdom in Relation to Salvation-History in the Psalms'. Dissertation, ThD, Union Theological Seminary, Richmond, Virginia, 1973.

— *Gospel and Wisdom: Israel's Wisdom Literature in the Christian Life*. Exeter: Paternoster, 1987.

Good, E.M. 'The 'Blessing' on Judah, Gen. 49:8-12'. *JBL* 82 (1963): 427-432.

— *Irony in the Old Testament*. Bible and Literature Series, 3. 2nd edn. Sheffield: Almond Press, 1981.

Gordon, R.P. 'A house divided: wisdom in Old Testament narrative traditions'. In *Wisdom in ancient Israel: Essays in honour of J.A. Emerton*. Edited by J. Day, R.P. Gordon and H.G.M. Williamson. Cambridge: Cambridge University Press, 1995, 94-105.

Görg, M. 'Potifar und Potifera'. *BN* 85 (1996): 8-10.

Gottlieb, I.B. '*Sof Davar*: Biblical Endings'. *Prooftexts* 11 (1991): 213-224.

Green, B. *"What Profit for Us?" Remembering the Story of Joseph*. Lanham: University Press of America, 1996.

— The Determination of Pharaoh: His Characterization in the Joseph Story (Genesis 37-50)'. In *The World of Genesis: Persons, Places, Perspectives*. JSOTSup, 257. Edited by P.R. Davies and D.J.A. Clines. Sheffield: Sheffield Academic Press, 1998, 150-171.

Greenstein, E.L. 'An Equivocal Reading of the Sale of Joseph'. In *Literary Interpretations of Biblical Narratives II*. Edited by K.R.R. Gros Louis. Nashville: Abingdon, 1982, 114-125.

Gunkel, H. *The Legends of Genesis: The Biblical Saga and History*. Translated by W.H. Carruth. New York: Schocken, 1964.

— *Genesis*. Mercer Library of Biblical Studies. Translated by M.E. Biddle. Macon: Mercer University Press, 1997.

Gunn, D. *The Story of King David: Genre and Interpretation*. JSOTSup, 6. Sheffield: JSOT Press, 1978.

— *The Fate of King Saul: An Interpretation of a Biblical Story*. JSOTSup, 14. Sheffield: JSOT Press, 1980.

Hallo, W.W. 'The First Purim'. *BA* 46 (1983): 19-26.

Hamilton, V.P. *Handbook on the Pentateuch*. Grand Rapids: Baker, 1982.

— *The Book of Genesis Chapters 18-50*. NICOT. Grand Rapids: Eerdmans, 1995.

Harris, S.L. *Proverbs 1-9: A Study of Inner-Biblical Interpretation*. SBLDS, 150. Atlanta: Scholars, 1995.

Hartley, J.E. *Genesis*. NIBC. Peabody: Hendrickson/Carlisle: Paternoster, 2000.

Hasel, G.F. *The Remnant: The History and Theology of the Remnant Idea from Genesis to Isaiah*. 3rd edn. Berrien Springs: Andrews University Press, 1980.

Heaton, E.W. 'The Joseph Saga'. *ExpTim* 59 (1947-8): 134-136.

— *The Hebrew Kingdoms*. New Clarendon Bible: Old Testament, 3. Oxford: Oxford University Press, 1968.

— *Solomon's New Men*. London: Thames and Hudson, 1974.

Heck, J.D. 'A History of Interpretation of Genesis 49 and Deuteronomy 33'. *BSac* 147 (1990): 16-31.

van Heerden, W. 'A bright spark is not necessarily a wise person. Old Testament and contemporary perspectives on wisdom and intelligence'. *Old Testament Essays* 9 (1996): 512-526.

Hempel, J. *Geschichten und Geschichte im Alten Testament bis zur persischen Zeit*. Güttersloh: Gerd Mohn, 1964.

Hendel, R.S. *The Epic of the Patriarch: The Jacob Cycle and the Narrative Traditions of Canaan and Israel*. HSM, 42. Atlanta: Scholars, 1987.

Hengstenberg, E.W. *History of the Kingdom of God Under the Old Testament*. 2 vols. Cherry Hill: Mack, 1972.

Herbert, A.S. *Genesis 12-50*. Torch Bible Commentaries. London: SCM, 1962.

Hess, R.S. 'The Genealogies of Genesis 1-11 and Comparative Literature'. *Bib* 70 (1989): 241-254.

Hettema, T.L. *Reading for Good: Narrative Theology and Ethics in the Joseph Story from the Perspective of Ricoeur's Hermeneutics*. Studies in Philosophical Theology, 18. Kampen: Kok Pharos, 1996.

Hirth, V. 'Jakobs Segen über Ephraim und Manasse (Gen. 48,15f.) als Beispiel frühisraelitischer familiärer Frömmigkeit'. *BN* 86 (1997): 44-48.

Hoftijzer, J. *Die Verheissungen an die drei Erzväter*. Leiden: E.J. Brill, 1956.

Hollander, H.W. *Joseph as an Ethical Model in the Testaments of the Twelve Patriarchs*. SVTP, 6. Leiden: E.J. Brill, 1981.

— 'The Ethical Character of the Patriarch Joseph'. In *Studies on the Testament of Joseph*. Edited by G.W.E. Nickelsburg. Missoula: Scholars, 1975, 47-104.

Hollis, S.T. 'The Woman in Ancient Examples of the Potiphar's Wife Motif, K 2111'.

In *Gender and Difference in Ancient Israel*. Edited by P.L. Day. Minneapolis: Fortress, 1989, 28-42.

Honeyman, A.M. 'The Occasion of Joseph's Temptation', *VT* 2 (1952): 85-87.

Hopkins, D.C. *The Highlands of Canaan*. Social World of Biblical Antiquity, 3. Sheffield: Almond Press, 1985.

Hubbard, D.A. 'The Wisdom Movement and Israel's Covenant Faith'. *TynBul* 17 (1966): 3-33.

Humphreys, C.J. and R.S. White, 'The Eruption of Santorini and the Date and Historicity of Joseph'. *Science & Christian Belief* 7 (1995): 151-162.

Humphreys, W.L. 'The Motif of the Wise Courtier in the Old Testament'. Dissertation, PhD, Union Theological Seminary, New York, 1970.

— 'A Life-Style for Diaspora: A Study in the Tales of Esther and Daniel'. *JBL* 92 (1973): 211-223.

— 'Joseph Story, The'. In *Interpreter's Dictionary of the Bible, Supplementary Volume*. Nashville: Abingdon, 1976, 491-493.

— *Crisis and Story: Introduction to the Old Testament*. Palo Alto: Mayfield, 1979.

— *Joseph and His Family: A Literary Study*. Studies on Personalities of the Old Testament. Columbia: University of South Carolina Press, 1988.

Hurowitz, V.A. 'Joseph's Enslavement of the Egyptians (Genesis 47:13-26) in the Light of Famine Texts from Mesopotamia'. *RB* 101 (1994): 355-362.

Husser, J.-M. *Le songe et la parole: Etude sur le rêve et sa fonction dans l'ancien Israël*. BZAW 210. Berlin: Walter de Gruyter, 1994.

Jackson, B.S. 'Practical Wisdom and Literary Artifice in the Covenant Code'. In *The Jerusalem 1990 Conference Volume*. Jewish Law Association Studies, 6. Edited by B.S. Jackson and S.M. Passamaneck. Atlanta: Scholars, 1992, 65-92.

Jacob, B. *The First Book of the Bible Genesis*. Edited by E.I. Jacob and W. Jacob. New York: KTAV, 1974.

Jacobson, H. 'A Legal Note on Potiphar's Wife'. *HTR* 69 (1976): 177.

Jagersma, H. *A History of Israel in the Old Testament Period*. Translated by J. Bowden. Philadelphia, Fortress, 1982.

Jamieson-Drake, D.W. *Scribes and Schools in Monarchic Judah*. JSOTSup, 109. Sheffield: Almond Press, 1991.

Janssen, J.M.A. 'Egyptological Remarks on the Story of Joseph in Genesis'. *Jaarbericht van het Voorzatiatisch-Egyptische Genootschap: Ex Oriente Lux* 14 (1956): 63-72.

Janzen, J.G. *Abraham and All the Families of the Earth: A Commentary on the Book of Genesis 12-50*. International Theological Commentary. Grand Rapids: Eerdmans, 1993.

Jeansonne, S.P. *The Women of Genesis*. Minneapolis: Fortress, 1990.

Jeffers, A. 'Divination by Dreams in Ugaritic Literature and in the Old Testament', *Irish Biblical Studies* 12 (1990): 167-183.

Jenks, A.W. *The Elohist and North Israelite Traditions*. SBLMS, 22. Missoula: Scholars, 1977.

Johnson, M.D. *The Purpose of the Biblical Genealogies With Special Reference to the Setting of the Genealogies of Jesus*. SNTSMS, 8. Cambridge: Cambridge University Press, 1969.

Kautzsch, E. *Gesenius' Hebrew Grammar*. Revised and translated by A.E. Cowley. Oxford: Clarendon, 1910.

Kebekus, N. *Die Joseferzählung: Literarkritische und redaktionsgeschichtliche*

Untersuchungen zu Genesis 37-50. Münster: Waxmann, 1990.

Keil C.F. and F. Delitzsch, *Biblical Commentary on the Old Testament, Volume 1: The Pentateuch.* Translated by J. Martin. Grand Rapids: Eerdmans, 1951.

Kendall, R.T. *God meant it for good.* Wheaton: Tyndale House, 1986.

Kidner, D. *Proverbs.* TOTC. London: Inter-Varsity Press, 1964.

— *Genesis.* TOTC. London: Tyndale, 1967.

King, J.R. 'The Joseph Story and Divine Politics: A Comparative Study of a Biographic Formula from the Ancient Near East'. *JBL* 106 (1987): 577-594.

Kitchen, K.A. 'The Term *Nsq* in Genesis XLI, 40'. *ExpTim* 69 (1957): 30.

— 'Review. Joseph en Égypte: Genèse chap. 37-50 à la lumière des études égyptologiques récentes by J. Vergote'. *JEA* 47 (1961): 158-164.

— *Ancient Orient and Old Testament.* London: Tyndale, 1966.

— 'Joseph'. In *Illustrated Bible Dictionary.* 3 vols. Edited by J.D. Douglas and N. Hillyer. Leicester: Intervarsity Press, 1980, 2:812-815.

— 'Joseph'. In *The International Standard Bible Encyclopedia.* 4 vols. Edited by G.W. Bromiley. Grand Rapids: Eerdmans, 1982, 2:1126-1130.

Klein, L.R. *The Triumph of Irony in the Book of Judges.* Bible and Literature Series, 14. Sheffield: Almond Press, 1989.

Knauf, E.A. 'Midianites and Ishmaelites'. In *Midian, Moab and Edom: The History and Archaeology of Late Bronze and Iron Age Jordan and North-West Arabia.* JSOTSup, 24. Edited by J.F.A. Sawyer and D.J.A. Clines. Sheffield: JSOT Press, 1983, 147-162.

Knipping, B.R. 'Textwahrnehmung 'häppchenweise': Bemerkungen zu H. Schweizers 'Die Josefsgeschichte' und zu seiner Literarkritik'. *BN* 62 (1992): 61-95.

Koenen, K. 'Zur Bedeutung von Gen 37,15-17 im Kontext der Josephs-Erzählung und von B 21-29 in dem der ägyptischen Sinuhe-Erzählung'. *BN* 86 (1997): 51-56.

Kornfeld, W. 'L'Adultère dans l'Orient antique'. *RB* 57 (1950): 92-109.

Kriel, J.R. 'Esther: The story of a girl or the story of her God?'. *Theologia Evangelica* 19 (1986): 2-14.

Krüger, T. 'Genesis 38 - ein "Lehrstück" alttestamentlicher Ethik'. In *Konsequente Traditionsgeschichte. Festschrift für Klaus Baltzer zum 65. Geburtstag.* OBO, 126. Edited by R. Bartelmus, T. Krüger and H. Utzschneider. Freiburg: Universitätsverlag Freiburg, 1993, 205-226.

Kselman, J.S. 'Genesis'. In *Harper's Bible Commentary.* Edited by J.L. Mays. San Francisco: Harper & Row, 1988, 85-128.

— 'The Book of Genesis: A Decade of Scholarly Research'. *Int* 45 (1991): 380-392.

Kugel, J.L. 'The Case Against Joseph'. In *Lingering over Words: Studies in Ancient Near Eastern Literature in Honor of William L. Moran.* Harvard Semitic Studies, 37. Edited by T. Abusch, J. Huchnergard and P. Steinkeller. Atlanta: Scholars, 1990, 271-287.

— 'Introduction to the Psalms and Wisdom'. In *Harper's Bible Commentary.* Edited by J.L. Mays. San Francisco: Harper & Row, 1988, 396-406.

— *In Potiphar's House.* San Francisco: Harper, 1990.

— 'Wisdom and the Anthological Temper'. *Prooftexts* 17 (1997): 9-32.

LaCocque, A. 'An Ancestral Narrative: The Joseph Story'. In *Thinking Biblically: Exegetical and Hermeneutical Studies.* Edited by A. LaCocque and P. Ricoeur. Translated by D. Pellauer. Chicago: University of Chicago Press, 1998, 365-397.

Lambe, A.J. 'Genesis 38: Structure and Literary Design'. In *The World of Genesis:*

Persons, Places, Perspectives. JSOTSup, 257. Edited by P.R. Davies and D.J.A. Clines. Sheffield: Sheffield Academic Press, 1998, 150-171.

Lange, J.P. *A Commentary on the Holy Scriptures: Genesis*. Translated by T. Lewis and A. Gosman. Edinburgh: T & T Clark, 1868.

Lawson, G. *Lectures on the History of Joseph*. London: Banner of Truth, 1972, originally 1807.

Layton, S.C. 'The Steward in Ancient Israel: A Study of Hebrew (ʾăšer) ʿal-habbayit in its Near Eastern Setting'. *JBL* 109 (1990): 633-649.

Lebram, J.C.H. 'Nachbiblische Weisheitstraditionen'. *VT* 15 (1965): 167-237.

Lee, S. *Creation and Redemption in Isaiah 40-55*. Jian Dao Dissertation Series, 2. Hong Kong: Alliance Biblical Seminary, 1995.

van Leeuwen, R.C. *Context and Meaning in Proverbs 25-27*. SBLDS, 96. Atlanta: Scholars, 1988.

Leibowitz, N. *Studies in Bereshit (Genesis)*. Translated by A. Newman. Jerusalem: World Zionist Organization, 1976.

Lemaire, A. *Les Écoles et la formation de la Bible dans l'ancien Israël*. OBO, 39. Fribourg: Éditions Universitaires, 1981.

— 'Sagesse et écoles'. *VT* 34 (1984): 270-281.

— 'The Sage in School and Temple'. In *The Sage in Israel and the Ancient Near East*. Edited by J.G. Gammie and L.G. Perdue. Winona Lake: Eisenbrauns, 1990, 165-181.

Leupold, H.C. *Exposition of Genesis*. Vol. 2. Grand Rapids: Baker, 1953.

Lévêque, J. 'Le contrepoint théologique apporté par la réflexion sapientielle'. In *Questions disputées d'Ancien Testament*. BETL, 33. Edited by C. Brekelmans. Leuven: Leuven University Press, 1974, 183-202.

Licht, J. *Storytelling in the Bible*. Jerusalem: Magnes, 1978.

Lichtenstein, M.H. 'Idiom, Rhetoric and the Text of Genesis 41: 16'. *The Journal of the Ancient Near Eastern Society* 19 (1989): 85-94.

Loader, J.A. 'Chokma - Joseph - Hybris'. In *Studies in the Pentateuch*. Ou Testamentiese Werkgemeenskap in Suid-Afrika, 17 & 18: Old Testament Essays. Edited by W.C. van Wyk. Pretoria: Ou Testamentiese Werkgemeenskap in Suid-Afrika, 1974/75, 21-31.

— 'Jedidah or: Amadeus. Thoughts on the Succession Narrative and Wisdom'. In *Studies in the Succession Narrative*. Ou Testamentiese Werkgemeenskap in Suid-Afrika, 27 & 28: Old Testament Essays. Edited by W.C. van Wyk. Pretoria: Ou Testamentiese Werkgemeenskap in Suid-Afrika, 1986, 167-201.

Lockwood, P.F. 'Tamar's Place in the Joseph Cycle'. *Lutheran Theological Journal* 26 (1992): 35-43.

Lohfink, N. 'Die Ursünden in der priesterlichen Geschichtserzählung'. In *Die Zeit Jesu*. Festscrift H. Schlier. Edited by G. Bornkamm and K. Rahner. Freiburg: Herder, 1970, 38-57.

Longacre, R.E. 'Who Sold Joseph into Egypt?'. In *Interpretation and History: Essays in Honour of Allan A. Macrae*. Edited by R. Laird Harris, S.-H. Quek, and J.R. Vannoy. Singapore: Christian Life, 1986, 75-92.

— *Joseph: A Story of Divine Providence: A Text Theoretical and Textlinguistic Analysis of Genesis 37 and 39-48*. Winona Lake: Eisenbrauns, 1989.

Longman, T. *Literary Approaches to Biblical Interpretation*. Foundations of Contemporary Interpretation, 3. Grand Rapids: Academie, 1987.

Lowenthal, E.I. *The Joseph Narrative in Genesis*. New York: KTAV, 1973.

McComiskey, T.E. *The Covenants of Promise. A Theology of the Old Testament Covenants*. Leicester: Inter-Varsity Press, 1985.

McCurley, F.R. *Genesis, Exodus, Leviticus, Numbers*. Proclamation Commentaries. Philadelphia: Fortress, 1979.

McGuire, E.M. 'The Joseph Story: A Tale of Son and Father'. In *Images of Man and God: Old Testament Short Stories in Literary Focus*. Bible and Literature Series. 1. Edited by B.O. Long. Sheffield: Almond Press, 1981, 9-25.

McKay, H.A. 'Confronting Redundancy as Middle Manager and Wife: The Feisty Woman of Genesis 39'. *Semeia* 87 (1999): 219-231.

McKenzie, B.A. 'Jacob's Blessing on Pharaoh: An Interpretation of Gen 46:31-47:26'. *WTJ* 45 (1983): 386-399.

Magness, J.L. *Sense and Absence*. Atlanta: Scholars, 1986.

Maher, M. *Genesis*. Old Testament Message, 2. Wilmington: Glazier, 1982.

Mann, T.W. *Divine Presence and Guidance in Israelite Traditions: The Typology of Exaltation*. John Hopkins Near Eastern Studies. Baltimore: John Hopkins, 1977.

— '"All the Families of the Earth". The Theological Unity of Genesis'. *Int* 45 (1991): 341-353.

— *The Book of the Torah*. Atlanta: John Knox, 1988.

Marcus, D. '"Lifting up the Head': On the Trail of a Word Play in Genesis 40'. *Prooftexts* 10 (1990): 17-27.

Marshall, I.H. 'Climbing Ropes, Ellipses and Symphonies: the Relation between Biblical and Systematic Theology'. In *A Pathway into the Holy Scripture*. Edited by P.E. Satterthwaite and D.F. Wright. Grand Rapids: Eerdmans, 1994, 199-219.

Martens, E.A. *God's Design. A Focus on Old Testament Theology*. 3rd edn. N. Richland Hills: Bibal, 1998.

Martin-Achard, R. 'Problèmes soulevés par l'étude de l'histoire biblique de Joseph'. *RTP* 21 (1972): 94-102.

— 'A propos de la bénédiction de Juda en Genèse 49,8-12 (10)'. In *De la Tôrah au Messie*. Edited by M. Carrez, J. Doré and P. Grelot. Paris: Desclée, 1981, 121-134.

Mathewson, S.D. 'An Exegetical Study of Genesis 38'. *BSac* 146 (1989): 373-392.

Matthews, V.H. 'The Anthropology of Clothing in the Joseph Narrative'. *JSOT* 65 (1995): 25-36.

Melchin, K.R. 'Literary Sources in the Joseph Story'. *ScEs* 31 (1979): 93-101.

Menn, E.M. *Judah and Tamar (Genesis 38) in Ancient Jewish Exegesis: Studies in Literary Form and Hermeneutics*. Supplements to the Journal for the Study of Judaism, 51. Leiden: E.J. Brill, 1997.

van der Merwe, B.J. 'Joseph as Successor of Jacob'. In *Studia Biblica et Semitica*. Edited by W.C. van Unnik and A.S. van der Woude. Wageningen: Veenman & Zonen, 1966, 221-232.

Mettinger, T.N.D. *Solomonic State Officials*. CBOTS, 5. Lund: CWK Gleerups, 1971.

Meyer, F.B. *Joseph: Beloved - Hated - Exalted*. London: Lakeland, 1975.

Miscall, P.D. 'The Jacob and Joseph Stories as Analogies'. *JSOT* 6 (1978): 28-40.

Moberly, R.W.L. *At the Mountain of God*. JSOTSup, 22. Sheffield: JSOT Press, 1983.

— *The Old Testament of the Old Testament. Patriarchal Narratives and Mosaic Yahwism*. Overtures to Biblical Theology. Minneapolis: Fortress, 1992.

Monroe, J. 'Joseph as a Statesman'. *BSac* 54 (1897): 484-500.

Morgan, D.F. 'Wisdom and the Prophets'. In *Studia Biblica 1978: I*. JSOTSup, 11. Sheffield: JSOT Press, 1979, 209-244.

— *Wisdom in the Old Testament Traditions*. Oxford: Basil Blackwell, 1981.

Morimura, N. 'The Story of Tamar: A Feminist Interpretation of Genesis 38'. *Japan Christian Review* 59 (1993): 55-67.

Morris, H.M. *The Genesis Record: A Scientific and Devotional Commentary on the Book of Beginnings*. Grand Rapids: Baker, 1976.

Muilenburg, J. 'Form Criticism and Beyond'. *JBL* 88 (1969): 1-18.

Müller, H.-P. 'Magisch-mantische Weisheit und die Gestalt Daniels'. *Ugarit-Forschungen* 1 (1969): 79-94.

— 'Die weisheitliche Lehrerzählung im Alten Testament und seiner Umwelt'. *Die Welt des Orients* 9 (1977): 77-98.

Murtagh, J. 'The Egyptian Colouring of Genesis and Exodus'. *Irish Ecclesiastical Record* 107 (1967): 253-260.

Murphy, R.E. 'Wisdom and Yahwism'. In *No Famine in the Land: Studies in Honor of John L. McKenzie*. Edited by J.W. Flanagan and A.W. Robinson. Claremont: Scholars, 1975, 117-126.

— 'Religious Dimensions of Israelite Wisdom'. In *Ancient Israelite Religion: Essays in Honor of Frank Moore Cross*. Edited by P.D. Miller, P.D. Hanson and S.D. McBride. Philadelphia: Fortress, 1987, 449-458.

— *The Tree of Life: An Exploration of Biblical Wisdom Literature*. ABRL. 2nd edn. Grand Rapids: Eerdmans, 1996.

Nel, P.J. 'The Genres of Biblical Wisdom Literature'. *JNSL* 9 (1981): 129-142.

Nicol, G.G. 'Story-Patterning in Genesis'. In *Text as Pretext. Essays in Honour of Robert Davidson*. JSOTSup, 138. Edited by R.P. Carroll. Sheffield: Sheffield Academic Press, 1992, 215-233.

Niditch, S. and R. Doran. 'The Success Story of the Wise Courtier: A Formal Approach'. *JBL* 96 (1977): 179-193.

Niditch, S. 'The Wronged Woman Righted: An Analysis of Genesis 38'. *HTR* 72 (1979): 143-149.

— *Underdogs and Tricksters*. San Francisco: Harper & Row, 1987.

— 'Genesis'. In *The Women's Bible Commentary*. Edited by C.A. Newsom and S.H. Ringe. London: SPCK, 1992, 10-25.

Nohrnberg, J.C. 'Princely Characters'. In *"Not in Heaven": Coherence and Complexity in Biblical Narrative*. Edited by J.S. Rosenblatt and J.C. Sitterson. Bloomington: Indiana University Press, 1991, 58-97.

Noth, M. *A History of Pentateuchal Traditions*. Translated by B.W. Anderson. Englewood Cliffs: Prentice-Hall, 1972.

O'Brien, M.A. 'The Contribution of Judah's Speech, Genesis 44:18-34, to the Characterization of Joseph'. *CBQ* 59 (1997): 429-447.

O'Callaghan, M. 'The Structure and Meaning of Genesis 38: Judah and Tamar'. *Proceedings of the Irish Biblical Association* 5 (1981): 72-88.

O'Connor, M. *Hebrew Verse Structure*. Winona Lake: Eisenbrauns, 1980.

Olson, D.T. *The Death of the Old and the Birth of the New: The Framework of the Book of Numbers and the Pentateuch*. Brown Judaic Studies, 71. Chico: Scholars, 1985.

Oppenheim, A.L. 'The Interpretation of Dreams in the Ancient Near East'. *Transactions of the American Philosophical Society* 46 (1956): 179-373.

Otto, E. 'Die 'synthetische Lebensauffassung' in der frühköniglichen Novellistik Israels'. *ZTK* 74 (1977): 371-400.

Paap, C. *Die Josephsgeschichte Genesis 37-50: Bestimmungen ihrer literarischen*

Gattung in der zweiten Hälfte des 20. Jahrhunderts. Europäische Hochschulschriften, 23, Theologie, Band 534. Frankfurt am Main: Peter Lang, 1995.

Patrick, D. *The Rendering of God in the Old Testament*. Overtures to Biblical Theology. Philadelphia: Fortress, 1981.

Peacock, H.F. 'Translating "Mercy", "Steadfast love", in the book of Genesis'. *The Bible Translator* 31 (1980): 201-207.

Peck, J. 'Note on Genesis 37,2 and Joseph's Character'. *ExpTim* 82 (1970/1971): 342-343.

Perdue, L.G. *Wisdom and Creation: The Theology of Wisdom Literature*. Nashville: Abingdon, 1994.

Pink, A.W. *Gleanings in Genesis*. Chicago: Moody, 1922.

Pirson, R. 'What is Joseph Supposed to Be? On the Interpretation of נַעַר in Genesis 37:2'. *Recycling Biblical Figures: Papers Read at a NOSTER Colloquium in Amsterdam, 12-13 May 1997*. Leiden: Deo, 1999, 81-92.

— 'The Sun, The Moon and Eleven Stars. An Interpretation of Joseph's Second Dream'. In *Studies in the Book of Genesis: Literature, Redaction and History*. Edited by A. Wénin. BETL 155. Leuven: Leuven University Press, 2001, 561-568.

— *The Lord of the Dreams: A Semantic and Literary Analysis of Genesis 37-50*. JSOTSup, 355. Sheffield: Sheffield Academic Press, 2002.

Plaut, W.G. 'Genesis'. In *The Torah: A Modern Commentary*. New York: Union of American Hebrew Congregations, 1981, 3-318.

Plum, K.F. 'Genealogy as Theology'. *SJOT* 1 (1989): 66-92.

Polzin, R. *Moses and the Deuteronomist*. New York: Seabury, 1980.

Poythress, V.S. *Symphonic Theology: The Validity of Multiple Perspectives in Theology*. Grand Rapids: Academie, 1987.

Preuss, H.D. 'Ich will mit dir sein'. *ZAW* 80 (1968): 139-173.

Priest, J.F. 'Where Is Wisdom to be Placed?'. *JAAR* 31 (1963): 275-282.

Prouser, O.H. 'The Truth about Women and Lying'. *JSOT* 61 (1994):15-28.

de Pury, A. *Promesse Divine et Légende Cultuelle dans le Cycle de Jacob: Genèse 28 et les traditions patriarcales*. Études Bibliques, 2 vols. Paris: J. Gabalda, 1975.

von Rad, G. 'The Theological Problem of the Old Testament Doctrine of Creation'. In *The Problem of the Hexateuch and other essays*. Translated by E.W.T. Dicken. London: SCM, 1984, 131-143.

— 'The Joseph Narrative and Ancient Wisdom'. In *The Problem of the Hexateuch and other essays*. Translated by E.W.T. Dicken. London: SCM, 1984, 292-300.

— 'The Story of Joseph'. In *God at Work in Israel*. Translated by J.H. Marks. Nashville: Abingdon, 1980, 19-35.

— *Genesis*. Old Testament Library. Revised edn. Translated by J.H. Marks and J. Bowden. London: SCM, 1972.

— *Wisdom in Israel*. Translated by J.D. Martin. London: SCM, 1972.

Radday, Y.T. 'Humour in Names'. In *On Humour and the Comic in the Hebrew Bible*. JSOTSup, 92. Edited by Y.T. Radday and A. Brenner. Sheffield: Almond Press, 1990, 59-97.

Rainy, R. 'Joseph's Forgetting'. *The Expositor* 3rd Series. 4 (1886): 401-411.

Rand, H. 'The Testament of Jacob, An Analysis of Gen. 49:18'. *The Jewish Bible Quarterly/Dor le Dor* 18 (1989-1990): 101-106.

Redford, D.B. *A Study of the Biblical Story of Joseph (Genesis 37-50)*. VTSup, 20. Leiden: E.J. Brill, 1970.

— *Egypt, Canaan, and Israel in Ancient Times*. Princeton: Princeton University Press, 1992.

Reis, P.T. 'Dead Men Tell No Tales: On the Motivation of Joseph's Brothers'. *Conservative Judaism* 44 (1992): 57-60.

Renaud, B. 'Les généalogies et la structure de l'histoire sacerdotale dans le livre de la Genèse'. *RB* 97 (1990): 5-30.

Rendsburg, G.A. *The Redaction of Genesis*. Winona Lake: Eisenbrauns, 1986.

— 'David and his Circle in Genesis XXXVIII'. *VT* 36 (1986): 438-446.

— 'Israelian Hebrew Features in Genesis 49'. *Maarav* 8 (1992): 161-170.

Rendtorff, R. *The Problem of the Process of Transmission in the Pentateuch*. JSOTSup, 89. Translated by J.J. Scullion. Sheffield: Sheffield Academic Press, 1990.

— 'The Future of Pentateuchal Criticism'. *Henoch* 6 (1984): 1-14.

Resch, A. *Der Traum im Heilsplan Gottes*. Freiburg: Herder, 1964.

Revell, E.J. 'Midian and Ishmael in Genesis 37: Synonyms in the Joseph Story'. In *The World of the Arameans I: Biblical Studies in Honour of Paul-Eugène Dion*. Edited by P.M.M. Daviau, J.W. Wevers and M. Weigl. JSOTSup, 324. Sheffield: Sheffield Academic Press, 2001, 70-91.

Richter, W. 'Traum und Traumdeutung im AT: Ihre Form und Verwendung'. *BZ* 7 (1963): 202-220.

Ringgren, H. 'Die Versuchung Josefs (Gen 39)'. In *Die Väter Israels: Beitrage zur Theologie der Patriarchenüberlieferungen im Alten Testament*. Festschrift J. Scharbert zum 70. Edited by M. Görg. Stuttgart: Katholisches Bibelwerk, 1989, 267-270.

Robertson, E. *The Old Testament Problem*. Manchester: Manchester University Press, 1950.

Robertson, D. *The Old Testament and the Literary Critic*. Guides to Biblical Scholarship, Old Testament Series. Philadelphia: Fortress, 1977.

Robinson, B.P. *Israel's Mysterious God*. Newcastle: Grevatt & Grevatt, 1986.

Robinson, I. '*běpetaḥ ʿênayim* in Genesis 38:14'. *JBL* 96 (1977): 569.

Robinson, R.B. 'Literary Functions of the Genealogies of Genesis'. *CBQ* 48 (1986): 595-608.

Roop, E.F. *Genesis*. Believers Church Bible Commentary. Scottdale: Herald, 1987.

Rosenthal, L.A. 'Die Josephsgeschichte mit den Büchern Ester und Daniel verglichen'. *ZAW* 15 (1895): 278-284.

Ross, A.P. *Creation and Blessing: A Guide to the Study and Exposition of the Book of Genesis*. Grand Rapids: Baker, 1988.

le Roux, J.H. 'The study of wisdom literature in South Africa'. *Old Testament Essays* 4 (1991): 342-361.

Rudolph, W. 'Die Josephsgeschichte'. In *Der Elohist als Erzähler*. BZAW, 63. Edited by P. Volz and W. Rudolph. Giessen: Töpelmann, 1933, 145-184.

Ruppert, L. *Die Josephserzählung der Genesis: Ein Beitrag zur Theologie der Pentateuchquellen*. SANT, 11. Munich: Kösel, 1965.

— 'Zur neueren Diskussion um die Josefsgeschichte der Genesis'. *BZ* 33 (1989): 92-97.

Ryken, L. *Words of Delight: A Literary Introduction to the Bible*. Grand Rapids: Baker, 1987.

Sæbø, M. 'Divine names and epithets in Genesis 49:24b-25a: some methodological and traditio-historical remarks'. In *History and Traditions of Early Israel: Studies Presented to Eduard Nielsen May 8th 1993*. Edited by A. Lemaire and B. Otzen.

Leiden: E.J. Brill, 1993, 115-132.

Sailhamer, J.H. *The Pentateuch as Narrative: A Biblical-Theological Commentary.* Library of Biblical Interpretation. Grand Rapids: Zondervan, 1992.

— 'Genesis'. In *The Expositor's Bible Commentary.* Vol. 2. Grand Rapids: Zondervan, 1990, 1-284.

Salm, E. *Juda und Tamar: Eine exegetische Studie zu Gen 38.* Forschung zur Bibel, 76. Würzburg: Echter, 1996.

Samuel, M. 'Joseph - The Brilliant Failure'. *Bible Review* 2 (1986): 38-51, 68.

Sarna, N.M. *Understanding Genesis.* New York: McGraw Hill, 1966.

— 'Joseph'. In *Encyclopedia Judaica.* Vol. 10. Jerusalem: Keter, 1972, 202-209.

— *The JPS Torah Commentary: Genesis.* Philadelphia: Jewish Publication Society, 1989.

Savage, M. 'Literary Criticism and Biblical Studies: A Rhetorical Analysis of the Joseph Narrative'. In *Scripture in Context: Essays on the Comparative Method.* Pittsburgh Theological Monograph Series, 34. Edited by C.D. Evans, W.W. Hallo and J.B. White. Pittsburgh: Pickwick, 1980, 79-100.

Savran, G. 'The Character as Narrator in Biblical Narrative'. *Prooftexts* 5 (1985): 1-17.

— *Telling and Retelling: Quotation in Biblical Narrative.* Bloomington: Indiana University Press, 1988.

Sayce, A.H. *The Early History of the Hebrews.* London: Rivingtons, 1897.

Scharbert, J. 'Der Sinn der Toledot-Formel in der Priesterschrift'. In *Wort - Gebot - Glaube: Beiträge zur Theologie des Alten Testaments. Walter Eichrodt zum 80. Geburtstag.* ATANT, 59. Edited by H.J. Stoebe, J.J. Stamm and E. Jenni. Zurich: Zwingli Verlag, 1970, 45-56.

— *Genesis 12-50.* Die Neue Echter Bibel. Würzburg: Echter, 1986.

Schimmel, S. 'Joseph and his Brothers: A Paradigm for Repentance'. *Judaism* 37 (1988): 60-65.

Schmid, H. *Wesen und Geschichte der Weisheit.* BZAW, 101. Berlin: Töpelmann, 1966.

Schmidt, L. *Literarische Studien zur Josephsgeschichte.* BZAW, 167. Berlin: Walter de Gruyter 1986.

Schmitt, H.-C. *Die Nichtpriesterliche Josephsgeschichte: Ein Beitrag zur neusten Pentateuchkritik.* BZAW, 154. Berlin: Walter de Gruyter, 1980.

Schroer, S. 'Wise and Counselling Women in Ancient Israel: Literary and Historic Ideals of the Personified Ḥokmä'. In *A Feminist Companion to Wisdom Literature.* Feminist Companion to the Bible, 9. Edited by A. Brenner. Sheffield: Sheffield Academic Press, 1995, 67-84.

Schultz, R.L. 'Unity or Diversity in Wisdom Theology? A Canonical and Covenantal Perspective'. *TynBul* 48 (1997): 271-306.

Schüngel-Straumann, H. 'Tamar'. *BK* 39 (1984): 148-157.

Schwartz, R.M. 'Joseph's Bones and the Resurrection of the Text: Remembering in the Bible'. In *The Book and the Text.* Edited by R.M. Schwartz. Oxford: Basil Blackwell, 1990, 40-59.

Schweizer, H. *Die Josefsgeschichte: Konstituierung des Textes.* 2 vols. Tübingen: Francke, 1991.

— 'Leckere Häppchen oder dicke Mehlsoße?'. *BN* 63 (1992): 52-57.

— 'Angst vor Wahrnehmung solo? Zu: Objektive Ergebnisse bei textinterner Literarkritik? Einige Anmerkungen zur Subjektivität literarkritischer Beobachtungen in Harald Schweizers Studie "Die Josefsgeschichte" von Bernd Willmes: BN 67

(1993) 54-86'. *BN* 69 (1993): 24-28.

Scobie, C.H.H. 'The Place of Wisdom in Biblical Theology'. *Biblical Theology Bulletin* 14 (1984): 43-48.

Scott, R.B.Y. 'Solomon and the Beginnings of Wisdom in Israel'. In *Wisdom in Israel and in the Ancient Near East*. VTSup, 3. Edited by M. Noth and D.W. Thomas. Leiden: E.J. Brill, 1955, 262-279.

— 'The Study of Wisdom Literature'. *Int* 24 (1970): 20-45.

— *The Way of Wisdom in the Old Testament*. (New York: Macmillan, 1971).

Scullion, J.J. 'The God of the Patriarchs'. *Pacifica* 1 (1988): 141-156.

— '"Die Genesis ist eine Sammlung von Sagen" (Hermann Gunkel) Independent Stories and Redactional Unity in Genesis 12-36'. In *»Wünschet Jerusalem Frieden« IOSOT Congress Jerusalem 1986*. Edited by M. Augustin and K.-D. Schunck. Frankfurt am Main: Peter Lang, 1988, 243-247.

— *Genesis: A Commentary for Students, Teachers, and Preachers*. Old Testament Studies, 6. Collegeville: Liturgical Press, 1992.

Seebass, H. *Geschlichtliche Zeit und theonome Tradition in der Joseph-Erzählung*. Gütersloh: Gerd Mohn, 1978.

— 'Die Stämmesprüche Gen 49:3-27'. *ZAW* 96 (1984): 333-350.

— 'The Joseph Story, Genesis 48 and the Canonical Process'. *JSOT* 35 (1986): 29-53.

Segal, E. 'Human Anger and Divine Intervention in Esther'. *Prooftexts* 9 (1989): 247-256.

Seybold, D.A. 'Paradox and Symmetry in the Joseph Narrative' In *Literary Interpretations of Biblical Narratives*. Edited by K.R.R. Gros Louis, J.S. Ackerman, and T.S. Warshaw. Nashville: Abingdon, 1974, 59-73.

Sheppard, G.T. *Wisdom as a Hermeneutical Construct: A Study in the Sapientializing of the Old Testament*. BZAW, 151. Berlin: Walter de Gruyter, 1980.

Shevitz, D.R. 'Joseph: A Study in Assimilation and Power', *Tikkun* 8 (Jan/Feb 1993): 51-52, 76-77.

Shupak, N. 'Egyptian "prophetic" writings and biblical wisdom literature'. *BN* 54 (1990): 81-102.

— *Where can Wisdom be found? The Sage's Language in the Bible and in Ancient Egyptian Literature*. OBO, 130. Fribourg: University Press, 1993.

— 'סיפור יוסף - בין אגדה להיסטוריה' In *Texts, Temples, and Traditions: A Tribute to Menahem Haran*. Edited by M.V. Fox, V.A. Hurowitz, A. Hurvitz, M.L. Klein, B.J. Schwartz and N. Shupak. Winona Lake: Eisenbrauns, 1996. 125-133, 412.

da Silva, A. *La symbolique des rêves et des vêtements dans l'histoire de Joseph et de ses frères*. Héritage et projet, 52. Québec: Fides, 1994.

Simon, U. *Story and Faith in the Biblical Narrative*. London: SPCK, 1975.

Skinner, J. *A Critical and Exegetical Commentary on Genesis*. ICC. Edinburgh: T. & T. Clark, 1910.

Smith, G.V. 'Is There a Place for Job's Wisdom in Old Testament Theology?'. *Trinity Journal* 13NS (1992): 3-20.

Soggin, J.A. 'Judah and Tamar (Genesis 38)'. In *Of Prophets' Visions and the Wisdom of Sages*. JSOTSup, 162. Edited by H.A. McKay and D.J.A. Clines. Sheffield: JSOT Press, 1993, 281-287.

— 'Notes on the Joseph Story'. In *Understanding Poets and Prophets: Essays in Honour of George Wishart Anderson*. JSOTSup, 152. Edited by A.G. Auld. Sheffield: Sheffield Academic Press, 1993, 336-349.

Spangenberg, I.J.J. 'Old Testament Theology and Wisdom Literature'. *Theologica Evangelica* 25 (1992): 2-7.

Speiser, E.A. *Genesis*. Anchor Bible. New York: Doubleday, 1964.

Sperling, S.D. 'Genesis 41:40: A New Interpretation'. *The Journal of the Ancient Near Eastern Society of Columbia University* 10 (1978): 113-119.

Spero, S. 'The Funeral of Jacob: A Joint Hebrew-Egyptian Affair', *Jewish Bible Quarterly* 26 (1998): 20-25.

Spina, F.A. 'Qoheleth and the Reformation of Wisdom'. In *The Quest For the Kingdom of God: Studies in Honor of George E. Mendenhall*. Edited by H.B. Huffmon, F.A. Spina and A.R.W. Green. Winona Lake: Eisenbrauns, 1983, 267-279.

Sternberg, M. *The Poetics of Biblical Narrative*. Bloomington: Indiana University Press, 1985.

Steinberg, N. 'The Genealogical Framework of the Family Stories in Genesis'. *Semeia* 46 (1989): 41-50.

Steiner, F. 'Enslavement and the Early Hebrew Lineage System. An Explanation of Genesis 47:29-31; 48:1-16'. In *Anthropological Approaches to the Old Testament*. Issues in Religion and Theology, 8. Edited by B. Lang. Philadelphia: Fortress, 1985, 21-25.

Syrén, R. *The Forsaken First-Born: A Study of a Recurrent Motif in the Patriarchal Narratives*. JSOTSup, 133. Sheffield: Sheffield Academic Press, 1993.

Tawil, H. 'Hebrew *hṣlḥ/ṣlḥ*, Akkadian *ešēru/šūšuru*: A Lexicographical Note'. *JBL* 95 (1976): 405-413.

Tengström, S. *Die Toledotformel und die literarische Struktur der priesterlichen Erweiterungsschicht im Pentateuch*. CBOTS, 17. Uppsala: Almqvist & Wiksell, 1981.

Thomas, J.H. 'Philosophy and the Critical Study of Wisdom Literature'. *HeyJ* 20 (1979): 290-294.

Thompson, T.L. and D. Irvin. 'The Joseph and Moses Narratives'. In *Israelite and Judean History*. Edited by J.H. Hayes and J.M. Miller. London: SCM, 1977, 149-212.

Thompson, T.L. *The Origin Tradition of Ancient Israel*. JSOTSup, 55. Sheffield: JSOT Press, 1987.

Trible, P. *Rhetorical Criticism: Context, Method, and the Book of Jonah*. Guides to Biblical Scholarship, Old Testament Series. Minneapolis: Fortress, 1994.

Tucker, G. 'Jacob's Terrible Burden: In the Shadow of the Text'. *Bible Review* 10 (1994): 25-28.

Turner, L.A. *Announcements of Plot in Genesis*. JSOTSup, 96. Sheffield: JSOT Press, 1990.

VanGemeren, W.A. *The Progress of Redemption: The Story of Salvation from Creation to the New Jerusalem*. Grand Rapids: Academie, 1988.

de Vaux, R. *La Genèse*. Paris: Éditions du Cerfs, 1953.

— *Ancient Israel: Its Life and Institutions*. Translated by J. McHugh. New York: McGraw-Hill, 1961.

de Vaux, R. *The Early History of Israel*. Translated by D. Smith. London: Darton, Longman & Todd, 1978.

Vawter, B. 'The Canaanite Background of Genesis 49'. *CBQ* 17 (1955): 1-18.

— *On Genesis: A New Reading*. New York: Doubleday, 1977.

Vergote, J. *Joseph en Égypte: Genèse 37-50 à la lumière des études égyptologiques récentes*. Orientalia et Biblica Lovaniensia, 3. Louvain: Publications Universitaires, 1959.

Vetter, D. *Jahwes mit-Sein als Ausdruck des Segens*. Arbeiten zur Theologie, 5. Stuttgart: Calwer Verlag, 1971.

Vreeland, G.D. 'The Joseph Narrative - Genesis 37-39: An analysis of three modern textual approaches'. Dissertation, PhD, Trinity Evangelical Divinity School, 1994.

Waltke, B.K. and M. O'Connor. *An Introduction to Biblical Hebrew Syntax*. Winona Lake: Eisenbrauns, 1990.

Walton, J.H. *Covenant: God's Purpose, God's Plan*. Grand Rapids: Zondervan, 1994.

Ward, W.A. 'The Egyptian Office of Joseph'. *JSS* 5 (1960): 144-150.

Warning, W. 'Terminological Patterns and Genesis 38'. *AUSS* 38 (2000): 293-305.

— 'Terminological Patterns and Genesis 39'. *JETS* 44 (2001): 409-419.

Webb, B.G. *The Book of the Judges: An Integrated Reading*. JSOTSup, 46. Sheffield: JSOT Press, 1987.

Weeks, S.D.E. 'Joseph, Dreams and Wisdom'. Dissertation, MPhil, Oxford University, 1989.

— *Early Israelite Wisdom*. Oxford Theological Monographs. Oxford: Clarendon, 1994.

Weimar, P. 'Die Toledot-Formel in der priesterschriftlichen Geschichtsdarstellung'. *BZ* 18 (1974): 65-93.

Wenham, G.J. *Genesis 16-50*. WBC. Dallas: Word, 1994.

— *Numbers*. OTG. Sheffield: Sheffield Academic Press, 1997.

Wessels, J.P.H. 'The Joseph story as a wisdom novelette'. *Old Testament Essays* 2 (1984): 39-60.

West, G. 'Difference and Dialogue: Reading the Joseph Story with Poor and Marginalized Communities in South Africa'. *BibInt* 2 (1994): 152-170.

West, S.A. 'Judah and Tamar - A Scriptural Enigma'. *Dor le Dor* 12 (1984): 246-252.

Westermann, C. *Genesis 37-50*. Translated by J.J. Scullion. Minneapolis: Augsburg, 1986.

— *Joseph: Studies of the Joseph Stories in Genesis*. Translated by O. Kaste. Edinburgh: T & T Clark, 1996.

— *The Promises to the Fathers*. Translated by D.E. Green. Philadelphia: Fortress, 1980.

— *Roots of Wisdom: The Oldest Proverbs of Israel and Other Peoples*. Translated by J.D. Charles. Louisville: Westminster John Knox, 1995.

Whedbee, J.W. *Isaiah & Wisdom*. Nashville: Abingdon, 1971.

White, H.C. 'The Joseph Story: A Narrative Which "Consumes" its Content'. *Semeia* 31 (1985): 49-69.

— *Narration and Discourse in the Book of Genesis*. Cambridge: Cambridge University Press, 1991.

Whybray, R.N. *Wisdom in Proverbs*. SBT, 45. London: SCM, 1965.

— 'The Joseph Story and Pentateuchal Criticism'. *VT* 18 (1968): 522-528.

— *The Intellectual Tradition in the Old Testament*. BZAW, 135. Berlin: Walter de Gruyter, 1974.

— 'Wisdom Literature in the Reigns of David and Solomon'. In *Studies in the Period of David and Solomon and Other Essays*. Edited by T. Ishida. Winona Lake: Eisenbrauns, 1982, 13-26.

— *The Making of the Pentateuch: A Methodological Study*. JSOTSup, 53. Sheffield: JSOT Press, 1987.

— 'The Social World of the Wisdom Writers'. In *The World of Ancient Israel*. Edited by R.E. Clements. Cambridge: Cambridge University Press, 1989, 227-250.

— 'Yahweh-sayings and their Contexts in Proverbs, 10,1-22,16'. In *La sagesse de l'Ancien Testament*. 2nd edn. Edited by M. Gilbert. BETL 51. Leuven: Leuven University Press, 1990, 153-165.

— 'The Sage in the Israelite Royal Court'. In *The Sage in Israel and the Ancient Near East*. Edited by J.G. Gammie and L.G. Perdue. Winona Lake: Eisenbrauns, 1990, 133-139.

— *The Composition of the Book of Proverbs*. JSOTSup, 168. Sheffield: Sheffield Academic Press, 1994.

Wildavsky, A. *Assimilation versus Separation: Joseph the Administrator and the Politics of Religion in Biblical Israel*. New Brunswick: Transaction, 1993.

— 'Survival Must not be Gained through Sin: The Moral of the Joseph Stories Prefigured through Judah and Tamar'. *JSOT* 62 (1994): 37-48.

Williams, J.G. 'Number Symbolism and Joseph as Symbol of Completion'. *JBL* 98 (1979): 86-87.

— *Those Who Ponder Proverbs: Aphoristic Thinking and Biblical Literature*. Bible and Literature Series, 2. Sheffield: Almond Press, 1981.

Willmes, B. 'Objektive Ergebnisse bei textinterner Literarkritik? Einige Anmerkungen zur Subjektivität literarkritischer Beobachtungen in H. Schweizers Studie 'Die Josefsgeschichte''. *BN* 67 (1993): 54-86.

Wills, L.M. *The Jew in the Court of the Foreign King: Ancient Jewish Court Legends*. HDR, 26. Minneapolis: Fortress, 1990.

Wills, L.M. 'Observations on "Wisdom Narratives" in Early Biblical Literature'. In *Of Scribes and Scrolls: Studies on the Hebrew Bible, Intertestamental Judaism, and Christian Origins. Presented to John Strugnell on the Occasion of His Sixtieth Birthday*. Edited by H.W. Attridge, J.J. Collins and T.H. Tobin. Lanham: University Press of America, 1990, 57-66.

Wilson, L. 'The Place of Wisdom in Old Testament Theology'. *RTR* 49 (1990): 60-69.

Wilson, L. 'The Book of Job and the Fear of God'. *TynBul* 46 (1995): 59-79.

Wilson, R.R. *Genealogy and History in the Biblical World*. New Haven: Yale, 1977.

Wintermute, O. 'Joseph Son of Jacob'. In *Interpreter's Dictionary of the Bible*. 4 vols. Edited by G.A. Buttrick. Nashville: Abingdon, 1962, 2:981-986.

van Wolde, E. 'Texts in Dialogue with Texts: Intertextuality in the Ruth and Tamar Narratives'. *BibInt* 5 (1997): 1-28.

Wolff, H.W. 'The Kerygma of the Yahwist'. Translated by W.A. Benware. In *The Vitality of Old Testament Traditions*. 2nd edn. Edited by W. Brueggemann and H.W. Wolff. Atlanta: John Knox, 1982, 41-66.

Woudstra, M.H. 'The *Toledot* of the Book of Genesis and their Redemptive-Historical Significance'. *CTJ* 5 (1970): 184-189.

Wright, C.J.H. *Living as the People of God*. Leicester: Inter-Varsity Press, 1983.

Wright, G.R.H. 'The Positioning of Genesis 38'. *ZAW* 94 (1982): 523-529.

Yohannan, J.D. *Joseph and Potiphar's Wife in World Literature. An Anthology of the Story of the Chaste Youth and the Lustful Stepmother*. New York: New Directions, 1968.

Zeitlin, S. 'Dreams and Their Interpretation from the Biblical Period to the Tannaitic Time: An Historical Study'. *Jewish Quarterly Review* 66 (1975): 1-18.

Zimmerli, W. 'Promise and Fulfillment', Translated by J. Wharton. In *Essays on Old Testament Interpretation*. Edited by C. Westermann, English translation edited by

J.L. Mays. London: SCM, 1963, 89-122.

Zimmerli, W. 'The Place and Limit of the Wisdom in the Framework of the Old Testament Theology'. *SJT* 17 (1964): 146-158.

Zimmerli, W. *Man and his Hope in the Old Testament*. SBT, 20. London: SCM, 1971.

Zobel, H.-J. *Stammesspruche und Geschichte: Die Angaben der Stammessprüche von Gen 49, Dtn 33 and Jdc 5 über die politischen und kultischen Zustände in damaligen "Israel"*. BZAW, 95. Berlin: Walter de Gruyter, 1965.

Author Index

Biblical Index

Paternoster Biblical Monographs

(All titles uniform with this volume)

Joseph Abraham
Eve: Accused or Acquitted?
A Reconsideration of Feminist Readings of the Creation Narrative Texts in Genesis 1–3
Two contrary views dominate contemporary feminist biblical scholarship. One finds in the Bible an unequivocal equality between the sexes from the very creation of humanity, whilst the other sees the biblical text as irredeemably patriarchal and androcentric. Dr. Abraham enters into dialogue with both camps as well as introducing his own method of approach. An invaluable tool for anyone who is interested in this contemporary debate.
2002 / ISBN 0-85364-971-5 / xxiv + 272pp

Paul Barker
The Triumph of Grace in Deuteronomy
This book is a textual and theological analysis of the interaction between the sin and faithlessness of Israel and the grace of Yahweh in response, looking especially at Deuteronomy chapters 1–3, 8–10 and 29–30. The author argues that the grace of Yahweh is determinative for the ongoing relationship between Yahweh and Israel and that Deuteronomy anticipates and fully expects Israel to be faithless.
2004 / ISBN 1-84227-226-8 / xxii + 270pp

Jonathan F. Bayes
The Weakness of the Law
God's Law and the Christian in New Testament Perspective
A study of the four New Testament books which refer to the law as weak (Acts, Romans, Galatians, Hebrews) leads to a defence of the third use in the Reformed debate about the law in the life of the believer.
2000 / ISBN 0-85364-957-X / xii + 244pp

Mark Bonnington
The Antioch Episode of Galatians 2:11-14 in Historical and Cultural Context
The Galatians 2 'incident' in Antioch over table-fellowship suggests significant disagreement between the leading apostles. This book analyses the background to the disagreement by locating the incident within the dynamics of social interaction between Jews and Gentiles. It proposes a new way of understanding the relationship between the individuals and issues involved.
2004 / ISBN 1-84227-050-8 / approx. 350pp

May 2004

Mark Bredin
Jesus, Revolutionary of Peace
A Nonviolent Christology in the Book of Revelation
This book aims to demonstrate that the figure of Jesus in the Book of Revelation can best be understood as an active nonviolent revolutionary.
2003 / ISBN 1-84227-153-9 / xviii + 262pp

Daniel J-S Chae
Paul as Apostle to the Gentiles
His Apostolic Self-awareness and its Influence on the Soteriological Argument in Romans
Opposing 'the post-Holocaust interpretation of Romans', Daniel Chae competently demonstrates that Paul argues for the equality of Jew and Gentile in Romans. Chae's fresh exegetical interpretation is academically outstanding and spiritually encouraging.
1997 / ISBN 0-85364-829-8 / xiv + 378pp

Luke L. Cheung
The Genre, Composition and Hermeneutics of the Epistle of James
The present work examines the employment of the wisdom genre with a certain compositional structure and the interpretation of the law through the Jesus' tradition of the double love command by the author of the Epistle of James to serve his purpose in promoting perfection and warning against doubleness among the eschatologically renewed people of God in the Diaspora.
2003 / ISBN 1-84227-062-1 / xvi + 372pp

Andrew C. Clark
Parallel Lives
The Relation of Paul to the Apostles in the Lucan Perspective
This study of the Peter-Paul parallels in Acts argues that their purpose was to emphasize the themes of continuity in salvation history and the unity of the Jewish and Gentile missions. New light is shed on Luke's literary techniques, partly through a comparison with Plutarch.
2001 / 1-84227-035-4 / xviii + 386pp

Andrew D. Clarke
Secular and Christian Leadership in Corinth
A Socio-Historical and Exegetical Study of 1 Corinthians 1–6
This volume is an investigation into the leadership structures and dynamics of first-century Roman Corinth. These are compared with the practice of leadership in the Corinthian Christian community which are reflected in 1 Corinthians 1–6, and contrasted with Paul's own principles of Christian leadership.

2004 / ISBN 1-84227-229-2 / xii + 188pp

Stephen Finamore
God, Order and Chaos
René Girard and the Apocalypse
Readers are often disturbed by the images of destruction in the book of Revelation and unsure why they are unleashed after the exaltation of Jesus. This book examines past approaches to these texts and uses René Girard's theories to revive some old ideas and propose some new ones.

2004 / ISBN 1-84227-197-0 / approx. 344pp

Scott J. Hafemann
Suffering and Ministry in the Spirit
Paul's Defence of His Ministry in II Corinthians 2:14–3:3
Shedding new light on the way Paul defended his apostleship, the author offers a careful, detailed study of 2 Corinthians 2:14–3:3 linked with other key passages throughout 1 and 2 Corinthians. Demonstrating the unity and coherence of Paul's argument in this passage, the author shows that Paul's suffering served as the vehicle for revealing God's power and glory through the Spirit.

2000 / ISBN 0-85364-967-7 / xiv + 262pp

Douglas S. McComiskey
Lukan Theology in the Light of the Gospel's Literary Structure
Luke's Gospel was purposefully written with theology embedded in its patterned literary structure. A critical analysis of this cyclical structure provides new windows into Luke's interpretation of the individual pericopes comprising the Gospel and illuminates several of his theological interests.

2004 / ISBN 1-84227-148-2 / approx. 400pp

Stephen Motyer
Your Father the Devil?
A New Approach to John and 'The Jews'
Who are 'the Jews' in John's Gospel? Defending John against the charge
of anti-semitism, Motyer argues that, far from demonizing the Jews, the
Gospel seeks to present Jesus as 'Good News for Jews' in a late first
century setting.
1997 / ISBN 0-85364-832-8 / xiv + 260pp

Esther Ng
Reconstructing Christian Origins?
The Feminist Theology of Elizabeth Schüssler Fiorenza: An Evaluation
In a detailed evaluation, the author challenges Elizabeth Schüssler
Fiorenza's reconstruction of early Christian origins and her underlying
presuppositions. The author also presents her own views on women's roles
both then and now.
2002 / ISBN 1-84227-055-9 / xxiv + 468pp

Robin Parry
Old Testament Story and Christian Ethics
The Rape of Dinah as a Case Study
What is the role of story in ethics and, more particularly, what is the role of
Old Testament story in Christian ethics? This book, drawing on the work
of contemporary philosophers, argues that narrative is crucial in the ethical
shaping of people and, drawing on the work of contemporary Old
Testament scholars, that story plays a key role in Old Testament ethics.
Parry then argues that when situated in canonical context Old Testament
stories can be reappropriated by Christian readers in their own ethical
formation. The shocking story of the rape of Dinah and the massacre of the
Shechemites provides a fascinating case study for exploring the parameters
within which Christian ethical appropriations of Old Testament stories can
live.
2004 / ISBN 1-84227-210-1 / approx. 350pp

David Powys
'Hell': A Hard Look at a Hard Question
The Fate of the Unrighteous in New Testament Thought
This comprehensive treatment seeks to unlock the original meaning of
terms and phrases long thought to support the traditional doctrine of hell. It
concludes that there is an alternative – one which is more biblical, and
which can positively revive the rationale for Christian mission.
1997 / ISBN 0-85364-831-X / xxii + 478pp

Rosalind Selby
The Comical Doctrine
Can a Gospel Convey Truth?
This book argues that the Gospel breaks through postmodernity's critique of truth and the referential possibilities of textuality and its gift of grace. With a rigorous, philosophical challenge to modernist and postmodernist assumptions, it offers an alternative epistemology to all who would still read with faith *and* with academic credibility.
2004 / ISBN 1-84227-212-8 approx. 350pp

Kevin Walton
Thou Traveller Unknown
The Presence and Absence of God in the Jacob Narrative
The author offers a fresh reading of the story of Jacob in the book of Genesis through the paradox of divine presence and absence. The work also seeks to make a contribution to Pentateuchal studies by bringing together a close reading of the final text with historical critical insights, doing justice to the text's historical depth, final form and canonical status.
2003 / ISBN 1-84227-059-1 / xvi + 238pp

Alistair Wilson
When Will These Things Happen?
A Study of Jesus as Judge in Matthew 21–25
This study seeks to allow Matthew's carefully constructed presentation of Jesus to be given full weight in the modern evaluation of Jesus' eschatology. Careful analysis of the text of Matthew 21–25 reveals Jesus to be standing firmly in the Jewish prophetic and wisdom traditions as he proclaims and enacts imminent judgement on the Jewish authorities then boldly claims the central role in the final and universal judgement.
2004 / ISBN 1-84227-146-6 / xvi + 292pp

Lindsay Wilson
Joseph Wise and Otherwise
The Intersection of Covenant and Wisdom in Genesis 37–50
This book offers a careful literary reading of Genesis 37–50 that argues that the Joseph story contains both strong covenant themes and many wisdom-like elements. The connections between the two helps to explore how covenant and wisdom might intersect in an integrated biblical theology.
2004 / ISBN 1-84227-140-7 approx. 350pp

Stephen I. Wright
The Voice of Jesus
Studies in the Interpretation of Six Gospel Parables
This literary study considers how the 'voice' of Jesus has been heard in different periods of parable interpretation, and how the categories of figure and trope may help us towards a sensitive reading of the parables today.

2000 / ISBN 0-85364-975-8 / xiv + 280pp

Paternoster Theological Monographs

(All titles uniform with this volume)

Emil Bartos
Deification in Eastern Orthodox Theology
An Evaluation and Critique of the Theology of Dumitru Staniloae
Bartos studies a fundamental yet neglected aspect of Orthodox theology: deification. By examining the doctrines of anthropology, christology, soteriology and ecclesiology as they relate to deification, he provides an important contribution to contemporary dialogue between Eastern and Western theologians.

1999 / ISBN 0-85364-956-1 / xii + 370pp

James Bruce
Prophecy, Miracles, Angels *and* Heavenly Light?
The Eschatology, Pneumatology and Missiology of Adomnán's Life of Columba
This book surveys approaches to the marvellous in hagiography, providing the first critique of Plummer's hypothesis of Irish saga origin. It then analyses the uniquely systematized phenomena in the *Life of Columba* from Adomnán's seventh-century theological perspective, identifying the coming of the eschatological Kingdom as the key to understanding.

2004 / ISBN 1-84227-227-6 / approx. 400pp

Colin J. Bulley
The Priesthood of Some Believers
Developments from the General to the Special Priesthood in the Christian Literature of the First Three Centuries
The first in-depth treatment of early Christian texts on the priesthood of all believers shows that the developing priesthood of the ordained related closely to the division between laity and clergy and had deleterious effects on the practice of the general priesthood.

2000 / ISBN 1-84227-034-6 / xii + 336pp

May 2004

Iain D. Campbell
Fixing the Indemnity
The Life and Work of George Adam Smith
When Old Testament scholar George Adam Smith (1856–1942) delivered the Lyman Beecher lectures at Yale University in 1899 he confidently declared that 'modern criticism has won its war against traditional theories. It only remains to fix the amount of the indemnity.' In this biography, Iain D. Campbell assesses Smith's critical approach to the Old Testament and evaluates its consequences, showing that Smith's life and work still raises questions about the relationship between biblical scholarship and evangelical faith.
2004 / ISBN 1-84227-228-4 / approx. 276pp

Sylvia W. Collinson
Making Disciples
The Significance of Jesus' Educational Strategy for Today's Church
This study examines the biblical practice of discipling, formulates a definition, and makes comparisons with modern models of education. A recommendation is made for greater attention to its practice today.
2004 / ISBN 1-84227-116-4 / approx. 320pp

Stephen M. Dunning
The Crisis and the Quest
A Kierkegaardian Reading of Charles Williams
Employing Kierkegaardian categories and analysis, this study investigates both the central crisis in Charles Williams's authorship between hermetism and Christianity (Kierkegaard's Religions A and B), and the quest to resolve this crisis, a quest that ultimately presses the bounds of orthodoxy.
2000 / ISBN 0-85364-985-5 / xxiv + 254pp

Keith Ferdinando
The Triumph of Christ in African Perspective
A Study of Demonology and Redemption in the African Context
The book explores the implications of the gospel for traditional African fears of occult aggression. It analyses such traditional approaches to suffering and biblical responses to fears of demonic evil, concluding with an evaluation of African beliefs from the perspective of the gospel.
1999 / ISBN 0-85364-830-1 / xviii + 450pp

Andrew Goddard
Living the Word, Resisting the World
The Life and Thought of Jacques Ellul
This work offers a definitive study of both the life and thought of the French Reformed thinker Jacques Ellul (1912-1994). It will prove an indispensable resource for those interested in this influential theologian and sociologist and for Christian ethics and political thought generally.
2002 / ISBN 1-84227-053-2 / xxiv + 378pp

Ruth Gouldbourne
The Flesh and the Feminine
Gender and Theology in the Writings of Caspar Schwenckfeld
Caspar Schwenckfeld and his movement exemplify one of the radical communities of the sixteenth century. Challenging theological and liturgical norms, they also found themselves challenging social and particularly gender assumptions. In this book, the issues of the relationship between radical theology and the understanding of gender are considered.
2004 / ISBN 1-84227-048-6 / approx. 304pp

Roger Hitching
The Church and Deaf People
A Study of Identity, Communication and Relationships with Special Reference to the Ecclesiology of Jürgen Moltmann
In *The Church and Deaf People* Roger Hitching sensitively examines the history and present experience of deaf people and finds similarities between aspects of sign language and Moltmann's theological method that 'open up' new ways of understanding theological concepts.
2003 / ISBN 1-84227-222-5 / xxii + 236pp

John G. Kelly
One God, One People
The Differentiated Unity of the People of God in the Theology of Jürgen Moltmann
The author expounds and critiques Moltmann's doctrine of God and high-lights the systematic connections between it and Moltmann's influential discussion of Israel. He then proposes a fresh approach to Jewish-Christian relations building on Moltmann's work using insights from Habermas and Rawls.
2004 / ISBN 0-85346-969-3 / approx. 350pp

Mark F.W. Lovatt
Confronting the Will-to-Power
A Reconsideration of the Theology of Reinhold Niebuhr
Confronting the Will-to-Power is an analysis of the theology of Reinhold Niebuhr, arguing that his work is an attempt to identify, and provide a practical theological answer to, the existence and nature of human evil.
2001 / ISBN 1-84227-054-0 / xviii + 216pp

Neil B. MacDonald
Karl Barth and the Strange New World within the Bible
Barth, Wittgenstein, and the Metadilemmas of the Enlightenment
Barth's discovery of the strange new world within the Bible is examined in the context of Kant, Hume, Overbeck, and, most importantly, Wittgenstein. MacDonald covers some fundamental issues in theology today: epistemology, the final form of the text and biblical truth-claims.
2000 / ISBN 0-85364-970-7 / xxvi + 374pp

Gillian McCulloch
The Deconstruction of Dualism in Theology
With Reference to Ecofeminist Theology and New Age Spirituality
This book challenges eco-theological anti-dualism in Christian theology, arguing that dualism has a twofold function in Christian religious discourse. Firstly, it enables us to express the discontinuities and divisions that are part of the process of reality. Secondly, dualistic language allows us to express the mysteries of divine transcendence/immanence and the survival of the soul without collapsing into monism and materialism, both of which are problematic for Christian epistemology.
2002 / ISBN 1-84227-044-3 / xii + 282pp

Leslie McCurdy
Attributes and Atonement
The Holy Love of God in the Theology of P.T. Forsyth
Attributes and Atonement is an intriguing full-length study of P.T. Forsyth's doctrine of the cross as it relates particularly to God's holy love. It includes an unparalleled bibliography of both primary and secondary material relating to Forsyth.
1999 / ISBN 0-85364-833-6 / xiv + 328pp

Nozomu Miyahira
Towards a Theology of the Concord of God
A Japanese Perspective on the Trinity
This book introduces a new Japanese theology and a unique Trinitarian formula based on the Japanese intellectual climate: three betweennesses and one concord. It also presents a new interpretation of the Trinity, a co-subordinationism, which is in line with orthodox Trinitarianism; each single person of the Trinity is eternally and equally subordinate (or serviceable) to the other persons, so that they retain the mutual dynamic equality.
2000 / ISBN 0-85364-863-8 / xiv + 256pp

Eddy José Muskus
The Origins and Early Development of Liberation Theology in Latin America
With Particular Reference to Gustavo Gutiérrez
This work challenges the fundamental premise of Liberation Theology, 'opting for the poor', and its claim that Christ is found in them. It also argues that Liberation Theology emerged as a direct result of the failure of the Roman Catholic Church in Latin America.
2002 / ISBN 0-85364-974-X / xiv + 296pp

Anna Robbins
Methods in the Madness
Diversity in Twentieth-Century Christian Social Ethics
The author compares the ethical methods of Walter Rauschenbusch, Reinhold Niebuhr and others. She argues that unless Christians are clear about the ways that theology and philosophy are expressed practically they may lose the ability to discuss social ethics across contexts, let alone reach effective agreements.
2004 / ISBN 1-84227-211-X / xvi + 320pp

Ed Rybarczyk
Beyond Salvation
Eastern Orthodoxy and Classical Pentecostalism on becoming like Christ
At first glance eastern Orthodoxy and Classical Pentecostalism seem quite distinct. This groundbreaking study shows that they share much in common, especially as it concerns the experiential elements of following Christ. Both traditions assert that authentic Christianity transcends the wooden categories of modernism.
2003 / ISBN 1-84227-144-X / xii + 356pp

Signe Sandsmark
Is World View Neutral Education Possible and Desirable?
A Christian Response to Liberal Arguments
(Published jointly with The Stapleford Centre)
This book discusses reasons for belief in world view neutrality, and argues that 'neutral' education will have a hidden, but strong world view influence. It discusses the place for Christian education in the common school.
2000 / ISBN 0-85364-973-1 / xiv + 182pp

Hazel Sherman
Reading Zechariah
The Allegorical Tradition of Biblical Interpretation through the Commentaries of Didymus the Blind and Theodore of Mopsuestia
A close reading of the commentary on Zechariah by Didymus the Blind alongside that of Theodore of Mopsuestia suggests that popular categorising of Antiochene and Alexandrian biblical exegesis as 'historical' or 'allegorical' is inadequate and misleading.
2004 / ISBN 1-84227-213-6 / approx. 280pp

Andrew Sloane
On Being a Christian in the Academy
Nicholas Wolterstorff and the Practice of Christian Scholarship
An exposition and critical appraisal of Nicholas Wolterstorff's epistemology in the light of the philosophy of science, and an application of his thought to the practice of Christian scholarship.
2003 / ISBN 1-84227-058-3 / xvi + 274pp

Daniel Strange
The Possibility of Salvation Among the Unevangelised
An Analysis of Inclusivism in Recent Evangelical Theology
For evangelical theologians the 'fate of the unevangelised' impinges upon fundamental tenets of evangelical identity. The position known as 'inclusivism', defined by the belief that the unevangelised can be ontologically saved by Christ whilst being epistemologically unaware of him, has been defended most vigorously by the Canadian evangelical Clark H. Pinnock. Through a detailed analysis and critique of Pinnock's work, this book examines a cluster of issues surrounding the unevangelised and its implications for christology, soteriology and the doctrine of revelation.
2002 / ISBN 1-84227-047-8 / xviii + 362pp

G. Michael Thomas
The Extent of the Atonement
A Dilemma for Reformed Theology from Calvin to the Consensus
This is a study of the way Reformed theology addressed the question, 'Did Christ die for all, or for the elect only?', commencing with John Calvin, and including debates with Lutheranism, the Synod of Dort and the teaching of Moïse Amyraut.
1997 / ISBN 0-85364-828-X / x + 278pp

Mark D. Thompson
A Sure Ground on which to Stand
*The Relation of Authority and Interpretive Method in
Luther's Approach to Scripture*
The best interpreter of Luther is Luther himself. Unfortunately many modern studies have superimposed contemporary agendas upon this sixteenth-century Reformer's writings. This fresh study examines Luther's own words to find an explanation for his robust confidence in the Scriptures, a confidence that generated the famous 'stand' at Worms in 1521.
2004 / ISBN 1-84227-145-8 / xvi + 322pp

Graham Tomlin
The Power of the Cross
Theology and the Death of Christ in Paul, Luther and Pascal
This book explores the theology of the cross in St Paul, Luther and Pascal. It offers new perspectives on the theology of each, and some implications for the nature of power, apologetics, theology and church life in a postmodern context.
1999 / ISBN 0-85364-984-7 / xiv + 344pp

Graham J. Watts
Revelation and the Spirit
*A Comparative Study of the Relationship between the Doctrine of
Revelation and Pneumatology in the Theology of Eberhard Jüngel and of
Wolfhart Pannenberg*
The relationship between revelation and pneumatology is relatively unexplored. This approach offers a fresh angle on two important twentieth century theologians and raises pneumatological questions which are theologically crucial and relevant to mission in a post modern culture.
2004 / ISBN 1-84227-104-0 / xxii + 232pp

Nigel G. Wright
Disavowing Constantine
Mission, Church and the Social Order in the Theologies of
John Howard Yoder and Jürgen Moltmann
This book is a timely restatement of a radical theology of church and state
in the Anabaptist and Baptist tradition. Dr Wright constructs his argument
in dialogue and debate with Yoder and Moltmann, major contributors to a
free church perspective.
2000 / ISBN 0-85364-978-2 / xvi + 252pp

The Paternoster Press
PO Box 300,
Carlisle,
Cumbria CA3 0QS,
United Kingdom
Web: www.paternoster-publishing.com

May 2004